CoffeeScript in Action

CoffeeScript in Action

PATRICK LEE

MANNING
SHELTER ISLAND

Manning Publications Co.
20 Baldwin Road
PO Box 261
Shelter Island, NY 11964

Development editors:	Renae Gregoire, Jennifer Stout
Copyeditor:	Linda Recktenwald
Proofreaders:	Andy Carroll, Katie Tennant
Technical proofreader:	Doug Warren
Typesetter:	Dennis Dalinnik
Illustrator:	Nick Marino
Cover designer:	Marija Tudor

ISBN: 9781617290626
Printed in the United States of America
2 3 4 5 6 7 8 9 10 – EBM – 19 18 17 16 15 14

brief contents

contents

preface

I've long thought that the things that will ultimately resonate the most with people don't reveal themselves immediately. Instead, they might initially present themselves as slightly interesting but not striking. I've seen this with music, film, literature, and every other aspect of human experience that I've looked at for any substantial amount of time. I've also seen this with at least two programming languages, JavaScript and CoffeeScript.

My early reaction to JavaScript was dismissive. Strangely, or not, years later I would be working almost exclusively in it. My early reaction to CoffeeScript was also dismissive. "Here we go," I thought. "Yet another tool created because people don't understand JavaScript!" I was wrong about CoffeeScript just like I was wrong about JavaScript.

CoffeeScript is not about avoiding JavaScript—it is about understanding JavaScript. This applies to both people who are already familiar with JavaScript and people who are not familiar with JavaScript. Learning CoffeeScript helps people to understand Java-Script. At the same time, for many people it makes writing JavaScript programs simpler and more enjoyable, which means that it makes sense for them to use CoffeeScript instead of JavaScript.

acknowledgments

Thanks to Jeremy Ashkenas for creating CoffeeScript. Thanks to Michael Stephens at Manning for picking up a book on CoffeeScript, and to my editors at Manning—Bert Bates, James Hatheway, Jennifer Stout, and Renae Gregoire—who worked with me at various stages of manuscript development. Thanks also to Kevin Sullivan, Linda Recktenwald, Andy Carroll, Katie Tennant, and Mary Piergies, as well as technical proofreader Doug Warren, who worked with me during production—I was very impressed. Finally, thanks to publisher Marjan Bace for having patience with a book that took much longer to complete than anybody had initially expected.

Thanks to all the family, friends, and colleagues who read and provided feedback on early drafts. Thanks to the ThoughtWorks Sydney office for their patience with me while I balanced consulting with authoring.

Thanks to Nick Marino for the illustrations that brought Agtron and Scruffy to life, and for making sense of my sometimes-bizarre scripts.

Thanks also to the MEAP readers who provided feedback on the chapters as they were being written, and to the following reviewers who read the chapters at various stages during the development of the manuscript: Andrew Broman, Brett Veenstra, Carl Witty, Carlos Santiago, Cleland Early, Daniel Bretoi, David Hunter, Guy Mackenzie, Ian Phillips, Jeff Foster, John Shea, Julian Parry, Ken Chien, Logan Johnson, Musannif Zahir, Olivier Broqueville, Peter Fries, Phily Austria, Robert Henley, and Sergey Seletskyy, and to Tim Moore and Mikkel Bergmann (who provided many important insights).

Finally, a special thanks to those who had to stand living with me while I wrote: thanks to Kandy and to Leigh.

about this book

This is a language book. It doesn't try to comprehensively detail libraries, frameworks, or other ancillary matters. Instead, it concentrates *only* on teaching the CoffeeScript programming language from syntax, through composition, to building, testing, and deploying applications. Although this book is full of complete, working programs, they're all manufactured (contrived, if you will) slaves to the core goal of helping you learn to program in CoffeeScript. You'll find this book to be a useful reference because of its breadth and depth, but it isn't comprehensive. The web made comprehensive programming references obsolete long ago.

If you want to learn the CoffeeScript *language*, then this book is for you. If, instead, you want to eschew that learning in favor of ready-made instructions for using Coffee-Script with one framework or another, then this is probably not the book for you. Although references to popular frameworks are given, this book concentrates on Coffee-Script as a language. This book balances server-side and client-side uses of CoffeeScript as appropriate to each individual topic.

Roadmap

This book follows a three-act structure in which you, the hero, journey to the heart of CoffeeScript before emerging with a thorough grasp of it.

Part 1 sets up your core understanding of the language. When you begin your apprenticeship in chapter 1, you'll learn the motivations for creating CoffeeScript and why you are embarking on your journey. In chapter 2 you'll be immersed in the syntax of the language and begin to absorb it. In chapter 3 you'll learn about functions from the ground up, and in chapter 4 you'll do the same with objects.

In part 2 you'll learn how to wield your new understanding of CoffeeScript. Chapter 5 will have you pulling apart objects and putting them together, and chapter 6 will have you creating functions from functions, and from functions that create functions. In chapter 7 you'll hone your craft, technique, and style. After that comes chapter 8, which leads you right to the heart of CoffeeScript where you'll learn to change the language itself. Finally prepared, in chapter 9 you'll enter the dragon's lair of asynchronous programs.

In part 3 your travels will take you further from home where you'll learn how to build entire applications. This starts in chapter 10 where you'll learn about test-driven development. In chapter 11 you'll learn about building user interfaces for web browsers. In chapter 12 you'll wrap everything up by building and packaging applications, ready for the world to see. Finally, chapter 13 looks at the future and where you, the journeyman, are headed with CoffeeScript.

Prerequisites

This book doesn't assume any knowledge of CoffeeScript. Although some familiarity with JavaScript will make things easier, no level of JavaScript experience is assumed. What *is* assumed is some experience with programming (any language will do) and a basic grasp of web development concepts. Finally, although the Node.js platform is used throughout the book, no prior knowledge of Node.js is assumed.

Code conventions

Any source code listings inline within the text, such as read 'book', are formatted using a fixed-width font. Blocks of code are also formatted in a fixed-width font, separated from page content:

```
read = (material) ->
  console.log "Reading #{material}"

read 'CoffeeScript in Action'
```

Within blocks of code, a # character at the start of a line indicates that what follows the # is the result of evaluating the immediately preceding line:

```
read = (material) ->
  console.log "Reading #{material}"

read 'CoffeeScript in Action'
# Reading CoffeeScript in Action
```

In this way, all of the code snippets can be pasted directly into a CoffeeScript prompt, where the output you see should match the comment. A similar approach is taken with JavaScript code snippets where # is replaced with //:

```
'Raw' + ' JavaScript'
// 'Raw JavaScript'
```

Formatted code snippets can be copied and pasted from HTML files, one for each chapter, which are available for download from the publisher's website and also from links inside eBook versions of *CoffeeScript in Action*.

Invoking programs on the command line is shown by prefixing each line with a >. Expected output is prefixed with a #:

```
> coffee -e "console.log(3 + 4);"
# 7
```

Being prefixed with a >, the command-line examples have the disadvantage that they can't be pasted directly into a prompt. Occasionally, to provide a clear distinction between general command lines and the prompt for a particular program, the listing is prefixed with the name of the program prompt followed by a >:

```
node>
```

Before you can run any of this code, you need to have CoffeeScript installed.

Installing CoffeeScript

This book assumes that you have Node.js installed. To install Node.js, visit the website at http://nodejs.org and follow the instructions for your system. Once you have Node.js installed, you'll be able to run Node.js from the command line:

```
> node
```

This will land you in the Node.js prompt, into which you can enter raw JavaScript:

```
node> 1 + 2;
// 3
```

To exit, enter Ctrl-C twice:

```
node> <CTRL-C>
// (^C again to quit)
node> <CTRL-C>
>
```

Installing Node.js also installs npm (Node packaged modules), which you'll use for installing packages. Use npm to install CoffeeScript for all users on your system:

```
> npm install -g coffee-script
```

You now have CoffeeScript installed. Enter coffee into your command line:

```
> coffee
```

This launches you into a CoffeeScript prompt that will be your constant companion throughout this book. The command has other functionality besides the prompt, which you can see via --help:

```
> coffee --help
```

This will list the options. The meaning of particular options is given later in this book where needed, but not all options are covered.

As with Node.js, to exit this prompt, enter Ctrl-C twice.

Code downloads

All of the book's listings are available in the downloadable code from the publisher's website at www.manning.com/CoffeeScriptinAction and also on GitHub at https://github.com/boundvariable/coffeescript-in-action. When you obtain the downloadable code, go to the directory containing it and run the command npm install. Suppose you have the downloadable code at ~/src/coffeescript-in-action:

```
> cd ~/src/coffeescript-in-action
> npm install
```

You'll see npm install some packages that you'll need. Once that's done, you're ready to start running the listings.

The downloadable code is organized into directories corresponding to chapter numbers, with each chapter folder containing a "listings" folder with files named to correspond to listing numbers for that chapter. Where possible, code listings are standalone programs, and you can run them by passing them to the coffee command. Suppose you wanted to run the imaginary listing 77 from chapter 77:

```
> coffee 77/listings/77.coffee
```

Some code listings in the book are complete programs that aren't made to run on the command line but require a browser to run. In those cases, a command-line server program that will enable you to run them is provided either as one of the listings or along with the listings. Wherever that is the case, instructions are provided for running the server.

Exercises

Throughout the book you'll find some recommended exercises designed to help you better understand the concepts presented. The exercises range from small and closely defined to more open-ended exercises intended for exploration.

Author Online

Purchase of *CoffeeScript in Action* includes free access to a private web forum run by Manning Publications where you can make comments about the book, ask technical questions, and receive help from the author and other users. To access the forum and subscribe to it, point your web browser to www.manning.com/CoffeeScriptinAction. This page provides information on how to get on the forum once you're registered, what kind of help is available, and the rules of conduct on the forum.

Manning's commitment to our readers is to provide a venue where a meaningful dialog among individual readers and between readers and the author can take place. It's not a commitment to any specific amount of participation on the part of the author, whose contribution to the book's forum remains voluntary (and unpaid). We suggest you try asking the author some challenging questions, lest his interest stray!

The Author Online forum and the archives of previous discussions will be accessible from the publisher's website as long as the book is in print.

about the cover illustration

The figure on the cover of *CoffeeScript in Action* is captioned "Man from Dalj, Slavo-nia, Croatia." The illustration is taken from a reproduction of an album of Croatian traditional costumes from the mid-nineteenth century by Nikola Arsenovic, published by the Ethnographic Museum in Split, Croatia, in 2003. The illustrations were obtained from a helpful librarian at the Ethnographic Museum in Split, itself situated in the Roman core of the medieval center of the town: the ruins of Emperor Diocle-tian's retirement palace from around AD 304. The book includes finely colored illus-trations of figures from different regions of Croatia, accompanied by descriptions of the costumes and of everyday life.

Dalj is a village in eastern Croatia, on the border with Serbia, near the confluence of the Drava and Danube rivers. The figure on the cover is wearing a black woolen jacket over black woolen pants, both richly embroidered in the red and blue colors typical for this region.

Dress codes and lifestyles have changed over the last 200 years, and the diversity by region, so rich at the time, has faded away. It is now hard to tell apart the inhabitants of different continents, let alone of different hamlets or towns separated by only a few miles. Perhaps we have traded cultural diversity for a more varied personal life—cer-tainly for a more varied and fast-paced technological life.

Manning celebrates the inventiveness and initiative of the computer business with book covers based on the rich diversity of regional life of two centuries ago, brought back to life by illustrations from old books and collections like this one.

Part 1

Foundations

Although there are many theories about exactly how the process works, learning a new language is known to involve comprehensible input, comprehensible output, and reflection for you, the learner. This part of the book provides many opportunities for all three, and you'll get the most benefit if you take advantage of all those opportunities not only by reading the content and the code but also by running and experimenting with the examples, doing the exercises, and taking some time to consider the deeper implications of the underlying concepts.

Because this part covers CoffeeScript language fundamentals, your current experience level with CoffeeScript (and to an extent JavaScript) will affect how quickly you take it in.

The road to CoffeeScript

This chapter covers

- Why CoffeeScript matters
- How to get started
- The evolution of JavaScript
- Adapting to evolution by using CoffeeScript

CoffeeScript is a small, general-purpose programming language. It was created by Jeremy Ashkenas and first released in 2009. It's a compiled language: you write your program in CoffeeScript and then use the compiler to translate it to an equivalent JavaScript program. When you run your program, it's the compiled JavaScript that runs. Think of your CoffeeScript programs as being JavaScript programs underneath.

There are many programming languages that can compile to JavaScript, so many that they might even outnumber the programming languages that *don't* compile to JavaScript. CoffeeScript is rare among these languages because it keeps the core structure and semantics of JavaScript intact. CoffeeScript is essentially Java-Script. If it's essentially JavaScript though, why bother to use CoffeeScript? What's the benefit?

1.1   Why CoffeeScript?

CoffeeScript is a simple language, and there are two simple reasons for learning it. First, it fixes some problems in JavaScript that are unpleasant to work with. Second, understanding CoffeeScript will help you learn new ways of using JavaScript, and new ways of programming in general.

JavaScript is an elegant programming language with some unfortunate gnarled edges. It has problems that other popular programming languages don't have. Layers of these problems obscure the simple elegance of JavaScript and any programs you write with it. The goal of CoffeeScript is to peel back those layers. Think of your JavaScript programs as being CoffeeScript programs underneath.

Why CoffeeScript? One reason is that it can help you to make smaller and easier-to-understand programs that are easier to maintain. You say you don't have a problem with programs being large, difficult to understand, and difficult to maintain? Meet Agtron and Scruffy (figure 1.1).

Agtron and Scruffy have recently started working on a massive JavaScript program. This program contains more lines of JavaScript than Scruffy cares to count (though Agtron informs Scruffy that when he last looked it was 532,565). Agtron and Scruffy both consider the application they inherited to be disgusting. Scruffy thinks it's disgusting because he can't figure out what's going on. Agtron thinks it's disgusting because he *can* figure out what's going on. Why is the program disgusting? Because it's too big and the different components are too complicated and intertwined. The program is incomprehensible. Understanding how any of it works requires understanding of how *all* of it works.

How might CoffeeScript help? By simplifying JavaScript syntax and making each line easier to comprehend. That simplicity of expression will encourage you to compose programs that are, in turn, simpler and easier to comprehend. Your programs will become less complicated and not so intertwined. Simplifying small things, like syntax, can lead to simpler big things, like programs. Although it's not a panacea (it's possible to write incomprehensible garbage in CoffeeScript), learning

Figure 1.1   Meet
Agtron and Scruffy.

CoffeeScript will help you to write better programs. It's time to get started, time to write some CoffeeScript.

1.2 *Running CoffeeScript*

One thing you need to get out of the way is to make sure you're ready to start experimenting with CoffeeScript. Assuming you already have CoffeeScript installed (if not, refer to the "About this book" section before this chapter), open a console or terminal, type the word `coffee`, and press Enter. You see a prompt:

```
coffee>
```

You're now in the CoffeeScript REPL (pronounced like *ripple* but with an *e* instead of an *i*). Now enter some CoffeeScript and press Enter again:

```
coffee> 'CoffeeScript!'
'CoffeeScript!'
```

That's it, you've written CoffeeScript. To exit the REPL, press Ctrl-D (that's the Ctrl and D keys pressed simultaneously), and you'll be back to your regular command line. Why is it called a REPL? It stands for *Read-Eval-Print Loop*, and that's exactly what it does:

```
coffee> 'CoffeeScript!'   # Read 'CoffeeScript!'
                          # Evaluate 'CoffeeScript!'
'CoffeeScript!'           # Print the evaluation of 'CoffeeScript!'
coffee>                   # Loop (to start again)
```

By default, the CoffeeScript REPL will read only one line at a time before evaluating. In some cases you might want to evaluate two lines at a time. To do this, press Ctrl-V, and you'll see the prompt change. Now, regardless of how many times you press Enter, the REPL will continue to read until you press Ctrl-V again, at which point it will evaluate, print, and resume the loop:

```
coffee> CTRL-V

------> 'CoffeeScript!'    # Read
.......
.......
....... CTRL-V            # Eval
'CoffeeScript!'           # Print
coffee>                   # Loop
```

Now that you're familiar with the REPL, any time you are working with a single-line snippet of CoffeeScript, you can enter it into the REPL and see it evaluated:

```
'CoffeeScript!'
# 'CoffeeScript!'
```

When you see a snippet of CoffeeScript that requires the multiline mode, press Ctrl-V first and then type or paste it in, and finally press Ctrl-V again to see it evaluated.

Although the REPL is fun, and it will often be your companion as you learn Coffee-Script, you didn't come here for a lesson on how to use your keyboard. No, you came to learn about CoffeeScript, how to use it, and what it means. To begin, you want to know where you are and how you got here. How *did* you get here? The answer starts with a small historical detour, beginning with JavaScript.

1.3   JavaScript

To understand CoffeeScript and how it relates to JavaScript, you first need to know about some other languages that influenced JavaScript. Programming language influences can come in many forms, but the ones of significance in your understanding of CoffeeScript and JavaScript are the ones that led to the style, semantics, and syntax. The first influence for JavaScript in these three areas (and your starting place) is the C programming language and a humble little character called the *curly brace*.

1.3.1   C

The C programming language is one of the most widely used, and enduring, general-purpose programming languages of all time. JavaScript *deliberately* looks like the C programming language with many syntactical similarities. One of the most obvious similarities is the use of curly braces, { and }, to indicate the beginning and end of each block of code. JavaScript is not alone in sharing this syntax with C—many mainstream programming languages look like C. Why should it matter that JavaScript borrows syntax from C? It matters because the story of a programming language (like the story of any language) is, in many regards, a social one. Here's one account of that story.

Anybody who studied computer science when grunge music was popular knew that all the cool kids were using C with curly braces and that C programming was *real* programming, involving things like managing memory and manipulating strings as arrays of char pointers. The C programming language was the most grown-up thing to write besides assembly language, and the computer science departments in universities around the world were full of youth. Finally, and perhaps most importantly, most computer games at the time were written in C, and all those young people wanted to write computer games.

The schools of computer science were motivated to produce graduates who could get jobs, so the three most popular languages at the time were often taught. All three of these languages—C, C++, and Java—have curly braces. There were many less-popular languages with different styles, syntax, semantics, and ideas, but things found in unpopular places are easily ignored—regardless of whether they're good or bad. That's why JavaScript looks like the C programming language.

Despite being dressed in a curly-brace suit and semicolon top hat to look like C, JavaScript took two core ideas from other languages called Scheme and Self. As it happens, neither Scheme nor Self was quite so popular or looked very much like C, C++, or Java. So, although JavaScript looks very much like C, some of the core ideas are very much unlike C. To understand the friction this causes, you need to look closer at these two languages, Scheme and Self.

1.3.2 *Scheme*

Scheme is a general-purpose programming language created by Guy Steele and Gerald Sussman. It's considered a *dialect* of the programming language Lisp, which the late John McCarthy created when he was a young man. Lisp dialects don't look like the C programming language at all.

Over time, the popularity of Lisp dialects waned while the popularity of the C programming language grew. Finally, when Brendan Eich created the C-resembling JavaScript language to be used in the web browser of a company called Netscape, all of McCarthy's hair was gray. Lisp dialects might have been moderately popular choices for programming languages when men in rock bands had perms, but they were no longer popular by the time Eich created JavaScript. Because they weren't popular, there was no way that JavaScript was going to look like one of them. But Lisp contained some powerful programming ideas that JavaScript needed, so, syntax aside, there was nothing preventing it from being inspired by Lisp.

The ideas that JavaScript takes from Scheme have foundations in a mathematical system called *lambda calculus*. In terms of modern computer programming, some of these ideas fall under the term *functional programming*, which is the style of programming encouraged by Scheme. Functional programming very loosely means programming with functions (which you'll start to learn about in chapter 3). How about C? The style of programming encouraged by C is called *imperative programming*. JavaScript has the syntax of C, but it was inspired, in a small but important way, by the functional style of Scheme.

While the popularity of Lisp and the functional programming style was declining, another programming style called *object-oriented programming* was starting to gain popularity. An object-oriented language called Self was the basis of a core idea in JavaScript called *prototypes*.

1.3.3 *Self*

The Self programming language was created as a research project by David Ungar and Randall Smith based on a programming concept known as *prototypes*. Being based on prototypes, Self was very different from the popular object-oriented languages of the time (such as C++ and Java) that were based on *classes*. You'll learn more about classes and prototypes in later chapters, but for now, think of classes as being a more rigid and static approach, and prototypes as a more fluid and dynamic approach.

Self also had a different style than the other popular object-oriented languages of the time by preferring a small but powerful set of operations to more numerous and elaborate ones. This style was a direct inspiration in the creation of JavaScript, which took not only the idea of prototypes from Self but also this idea of having a small set of powerful primitive tools as a primary design goal. So, although JavaScript looks more like Java or C++ than it does Self, it has some core ideas taken directly from Self. It looks one way but acts another.

Although JavaScript looks like C (the syntax and to some extent the style and semantics), some of the key ideas (and to some extent the style and semantics) are borrowed from Self and Scheme. What happens when a language has many competing factors?

1.4   *Evolving JavaScript*

The inherent friction between the competing ideas behind JavaScript's creation is compounded by it now being the most widely used programming language in the world. The social aspect of JavaScript as a programming language has more influencing factors than most other programming languages, and the widespread use of JavaScript serves to amplify all of the influences. This is important in understanding the future of JavaScript because the people who use *any* language (JavaScript or otherwise) are those who shape it over time. To illustrate, consider a brief account of a particular *spoken* language.

1.4.1   *A little story about language*

Sometime around the fifth century, a West Germanic tribe invaded Britain and brought with them their language. As a result, the existing languages of the region (Celtic and Cornish) were mostly replaced with the West Germanic dialect of the invaders, leaving only a hint of Celtic and Cornish in modern English today. A few hundred years later some Vikings, who spoke a Scandinavian language, colonized parts of Northern Britain. They needed to speak the local language (now a West Germanic dialect) in order to trade with nearby people, but they didn't know it very well, so they spoke a simplified, broken version of it. The broken way they spoke the language changed the way everybody else spoke it, the language evolved as a result.

Later, in the eleventh century, the Norman French conquered England, and William the Conqueror became the king of England. During the Norman occupancy the official language of the region was Norman French, but English was still spoken by the commoners on the streets and on their farms. This is why English farm animals such as cows and pigs have one name, but the meats used in the restaurants by people speaking Norman French have other names such as beef and pork. The entire history of English is like this. When the printing press was invented, it had only the Latin alphabet, so English was changed again, one of the changes being to replace the thorn, þ, with the digraph th.

Now, you *might* think that a community doesn't shape a constructed programming language like JavaScript in the same way it shapes a spoken language like English, but a language that isn't shaped by a community is a dead language. A language can initially be constructed, but eventually it either evolves and changes as part of a community or it perishes. Just consider any one of the thousands of constructed spoken languages created in the history of mankind. Even Esperanto, perhaps the best-known constructed language, has today fewer than 1,000 native speakers.

1.4.2   *The lesson for JavaScript*

As the unavoidable language of the web, as the language used to create experiences in the web browser from its very inception, JavaScript is a melting pot of different language ideas. It's not a language used exclusively by JavaScript programmers; it's a language frequently used by people who typically program in another language. JavaScript is a language used by people who don't necessarily understand (or want to understand) every subtle nuance. Because of all these different people who use JavaScript, it has necessarily changed substantially over time. At least, the way it is used, the techniques, and the types of things written in JavaScript have changed substantially. Not the syntax, though; that hasn't changed much at all.

JavaScript was created in about the time it takes to get over a cold. The short time frame in which JavaScript was created (and subsequently standardized) led to some problems being set into the language—problems that are still in the process of being fixed many years later. So, take a language that was created in a matter of days, add in some competing ideas, give it to a whole lot of people who don't know it very well, and what happens? You can fill in the rest of *that* story yourself.

How does CoffeeScript fit into this picture? CoffeeScript changes JavaScript's syntax. CoffeeScript simplifies JavaScript so that it expresses those key ideas borrowed from Self and Scheme, as understood by users of the language today. In doing so, it also fixes some of the problems caused by JavaScript's quick birth. Sure, as with all things, these changes come with their own unique set of trade-offs. To see if those trade-offs are right for you, it's time to see what CoffeeScript does to JavaScript syntax and how it arrived at the changes that it did. Doing this starts with a simple thought experiment. What syntax can be taken away from a JavaScript program while still leaving the meaning intact?

1.5   *Creating CoffeeScript*

CoffeeScript starts with an experiment to remove as much nonessential syntax from JavaScript as possible. By working through that experiment, you can begin to understand CoffeeScript syntax and see how it differs from JavaScript. Relax if your JavaScript is still rusty at this point; just follow along and look at the syntax.

1.5.1   *Designing new syntax*

To arrive at CoffeeScript syntax, start with a small JavaScript program and see what can be removed without changing the meaning of the program. An uninteresting program serves this purpose well, so consider a function to square two numbers:

```
var square = function (x) {
  return x * x;
};
```

How much of the syntax is necessary? For a start, you can remove the semicolons:

```
var square = function (x) {
  return x * x
}
```

You can also remove the C-inspired curly braces:

```
var square = function (x)
  return x * x
```

You can also remove the `var` statement by making it implicit instead of explicit:

```
square = function (x)
  return x * x
```

The same applies to the `return` statement. Remove that also:

```
square = function (x)
  x * x
```

Finally, the `function` keyword is important and used frequently, but suppose you replace it with something that doesn't take so long to read or type:

```
square = (x) ->
  x * x
```

Now you have CoffeeScript. Think of it as JavaScript after a little bit of spring cleaning (see figure 1.2). Most Ruby or Python developers will immediately find this new syntax comfortable and familiar, whereas most C, C++, or Java programmers will immediately find it alien. But the familiarity of the syntax isn't important. What *is* important is how the new syntax fits how people think about the programs written using it. Why? Because a more natural syntax can not only make your life as a programmer easier; it

Figure 1.2 Agtron and Scruffy doing some spring cleaning of the JavaScript syntax

can also help you start to think differently about your programs by letting you concentrate on other things—like the problems you're trying to solve with the language. In that way, learning CoffeeScript can help you learn new ways of programming.

1.5.2 Achieving new syntax

Deciding on the syntax that you want is a good start. What you need now is some way for the new CoffeeScript syntax to actually work. In order for your CoffeeScript program to execute as a JavaScript program, you need something that can take CoffeeScript,

```
square = (x) ->
  x * x
```

and turn it into the equivalent executable JavaScript:

```
var square = function (x) {
  return x * x;
};
```

That's exactly what a compiler is for, and it's exactly what the CoffeeScript compiler does. On the command line again, if you have a file called square.coffee containing the CoffeeScript, then you convert it to a JavaScript file like so:

```
> coffee -c square.coffee
```

Once that's done, you'll have a new file called square.js containing your newly compiled JavaScript program. That leaves just one question: If the CoffeeScript program must be compiled first, then how does the REPL work? Well, it's read-eval-print, right? The CoffeeScript is simply compiled before evaluation:

```
square = (x) -> x * x       # Read
                            # Compile to JavaScript
                            # Evaluate the resulting JavaScript
# [Function]                # Print

                            # Loop

square 2                    # Read
                            # Compile to JavaScript
                            # Evaluate the resulting JavaScript
# 4                         # Print

                            # Loop
```

Without needing to fully understand the CoffeeScript shown here, you see that it can be converted to JavaScript on the fly as you enter it into the REPL. Whether entered into the REPL or written to a file to be compiled later, all of your CoffeeScript is converted to JavaScript before it runs. The CoffeeScript compiler gives you the CoffeeScript syntax that makes it easy for you to express your program the way you want.

1.6   *Summary*

CoffeeScript is the JavaScript you're already using—just with a new syntax. Remember those Vikings? They changed English forever because they didn't know or care how to handle the nuances of the language. The same goes for JavaScript, the most widely used programming language in the world. It won't remain unchanged in the face of all the different people who are starting to use it, and recent revisions to the language specification that take inspiration from the community (and CoffeeScript in at least one case) are clear evidence of that. Whether you plan to stick with JavaScript syntax at all costs or you're looking to move away from it, you'll be better off for your new understanding of CoffeeScript. Read on in the next chapter when you're ready to take a deeper look at the syntax.

Simplified syntax

This chapter covers

- Basic syntax and structure
- Expressions and operators
- An introduction to strings, arrays, objects, and functions
- How to run CoffeeScript programs

Before going to a country where you don't speak the language, you might spend some time listening to the language to get a feel for it or maybe learn some essential canned phrases to help you get around. Think of CoffeeScript in the same way. As you're immersed in the syntax of CoffeeScript, you'll start to build your understanding.

In this chapter, you'll learn about expressions, operators, and statements, as well as how they work in CoffeeScript and how they're related to the JavaScript equivalents. You'll explore fundamental building blocks of CoffeeScript programs with strings, arrays, comments, and regular expressions. You'll begin with a program.

13

2.1   Your first program

Imagine a small program that controls a coffee machine (called the Barista). This coffee machine serves different styles of coffee, some with milk and some without, but it doesn't serve any coffee styles containing milk after midday. Now imagine you find an existing implementation of this CoffeeScript program, as shown in the following listing.

Listing 2.1   The coffee machine

```
houseRoast = null

hasMilk = (style) ->
  switch style
    when "latte", "cappuccino"           A function to
      yes                                determine if a style
    else                                 of coffee has milk
      no

makeCoffee = (requestedStyle) ->
  style = requestedStyle || 'Espresso'
  if houseRoast?                         A function to make
    "#{houseRoast} #{style}"             the coffee; returns
  else                                   a string
    style

barista = (style) ->
  time = (new Date()).getHours()
  if hasMilk(style) and time > 12 then "No!"    A function
  else                                          that coffee is
    coffee = makeCoffee style                   requested from
    "Enjoy your #{coffee}!"
```

You don't yet fully grasp CoffeeScript, but already you can get a feel for the basic structure. An equivalent JavaScript program has a very similar structure but slightly different syntax, as you'll see in listing 2.2. Compare these programs side by side and you'll begin to understand the syntax features that CoffeeScript removes and appreciate *why* it removes them.

> **Why remove?**
>
> Claude Debussy is quoted as saying that "music is the space between the notes." CoffeeScript syntax is defined as much by what is missing as by what is present. Part of the thought experiment behind CoffeeScript is to take patterns written frequently in JavaScript, look at them, and ask, "How much of this is necessary?"

2.1.1   Comparing CoffeeScript to JavaScript

The CoffeeScript implementation of the coffee machine appears side by side with an equivalent JavaScript implementation in the next listing. See how many differences you can spot.

Listing 2.2 Comparing CoffeeScript to JavaScript

CoffeeScript

```
hasMilk = (style) ->
  switch style
    when "latte", "cappuccino"
      yes
    else
      no
```

JavaScript

```
var hasMilk = function (style) {
  switch (style) {
    case "latte":
    case "cappuccino":
      return true;
    default:
      return false;
  }
};
```

JavaScript requires var declaration

Top level, not indented

```
makeCoffee = (style) ->
  style || 'Espresso'
```

```
var makeCoffee = function (style) {
  return style || 'Espresso';
};
```

Indentation inside function

Indentation inside if

Indentation inside else

```
barista = (style) ->
  now = new Date()
  time = now.getHours()
  if hasMilk(style) and time > 12
    "No!"
  else
    coffee = makeCoffee style
    "Enjoy your #{coffee}!"
```

```
var barista = function (style) {
  var now = new Date();
  var time = now.getHours();
  var coffee;
  if (hasMilk(style) && time > 12) {
    return "No!";
  } else {
    coffee = makeCoffee(style);
    return "Enjoy your "+coffee+"!";
  }
};
```

```
barista "latte"
```

```
barista("latte");
```

Returns either "No!" or "Enjoy your latte!" depending on the time of day

When you compare the CoffeeScript and JavaScript in listing 2.2, you'll notice four key things that CoffeeScript is missing. It has no var statements, semicolons, return statements, or curly braces.

VAR STATEMENTS

In JavaScript, unless you're in strict mode it's possible to accidentally assign variables on the global object, in the global scope. If you don't know what that means, for now just know it's a bad thing. CoffeeScript always defines new variables in the current scope, protecting you from this unfortunate feature in JavaScript.

SEMICOLONS

In CoffeeScript there are no semicolons.[1] Although they're allowed, you never need them, and they shouldn't be used.

---

[1] Sure, ECMA-262 says that JavaScript parsers should do automatic semicolon insertion, but the potential for errors in JavaScript has resulted in frequent advice to always use them.

RETURN STATEMENTS

The `return` keyword is absent from CoffeeScript. In CoffeeScript the last expression in the function is returned without any `return` statement. This is called an *implicit return*. Although required occasionally, explicit `return` statements are rarely used in CoffeeScript.

CURLY BRACES

In CoffeeScript there are no curly braces used to mark out blocks of code. In order to remove the need for curly braces and other block-delimiting characters, newlines and the indentation level for each line of code are meaningful. This is referred to as *significant whitespace* or sometimes as the *offside rule.*[2] Indentation matters in CoffeeScript programs, so you must be careful to indent consistently. Always use either two, three, or four spaces in CoffeeScript. Two spaces is the most common. If you use mixed indentation (sometimes using two, sometimes using five, sometimes using four), then your CoffeeScript might still compile, but it will almost certainly not do what you want it to. Almost all CoffeeScript programs you'll find in the wild use spaces. Using tabs is not recommended.

As you now turn your attention to expressions and some basic language features of CoffeeScript, keep the rules about `var`, semicolons, `return` statements, and curly braces in the back of your mind until you encounter them again. Unfortunately, reading about basic language features is a little bit like reciting the alphabet or playing musical scales. On the upside, once you see these basic features, you're better prepared for the real fun stuff.

2.2 *Simple expressions*

An expression is something that can be *evaluated*. An expression has a value. Almost everything in CoffeeScript is an expression. CoffeeScript even goes to some effort to make some things expressions that aren't expressions in the underlying JavaScript. This emphasis on expressions means that they're a good place to start exploring the syntax of CoffeeScript—starting with small expressions and moving on to larger ones.

All of the examples in this section can be run on the CoffeeScript Read-Eval-Print Loop (REPL). Start your REPL:

```
> coffee
coffee>
```

Ready?

2.2.1 *Literal values*

The smallest expressions in CoffeeScript are ones that evaluate to themselves. When you type them into the REPL and press Enter, you see the same thing shown on the

---

[2] Significant indentation will already be familiar to Python and F# programmers and anybody who has used HAML or SASS.

next line. These expressions are called *literal values*, and the notation used to write them is called *literal notation*:

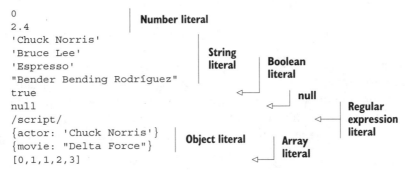

```
0
2.4
'Chuck Norris'
'Bruce Lee'
'Espresso'
"Bender Bending Rodríguez"
true
null
/script/
{actor: 'Chuck Norris'}
{movie: "Delta Force"}
[0,1,1,2,3]
```

The CoffeeScript literal values shown here are exactly the same in JavaScript. Not all literal values are the same though, so everybody (even seasoned JavaScript programmers) needs to learn something about literal values in CoffeeScript.

FUNCTION

One very important expression that's different from JavaScript is the *function literal*:

```
(x) -> x
```

In JavaScript, the function literal requires a bit more typing:

```
function (x) { return x; }
```

Functions are used all the time in both JavaScript and CoffeeScript. Removing the function keyword, curly braces, and return statements for CoffeeScript reduces the amount of boilerplate and gives your code greater prominence over language syntax.

OBJECT

The curly braces on an object are optional in CoffeeScript:

```
movie: "Delta Force"
# { movie: "Delta Force"}
```

BOOLEAN ALIASES

CoffeeScript has aliases for the literal values true and false:

```
on
# true
yes
# true
off
# false
no
# false
```

REGULAR EXPRESSIONS

Like JavaScript, a regular expression literal in CoffeeScript begins and ends with a forward slash /:

```
/abc/
# /abc/
```

Unlike JavaScript, though, a regular expression must not start with a literal space:

```
/ abc/
# error: unexpected /
```

Once you have expressions, you need a way to name things. You need variables.

2.2.2 *Variables*

Names that refer to local values are called *variables*. A name should contain only letters, numbers, and underscores. Other characters are permitted, such as π (pi) and $ (dollar sign), but you don't need them. A variable name must not be one of the reserved names. A list of reserved words that you can't use for names is in appendix A.

UNDEFINED

When you use a name that hasn't had any value assigned to it, you get an error telling you that the name is not defined:

```
pegasus
# ReferenceError: pegasus is not defined
```

Names that aren't defined have a special type called *undefined*. To define a variable, you assign a value to a name. This causes the variable to *reference* that value:

```
answer = 42
neighborOfTheBeast = 668
blameItOnTheBoogie = yes
texasRanger = {actor: 'Chuck Norris'}
```

When you evaluate a variable, you get the value referenced by it:

```
answer
# 42
```

If you assign a new value to the variable, the name will then evaluate to that new value:

```
texasRanger = true
texasRanger
# true
```

In CoffeeScript you can assign anything you want to a variable regardless of what was previously assigned to it. Any language that allows this is called *dynamically typed*.

To create a variable, you have to assign a value to it. When you do that, you use an operator.

2.3 *Operators*

Simple expressions are important, but in order to do things with those expressions (like assign a value to a variable) you need some operators to go with them. Coffee-Script has many operators that work exactly the same as they do in JavaScript:

```
+  -  !  /  %  >  <  >=  <=  .  &&  ||  *
```

Other operators from JavaScript, such as the ternary operator, are either different or unavailable in CoffeeScript, so for the time being you should avoid using them.

It's now time to look at the essential operators that provide basic syntax to Coffee-Script, some of the new operators that CoffeeScript introduces, and how operators are used to combine expressions. All of the examples in this section can be run on the Coffee-Script REPL. Type them all into the REPL, see the results, and experiment with them.

2.3.1 Essentials

Some operators come from JavaScript with only minor changes and, in some cases, aliases. The operator precedence rules are unchanged from JavaScript.

ASSIGNMENT

This operator is provided by the = symbol. Use it when you need to assign a value to a name:

```
wuss = 'A weak or ineffectual person'
chuckNorris = 'Chuck Norris'
```

CoffeeScript doesn't let you accidentally declare global variable names—you don't want global variables.

NEGATION

This operator is provided by ! or the alias not. Use it to get true or false depending on whether the value is truthy or falsy:

```
!true
# false
```

> **Falsy values**
>
> The values null, false, '', undefined, and 0 are called *falsy* values in CoffeeScript because they have the value false when coerced to a boolean, such as when used in an if clause. All other values in CoffeeScript will have the value true, making them *truthy*. You can observe this on the REPL by evaluating each of them prefixed with !!, such as !!'', which will give you false.

EQUALITY AND INEQUALITY

These operators are provided by ==, !=, or the aliases is and isnt, respectively. Use them to determine whether two values are equal or not:

```
chuckNorris = 'Chuck Norris'
weak = 'weak'
chuckNorris is weak
# false
chuckNorris isnt weak
# true
```

Be careful; isnt and is not are *not* the same thing in CoffeeScript:

```
5 isnt 6        ⟵  Means 5 and 6 are
# true             not the same value
5 is not 6    ⟵  Means 5 is the same
# false            value as not 6
```

The lesson is to avoid using `is not` in CoffeeScript and instead use `isnt` to test for inequality.

TYPE COERCION

Unlike in JavaScript, the equality and inequality operators in CoffeeScript aren't *type coercive*. They're equivalent to `===` and `!==` in JavaScript:

```
'' == false
# false
```

What does it mean that these operators aren't type coercive? Well, if the equality operator in CoffeeScript were type coercive, then the expression `1 == '1'` would evaluate to `true` because the operator would try coercing the values when it compares them:

```
1 == '1'
# false
```

In CoffeeScript the equality operator requires that both sides have the same value, not that they can be coerced into the same value. If you want a value to be coerced, then you should do it yourself. Read on to find out how.

ADD AND SUBTRACT

These operators are provided by `+` and `-`. Use `+` only with numbers or strings:

```
3 + 3
# 6
'string' + ' concatenation'
# 'string concatenation'
```

When you add a string to a number, the `+` operator will coerce the number to a string:

```
4 + '3'
# '43'
```

Use `-` only with numbers,

```
3 - 3
# 0
```

not with strings, which will evaluate to the primitive value that means *not a number* (`NaN`):

```
'apples' - 'oranges'
# NaN
```

If you get `NaN`, it usually means something has gone wrong.

MULTIPLY AND DIVIDE

These operators are provided by `*` and `/`. Use them with numbers. They work exactly the same as in JavaScript:

```
3*3
# 9
```

When you multiply a string by a number, the `*` operator will attempt to coerce the string into a number:

```
'3'*3
# 9
```

If the string can't be coerced into a number, then you get NaN:

```
'bork'*3
# NaN
```

You tried to multiply a string by a number and something went wrong.

MODULO

Modulo is the division remainder. Use it to see if a number is evenly divisible by another number:

```
3%2
# 1

4%2
# 0

not (3%2)
# false

not (4%2)
# true
```

COMPARISON

These operators are provided by <, >, <=, and >=. Use them when you want to compare number values or string values:

```
42 > 0
# true

42 >= 42
# true
```

Numbers are compared exactly how you'd expect:

```
time = 13
time > 12
# true
```

Strings are too. They're compared alphabetically:

```
'Aardvark' < 'Zebra'
# true
```

When you try to compare things that can't reasonably be compared, you get false:

```
2 > 'giraffe'
# false
```

THE GUARD (LOGICAL AND)

This operator is provided by && or the alias and. You use it when you want to evaluate an expression only if another expression is true:

```
chuckNorris is weak and pickFight
```

You evaluate the guard by first looking to the left of the and operator:

```
chuckNorris is weak
# false
```

If that evaluates to `false`, the expression to the right of the and operator isn't evaluated. The value of the expression then will be the value of the left-hand side:

```
chuckNorris is weak and pickFight
# false
```

THE DEFAULT (LOGICAL OR)

The counterpart of the guard, default, is provided by `||` or the alias or. You use it to evaluate an expression only if another expression is `false`:

```
runAway = 'Running away!'
chuckNorris is weak or runAway
```

The coffee machine program uses the default operator to provide a default style of coffee:

```
makeCoffee = (requestedStyle) ->
 requestedStyle || 'Espresso'

makeCoffee()
# 'Espresso'
```

Evaluate the default in your head by first looking to the left of the or:

```
chuckNorris is weak
# false
```

When that evaluates to `false`, the expression to the right of the or *is* evaluated:

```
runaway
# 'Running away!'
```

That's the opposite of how the guard operator works.

FUNCTION INVOCATION

A function is invoked by placing a value after it. Consider the `makeCoffee` function:

```
makeCoffee = (style) ->
  style || 'Espresso'
```

Invoke it with the value `'Cappuccino'`:

```
makeCoffee 'Cappuccino'
# 'Cappuccino'
```

The last value evaluated in a function is the value you get when that function is invoked. In this example, `'Cappuccino'` is the last value evaluated. Function values are covered in depth in chapter 3.

NEW

You use the new operator to get an instance of a class of object. Following are the date and time when this sentence was first written:

```
new Date()
# Sun, 21 Aug 2011 00:14:34 GMT
```

PROPERTY ACCESS

This operator is provided by `.` or by `[]`. You use them to access a property on an object:

```
texasRanger = actor: 'Chuck Norris'
texasRanger.actor
# 'Chuck Norris'
```

An object defining a single property, actor

Square brackets are useful when you have the property name in a value:

```
movie = title: 'Way of the Dragon', star: 'Bruce Lee'
myPropertyName = 'title'
movie[myPropertyName]
# 'Way of the Dragon'
```

An object defining two properties: title and star

A date object has a `getHours` property that can be used to get the hours part of a date. You can invoke that function on the date object created using the `new` operator:

```
now = new Date()
# Sun, 21 Aug 2011 00:14:34 GMT
now.getHours()
# 0
```

Objects and properties are covered in depth in chapter 4. You can now turn your eyes to types of things in CoffeeScript.

2.3.2 Types, existential, and combining operators

CoffeeScript has some operators that are not in JavaScript. These operators provide cleaner syntax for some common JavaScript idioms. One of these, called the existential operator, is useful for expressions such as "is there a house roast?"

```
houseRoast?
```

To understand the existential operator, you need to understand `undefined`, `null`, and types.

UNDEFINED

A variable that hasn't been assigned a value doesn't reference anything and so has the value `undefined`. When you evaluate an undefined value, you get a reference error (as you saw earlier with Pegasus):

```
pegasus
# ReferenceError: pegasus is not defined
```

NULL

A variable that is defined can have the `null` value. The `null` value is equal to itself:

```
reference = null
reference == null
# true
```

TYPES

CoffeeScript is dynamically and weakly typed, which means that the `typeof` operator was never going to be particularly useful. Also, the type of `null` is object:

```
typeof null
# 'object'
```

This problem in JavaScript makes `typeof` barely worth the pixels it appears on.

Programmers who normally use a language that's statically typed need to suspend disbelief as they learn how to solve the same problems without types. Techniques for doing so are covered in chapter 7. For now, remember that CoffeeScript is dynamically and weakly typed:

```
dynamicAndWeak = '3'
weakAndDynamic = 5
dynamicAndWeak + weakAndDynamic
# '35'
dynamicAndWeak = 3
dynamicAndWeak + weakAndDynamic
# 8
```

5 is coerced by + operator to '5'

Used to reference a string, now references a number

There are no type declarations, and the types of variables can change (remember, this is dynamic typing). Also, the addition operator works differently in the two examples because of type coercion (this is known as weak typing). *Don't rely on types in CoffeeScript.*

EXISTENTIAL OPERATOR

The existential operator is provided by `?`. You use it to evaluate whether something is defined *and* has a value other than `null` assigned to it:

```
pegasus?
# false
roundSquare?
# false
pegasus = 'Horse with wings'
pegasus?
# true
```

When something hasn't been defined, it has the *undefined* type:

```
typeof roundSquare
# 'undefined'
```

But *undefined* has an uncomfortable place in JavaScript, and type checks should generally be avoided. Here's a common phrase from JavaScript:

```
typeof pegasus !== "undefined" and pegasus !== null
#false
```

With the existential operator, you have a simpler way to express the same thing:

```
pegasus?
# false
```

CoffeeScript has other more advanced but less commonly used operators that are covered in chapter 7. For now, you can get by just fine with the basic operators.

COMBINING EXPRESSIONS

Operators can be used as parts of expressions, and one expression can be made up of multiple expressions. Operators are used to connect expressions, and connecting expressions using operators results in another expression, as shown in figure 2.1.

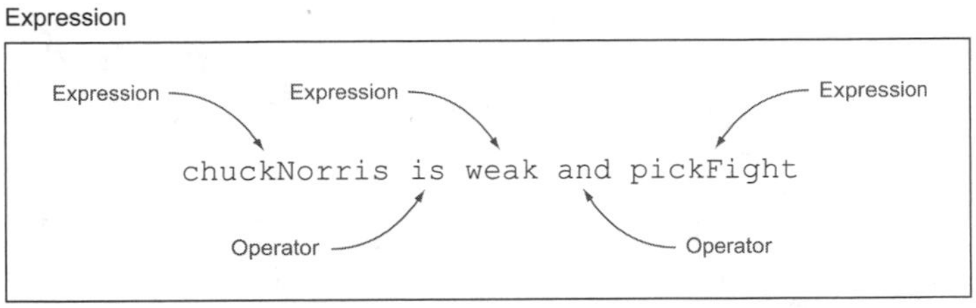

Figure 2.1 Expression anatomy

2.3.3 Exercises

To learn CoffeeScript, you need to write CoffeeScript. At the end of some sections in this book is a set of exercises for you to attempt. The answers to the exercises for all sections are in appendix B.

Suppose you just obtained two items, a torch and an umbrella. One of the items you purchased, and the other was a gift, but you're not sure which is which. Both of these are objects:

```
torch = {}
umbrella = {}
```

Either the torch or the umbrella has a `price` property, but the other does not. Write an expression for the combined cost of the torch and umbrella. *Hint: Use the default operator.*

2.4 Statements

Expressions and operators are important, but you'll also need to use statements to work effectively in CoffeeScript. Statements are executed but don't produce a value. When expressions are executed, they *do* produce a value:

```
balance = 1000
while balance > 0
  balance = balance - 100
```

Here, the `while` keyword is a statement, so it doesn't have a value but is an instruction only. In comparison, `balance - 100` is an expression and it has a value. That value is assigned to the variable `balance`.

In CoffeeScript you should always prefer expressions because expressions will lead to simpler programs—you'll learn more about that in later chapters. This section takes some common statements from JavaScript and demonstrates how they're used in CoffeeScript as part of an expression. Before getting to the individual examples, you'll look at the basic syntactic parts, or anatomy, of an expression.

2.4.1 Anatomy

Things that are only statements in JavaScript can be used as expressions in CoffeeScript. An example of this is the `if` statement, as shown by figure 2.2.

In JavaScript an `if-else` block like this can't be used as an expression. In Coffee-Script it can be.

Statement / expression in CoffeeScript

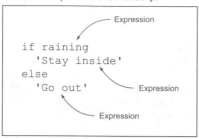

The equivalent JavaScript is a pure statement

Figure 2.2   Expression and statement anatomy

2.4.2   *Statements as expressions*

Things that are only statements in other languages, including JavaScript, can be used in CoffeeScript as expressions for the values they produce. Ruby programmers and Lisp programmers will be familiar with the idea that *everything is an expression*, but if you come from a language that doesn't do this, then it's time for some reeducation.

IF STATEMENTS

These are provided by `if` and optional `else` keywords. Use them when you want different things to be evaluated, depending on whether a particular value is `true` or `false`:

```
if raining
  'Stay inside'
else
  'Go out'
```

You can imagine the equivalent JavaScript. It has parentheses and curly braces. More importantly, though, an `if` block is also an expression in CoffeeScript; it has a value and can be assigned to a variable:

```
raining = true

activity = if raining
    'Stay inside'
  else
    'Go out'

activity
# 'Stay inside'
```

> ### Don't use ternary expressions
> CoffeeScript compiles an `if` statement used in an expression to use JavaScript's ternary expression. The ternary operator looks like `raining ? 'Go out' : 'Stay inside'`. If you're a JavaScript developer, don't use the ternary operator directly in Coffee-Script—it won't work.

SWITCH STATEMENTS

These are provided by the switch and when keywords, with the default option using the else keyword. Use them when you want different things to be evaluated depending on the value of an expression. The switch is often a good replacement for multiple if, else blocks:

```
connectJackNumber = (number) ->
  "Connecting jack #{number}"

receiver = 'Betty'

switch receiver
  when 'Betty'
    connectJackNumber 4
  when 'Sandra'
    connectJackNumber 22
  when 'Toby'
    connectJackNumber 9
  else
    'I am sorry, your call cannot be connected'

# 'Connecting jack 4'
```

You can use a switch block in an expression in the same way you can use an if block in an expression:

```
month = 3
monthName = switch month
  when 1
    'January'
  when 2
    'February'
  when 3
    'March'
  when 4
    'April'
  else
    'Some other month'

monthName
# 'March'
```

Use a switch to determine if a style of coffee has milk in it:

```
style = 'latte'
milk = switch style
  when "latte", "cappuccino"
    yes
  else
    no

milk
# true
```

Only one block of the switch is evaluated (there is no fall-through). A switch at the end of a function returns the evaluation of one block:

```
hasMilk = (style) ->
  switch style
    when "latte", "cappuccino"
      yes
    else
      no
```

◁— **Match multiple options.**

```
hasMilk 'espresso'
# false
```

The when keyword takes multiple options, each separated by a comma. If there is no else clause and none of the when clauses are matched, then evaluating the switch expression results in the value undefined:

```
pseudonym = 'Thomas Veil'

identity = switch pseudonym
  when 'Richard Bachman'
    'Stephen King'
  when 'Ringo Starr'
    'Richard Starkey'

identity
#
```

identity is declared but has the value undefined. Evaluating it on the REPL results in an empty line.

LOOPS

Loops are provided by the while, until, or loop keywords. Use them to do something, such as clean, repeatedly:

```
clean = (what) ->
  if what is 'House'
    'Now cleaning house'
  else
    'Now cleaning everything'

clean 'House'
# 'Now cleaning house'
```

You can continue cleaning the house while a variable messy is truthy:

```
messy = true
while messy
  clean 'House'
  messy = false
```

◁— **This particular while loop exits the first time around. Without assigning true to the messy variable, the loop won't exit.**

Or you can use an until statement. Suppose you have a variable spotless that is truthy when things are clean. You can use that instead of while:

```
spotless = false
until spotless
  clean 'Everything'
  spotless = true
```

This until loop exits the first time around. Without assigning true to the spotless variable, the loop won't exit.

Some things never end, though, and that's what the loop keyword is for:

```
loop clean 'Everything'
```

◁— **If you run this on the REPL, it will eventually exit with FATAL ERROR: JS Allocation failed - process out of memory.**

Loops are expressions, so they have a value, and if you have a loop that terminates, you can get the value:

```
x = 0
evenNumbers = while x < 6
  x = x + 1
  x * 2

evenNumbers
# [2, 4, 6, 8, 10, 12]
```

Most likely you won't use these looping constructs in CoffeeScript very often. They are there if you need them, though.

Finally, if you really need to, you can get out of a while, until, or for by using the break keyword. If you aren't familiar with the break keyword, then happily move on.

EXCEPTION BLOCKS

These are provided by the try, catch, and finally keywords. Use them to deal with *exceptional* circumstances inside a block of code. You should use the finally block to clean up after yourself. Exceptions are created with the throw statement. A try can also have a catch, a finally, or both:

```
flyAway = (animal) ->
  if animal is 'pig'
    throw 'Pigs cannot fly'
  else
    'Fly away!'

peter = 'pig'
try
  flyAway peter
catch error
  error
finally
  'Clean up!'
```

Of course, pigs don't fly, so any attempt to make one fly is an exceptional circumstance. In this example, if the animal is 'pig', then the catch block is evaluated, resulting in 'Pigs cannot fly'.

A try...catch also works as an expression. If no exception is thrown, then the value of the try is the value of the try expression:

```
charlotte = 'spider'
whatHappened = try
  flyAway charlotte
catch error
  error

whatHappened
# Fly away!
```

On the other hand, if an exception is thrown, then the value of the entire expression is the value of the catch:

```
whatHappened = try
  flyAway peter
catch error
  error

whatHappened
# Pigs cannot fly
```

Any variables assigned in a try, catch, or finally will be defined:

```
try definedOutsideTheTry = true
definedOutsideTheTry
# true
```

Finally, while it is possible, as shown here, to write a try without a catch, it's generally not a good idea to ignore exceptions. Deal with them.

INLINE BLOCKS

These are provided by the then keyword immediately after an if, case, or catch keyword to supply an expression as a block without a newline or indentation:

```
year = 1983
if year is 1983 then hair = 'perm'

hair
# 'perm'
```

Or for a while:

```
while messy then clean 'Everything'
```

Or inside a switch:

```
lastDigit = 4
daySuffix = switch lastDigit
  when 1 then 'st'
  when 2 then 'nd'
  when 3 then 'rd'
  else 'th'
```

An inline then is useful when the expression is small:

```
time = 15
allowed = if time < 12 then 'Yes' else 'No!'
allowed
# 'No!'
```

SUFFIX IF

An if statement can also go after an expression:

```
hair = 'permed' if year is 1983
```

Putting the if statement after the expression is more readable in some circumstances, so you should decide which version to use based on context.

2.4.3 *Pure statements*

If a statement isn't used as part of an expression but is used only to tell the computer to do something, then that's a *pure statement*. Some statements in JavaScript are only for control flow—there's no way for CoffeeScript to provide an expression version of those statements.

BREAK, CONTINUE, RETURN

The break, continue, and return statements can't be used as expressions. You might occasionally need return, but you should avoid break and continue. You might see this common idiom in other programming languages for reading line by line:

```
loop
  line = reader.readLine()
  if not line then break
```
> Loop over the lines of the file
> until there are no lines left.

Although it's possible to do that, it's not how you do things in CoffeeScript. In general, avoid using break, continue, or return. Use expressions instead.

2.4.4   Exercise

Suppose you have a variable animal that contains a string with the singular name for one of the animals: antelope, baboon, badger, cobra, or crocodile. Write some code to get the collective name for the animal. The collective names for the possible animals in the same order are herd, rumpus, cete, quiver, and bask:

```
animal = 'crocodile'
# <rest of answer goes here>
collective
# bask
```

2.5   Strings

It's possible to write CoffeeScript programs using only expressions containing the literal values already shown, but other language features and libraries provide convenient ways to do common tasks. Every program deals with text at some point, so it's useful to have some more string tools in your string toolbox. This section demonstrates some of the built-in string methods from JavaScript that are useful in Coffee-Script. This section also introduces string interpolation, which provides an elegant way to use variables inside strings.

2.5.1   Methods

CoffeeScript strings have all of the same built-in methods as JavaScript strings. Here are some of the most useful string methods.

SEARCHING

Use the search method on a string to find another string within:

```
'haystack'.search 'needle'
# -1

'haystack'.search 'hay'
# 0

'haystack'.search 'stack'
# 3
```

The number returned by search is the index in the string at which the match starts. If it returns -1, then no match was found. If it returns 0, the match starts at the beginning of the string.

Suppose you have all of the coffee drinks you serve containing milk in a string:

```
'latte,mocha,cappuccino,flat white,eiskaffee'
```

How do you write a new hasMilk function to use instead of a switch?

```
milkDrinks = 'latté,mocha,cappuccino,flat white,eiskaffee'

hasMilk = (style) ->
  milkDrinks.search(style) isnt -1

hasMilk 'mocha'
# true

hasMilk 'espresso romano'
# false
```

REPLACING

You use the replace method on a string when you want to replace one substring with another:

```
'haystack'.replace 'hay', 'needle'
# 'needlestack'
```

Suppose you want to fix the spelling of a coffee drink:

```
milkDrinks.replace 'latté', 'latte'
```

UPPERCASE AND LOWERCASE

There's a convenient way to convert a string to either all lowercase or all uppercase:

```
'Cappuccino'.toLowerCase()
# 'cappuccino'

'I am shouting!'.toUpperCase()
# 'I AM SHOUTING!'
```

SPLITTING

Use split when you want to split a string into an array of strings. You can split a string on the comma character using the /,/ regular expression literal:

```
'Banana,Banana'.split /,/
# [ 'Banana', 'Banana' ]

'latte,mocha,cappuccino,flat white,eiskaffee'.split /,/
# [ 'latte', 'mocha', 'cappuccino', 'flat white', 'eiskaffee' ]
```

That's enough string methods for now. On to something that JavaScript doesn't have.

2.5.2   *Interpolation*

Suppose you're displaying a web page to a user, and you want to include their name in the web page. You have the name in a variable:

```
userName = 'Scruffy'
```

Use interpolation. Provided by #{} inside double-quoted string literals, interpolation injects values into a string:

```
"Affirmative, Dave. I read you."
```

Use string interpolation to replace *Dave* with the actual username:

```
"Affirmative, #{userName}. I read you."
```

You might do the same with a style of coffee:

```
coffee = 'Ristresso'
"Enjoy your #{coffee}!"
# 'Enjoy your Ristresso!'
```

Without interpolation you'd have to add strings, which is tedious:

```
"Affirmative," + userName + ". I read you."
```

Imagine that you want to write a program that displays the string "Hi, my name is Scruffy. Today is Tuesday," where Tuesday is replaced with the current day of the week:

```
userName = 'Scruffy'

dayOfWeek = new Date().getDay()        ◄─── Use the getDay method
                                            of a date to get the day
                                            as a number.
dayName = switch dayOfWeek
  when 0 then 'Sunday'
  when 1 then 'Monday'
  when 2 then 'Tuesday'                Switch on the
  when 3 then 'Wednesday'             number to get the
  when 4 then 'Thursday'             name of the day.
  when 5 then 'Friday'
  when 6 then 'Saturday'
                                                          Use string
"Hi, my name is #{userName}. Today is #{dayName}."  ◄─┘  interpolation to
                                                          display the message.
```

2.5.3   *Exercise*

Get the collective animal name to be output in a string like the following:

```
"The collective of cobra is quiver"
```

2.6   *Arrays*

An *array* is an ordered set of values where a particular value is retrieved using the index of the value in the array. So far you've seen array literals in the form [1,2,3]. There are some features of arrays in CoffeeScript that you need to know, in particular, ranges and comprehensions. Just as there are features that make working with strings easier, there are features that make working with arrays easier.

Items in an array are accessed in order by using square brackets, with the first item being 0:

```
macgyverTools = ['Swiss Army knife', 'duct tape']
macgyverTools[0]
# 'Swiss Army knife'
```

```
macgyverTools[1]
# 'duct tape'
```

This section covers the basic use of arrays, how to transform them, how to extract values from them, and how to comprehend their contents.

2.6.1 *length, join, slice, and concat*

It's now time to explore some built-in properties and methods from JavaScript for arrays that you'll commonly need. None of them modify the original array.

LENGTH

All arrays have a `length` property that returns one greater than the index of the last item in the array:

```
fence = ['fence pail', 'fence pail']
fence.length
# 2
```

An item at any position in an array will affect the length of that array:

```
fence[999] = 'fence pail'
fence.length
# 1000
```

JOIN

Use `join` to convert an array into a string. It takes a string to use as the joining text between each item:

```
['double', 'barreled'].join '-'
# 'double-barreled'
```

SLICE

Use `slice` to extract part of an array:

```
['good', 'bad', 'ugly'].slice 0, 2
# ['good', 'bad']
```

When you use `slice`, the first number is the start index and the second number is the finish index. The item at the finish index isn't included in the result:

```
[0,1,2,3,4,5].slice 0,1
# [0]

[0,1,2,3,4,5].slice 3,5
# [3,4]
```

CONCAT

Use `concat` to join two arrays together:

```
['mythril', 'energon'].concat ['nitron', 'durasteel', 'unobtanium']
# [ 'mythril', 'energon', 'nitron', 'durasteel', 'unobtanium' ]
```

The array methods described don't modify the existing array:

```
potatoes = ['coliban', 'desiree', 'kipfler']

saladPotatoes = potatoes.slice 2,3
saladPotatoes
# ['kipfler']
```

```
potatoes
# ['coliban', 'desiree', 'kipfler']

potatoes.join 'mayonnnaise'

potatoes
# ['coliban', 'desiree', 'kipfler']

potatoes.concat ['pumpkin']

potatoes
# ['coliban', 'desiree', 'kipfler']
```

Enough potatoes. Time to look at the in operator.

2.6.2 *in*

In CoffeeScript the in operator has particular meaning for arrays. In JavaScript the in operator is used for objects, but in CoffeeScript it's used for arrays (the of operator is used for objects). Be mindful of that difference.

CONTAINS

This is provided by in for an array. Use it to determine if an array contains a particular value:

```
'to be' in ['to be', 'not to be']
# true

living = 'the present'
living in ['the past', 'the present']
# true
```

Suppose you split a string of beverages containing milk into an array:

```
milkBeverages = 'latte,mocha,cappuccino'.split /,/
```

The in operator shows if a particular beverage is present:

```
'mocha' in milkBeverages
```

2.6.3 *Ranges*

Ranges are provided by two or three dots between two numbers. Use a range when you need a short way of expressing an array containing a sequence of numerical values. Use two dots to include the upper bound:

```
[1..10]
# [ 1,2,3,4,5,6,7,8,9,10 ]

[5..1]
# [ 5,4,3,2,1 ]
```

Use three dots to exclude the upper bound:

```
[1...10]
# [ 1,2,3,4,5,6,7,8,9 ]
```

Range extraction also provides an alternative to the slice method for getting part of an array:

```
['good', 'bad', 'ugly'][0..1]
# ['good', 'bad']
```

2.6.4 *Comprehensions*

Comprehensions provide a way to look at the array of things (such as ingredients in a recipe) and to manipulate the values without having to use loops. CoffeeScript provides a rich set of comprehensions that can apply to either arrays or objects.

FOR...IN... COMPREHENSION

Array comprehensions allow you to evaluate an expression for each item in an array. Here's a one-line comprehension that's easy to experiment with on the REPL:

```
number for number in [9,0,2,1,0]
# [9,0,2,1,0]
```

Using the name `number` in the comprehension declares it as a variable. You can use any variable name you like:

```
x for x in [9,0,2,1,0]
# [9,0,2,1,0]
```

However, it is best to use a different variable name just for the constructor (you'll learn more about why later on). Now use a comprehension to add 1 to every item in the array:

```
number + 1 for number in [9,0,2,1,0]
# [10,1,3,2,1]
```

Use a comprehension to convert every item to a 0:

```
0 for number in [9,0,2,1,0]
# [0,0,0,0,0]
```

The name after the `for` keyword in a comprehension creates a variable with that name. It's possible to access the variable outside of the comprehension:

```
letter for letter in ['x','y','z']
# [x,y,z]

letter
# 'z'
```

But it's a very bad idea to do so. Leave comprehension variables in the comprehensions where they belong.

USING COMPREHENSIONS

Imagine you're making a chocolate cake. You have the ingredients supplied as an array of strings:

```
ingredients = [
  'block of dark chocolate'
  'stick butter'
  'cup of water'
  'cup of brown sugar'
  'packet of flour'
  'egg'
]
```

Suppose you want to make a cake that's twice as big. Make a new ingredients list that puts *2x* in front of all of the ingredients:

```
doubleIngredients = ("2x #{ingredient}" for ingredient in ingredients)

doubleIngredients
# [
#    '2x block of dark chocolate'
#    '2x stick butter'
#    '2x cup of water'
#    '2x cup of brown sugar'
#    '2x packet of flour'
#    '2x egg'
# ]
```

How do you mix all these ingredients? Suppose you have a `mix` function:

```
mix = (ingredient) ->
  "Put #{ingredient} in the bowl"
```

Invoke it for each item in the array:

```
instructions = (mix ingredient for ingredient in doubleIngredients)
```

Here, the function `mix` is invoked with the value of each ingredient and the result of all that is assigned to the instructions variable that now references an array:

```
[
  'Put 2x block of dark chocolate in the bowl'
  'Put 2x stick butter in the bowl'
  'Put 2x cup of water in the bowl'
  'Put 2x cup of brown sugar in the bowl'
  'Put 2x packet of flour in the bowl'
  'Put 2x egg in the bowl'
]
```

Notice the absence of loops. Comprehensions can simplify your code. Remember the `switch` statement from listing 2.1?

```
hasMilk = (style) ->
  switch style
    when 'latte', 'cappuccino', 'mocha'
      yes
    else
      no
```

Suppose you have some coffee styles in an array:

```
styles = ['cappuccino', 'mocha', 'latte', 'espresso']
```

Create a new comprehension with the result of invoking `hasMilk` for each item in the array:

```
hasMilk style for style in styles
# [true, true, true, false]
```

You can see Agtron use a comprehension when replying to Scruffy's array of beverages in figure 2.3.

Figure 2.3 Don't repeat yourself. Use a comprehension.

THE WHEN COMPREHENSION GUARD

A when at the end of a comprehension works like a guard; to make a flourless chocolate cake, you remove the flour from the ingredients:

```
mix = (ingredient) -> "Mixing #{ingredient}"
for ingredient in ingredients when ingredient.search('flour') < 0
  mix ingredient
```

Similarly, to get only the even numbers from a range of numbers, use a for..in comprehension with a when guard against odd numbers:

```
num for num in [1..10] when not (num%2)
# [ 2, 4, 6, 8, 10]
```

THE BY COMPREHENSION GUARD

Use by to perform an array comprehension in jumps. For example, people experimenting with something called polyphasic sleep might sleep every six hours:

```
day = [0..23]
sleep = (hour) -> "Sleeping at #{hour}"
sleep hour for hour in day by 6
# [ 'Sleeping at 0','Sleeping at 6','Sleeping at 12','Sleeping at 18' ]
```

Suppose you want to select every second person in an array; you can use the by keyword to do so:

```
person for person in ['Kingpin', 'Galactus', 'Thanos', 'Doomsday'] by 2
# ['Kingpin', 'Thanos']
```

MULTIPLY AN ARRAY

Suppose you have an array of your lucky numbers:

```
luckyNumbers = [3,4,8,2,1,8]
```

How do you multiply every item in the array by 2? Here's the *wrong* answer:

```
i = 0
twiceAsLucky = []

while i != luckyNumbers.length
  twiceAsLucky[i] = luckyNumbers[i]*2
  i = i + 1
# [1,2,3,4,5,6]

twiceAsLucky
# [6,8,16,4,2,16]
```

> **Depending on your REPL version, this while loop might even generate REPL output that you don't need!**

You can write a more concise solution using a comprehension:

```
number * 2 for number in luckyNumbers
```

Comprehensions help you to write simpler code that matches your intentions without having to worry about intermediate variables and loop counters.

2.6.5 Exercise

Suppose you have a string containing animal names:

```
animals = 'baboons badgers antelopes cobras crocodiles'
```

Write a program to output the following:

```
['A rumpus of baboons',
 'A cete of badgers',
 'A herd of antelopes',
 'A quiver of cobras',
 'A bask of crocodiles']
```

2.7 Heres for comments, docs, and regexes

CoffeeScript provides variants of strings, comments, and regular expression literals that can contain whitespace, such as newlines. All of these are indicated with syntax similar to their nonwhitespace counterparts but have a triple of the character for opening and closing the literal. Because they can contain literal whitespace, here-docs, herecomments, and heregexes are useful where formatting needs to be preserved and also for retaining clarity in code that would be difficult to read if the whitespace wasn't preserved.

2.7.1 Comments

Standard comments use a single # and continue to the end of the line:

```
# This is a comment
```

These standard CoffeeScript comments aren't included in the compiled JavaScript.

HERECOMMENTS

The CoffeeScript block comment called the *herecomment* is included as a block comment in the compiled JavaScript. Start and finish a block comment with three consecutive hashes (###):

```
###
This is a herecomment
It will be a block comment in the generated JavaScript
###
```

This herecomment will appear in the compiled JavaScript as a block comment:

```
/*
This is a herecomment
It will be a block comment in the generated JavaScript
*/
```

2.7.2   *Heredocs*

These are written as literal strings that contain literal whitespace. Use a heredoc when your text maintains whitespace for formatting:

```
'''
This
String
Contains
Whitespace
'''
```

Aside from maintaining whitespace, heredocs work like any other string literal. They can be assigned to a variable:

```
stanza = '''
Tyger! Tyger! burning bright
In the forests of the night,
What immortal hand or eye
Could frame thy fearful symmetry?
'''
```

When used with double-quoted strings, heredocs support string interpolation:

```
title = 'Tiny HTML5 document'
doc = """
<!doctype html>
<title>#{title}</title>
<body>
"""

doc
# '<!doctype html>\n<title>Tiny HTML5 document</title>\n<body>'
```

The literal newlines in the heredoc appear as \n newline characters in a string when the heredoc is evaluated.

2.7.3 Heregexes

CoffeeScript has the same regular expression support as the underlying JavaScript runtime with regular expression literals contained within single forward slashes:

```
/[0-9]/
```

CoffeeScript also supports a notation for regular expressions containing whitespace such as newlines. These *heregexes* are written between triple forward slashes; they're useful when writing more complicated regular expressions that have a reputation for being impenetrable to understanding:

```
leadingWhitespace = ///
  ^\s\s*  # start and pre-check optimizations for performance
///g
```

Syntax and language features are important, but they don't write programs for you. In the next section, you'll write a toy program and run it in the two environments that will be used the most in this book: web browsers and Node.js.

2.8 Putting it together

To learn a programming language, you need to write programs with it. By looking at a program here, you'll also get context and examples for housekeeping, such as how to run the program once it's written.

Some of the code listings in this section might use techniques that are unfamiliar to you. Those techniques will be clear to you after chapter 3.

2.8.1 Running in a browser

To run CoffeeScript programs in a web browser, you should compile them to JavaScript and then include the JavaScript file in your HTML document. Suppose you have the barista program in a file called barista.coffee. First, go to the command line and use `coffee` to compile the script:

```
> coffee -c barista.coffee
```

This generates a barista.js file that you then include in an HTML document as a script:

```
<!doctype html>
<title>Barista</title>
<body>
<form id='order'>
<input id='request' />
<input type='submit' value ='order' />
</form>
The barista.
<div id='response'></div>
</body>
<script src='barista.js'></script>
</html>
```

If you load that file in your web browser, then the barista.js script is executed. In the following listing you see a browser-based implementation of the barista program. The browser version has the house roast specified at the top of the file.

Listing 2.3   A browser barista (barista.coffee)

```coffee
houseRoast = 'Yirgacheffe'

hasMilk = (style) ->
  switch style.toLowerCase()
    when 'latte', 'cappuccino', 'mocha'
      yes
    else
      no

makeCoffee = (requestedStyle) ->
  style = requestedStyle || 'Espresso'
  console.log houseRoast
  if houseRoast?
    "#{houseRoast} #{style}"
  else
    style

barista = (style) ->
  time = (new Date()).getHours()
  if hasMilk(style) and time > 12 then "No!"
  else
    coffee = makeCoffee style
    "Enjoy your #{coffee}!"

order = document.querySelector '#order'
request = document.querySelector '#request'
response = document.querySelector '#response'

order.onsubmit = ->
  response.innerHTML = barista(request.value)
  false
```

> When the order element (a form) is submitted, then evaluate the following function.

> Find the parts of the HTML document that you need to interact with. Assign references to them to variables.

> Return false from the function so that the order form doesn't submit.

> Use innerHTML to set the content of the response element to be the order response.

This program accepts the coffee order from an input field and displays the response in the web page.

2.8.2   Running on the command line

If you run CoffeeScript from a standard install on the command line and provide a CoffeeScript file (such as the one from listing 2.4), then the program in the file will be executed:

```
> coffee 2.4.coffee
You need to specify an order.
```

The output of the program indicates that you need to specify an order. You do that with arguments.

PROGRAM ARGUMENTS

Any Node.js program run on the command line has access to the command-line arguments passed to it via the process. The first command-line argument is available at process.argv[2]. Suppose the program is invoked as follows:

```
> coffee 2.4.coffee 'Cappuccino'
```

Here, the program process.argv[2] is 'Cappuccino'. What happened to argv[0] and argv[1]? They're reserved for other properties. The process.argv[0] is the runtime (in this case, coffee) and the process.argv[1] is the filesystem path for the program executed (in this case, the full path to the 2.4.coffee file).

THE FILESYSTEM MODULE

The other essential task in a Node.js program is to read files. For example, suppose your command-line barista program needs to read the house roast from a file before serving a coffee. To do this in Node, you'll require the filesystem module:

```
fs = require 'fs'
```

At this point you don't need to know much about how the module system works. It's covered in depth in chapter 12. Back to the program, though; in the next listing you see a full implementation of the command-line barista program.

Listing 2.4 A command-line barista

```
fs = require 'fs'

houseRoast = null

hasMilk = (style) ->
  switch style.toLowerCase()
    when "latte", "cappuccino"
      yes
    else
      no

makeCoffee = (requestedStyle) ->
  style = requestedStyle || 'Espresso'
  if houseRoast?
    "#{houseRoast} #{style}"
  else
    style

barista = (style) ->
  time = (new Date()).getHours()
  if hasMilk(style) and time > 12 then "No!"
  else
    coffee = makeCoffee style
    "Enjoy your #{coffee}!"
```

```
main = ->
  requestedCoffee = process.argv[2]                    ⊣ Read the command-
  if !requestedCoffee?                                   line input.
    console.log 'You need to specify an order'
  else
    fs.readFile 'house_roast.txt', 'utf-8', (err, data) -> ⊣
      if data then houseRoast = data.replace /\n/, ''
      console.log barista(requestedCoffee)             ⊣
main()
```

Read the file containing the house roast and set it.

Call the barista program with the command-line argument.

The program in listing 2.4 expects to find a file called house_roast.txt that contains the name of the house roast. Suppose that file contains Yirgacheffe and that it's currently before midday. Here's some sample output:

```
> coffee 2.4.coffee
You need to specify an order.

> coffee 2.4.coffee 'Ristretto'
Enjoy your Yirgacheffe Ristretto!
```

The output you'll get when you invoke the program depends on the order and the time of day; experiment with it and explore how it works. The programs in listings 2.3 and 2.4 use some concepts in CoffeeScript and related to CoffeeScript (such as asynchronous programs and web browsers) that you might not yet fully grasp. That's fine; the following chapters will lead you to a better understanding of these concepts.

2.9 Summary

You've learned a lot of syntax in this second chapter. It was important to immerse you in the syntax so that you could begin to get used to it. You've learned that CoffeeScript makes programs easier to understand by emphasizing expressions, cleaning syntax by removing unnecessary characters, and providing succinct alternatives to some common JavaScript idioms (such as dealing with null and undefined values). In the next chapter you'll start to really do things with CoffeeScript. The next chapter is about functions.

First-class functions

If you asked a dozen JavaScript programmers what they thought JavaScript got wrong, you'd probably get a dozen different answers. If you asked those same dozen people what JavaScript got *right*, they'd probably all answer, "First-class functions." What does it mean that JavaScript has first-class functions, why does it matter, and how does CoffeeScript make functions even better? All will be answered in good time. First, though, what exactly is a function?

A *function* defines a transformation of input values called *parameters* to an output value called the *return* value. You define a function in CoffeeScript with *literal notation* using an arrow:

```
->
```

That isn't a very useful function, though. It has no parameters and no return value. The function parameters go to the left of the arrow, and the function *body* goes to the right of the arrow:

```
Parameters        Body
(a, b)    ->    a + b
```

When you *invoke* a function, you provide arguments, and the function transforms them to produce an output value:

```
add = (a, b) -> a + b

add 2, 3
# 5
```

Notice how this function is assigned to the variable add? That's an important detail that underpins most of this chapter. You see, functions don't just produce values; they *are* values. This means that a function can produce a function as its return value and take a function as an argument. This idea that functions are values is referred to as functions being *first-class* and leads to the powerful technique of gluing functions together, called *function composition*.

How does this relate to JavaScript? Functions are just as powerful in JavaScript, but unfortunately functions in JavaScript have some problems. CoffeeScript aims to address these problems and improve the syntax. In this chapter you'll learn how to use functions for events, callbacks, and higher-order programming and why CoffeeScript syntax is a clearer way to describe functions than the equivalent JavaScript.

3.1   Computation

Imagine your friends Agtron and Scruffy are having a party, and you've been tasked with writing a program to count the number of confirmed attendees. When the program counts the attendees for you, it performs a *computation*. Think of functions as being little computers—they perform computations. To grasp this metaphor, you need to start with some basics.

3.1.1   Basics

You can multiply the numbers 3 and 4 using the multiplication operator:

```
3 * 4
# 12
```

Here's a function to perform the same operation:

```
threeTimesFour = -> 3 * 4        Declaring a function literal evaluates to a
# [Function]                  ⊲  function, shown on the REPL as [Function]
```

When this function is invoked, it evaluates the expressions in the body of the function:

```
threeTimesFour()
# 12
```

The *last* expression evaluated inside the function is the evaluation of the function itself:

```
journey = ->
  'A call to adventure'
  'Crossing the chasm'
  'Transformation'
  'Atonement'
  'Back home'

journey()
# 'Back home'
```

Remember, to enter an expression that spans multiple lines into the REPL, you press Ctrl-V to start and Ctrl-V when you've finished.

The result of invoking the function is the string 'Back home', which is the last expression in the function body.

That `threeTimesFour` function isn't very useful, though. How do you multiply *any* two numbers? By using function parameters:

```
multiply = (a, b) -> a * b
multiply(2, 7)
# 14
```

Here the names a and b inside the parentheses are known as either parameters or arguments.

Multiplication is rather boring, though, especially when there's already an operator to do it for you. What are functions good for then? The *real* power of functions starts when you use them to define new things that don't have operators. Why? Because when you define things that don't have operators, you create your own language.

3.1.2 Custom operations

Consider a function to covert gigabytes to megabytes:

```
gigabytesToMegabytes = (gigabytes) -> gigabytes * 1024
```

This function defines an operation that isn't built into the language. Try it:

```
gigabytesToMegabytes 7
# 7168
```

What sorts of things do you define in a language? That depends on the problem you're solving.

KEEPING TRACK OF ATTENDEES

Time to get back to counting the list of party attendees. Imagine a list of confirmed attendees is emailed to you with the name of each confirmed attendee separated from the next by a comma. The list is too long to print here, but the first part of the list looks like this:

```
'Batman,Joker,Wolverine,Sabertooth,The Green Lantern,Sinestro'
```

Sounds like a fun party. Anyway, you don't want to manually count the new list every time it arrives in your inbox. How do you write a program to count the list for you?

CoffeeScript doesn't have a built-in operator or method to count the number of comma-separated words in a string, but it's possible to count them by using the `split` method for strings that you saw in chapter 2. Split the string into an array of strings, and then use the array's `length` property. Try it on the REPL:

```
text = 'Monday,Tuesday,Wednesday,Thursday,Friday,Saturday,Sunday'
daysInWeek = text.split(/,/)
daysInWeek.length
# 7

text = 'Spring,Summer,Autumn,Winter'
seasons = text.split(/,/)
seasons.length
# 4
```

Split the string on the comma character to get an array of words.

Use the length property of the array.

If you're a masochist, then you'll happily do that over and over again, and over and over again, every time you have another string. Otherwise, you can write a program to count the words and use that program each time you want to count. The following listing contains a CoffeeScript program that runs on Node.js and counts the number of words in a comma-separated string. It reads arguments from the command line using process.argv, which you saw in chapter 2.

Listing 3.1   Counting words

```
text = process.argv[2]

if text
  words = text.split /,/
  console.log "#{words.length} partygoers"
else
  console.log 'usage: coffee 3.1.coffee [text]'
```

Get the argument provided to the program.

Count the partygoers.

No string provided. Exit.

Use this program from the command line by typing coffee followed by the name of the file and then the arguments to the program:

```
coffee listing.3.1.coffee Batman,Joker,Wolverine,Sabertooth
```

What does this have to do with functions? Well, functions are a bit like miniprograms. Consider a function that counts comma-separated words in a string:

```
countWords = (text) -> text.split(/,/).length
# [Function]
```

Evaluates to a function.

Enter the one-line countWords function into your REPL and experiment:

```
countWords 'sight,smell,taste,touch,hearing'
# 5

countWords 'morning,noon,night'
# 3
```

Functions can do anything—think of the possibilities! Before writing more functions, though, you should review their different parts.

3.1.3   Anatomy

As you've seen, a function is written with parameters in parentheses on the left side of an arrow and the function body on the right. But not many functions will fit on one line. If the function body requires multiple lines, then you put the function body underneath, with each line of code indented one level. Refer to figure 3.1.

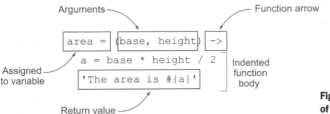

Figure 3.1 **Anatomy of a function**

INVOCATION

When you write the variable name of a function followed by one or more values, then the function is invoked:

```
countWords 'north,east,south,west'
# 4
```

Any function is invoked when followed by parameters or parentheses, even a function that's not assigned to a variable:

```
(-> 42)()
# 42
```

The significance of this odd-looking bit of syntax is explored later in the chapter.

ARGUMENTS

A function takes any number of values as arguments with a comma separating each argument from the next. These arguments specify values for the function parameters. Why do you need more than one argument? Well, consider a string of words separated by colons:

```
beerStyles = 'Porter:Pilsner:Stout:Lager:Bock'
```

The existing `countWords` function expects words separated by commas, so it doesn't work for this string. To solve this, add a second parameter to the function that you can use to pass a second argument to the function. This second argument specifies the character to use as the delimiter between each word:

```
countWords = (text, delimiter) ->
  words = text.split delimiter          ◁─  Split the string using the character
  words.length                              supplied in the argument.
```

Now the function works for strings delimited by different characters:

```
countWords('Josie:Melody:Valerie:Alexandra', ':')
# 4

countWords('halloween/scream/maniac', '/')
# 3

countWords('re#brown#tag#table', '#')
# 4

countWords(beerStyles, ':')
# 5
```

All those parentheses, though; are they necessary? No.

PARENTHESES

Parentheses around arguments are optional:

```
planets = 'Mercury,Venus,Earth,Mars,Jupiter,Saturn,Uranus,Neptune'
countWords(planets)            <─┐
# 8                              │  Invoke countWords
                                 │  with one argument.
countWords planets             <─┘
# 8
```

But parentheses aren't optional when you invoke a function *without any arguments*:

```
sayHello = -> 'Hello!'
sayHello()
# 'Hello!'
```

Without parentheses or arguments, the function itself is being evaluated, instead of the result of invoking the function:

```
sayHello                          │  Evaluates to
# [Function]                    <─┘  a function.
```

In general, you should omit parentheses where possible.

IMPLICIT RETURN

The return value for a function is the last expression evaluated when the function is invoked. In JavaScript a function requires an explicit `return` statement indicating the return value. If there is no such statement, then the return value is `undefined`:

```
returnsUndefined = function(a,b) {      In JavaScript the result of
  a + b;                                invoking a function that
};                                      has no return statement
                                        is undefined.
returnsUndefined();
// undefined
```

In CoffeeScript the only way to return `undefined` from a function is on purpose, by having it as the last expression evaluated:

```
returnsUndefined = ->
  return undefined          In CoffeeScript a function
                            returns undefined only if
returnsUndefined()          you make it.
# undefined
```

RETURN FROM INSIDE EXPRESSION

Remember the `countWords` function?

```
countWords = (text, delimiter) ->
  words = text.split delimiter
  words.length
```

The last expression evaluated is `words.length`. Suppose that this function doesn't quite do what you need it to—it has several problems. The first is that it gives an incorrect result for an empty string:

```
countWords '', ':'
# 1
```

It does that because that's how the `split` method works. Normally for `countWords`, the way that `split` works is fine for a single word:

```
'abc'.split /,/
# ['abc']
```

But an empty string looks just like a single word:

```
''.split /,/
# ['']
```

To fix the empty string problem in `countWords`, add an `if` inside it to check whether the text argument is empty or not:

```
countWords = (text, delimiter) ->
  if text                                      If text is a
    words = text.split(delimiter || /,/)       non-empty string
    words.length
  else                                         Else 0
    0

countWords ''          ◁──  Logs 0 to
# 0                          console
```

How does this affect the last expression in the function body? It now depends on whether the `if` or the `else` branch is evaluated. If the string is empty, then the `else` branch is evaluated[1] and the last expression is `0`. If the string is not empty, then the `if` branch is evaluated and the last expression is `words.length`.

EXPLICIT RETURN STATEMENT

You can return early from a function by using the `return` keyword followed by an expression. An alternative version of `countWords` with an explicit return statement follows:

```
count = (text, delimiter) ->
  return 0 unless text                ◁──  Return 0 unless text is
  words = text.split(delimiter || /,/)      a non-empty string.
  words.length
```

The `unless` keyword you see here isn't used all that often in CoffeeScript, but it's very handy and commonly used when returning early from a function. It's time for a quick detour about how `unless` works.

UNLESS

Putting `unless` after an expression has the opposite effect of putting `if` after an expression. This means that the following two expressions are equivalent:

```
eat berries if not poisonous
```

```
eat berries unless poisonous
```

---

[1] The `else` branch is evaluated when `text` is an empty string because an empty string is a falsy value. Remember, the falsy values are `null`, `false`, `0`, and `''`.

If the expression after the `unless` keyword is falsy, then the expression before the `unless` keyword won't be evaluated.

Back on track now, how does the CoffeeScript function syntax compare to the equivalent JavaScript?

3.1.4   *Comparison: JavaScript and CoffeeScript*

The next listing presents a side-by-side comparison of JavaScript and CoffeeScript for the latest `countWords` function. Variable names have been shortened to avoid clutter in the example.

Listing 3.2   Count words comparison

CoffeeScript
```
countWords = (s, del) ->
  if s
    words = s.split del
    words.length
  else
    0
```

JavaScript
```
var countWords = function (s, del) {
  var words;
  if (s) {
    words = s.split(del);
    return words.length;
  } else {
    return 0;
  }
}
```

CoffeeScript has less syntax than JavaScript for defining functions. Implicit returns aren't just syntax, though; they also help you think differently about how you write functions. In CoffeeScript, invoked functions have a value *by default*. This is a change in the *semantics* of functions that helps you more readily think of functions as expressions.

WHERE ARE THE NAMED FUNCTIONS?
JavaScript has named functions written by writing the `function` keyword followed by a name and a function definition:

```
function obi(wan) {
  return wan;
};

obi('kenobi');
```

JavaScript example

CoffeeScript, preferring expressions, *does not* have named functions but only function values assigned to variables.

3.1.5   *Exercises*

Use these exercises to ensure you understand functions as computations:

- Write a version of `countWords` that uses space for the word delimiter and ignores words shorter than three letters.
- Write a function that creates a new space-delimited string of words containing only every second word in the original space-delimited string. For example,

```
misquote = """we like only like think like when like we like are like
confronted like with like a like problem"""
everyOtherWord misquote
```

should return

```
'we only think when we are confronted with a problem'
```

That covers the core ideas behind functions. In order to get to more advanced usage, you now need to look at some real-world problems, warts and all, which will take you on the scenic route to uncovering the power of functions. With your patience in hand, you'll begin with events.

3.2 Events

Web browsers and Node.js have an event-driven programming model. The core idea of event-driven programming is that program flow reacts to events as they occur instead of prescribing the order in which things must occur. It's a bit like the difference between sitting in a pizza shop, watching your pizza get cooked, and having it home delivered. The home-delivered pizza is event driven—when the pizza is ready (the ready event), you will receive it, without having to wait around.

In CoffeeScript, *functions are used to handle events*. A function is registered as an event handler so that when the event occurs, the function is invoked. You'll see that in this section by looking at creating and handling events with callbacks.

> **PREREQUISITE: RUNNING ON THE CLIENT** Some parts of this section require that some CoffeeScript be embedded in an HTML document. Go back to the end of the previous chapter if you need a refresher on how to do that.

3.2.1 Browser events

A quick recap of the program you've been writing for Scruffy and Agtron's party is in order. So far you can count the number of guests attending the party by reading the attendee list from a file called partygoers.txt. Next, you need to create a website for the party that always shows the current attendee count. Scruffy started creating a site for the party, but he had to abandon the project at the last minute to tour Greenland as a xylophonist. Luckily, he had already started on it. You already have an HTML document:

```
<!doctype html>
<html>
<title>How many people are coming?</title>
<script src='attendees.js'></script>
<body>
<div id='how-many-attendees'>How many attendees?</div>
</body>
</html>
```

To get your CoffeeScript program to run in the browser when you load this document, you need to first compile it to a file called attendees.js.

The element that will hold the attendee count.

You want to replace the words *How many attendees?* with the current attendees count. Scruffy also left you some code that shows how to update the content:

```
document.querySelector('#how-many-attendees').innerHTML = 55
```

Update the content 'How many attendees?' with 55.

So, how do you update the content with the latest attendees? Forget about web browsers entirely for a minute and think about whether you've seen anything so far in CoffeeScript to do that. You haven't, but you're about to see something that gets you part of the way. It's called `setInterval`.

> **DOCUMENT.QUERYSELECTOR?**   The `document.querySelector` method is part of the Document Object Model (DOM) API that you use to manipulate things in a web browser. You'll find more about browsers in chapter 11.

3.2.2   Using timeouts and intervals to create events

Inside a browser there's a *global* `setInterval` method. It's a global method because you can invoke it anywhere in your program. The `setInterval` method is used to make something happen repeatedly, which is exactly what you want for updating the attendees count. First, though, there's another global method called `setTimeout` that's easier for you to experiment with.

The `setTimeout` method takes two arguments. The first argument is the function to be invoked, and the second argument is the duration (in milliseconds) from the current time that you want the function to be invoked. Try it on the REPL:

```
partyMessage = -> console.log "It's party time!"
setTimeout partyMessage, 1000          1000 milliseconds
# ... 1 second later                   is 1 second.
# It's party time!
```

The `setInterval` method works the same way, except that it invokes the function repeatedly. If you enter that into the REPL, then it will continue to be invoked until you exit the REPL or clear the interval.

```
interval = setInterval partyMessage, 1000
# ... 1 second later
# It's party time!
# ... 1 second later
# It's party time!
# and so on...                  To stop the interval,
clearInterval interval          you use clearInterval.
```

What does this have to do with functions and events? Continuing the scenic route, it's all about callbacks.

> **GLOBAL METHODS**   The `setTimeout` method belongs to a global object. The global object in a web browser is typically the browser's window object. Other environments have different global objects. Consult the reference for the specific environment.

CALLBACKS

A callback is a function that's invoked from somewhere else. You see, normally you invoke a function yourself, whenever you feel the need:

```
partyMessage()
# It's party time!
```

A function used as a callback is different. Instead of invoking the function, imagine giving it to Scruffy and asking him to invoke it later. *That's a callback.* Similarly, when you invoke `setTimeout` with `partyMessage`, you're telling `setTimeout` to invoke it later. You're using the `partyMessage` function as a callback.

These callback functions have a very important feature—they're *asynchronous*. What does that mean? To find out, try `setTimeout partyMessage` on the REPL again, but this time make the duration 5 seconds and enter the expression 1+1 before you see the party message appear. Be quick!

```
setTimeout partyMessage, 5000
1 + 1
# 2

# ... 5 seconds later
# It's party time!
```

Notice how the REPL evaluated the expression 1+1 before the timeout was complete? That's why asynchronous callbacks are important; you can go off and do other things while you're waiting for the response. That's exactly what Agtron does in figure 3.2 as he waits for Scruffy to call back.

If you created a timeout or interval that you decide you don't want, you use `clearTimeout` or `clearInterval` to clear it:

```
timeout = setTimeout partyMessage, 1000
clearTimeout timeout
```

The partyMessage callback won't be invoked because the timeout was cleared.

Figure 3.2 Callbacks are asynchronous.

Back to the task, use `setInterval` to update the attendee count in the HTML document every second:

```
updateAttendeesCount = ->
  document.querySelector('#how-many-attendees').innerHTML 55

setInterval updateAttendeesCount, 1000
```

> You can't just run this on the REPL. First, you must use the compiler to generate an attendees.js file that can be included in Scruffy's HTML document.

Updating with the value 55 every second isn't exactly what you need, though. Where does the actual attendee count come from? Just as you haven't seen anything in CoffeeScript to do something repeatedly, you also haven't seen anything[2] to read input or write output (called I/O). Indeed, there is no way *built into* the language to do I/O in CoffeeScript (or JavaScript). What do you use instead? You use callback functions.

3.3   *I/O*

Continuing the scenic route to the power of functions, you're presented with a new problem: there's no easy, built-in way to do I/O in CoffeeScript (or JavaScript). What can you do? The strategy so far for parts of the language you want but that are not built in has been to define a functions for them. It's the same with I/O; you define a function that specifies how to handle data resulting from I/O.

This method of doing I/O seems tedious at first but has two advantages. First, it means that I/O is asynchronous (something you'll learn much more about in chapter 9), and second, it means you don't have to look at the details of how the I/O is implemented. Instead, you concentrate on the callback function. But before you can ignore a detail, you need to appreciate what it is you're ignoring. The I/O details for fetching data in a web browser are commonly grouped under the term *Ajax*.

3.3.1   *Ajax*

Remember that party attendees website? You want the count to update every second, but so far you have no way to actually get the attendee count. Suppose the attendee count is available somewhere on the web; it doesn't matter where. To get that data into the website you use Ajax to fetch it. Time for a bit of wishful thinking: suppose you already have a `get` function that does the Ajax for you and that this `get` function accepts a callback function as an argument:

```
url = "http://www.coffeescriptinaction.com/3/data.js"
get url, (response) ->
  console.log response
```

> Use the get function to dispatch a request.

Figure 3.3 demonstrates how this works across the network.

The sequence diagram in figure 3.3 is more complicated than the callback you write. Now, the data.js file contains the number of party attendees and *you can get the contents of that file* with the `get` method, which does some Ajax for you. All this means

---

[2]   Excluding a brief encounter with fs.readFile in listing 2.4.

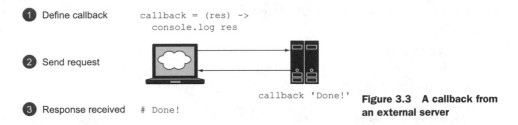

Figure 3.3 A callback from an external server

that you can use `setInterval` to regularly trigger a fetch of the latest attendee every second and display that in the HTML page. Here's the document again:

```
<!doctype html>
<title>How many people are coming?</title>
<script src='attendees.js'></script>
<body>
<div id='how-many-attendees'>How many attendees?</div>
</body>
</html>
```

Finally, here's the client-side script that brings all of this together:

```
showAttendees = ->
  url = "http://www.coffeescriptinaction.com/3/data.js"
  get url, (response) ->
    outputElement = document.querySelector("#how-many-attendees")
    outputElement.innerHTML = "#{response} attendees!"

setInterval(showAttendees, 1000)
```

> The callback inserts the contents of data.js into the web page.

> Request that showAttendees be invoked every 1000 milliseconds.

It took a while to get there, but that's how things work in a web browser. How about on Node.js then? Luckily, it works the same way.

3.3.2 *Event-driven file reading with Node.js*

Now imagine that you receive a new file called partygoers.txt containing the attendee list every time it changes and that you have access to this file. You already have a way to fetch the attendee count from a web browser, but how do you write a web server that serves up the attendee count by reading it from a file? Reading a file in Node.js looks a lot like the Ajax you just wrote:

```
fs = require 'fs'

readAttendeesList = (error, fileContents) ->
  console.log fileContents

fs.readFile 'partygoers.txt', readAttendeesList
```

> Require the Node.js filesystem module fs.

> Invoke fs.readFile with the file to read and a callback function to be invoked when it's done.

Great, now you can read the attendee file. The next step will be to serve the attendee count on the web somewhere so that the website can fetch it using Ajax. Before moving on, though, you might want to spend some time experimenting with file reading to become comfortable with it. Writing a version of a small utility called cat will help you do that.

A CAT PROGRAM

In the following listing is a simple program that's similar to the cat utility found on Unix-like operating systems. This program prints the contents of a file.

Listing 3.3   Cat utility

```
fs = require 'fs'

file = process.argv[2]
fs.readFile file, 'utf-8', (error, contents) ->
  if error
    console.log error
  else
    console.log contents
```

The readFile call needs to know what encoding the file has; use utf-8.

If there's an error reading the file, just console.log the error.

console.log the file if no error.

Ready to continue and serve a web page using Node.js? Ready for the surprise (or not)? Serving a website involves callback functions.

3.3.3   *Event-driven file serving with Node.js*

In the next listing, you see a web application that watches a local file for changes and displays the most recent value in a web page. When the file changes, the contents are read in and then assigned to a variable. The value of that variable is then used in the response to HTTP requests.

Listing 3.4   Serve the current contents of a file

```
fs = require 'fs'
http = require 'http'

sourceFile = 'myfile'
fileContents = 'File not read yet.'

readSourceFile = ->
  fs.readFile sourceFile, 'utf-8', (error, data) ->
    if error
      console.log error
    else
      fileContents = data

fs.watchFile sourceFile, readSourceFile

server = http.createServer (request, response) ->
  response.end fileContents

server.listen 8080, '127.0.0.1'
```

Require the filesystem and HTTP modules.

Set some vars for the app.

Function that asynchronously reads the source file.

Attach the file reader to file change events.

Listen on HTTP requests with event handler.

This program uses events for reading a file, for watching a file for changes, and for responding to incoming HTTP request events. Every one of these events is handled by a callback function defined in the program.

Although the module system is covered in depth in chapter 12, you'll see two modules used in this chapter. They are the filesystem module (`fs`) and the HTTP module (`http`).

FILESYSTEM MODULE

The Node.js filesystem module `fs` provides reading from and writing to local files. In listing 3.4 the `fs.readFile` method, which you've already seen, is used in addition to the `fs.watchFile` method.

The `fs.watchFile` method takes a file and callback function. The file is polled for changes; when a change is detected, the callback is invoked. The polling is implemented by Node.js interfacing with the operating system.

HTTP MODULE

The Node.js HTTP module provides low-level methods for making HTTP requests and serving HTTP responses. In listing 3.4 a server is created using `http.createServer` and then told to `listen` for incoming request events on port 8080 on the host 127.0.0.1.

3.3.4 Exercises

Use these exercises to build your confidence working with programs that contain functions:

- Add a word-counting function to the file-serving code in listing 3.4 so that the web server responds with the number of attendees to the party, given the following attendees list:

  ```
  'Talos,Gnut,Torg,Ash,Beta,Max,Bender'
  ```

- See what happens when you change the list of attendees in the file being watched from the previous exercise.

This ends the scenic route you took to understanding how central functions work in CoffeeScript. In order to achieve anything of practical value (like serving a website), you have to use callback functions. Functions are important, so you must become proficient at using them. This begins with the idea of higher-order functions.

3.4 Higher-order functions

Remember, *functions are values*. A function can be invoked by another function, supplied as an argument to another function, and be the return value of a function. Using these techniques, functions can be glued together. A function that glues together other functions, composing them, is a *higher-order function*.

Suppose you do roughly the same thing every day, a typical example being Monday:

```
monday = ->
  wake()
  work()
  sleep()
```

But on Thursday you go to train with your javelin-catching team:

```
thursday = ->
  wake()
  work()
  catchJavelins()
  sleep()
```

You could have a single function that switched on the day:

```
activities = (day) ->
  switch day
    when 'thursday' then catchJavelins()
```

But now you will be forever updating the `activities` function. Instead, how about a day function that looks like the following?

```
day = (freeTime) ->
  wake()
  work()
  freeTime()
  sleep()
```

Now you can define `thursday` using day and `catchJavelins`:

```
thursday = day catchJavelins
```

Now only `thursday` has to care about javelin catching. By using the `catchJavelins` function as a value composing `thursday`, you've made your life a little easier. This composition stuff sounds useful! How else can you compose with functions?

3.4.1 Invoking other functions

Imagine you want to check the attendee list to see if a particular person is attending. How do you write a program for that? You might think to start by using the `search` method on a string that you learned in chapter 2 (remember, `search` returns the value `-1` if it doesn't find a match). Consider a `contains` function that searches a string of comma-separated words:

```
contains = (text, word) -> (text.search word) isnt -1
randomWords = 'door,comeuppance,jacuzzi,tent,hippocampus,gallivant'

contains randomWords, 'tent'
# true
```

Remember, the isnt keyword is the CoffeeScript alias for !==.

Unfortunately, this `contains` function returns the wrong value for the word *camp* because the word *hippocampus* contains the word *camp*.

```
contains randomWords, 'camp'
#true
```

In case you missed the memo, false positives are not a design feature. You already have a function that splits these strings into individual words, so back to word counting—here's a one-liner:

```
wordCount = (text, delimiter) -> text.split(delimiter).length
```

Use this as the starting point for a correct `contains` function.

REUSE

To avoid duplication, you want to reuse this `wordCount` function, but sadly, it currently does too much for you to be able to reuse it. You need a function that splits the string into an array. So, take out the split and make it a separate function:

```
split = (text, delimiter) -> text.split delimiter
```

Now you can define `wordCount` as a function that invokes `split`:

```
wordCount = (text, delimiter) ->
  words = split(text, delimiter)
  words.length
```

Now define `contains` as a function that invokes `split` and uses the in operator on the array returned by the `split` function:

```
contains = (text, delimiter, word) ->
  words = split(text, delimiter)
  word in words
```

Because you're now looking for an actual word occurrence in an array instead of a match across the entire string, this new version of `contains` works correctly with the word *camp*:

```
contains randomWords, ',', 'camp'
# false
```

Invoking the `split` function from inside the `contains` function demonstrates another function composition—invoking one function from another.

3.4.2 *Example: Counting words in a file*

Counting words in comma-separated strings can be extended to a more general word-counting program similar to the wc utility on Unix-like operating systems. Here's a Node.js program for counting the number of words in a file. It demonstrates the techniques used so far, as well as revisiting array comprehensions.

Listing 3.5 Counting words

```
fs = require 'fs'

split = (text) ->            Split a string
  text.split /\W/g           into words.

count = (text) ->
  parts = split text
  words = (word for word in parts when word.trim().length > 0)     Count array.
  words.length

countMany = (texts) ->
  sum = 0
  for text in texts          Count in many
    sum = sum + count text   strings of text.
  sum
```

```
countWordsInFile = (fileName) ->
  stream = fs.createReadStream fileName
  stream.setEncoding 'ascii'
  wordCount = 0
  stream.on 'data', (data) ->
    lines = data.split /\n/gm
    wordCount = wordCount + countMany lines
  stream.on 'close', () ->
    console.log "#{wordCount} words"

file = process.argv[2]

if file
  countWordsInFile file
else
  console.log 'usage: coffee wordcount.coffee [file]'
```

Read the file in as a stream and perform a word count on each stream.

Get the filename from command-line argument.

Handle command line.

WHERE'S REDUCE?   If you're thinking that the countMany function could have just reduced the array instead of iterating manually, you're correct. If you don't know what reduce is, then that's fine too; carry on.

3.4.3   *Functions as arguments*

Good news! You've already seen functions used as arguments. For example, the setTimeout method takes a function as an argument:

```
invokeLater = -> console.log 'Please invoke in one second'
setTimeout invokeLater, 1000
```

This has uses other than callback functions, though.

SUMMING AN ARRAY

Just when you thought you had the party attendee count page covered, there's a problem. People are allowed to bring friends to the party, and those friends aren't being included in the attendee list. Instead, you're now getting emailed another *guests* file containing the number of friends each person is bringing. Like the attendee list, the guest list is too long to print here, but it's in this format:

```
'1,2,0,2,8,0,1,3'
```

You already have a split function to split comma-separated strings, but you'll need a way to add up the numbers returned. To do this you'll need a sum function that works as follows:

```
numbers = [1,2,0,2,8,0,1,3]
sum numbers
# 17
```

You haven't written the function yet, but that's how it should work.

WRITING ACCUMULATE

One way to add the numbers in an array is by keeping a total and adding each one in turn:

```
sum = (numbers) ->
  total = 0
  for number in numbers
    total = total + number
  total

sum [1..5]
# 15
```

> **Use a for comprehension to accumulate the total by adding each number in the range to the total as it goes through.**

Suppose you want to multiply the numbers instead of sum them. Do you write another function?

```
multiply = (initial, numbers) ->
  total = initial or 1
  for number in numbers
    total = total * number
  total
```

> **Can't start with a total of 0 if multiplying: 0x1x2x3x4x5 is 0.**

The `multiply` function looks almost exactly like the `sum` function! Now suppose you want to flatten an array of arrays so that `[[1,2],[2,2],[4,2]]` will become `[1,2,2,2,4,2]`. How do you do that? You *could* write yet another function that looks just like the last two:

```
flatten = (arrays) ->
  total = []
  for array in arrays
    total = total.concat array
  total
```

> **The concat method returns a new array of the two arrays combined.**

Now you have *three* similar functions. That's two too many. Instead of having different variants of the same function, if only you could avoid this repetition and have the common parts of the three functions in one place and the differences in another. Indeed you can! Extract the common parts of add, `multiply`, and `flatten` into a single function that takes another function as an argument. The function passed in as the argument will perform the parts that are different. Now, instead of using specific add, `multiply`, and `flatten` functions, you've abstracted away the common parts and made an accumulate function:

```
accumulate = (initial, numbers, accumulator) ->
  total = initial or 0
  for number in numbers
    total = accumulator total, number
  total
```

> **Add initial value and accumulator arguments.**

> **The total needs to be initialized; use 0 as the default.**

> **The accumulator function is invoked inside the comprehension.**

Inside `accumulate`, instead of there being a primitive operator such as + or *, you see the name of the argument, `accumulator`. Use the new `accumulate` function to sum an array:

```
sum = (acc, current) -> acc + current
accumulate(0, [5,5,5], sum)
# 15
```

> **Define a sum accumulator.**

> **Invoke accumulate with initial of 0, an array of numbers, and the sum function.**

Array of numbers

Sum array of numbers

$$1 \; + \; 2 \; + \; 3 \; + \; 4 \; + \; 5$$

sum: 1   3   6   10   15

Figure 3.4   Summing numbers with operator

Now use the `accumulate` function to flatten an array:

```
flatten = (acc,current) -> acc.concat current
accumulate([], [[1,3],[2,8]], flatten)
# [1,3,2,8]
```

Try to visualize this `accumulate` function to understand how it works.

VISUALIZING ACCUMULATE

Suppose you want to manually add the numbers from 1 through 5. Insert an addition operator between the numbers, as in figure 3.4.

When you use the `accumulate` function, you're doing the same thing, except that instead of an operator you insert a *function* between the numbers, as in figure 3.5.

You might visualize it as folding the function into the array. In some programming languages it's actually called *fold*, and when the function is inserted to the left (as in figure 3.5), it's called *fold left* or *foldl*.

> **RECURSION!**   If you think that the `flatten` function shown won't completely flatten deeply nested arrays such as `[1,[3,[4,5]]]`, then you're correct. Using recursion will be explored in chapter 6.

Before you had three similar functions to add, multiply, and flatten an array. Now you have one `accumulate` function that's an *abstraction* of the general idea of accumulating, or folding a function into an array or other data structure. The next important concept to learn for functions is *scope*. First, though, a quick mention of some syntax called *default arguments* that will tidy up some of what you've seen in this section.

Sum array of numbers

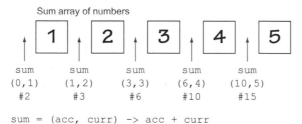

```
sum      sum      sum      sum      sum
(0,1)    (1,2)    (3,3)    (6,4)    (10,5)
 #2       #3       #6       #10      #15
```

```
sum = (acc, curr) -> acc + curr
```

Figure 3.5   Summing numbers by folding in a function

STRATEGY PATTERN   If you have a background in design patterns from object-oriented programming languages, you might recognize that the way a function is passed in here is essentially a lightweight strategy pattern. If you don't know design patterns, you've just learned your first one!

DEFAULT ARGUMENT VALUES

The `accumulate` function uses a default value of `0` for the total. Instead of having to do this in the body of the function, you can use a default argument value. So, instead of

```
accumulate = (initial, numbers, accumulator) ->
  total = initial or 0
  # <rest of function omitted>
```

you can use

```
accumulate = (initial=0, numbers, accumulator) ->
  total = initial
  # <rest of function omitted>
```

Try a basic version of this on the REPL:

```
logArgument = (logMe='default') -> console.log logMe
logArgument()
# 'default'

logArgument('not the default')
# 'not the default'
```

3.4.4   *Exercises*

It's time for some exercises to help you explore the concepts you've just learned:

- Use `accumulate` to create a `sumFractions` function that will sum fractions supplied as strings and return a fraction as a string. For example,

  ```
  sumFractions ['2/6', '1/4']
  ```

  should return `'7/12'` or an equivalent fraction such as `'14/24'`.

- Write a `keep` function that takes an array and returns a new array containing only the element of the array that meets a condition supplied by a function. For example,

  ```
  greaterThan3 = (n) -> n > 3
  keep [1,2,3,4], greaterThan3
  ```

  should return an array containing the single value `4`.

The next important composition technique involves using functions as return values and a concept called *closures*. In order to get there, you must first understand how the scope rules work inside functions.

3.5   Scope

Remember earlier when you defined a function called accumulate? Suppose this function is in a program you wrote and that one day your colleague Robin works on the program and adds this doozy to it:

```
accumulate = yes
```

Your program is broken and many of your tests fail. Just as individual programs have their own variables, you need a way to isolate individual components of your program so that a variable name in one part of the program doesn't accidentally overwrite or *clobber* the same variable name in another part of the program. You need *scope*.

3.5.1   Lexical function scope

All variables are lexically scoped to the body of a function and are defined only inside that function. In this section you'll see that implicit variable definitions in Coffee-Script can help prevent name collisions and global variables that can be a common affliction in JavaScript programs.

Functions are like programs with their own variables. If you first define a variable inside a function, then it can't be used outside the function:

```
scoped = ->
  secret = 'A secret'              ◁——| secret is defined
                                       | inside function
secret
# ReferenceError: secret is not defined
```

A variable that's scoped to a function is undefined outside of the function. This means you can have one part of the program where you use the name accumulate for one variable and another part of the program where Robin uses the name accumulate for a different variable:

```
subProgramOne = ->
  accumulate = (initial, numbers, accumulator) ->
    total = initial or 0
    for number in numbers
      total = accumulator total, number
    total

subProgramTwo = ->
  accumulate = yes
```

The two uses of accumulate in this example are different variables; functions provide scope.

3.5.2   No block scope

Function scope is the only lexical scope rule in CoffeeScript; there is no block scope. If subProgramOne and subProgramTwo are there only to provide scope, then there is no reason to assign them to variables. You can invoke a function literal directly:

```
(->
  name = 'Ren'
) ()

(->
  name = 'Stimpy'
) ()
```

This syntax is a bit clunky, so CoffeeScript provides an alternative way to invoke a function using the do keyword:

```
do ->
  name = 'Ren'

do ->
  name = 'Stimpy'
```

Putting the do keyword in front of a function has the same result as putting parentheses after one—invoking it.

3.5.3 *Implicit variable declarations*

As described, lexical function scope in CoffeeScript works exactly the same as it does in JavaScript. There's one crucial difference between CoffeeScript and JavaScript, though: in CoffeeScript all variable declarations are *implicit*. Variable declarations in JavaScript are *explicit* because to create a variable you need to use the var keyword:

```
var scope = function () {
  var x = 1;
  y = 2;
};
```

The variable x is explicitly scoped to the function by the var keyword.

The variable y is not scoped to the function because there is no var y anywhere in the function.

What happens in JavaScript when you assign a value to a variable that has not been explicitly scoped to the function with var? The variable is declared globally *for you*.[3] This is a massive problem in a browser environment where scripts from many sources that have potentially never been tested together are loaded into a single webpage sharing a single global scope.

It was one thing for Robin to accidentally clobber your variable; it's another thing for a website running your script to load another script that accidentally or even deliberately clobbers your variables. The previous example would be written in Coffee-Script as

```
scope = ->
  x = 1
  y = 2
```

The variables will be defined in the current function scope implicitly. It's not possible to create a global variable unless you're explicitly trying to.

---

[3] The fifth edition of the ECMAScript specification can help with this problem in JavaScript. See chapter 13.

CoffeeScript variables don't require a `var` keyword; when an assignment to a variable is made, the name is first looked for in the current scope. If it isn't found, then it's created in the current scope. Because it isn't possible to create a new local variable that already exists in an outer scope, CoffeeScript is said to not have variable *shadowing*:

```
outer = 1          ⟵— New variable declared
do ->
  outer = 2        ⟵⎤  Assignment to
  inner = 1        ⟵⎦  existing variable
outer
# 2                New variable
inner              declared
# ReferenceError
```

Implicit variable definition in CoffeeScript means that variables can't accidentally be defined on the global scope. CoffeeScript goes one step further, though; in order to stop variables being placed in the global scope at all, the CoffeeScript compiler wraps the code in each compiled file in a scope, essentially doing this:

```
do ->
  # <your program here>
```

Except your CoffeeScript program is compiled to JavaScript, so it's actually wrapped in this:

```
(function() {
  // <your compiled program goes here>
}).call(this);
```

This does the same thing—creates a scope—but it uses the `call` method on the function and passes `this` as the argument. Both `call` and `this` are still relevant to CoffeeScript; if you don't already know them from JavaScript, `this` is covered in chapter 4 and `call` is covered in chapter 6.

3.5.4 Nesting

Functions are first-class values. Not only can you call a function from another function and pass a function to another function, but you can also define a function inside another function where lexical function scope rules still apply. This means that *a function defined inside a function has access to all the variables in the outer function.*

Consider the existing array `flatten` function and how you invoke your `accumulate` function with it:

```
flatten = (acc,current) -> acc.concat current
accumulate([], [[1,3],[2,8]], flatten)
```

Any time you need to flatten an array, you'll need to remember two functions; that's one more than you need. Instead, define a single function that combines them:

```
flattenArray = (array) ->
  flatten = (acc,current) -> acc.concat current    ⟵⎤ Function defined inside
  accumulate([], array, flatten)                        another function
```

```
flattenArray [[1,3],[2,8]]
# [1,3,2,8]
```

To explore this, consider the following example that uses the existential operator to demonstrate which variables are defined where:

```
layerOne = ->
  first = yes
  second?            ←┘ False
  third?            ←┐ False
  layerTwo = ->
    second = yes
    first?           ←┘ True
    third?          ←┐ False
    layerThree = ->
      third = yes
      second?        ←┘ True
      first?        ←┐ True
```

The same rules apply no matter how far down you go. A lexical function scopes *all the way down*.

ARGUMENT SCOPE

Function arguments follow the same lexical scoping rules as function variables, with the exception that arguments with the same name will shadow. Compare this example

```
jones = (x) ->
  smith = (y) ->          x argument
    x         ←┘         to jones
    y                          y argument
                               to smith
```

with the following:

```
jones = (x) ->
  smith = (x,y) ->        x argument
    x         ←┘         to smith
    y                          y argument
                               to smith
```

Although you have access to the arguments passed to a containing function, if you use the same argument name for a function scoped inside that containing function, then the inner function won't have access to the outer function argument. The name of an argument will shadow the name of a variable or argument in an outer scope.

FUNCTIONS AS RETURN VALUES

Perhaps you're thinking at this point that as awesome as this all sounds, nested scopes don't seem to buy you much. Why would you want to nest functions like this? You're about to find out.

You see, there's one more thing you can do with functions as values: you can return a function from a function. Pause for a minute and think what might happen to the scoped variables when a function is returned from a function:

```
close = ->
  closedOver = 1          Return a function that
  -> closedOver    ←┘    uses closedOver variable
```

```
closure = close()
closure()
```

What will this return?

Invoke a function, returning a function

This is your introduction to closures.

3.6   *Closures*

To newcomers, the idea of *closures* is often shrouded in mystery, so it's useful to first look at where they come from. Peter Landin coined the term *closure*, with the meaning used in CoffeeScript, in 1964 when he was implementing a virtual machine called the SECD[4] machine. Strictly speaking, it means that functions *close over* the free variables in their lexical scope. This has some profound importance that you need to see in action to appreciate. In this section you'll learn how closures work and how they not only help you get away from problematic global state but also provide a new composition technique when functions are used as return values.

3.6.1   *Global state problems*

In listing 3.4 you saw the contents of a file stored in a variable after it was read, so that it could be used by another function. Suppose you have two files, tweedle.dum and tweedle.dee, and you always want to serve the contents of the one that was most recently modified. Suppose you want to implement this as a function that will serve the most recently modified file:

```
serveMostRecentFile 'tweedle.dum', 'tweedle.dee'
```

This will involve another piece of function glue—functions as return values.

3.6.2   *Functions as return values*

Suppose now you don't want to just serve the most recent file. Instead, you want to use the most recent file's contents somewhere else in your program. As it's written now, though, because you've contained the variables inside a scope, you're unable to access them in other parts of your program. You need a way to expose a specific variable from a scope to other parts of your program, without resorting to a global variable. To do this, you write another function. This function is going to use a new piece of programming glue that you've not seen yet, by using a *function as the return value from a function*. In order to get there and understand what's happening, it's worth first looking at a simple example of the concept to see how it works.

ABSTRACT EXAMPLE

A simple, abstract example that illustrates the concept of returning a function from a function is a good place to start:

---

[4] SECD stands for Stack Environment Code Dump.

```
makeIncrementer = ->
  n = 0                              Initialize the variable.
  ->
    n = n + 1                                    Return a function
    n                 Return n.    Increment the   from this function.
                                   variable n.
```

When you invoke `makeIncrementer`, you get back a function that increments the value of the variable n and returns the value:

```
incrementer = makeIncrementer()
incrementer()
# 1

incrementer()
# 2
```

> **IS IT AN OBJECT?** If closures are new to you but you're comfortable with objects, then you might think of a closure as an object. Suppose you had an `incrementer` object with a single method called `increment` that incremented an internal value and returned it. This would be essentially the same thing as the closure demonstrated in this section.

The returned function has access to the variables scoped to `makeIncrementer`. The returned function *closes over* the variables in scope, resulting in *closure*. Each time `makeIncrementer` is invoked, a new closure is created, meaning you can have several of them:

```
up = makeIncrementer()
oneMore = makeIncrementer()
up()
# 1

up()
# 2

up()
# 3

oneMore()
# 1
```

APPLIED EXAMPLE

This same technique can be used to create a function that will always return the contents of the most recently modified of two files:

```
makeMostRecent = (file1, file2) ->
  mostRecent = 'Nothing read yet.'

  sourceFileWatcher = (fileName) ->
    sourceFileReader = ->
      fs.readFile fileName, 'utf-8', (error, data) ->
        mostRecent = data
    fs.watch fileName, sourceFileReader
```

```
    sourceFileWatcher file1
    sourceFileWatcher file2

    getMostRecent = ->
      mostRecent
```

This function can be used like so:

```
mostRecentTweedle = makeMostRecent 'tweedle.dee', 'tweedle.dum'
```

If tweedle.dee has been changed most recently and it contained

```
Contrariwise
```

then invoking the returned function will produce that text:

```
mostRecentTweedle()
# Contrariwise
```
◁── **If you try this and see something starting with <Buffer...,then that's okay. The file has just been saved in a different file encoding than the UTF-8 encoding expected by sourceFileWatcher. You can ignore file encodings in this chapter.**

The mostRecent variable is a *free variable* inside the getMostRecent function because it's not defined inside its function but inside the outer makeMostRecent function. Directly inside makeMostRecent, the mostRecent variable is a *bound variable*.

Closure says that free variables are closed over by a function that has them available via lexical scope, meaning that the function assigned to getMostRecent always has access to the mostRecent variable regardless of when or where it's invoked. As a result, even though the makeMostRecent function has already been invoked, the function returned from it still has access to its bound variables, via closure.

CLOSURE AND ARGUMENTS
Function arguments are also closed over:

```
closedOverArgument = (x) ->
  -> x

five = closedOverArgument 5

nine = closedOverArgument 9

five()
# 5

nine()
# 9
```

In that sense, the arguments to a function act like locally defined variables. The scoping rules for arguments are the same as for variables with the exception that *argument names shadow* names in outer functions, whereas variable names don't.

3.6.3   *Extended example: using closure*

The new watchedFileReader function allows you to now solve the problem without having to have a global variable to share state around the program. Here's a modification of the program from listing 3.4 that uses closures and serves the combined contents of multiple files.

Listing 3.6 Serve multiple files

```
fs = require 'fs'
http = require 'http'

makeMostRecent = (file1, file2) ->
  mostRecent = 'Nothing read yet.'

  sourceFileWatcher = (fileName) ->
    sourceFileReader = ->
      fs.readFile fileName, 'utf-8', (error, data) ->
        mostRecent = data
    fs.watch fileName, sourceFileReader

  sourceFileWatcher file1
  sourceFileWatcher file2

  getMostRecent = ->
    mostRecent

makeServer = ->
  mostRecent = makeMostRecent 'file1.txt', 'file2.txt'

  server = http.createServer (request, response) ->
    response.write mostRecent()
    response.end()

  server.listen '8080', '127.0.0.1'

server = makeServer()                      <--- Create server
```

The earlier
makeMostRecent
function

Use
makeMostRecent
inside server

Using closure, you've been able to isolate two parts of your program and provide a way to get data from one part of a program to another.

3.7 Putting it together

You've looked at functions as discrete parts of a program that use values as arguments, contain expressions, and return values. You've also looked at functions themselves as values and at some of the powerful abstraction techniques that provides. All of this was done in the context of creating a website for Agtron and Scruffy's party. Finally, you have all of the building blocks to create the full solution.

The following listing provides the program to serve a web page with the total number of guests at Scruffy and Agtron's party using the techniques and concepts from this chapter. Note that this listing requires the compiler to be available as a module, so to run it you first need to run `npm install coffee-script` from the command line in the folder you want to run it from. Exactly what modules are and what `npm install` does are covered in chapter 12. For now, on to the listing.

Listing 3.7 The party website

```
fs = require 'fs'
http = require 'http'
coffee = require 'coffee-script'
```

Variables with
application state.

```coffeescript
attendees = 0
friends = 0
```

Count attendees in a string like ren,stimpy,horse.

```coffeescript
split = (text) ->
  text.split /,/g

accumulate = (initial, numbers, accumulator) ->
  total = initial or 0
  for number in numbers
    total = accumulator total, number
  total

sum = (accum, current) -> accum + current

attendeesCounter = (data) ->
  attendees = data.split(/,/).length
```

Count friends in a string like 1,2,3.

```coffeescript
friendsCounter = (data) ->
  numbers = (parseInt(string, 0) for string in split data)
  friends = accumulate(0, numbers, sum)
```

Read file and call strategy function with response.

```coffeescript
readFile = (file, strategy) ->
  fs.readFile file, 'utf-8', (error, response) ->
    throw error if error
    strategy response
```

Read file immediately and watch it for changes.

```coffeescript
countUsingFile = (file, strategy) ->
  readFile file, strategy
  fs.watch file, (-> readFile file, strategy)

init = ->
  countUsingFile 'partygoers.txt', attendeesCounter
  countUsingFile 'friends.txt', friendsCounter
```

Set up the two source files. Sample files are provided in the downloadable source.

```coffeescript
  server = http.createServer (request, response) ->
    switch request.url
      when '/'
        response.writeHead 200, 'Content-Type': 'text/html'
        response.end view
      when '/count'
        response.writeHead 200, 'Content-Type': 'text/plain'
        response.end "#{attendees + friends}"
  server.listen 8080, '127.0.0.1'
  console.log 'Now running at http://127.0.0.1:8080'
```

Listen handler on port 8080.

```coffeescript
  clientScript = coffee.compile '''
  get = (path, callback) ->
    req = new XMLHttpRequest()
    req.onload = (e) -> callback req.responseText
    req.open 'get', path
    req.send()

  showAttendees = ->
    out = document.querySelector '#how-many-attendees'
    get '/count', (response) ->
      out.innerHTML = "#{response} attendees!"

  showAttendees()
  setInterval showAttendees, 1000
  '''
```

Client/browser CoffeeScript.

```
view = """
<!doctype html>
<title>How many people are coming?</title>
<body>
<div id='how-many-attendees'></div>
<script>
#{clientScript}
</script>
</body>
</html>
"""

init()
```

HTML document as heredoc, rendered by HTTP handler.

This entire program is more complicated than anything you've seen before in Coffee-Script. But everything in it is either a general syntactic feature of CoffeeScript or a technique for using functions that you've learned in this chapter. It's apparent, though, that if this program were to get larger, then new tools and techniques for composing functions and programs and new ways of thinking about how to design them would be needed. For now, though, you have enough to start writing applications, from functions all the way down.

3.8 Summary

Functions are first-class values in CoffeeScript. They're used for structuring programs at several levels and allow you to group together multiple expressions, treating them like a single expression. By assigning function values to a variable, you have names for functions that you use to organize programs.

First-class functions used as callbacks are a fundamental I/O technique used both in the browser and on the client. You've seen repeatedly how this technique works in different contexts and how it allows I/O to be treated with the same techniques whether it's local file access or across a network. This idea has some important implications and advantages that will be explored later on.

Functions are combined by invoking them inside other functions, by passing them as arguments to other functions, and by using functions as return values from other functions. By gluing functions together, you can use them to create abstractions of other functions, as you saw in the `accumulator` function.

Closure provides a way to isolate parts of a program by containing the variables defined within them, and by passing closures around in your programs you can use them to carry data. In one sense, closures provide some of the features that you'll see objects provide in the next chapter but with a different conceptual model and a different sweet spot for where they're used.

Finally, CoffeeScript blends ideas from different programming languages. Although it supports some important functional programming techniques, it also supports techniques from object-based languages. You'll see those techniques in the next chapter.

Dynamic objects

4

This chapter covers

- Objects as data
- Object comprehensions
- An introduction to prototypes
- An introduction to classes

JavaScript objects are simple and powerful, but because they don't work quite like objects in other popular programming languages, they're often wrongly perceived as confusing and underpowered. With simplified and familiar syntax, CoffeeScript both eliminates the confusion and better exposes the inherent power of objects. Before diving in, though, what exactly is an object?

Objects are collections of named properties where each name maps to a value. The value of a property can be any valid CoffeeScript value. You write an empty object with a set of curly braces:

```
{}
```

That is an object, in *literal notation*. The literal notation for objects is small and convenient. It's used in the source code of programs to represent data and as a format for transferring data on the web.

Beyond being simple property containers, objects are also used for managing state and structuring programs. Objects in CoffeeScript are based on a concept called *prototypes*, which have the advantages of being dynamic and flexible but the disadvantages of being uncommon in other programming languages and unfamiliar to most programmers. It's classes, and not prototypes, that are a familiar concept in other programming languages, so CoffeeScript provides class syntax that allows programs to be structured using more familiar class-based techniques.

In this chapter you'll learn the syntax for defining objects, how object properties and values work as key-value stores, how to write comprehensions for objects, how to structure data using objects, how prototypes work, how functions are bound to objects, and finally how common behavior among many objects is efficiently achieved with CoffeeScript's class syntax.

4.1 Syntax

CoffeeScript has some types that you've encountered already. They are numbers, strings, booleans, functions, null, and undefined. Everything else is an object. Objects with properties and values are declared using either the literal brace notation familiar to JavaScript developers or a minimalist CoffeeScript syntax, described in this section.

4.1.1 Literals

One way to get a brand-new empty object, assigned to a variable, is with an object literal:

```
brandSpankingNewObject = {}
anotherOne = {}
```

To impress your friends, immediately start referring to this as *ex nihilo* object creation. *Ex nihilo* is a Latin term that means "out of nothing." An object created using the literal notation isn't created from something else—it's just *there*, out of nothing.

4.1.2 Properties

Objects contain properties. Each property has a name and associated value. An object with one property `title` and value `'Way of the Dragon'` looks like this:

```
{title: 'Way of the Dragon'}
```

A colon is used to separate the property name and value. When an object has more than one property, commas separate subsequent properties:

```
{title: 'Way of the Dragon', star: 'Bruce Lee'}
```

There is no restriction on the types of values that can be object properties. For example, a property can be an array:

```
{title: 'Way of the Dragon', actors: ['Bruce Lee', 'Chuck Norris']}
```

Or it can be another object. Here, the `info` property contains an object with properties named `budget` and `released`:

```
{title: 'Way of the Dragon', info: {budget: '$130000', released: '1972'}}
```

Because an object is a value, it can be assigned to a variable:

```
movie = {title: 'Way of the Dragon'}
```

4.1.3 YAML-style syntax

YAML (rhymes with *camel*) is a data format that uses significant whitespace, making it a natural fit for CoffeeScript. Objects are written either in the JavaScript style with curly braces and commas or with a syntax similar to YAML. Consider this valid Coffee-Script object:

```
{title: 'Enter the Dragon', info: {budget: '$850000', released: '1973'}}
```

It can also be expressed in the new YAML-style syntax:

```
title: 'Enter the Dragon'
info:
  budget: '$850000'
  released: '1973'
```

Either is acceptable, though the YAML-style syntax is more commonly used inside Coffee-Script programs, with the curly brace style often used when transferring data. The following listing shows a syntax comparison of two object literals related to Scruffy's favorite television show, *Futurama*.

Listing 4.1 Comparison of YAML literal with brace literal notation

YAML object literals

```
futurama =
  characters: [
    'Fry'
    'Leela'
    'Bender'
    'The Professor'
    'Scruffy'
  ]
  quotes: [
    'Good news everyone!'
    'Bite my shiny metal'
  ]
```

Both sides declare a variable with the name futurama that contains two properties named characters and quotes. The value of the characters property is an array containing five strings and the quotes property is an array with two strings.

Brace object literals

```
futurama = {
  characters: [
    'Fry',
    'Leela',
    'Bender',
    'The Professor',
    'Scruffy'
  ],
  quotes: [
    'Good news everyone!',
    'Bite my shiny metal'
  ]
}
```

That covers what objects look like; how about what they're used for? To start, the convenient literal notation for objects in CoffeeScript is useful for representing data such as key-value stores.

4.2 Key-value stores

A key-value store associates a set of keys with a set of values, each key being associated with one value. In CoffeeScript, objects are often used as key-value stores, similar to how a hash is used in Ruby, a hash table is used in Java, or a dictionary is used in Python.

Objects in CoffeeScript aren't hash tables in the strict sense of the word, but they are effective as key-value stores. In particular, the convenient object literal syntax and lack of ceremony make them very effective key-value stores. In this section you'll see how objects as key-value stores are used as data in a program and to name function arguments.

4.2.1 Data

Imagine you have phone numbers of your friends written on a piece of paper (figure 4.1). You want to write a program that stores these numbers and allows you to add new numbers, change existing numbers, and check whether you have the number for a particular person. How do you express what you see on the paper in CoffeeScript?

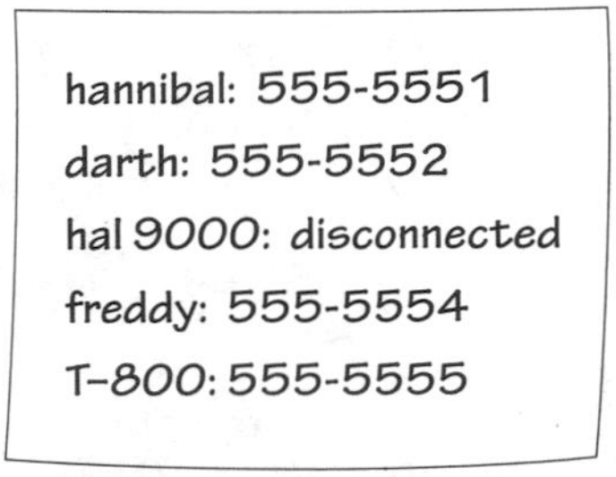

Express the list of phone numbers as an object with person names as the property names and phone numbers as the values. The object that you express as a key-value store looks similar to the paper version. Here it's assigned to a variable:

```
hannibal: 555-5551
darth: 555-5552
hal 9000: disconnected
freddy: 555-5554
T-800: 555-5555
```

Figure 4.1 Phone numbers

```
phoneNumbers =
  hannibal: '555-5551'
  darth: '555-5552'
  hal9000: 'disconnected'
  freddy: '555-5554'
  'T-800': '555-5555'
```

◁── **YAML-style object syntax used, no curly braces**

◁── **Quoted property because T-800 isn't a valid name**

Now that you have the object in your program, how do you use it?

ACCESSING PROPERTIES

Use dot notation on the object with the property name to get the corresponding value. For example, to call Darth, get his phone number by using the key `darth` on the object referenced by the `phoneNumbers` variable:

```
phoneNumbers.darth
# '555-5552'
```

Calling Hal to ask him if he's feeling better is similar:

```
phoneNumbers.hal9000
# 'disconnected'
```

This dot notation doesn't always work, though. Some properties don't play nice.

QUOTED PROPERTY NAMES AND SQUARE BRACKETS

How do you get the phone number for T-800? This doesn't work:

```
phoneNumbers.T-800
# NaN
```

Why doesn't it work? Look at it again:

```
phoneNumbers.T - 800
```

You can't use the minus symbol to access a property name because minus means subtraction. Instead, to use a property that's not a valid name, you put quotes around the property and *square brackets* around the quotes:

```
phoneNumbers['T-800']
# '555-5555'
```

Although properties that aren't valid names can't be accessed with dot notation, any property can be accessed using square brackets:

```
phoneNumbers['freddy']
# '555-5554'
```

In general, dot notation is easier to read, so it should be preferred for accessing any properties that don't contain special characters; that is, unless the property name is in a variable.

PROPERTY NAMES FROM VARIABLES

Because the property name inside the square brackets is a string, it can be provided by a variable:

```
friendToCall = 'hannibal'
phoneNumbers[friendToCall]
# '555-5551'

friendToCall = 'darth'
phoneNumbers[friendToCall]
# '555-5552'
```

The name of the key can be generated dynamically. If you aren't familiar with dynamic languages, leave that idea to settle for a little while before continuing.

ADDING A PROPERTY

By default, any objects you create are open, meaning they can be changed. Add a new phone number to your list by assignment:

```
phoneNumbers.kevin = '555-5556'
phoneNumbers['Agent Smith'] = '555-5557'
```

Now the object has those new friends in it, as if it were written like this:

```
phoneNumbers =
  hannibal:       '555-5551'
  darth:          '555-5552'
  hal9000:        'disconnected'
  freddy:         '555-5554'
  'T-800':        '555-5555'
  'kevin':        '555-5556'
  'Agent Smith': '555-5557'
```

Be careful because, although the numbers that were just added are shown at the end of the object, there's no requirement that object properties be in any particular order. Always consider object properties to be *unordered*.

CHANGING A PROPERTY

Properties can also be changed:

```
phoneNumbers.hannibal = '555-5525'
phoneNumbers.hannibal
# '555-55525'
```

Suppose you don't know what properties are in an object. You don't want to add to or change an object without knowing what properties it has.

CHECKING FOR A PROPERTY NAME

If you want to check if an object contains a property, use the of operator:

```
'hal9000' of phoneNumbers
# true

'skeletor' of phoneNumbers
# false
```

That covers basic object creation and manipulation. In listing 4.2 you see these object features together in a working phone book application. This listing uses some techniques you haven't seen yet, but those techniques are explained later in this chapter. The program, which runs on Node.js, doesn't persist changes to the phone book; each time you run it, the phone book will be reset.

Listing 4.2   A simple phone book

```
phonebook =
  numbers:
    hannibal: '555-5551'
    darth: '555-5552'
    hal9000: 'disconnected'
    freddy: '555-5554'
    'T-800': '555-5555'
  list: ->
    "#{name}: #{number}" for name, number of @numbers
  add: (name, number) ->
    if not (name of @numbers)
      @numbers[name] = number
  get: (name) ->
    if name of @numbers
      "#{name}: #{@numbers[name]}"
    else
      "#{name} not found"

console.log "Phonebook. Commands are add get list and exit."

process.stdin.setEncoding 'utf8'
stdin = process.openStdin()
```

The numbers object as a property of phonebook.

The methods of the phonebook object.

Read user commands entered into the console while the program is running by using stdin.

```
stdin.on 'data', (chunk) ->                              ◁─────── Listen on input
  args = chunk.split(' ')                                          events.
  command = args[0].trim()            Get the individual
  name - args[1].trim() if args[1]    arguments, trimming
  number = args[2].trim() if args[2]  any whitespace.
  switch command
    when 'add'
      res = phonebook.add(name, number) if name and number    Switch based on
      console.log res                                          the command
    when 'get'                                                 entered.
      console.log phonebook.get(name) if name
    when 'list'
      console.log phonebook.list()
    when 'exit'
      process.exit 1
```

What does listing 4.2 do when it runs? Try it on the REPL. When you start the program, it will wait for input:

```
> coffee phonebook.coffee
Phonebook. Commands are add, get, list and exit.
```

Now, list all the numbers by typing `list` and pressing Enter. You'll see the following:

```
hannibal: 555-5551
darth: 555-5552
hal9000: disconnected
freddy: 555-5554
T-800: 555-5555
```

To get a specific number, type `get` followed by the name you want and press Enter:

```
> get freddy
freddy: 555-5554
```

To add a new number or change an existing one, enter `add` followed by the name and then the number. That number will be added or changed and the new value logged to the console:

```
> add kevin 555-5556
kevin: 555-556
```

Of course, the key-value feature of CoffeeScript objects isn't just for creating phone books.

4.2.2 *Key-values for named arguments*

Imagine you're purchasing a Maserati (to keep your Ferrari from getting lonely) and that there are different options available to you for customizing it. Suppose that the order process is represented as a single function that passes an argument with your requested color:

```
orderMaserati = (color) ->            Returning formatted output using
  """Order summary            ◁────── a whitespace-preserving heredoc
  - Make: Gran Turismo S
  - Color: #{color}           ◁────── String interpolation
  """                                  into heredoc
```

The orderMaserati function takes a single argument color and returns a string using a whitespace-preserving heredoc with the color inserted into the string via *string interpolation* (see section 2.5.2). Scruffy likes metallic black, or *Nero Carbonio* as Maserati calls it, so he orders that:

```
orderMaserati 'Nero Carbonio'
# Order summary:
# - Make: Gran Turismo S
# - Color: Nero Carbonio
```

Maserati lets you customize more than just the color, though. How will the order function handle other options?

MULTIPLE ARGUMENTS

Suppose the interior color is also an option; the function definition gets more complicated:

```
orderMaserati = (exteriorColor, interiorColor) ->
  """Order summary:
  - Make: Gran Turismo

  Options:
  - Exterior color: #{exteriorColor}
  - Interior color: #{interiorColor}
  """
```

As the number of options and hence arguments grows, this will get unwieldy very quickly. How many arguments are too many?

TOO MANY ARGUMENTS

Perhaps the second argument doesn't seem so bad. How about a third?

```
orderMaserati = (exteriorColor, interiorColor, wheelRims) ->
  """Order summary:
  Make: Gran Turismo

  Options:
  Exterior color: #{exteriorColor}
  Interior color: #{interiorColor}
  Wheel rims: #{options.wheelRims}
  """
```

The next time you use this function, you'll find yourself wondering, *was it the interior or exterior color that went first?* That's no way to live. Instead, you need a way to pass any number of arguments into a function and not have to remember the order. You do this with an object.

AN OPTIONS ARGUMENT

Instead of having to pass each argument to the function in a particular order, use an object as a key-value store to pass all the options as one argument:

```
orderMaserati = (options) ->
  """Order summary:
  Make: Gran Turismo
```

```
Options:
Exterior color: #{options.exterior}
Interior color: #{options.interior}
Interior trim: #{options.trim}
Wheel rims: #{options.rims}
"""
```

Try to invoke this version of the function on the REPL:

```
orderMaserati exterior:'red', interior:'red', trim:'walnut', wheels:'18'
```

Your REPL might not show the line breaks and whitespace correctly, but the output is as follows:

```
Order summary:
Make: Gran Turismo

Options:
Exterior color: red
Interior color: red
Interior trim: walnut
Wheel rims: 18
```

Using an object as an options argument saves you from having to remember too many things when several configuration parameters have to be passed to a function. When you find yourself adding another similar argument for the third time, you should consider using an object. An object used this way for arguments is similar to *named arguments* in other programming languages. Actually, with CoffeeScript you can make it look even better, but that's a lesson saved for chapter 7.

> **THREE STRIKES REFACTOR**   Doing the same thing in your program three times should be your pain threshold for repetition before you use or create a new abstraction to avoid the duplication.

4.2.3   *Exercises*

Spend some time exploring objects as key-value stores by completing the following:

- Change listing 4.2 to add an `edit` command that allows existing phone book entries to be changed.
- Write a function that uses an options argument containing CSS property names and values and sets them as style properties on an object. Invoking the function should look like this:

```
element = {}
styles =
  width: '10px'
  color: 'red'
css element, styles
element.style.width
# '10px'
element.style.color
# 'red'
```

With objects as key-value stores providing such a convenient way for you to put data in your CoffeeScript, you'd expect equally convenient ways to actually do things with that data. There are; one of them is called *comprehensions*.

4.3 Comprehensions

When you first encountered comprehensions (see section 2.6.4), they were used for arrays. Objects have comprehensions too, and they're very useful. Imagine you have a website with two pages. You want to track how many views each page on your website gets and the total number of views for all pages. Your website pages live on real URLs, but for the sake of simplicity here, suppose they're just called *ren* and *stimpy*. Now, if the ren page has so far received 30 views and the stimpy page 10 views, that can be represented with an object literal as follows:

```
views =
  'ren': 30
  'stimpy': 10
```

As you've seen, storing a property on the object is done with assignment. Use this to increment the count:

```
views.ren = views.ren + 1
```

What you want to do is add up the existing views. You do that with a comprehension. In this section you'll learn how to use comprehensions to transform the properties and values of an object into other properties and values.

4.3.1 Object comprehensions

You saw previously that comprehensions allow you to deal with the elements of an array without having to write a bunch of boilerplate and iterate manually through every single thing in the array one by one, again and again and again. Here's a refresher in case you forgot:

```
number + 1 for number in [1,2,3,4,5]
# [2,3,4,5,6]
```

Object comprehensions in CoffeeScript work similarly to how array comprehensions work. They have a basic format similar to array comprehensions, except they use the word of:

```
expression for property of object
```

What does an object comprehension do? The following listing is a side-by-side comparison with the conceptually equivalent (but not compiled) JavaScript for...in loop.

Listing 4.3   Comprehension compared to `for...in` loop

CoffeeScript	JavaScript

```coffeescript
movie =
  title: 'From Dusk till Dawn'
  released: '1996'
  director: 'Robert Rodriguez'
  writer: 'Quentin Tarantino'


for property of movie
  console.log property
```

```javascript
var movie = {
  title: 'From Dusk till Dawn',
  released: '1996',
  director: 'Robert Rodriguez',
  writer: 'Quentin Tarantino'
}

for (var property in movie) {
  console.log(property);
}
```

In the basic case of listing 4.3 the JavaScript version is fine. How about getting an array of property names, though? Compare that in the next listing.

Listing 4.4   Comprehension as expression

CoffeeScript	JavaScript

```coffeescript
properties = (prop for prop of movie)
```

```javascript
var properties = [];
for (var prop in movie) {
  properties.push(prop);
}
```

The JavaScript version uses multiple statements and has to micromanage the state of the variables `properties` and `prop`. The CoffeeScript version does not.

COMPREHENDING PROPERTIES

The property names of an object are returned as an array using a comprehension:

```coffeescript
name for name of {bob: 152, john: 139, tracy: 209}
# ['bob', 'john', 'tracy']
```

Where is that useful? Well, imagine now that your website has four pages named by the paths to those pages. It looks like this:

```coffeescript
views =
  '/reviews/pool-of-radiance': 121
  '/reviews/summer-games': 90
  '/reviews/wasteland': 139
  '/reviews/impossible-mission': 76
```

A list of pages from this object is obtained using the following comprehension:

```coffeescript
page for page of views
```

This results in an array containing the page names:

```coffeescript
[ '/reviews/pool-of-radiance'
  '/reviews/summer-games'
  '/reviews/wasteland'
  '/reviews/impossible-mission' ]
```

COMPREHENDING VALUES

To get the property values from an object instead of the property names, use a slightly different comprehension format:

```
value for property, value of object
```

For example:

```
score for name, score of {bob: 152, john: 139, tracy: 209}
# [152, 139, 209]
```

The number of views for each page is obtained using the comprehension

```
count for page, count of views
```

for the four pages described earlier. This results in an array containing the page views for those pages:

```
[ 121, 90, 139, 76 ]
```

ALTERNATIVE FORMAT

So far you've seen comprehensions written on a single line:

```
expression for property, value of object
```

But it's also possible to have the expression indented underneath:

```
for property, value of object
  expression
```

When you do that, the *expression* is evaluated for each property in the object. For example, consider a comprehension to collect and sum the view count for all of the pages:

```
sum = 0
for page, count of views
  sum = sum + count
# [121, 211, 350, 426]
```

Use the indented style when the expression is long and needs to be on a separate line for readability. Now it's time to see all of this in action.

4.3.2 Example

To keep track of how many views each page gets, you need a function to increment the value stored against an individual page. Then, to get the total number of views for all pages, you'll need a function that sums all of the values of the object. The next listing is a first implementation of this program. A detailed discussion follows the listing.

Listing 4.5   Page views

```
views = {}                              ◁─── The views object,
                                             created ex nihilo
viewsIncrement = (key) ->        ┐
  views[key] ?= 0                │ An increment
  views[key] = views[key] + 1    ┘ helper function
```

```
total = ->
  sum = 0
  for own page, count of views
    sum = sum + count
  sum
```

A total function
to add up the
page views

REDUCE!   If you were expecting the sum to be done inside the `total` function with a `reduce` on the array, then rest assured that you can and should use `Array.reduce` in CoffeeScript.

Before moving along to more uses of objects, notice in listing 4.5 that there's a bit of syntax that looks a little foreign. What is the `?=` in `views[key] ?= 0` used for?

DEALING WITH UNDEFINED PROPERTIES

Suppose the `views` object doesn't yet have any properties. If there's a page called *donatello* that receives a view, how do you increment a `donatello` property that doesn't exist? The long way to do it is to first use the existential operator to see if it exists, and then initialize it if it doesn't:

```
if !views['donatello']?
  views['donatello'] = 1
```

This is a common pattern, so there's a shorter version of it called *existential assignment.* Put an existential operator in front of the assignment operator:

```
views['donatello'] ?= 0
```

You'll notice that the `viewsIncrement` function takes the name of the property as the argument key, which it uses as the property name. The specific case of `donatello` is then generalized:

```
views[key] =? 0
```

There's one other foreign word, though; what does that own keyword in listing 4.5 do?

OWN PROPERTIES

The `total` function adds an `own` to the comprehension, immediately after the `for` keyword:

```
for own url, count of views
```

Objects can get properties that weren't defined directly on them but somewhere else on the prototype chain. The prototype chain is described later in this chapter, but for now, be mindful that when an object is used as a key-value store, the comprehensions in that object should always include the `own` keyword.

> **TIP**   If you're using an object as a key-value store, always use `own` inside comprehensions on that object.

So far you've seen objects used for their key-value properties. By using objects as values, you can represent other structured data in CoffeeScript.

4.4 Structured data

Objects are useful not only for flat key-value data stores but also for data that has multiple levels (such as in listing 4.6). What's the difference? In a flat key-value store, each key maps to a single number, string, or boolean value (or even `null` or `undefined`). In contrast, when one of the keys maps to an object or array, then data can be nested. Think of the difference between a phone book that has names relating only to numbers and a phone book that has names relating to numbers, addresses, and birthdays. In this section you'll see how to use objects as values in other objects and how this means they can be used for structured data such as trees.

4.4.1 JSON

Imagine you wanted to get the status updates related to a particular topic from a popular social network. When you request data from the social network web service, the response you get back might look something like what's shown in the next listing.

Listing 4.6 JSON status updates

```
response = {
  "results": {
    "23446": {
      "user": "Guard",
      "text": "Found them? In Mercia?! The coconut's tropical!"
    },
    "23445": {
      "user": "Arthur",
      "text": "We found them."
    },
    "23443": {
      "user": "Guard",
      "text": "Where'd you get the coconuts?"
    }
  }
}
```

◁— The object has been fetched and assigned to the variable response.

This format is called JavaScript Object Notation (JSON). Being the language of the web, JavaScript's syntax for representing structured data has become a popular format for data interchange on the web. JSON is a subset of the literal syntax for objects in JavaScript. This means that valid JSON is a valid object literal in JavaScript and in CoffeeScript. But not every valid object literal is valid JSON. You can expect many web services to offer JSON as one of the supported data formats they provide.

4.4.2 Trees

The data that contains the status updates has a tree structure. For phone numbers, each property is mapped to a single string, shown in figure 4.2.

The response that you get back from the web service isn't a flat structure. The object has a property `results` with a value that is itself an object with three properties

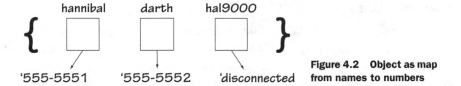

Figure 4.2   Object as map from names to numbers

defined, each of which has a value that's another object. This data looks more like a tree, as shown in figure 4.3.

You'll frequently encounter tree structures when writing CoffeeScript programs. Not only is any JSON data received by your application a tree structure, but HTML documents, with their nested elements, are also trees.

ACCESSING VALUES

For the `response` variable shown in listing 4.6, the value of the `results` property can be obtained with the familiar dot notation:

```
response.results

# { "23443":
#   { user: "Guard",
#     text: "Where\'d you get the coconuts?" },
#   "23445":
#     { user: "Arthur",
#         text: "We found them." },
#   "23446":
#   { user: "Guard",
#     text: "Found them? In Mercia?! The coconut\'s tropical!" }
# }
```

To access an object farther down the tree, you can use another dot to *refine* the selection:

```
response.results['23443'].user
# "Guard"

response.results['23445'].text
# "We found them."

response.results['23446']
# {user: "Guard", text: "Found them? In Mercia?! The coconut\'s tropical!"}
```

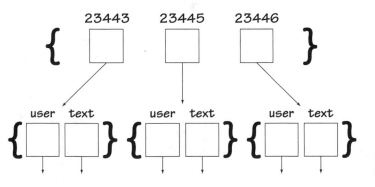

Figure 4.3   Object as tree

> **Wait a minute!**
> If you're thinking that a chain of object calls is a train wreck, then you're correct in the case of a method call returning another object that is then modified. In this case, though, the object is being used purely as data. All of the data is self-contained, and there's no indirection occurring.

You've seen CoffeeScript objects used as data and transformed with comprehensions. You'll need to do more with objects, though, and in CoffeeScript this means your objects will need to work with your functions. One piece of glue used with objects and functions is the binding of functions to objects.

4.5 Binding

When working with objects, you'll need some way to refer to them. One important way this is achieved in CoffeeScript is with binding. Binding in CoffeeScript works the same as in JavaScript, with the important addition of new syntax that makes it easier to deal with.

If you're coming from other programming languages, the way binding works in JavaScript and CoffeeScript can be counter to your expectations. For that reason, it's important to start at the beginning and take it slowly. First, remember that a first-class value function can be the value of an object property:

```
yourObject =
  someFunction: ->
```

When a function is accessed as a property of an object and invoked, then the object takes on a special behavior; it becomes `this` inside the function invocation:

```
yourObject.someFunction()
```

If you look at it, because of the presence of the property access, `yourObject` is the object on which the function was invoked. Another way to put it is to say that `yourObject` is the receiver of the function call (it's receiving the current message). That's not quite the whole story, though. Binding can be a little nuanced for the beginner, so to get to a full understanding, it's once again necessary to take a scenic route.

In this section you'll see why a dynamic `this` is useful and how to use it. You'll also see where a dynamic `this` isn't useful and how you can stop `this` from being dynamic by using the fat arrow. That's a head-spinning sentence! Sit back, relax, and take the scenic route. What is `this`?

4.5.1 this

Imagine you have an element in an HTML document and you want to change the contents of the element when it's clicked. This venerable problem, which you've seen before, has been around since the beginning of JavaScript. Here's the minimal HTML5 document:

```
<!doctype html>
<title>How many people are coming?</title>
<body>
<div id='#some-element'>Change this text</div>
```

Now suppose you assign a click handler:

```
someElement = document.querySelector('#some-element')
someElement.onclick = ->
  someElement.innerHTML 'Got clicked!'
```

That works okay, but what if there are two elements?

```
<!doctype html>
<title>How many people are coming?</title>
<body>
<div id='#some-element'>Change this text</div>
<div id='#some-other-element'>Change this text</div>
```

Now your handlers will look like this:

```
someElement = document.querySelector('#some-element')
someOtherElement = document.querySelector('#some-other-element')

someElement.onclick = ->
  someElement.innerHTML = 'Got clicked!'

someOtherElement.onclick = ->
  someOtherElement.innerHTML = 'Got clicked!'
```

You can smell the duplication! If the behavior is the same when the two elements are clicked, then you should be able to define one function that handles both events. How can you write a single function that works for both events?

---

innerHTML vs. html()

The `innerHTML` property is a standard property according to the W3C specification. If you are familiar with jQuery, you will know that it defines an `html` method that can be used to set the HTML content of a DOM element. In either case, it's a library method that allows you to change something about an object in an HTML document. Objects in HTML documents are special objects called host objects that you will learn more about in chapter 11.

ELEMENTS ARE RECEIVERS

Every time a function is invoked, some *object* is the receiver for that function invocation. In many cases, the receiver is unimportant to you, but when you're handling an event, the object that's receiving the event is important. When a function is handling a click event on an element in an HTML document, then the receiver is the element that was clicked, as shown in figure 4.4.

Inside the handling function, the receiver is available using the @ symbol or the this keyword. It can be helpful to think of @ in terms of the object you are *at* or this in terms of *this object* that is being used, right now.

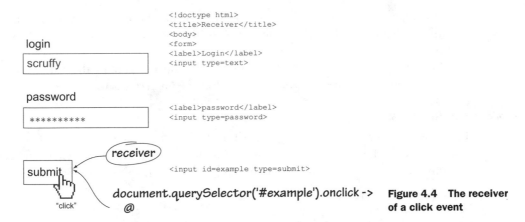

Figure 4.4   The receiver of a click event

Using the receiver, you can now rewrite the duplicated event handlers so that instead of having two handlers you can have just one. First, rewrite one event handler to use the receiver. Instead of this

```
someElement.onclick = ->
  someElement.innerHTML = 'Got clicked!'
```

it will look like this:

```
someElement.onclick = ->
  this.innerHTML = 'Got clicked!'
```

But this can get tedious to type, so CoffeeScript syntax lets you write it with @:

```
someElement.onclick = ->
  @innerHTML = 'Got clicked!'
```

Although you can put a dot after @, it's unnecessary:

```
@.innerHTML 'Got clicked!'
```
⟵ **Leave out the dot after @.
It's unnecessary.**

Use this technique to create a click-handling function that you can attach to both elements:

```
markAsClicked = ->
  @innerHTML = 'Got clicked!'
```
**Common click-
handling function**

```
someElement.onclick = markAsClicked
someOtherElement.onclick = markAsClicked
```
**Attach to click event
of two elements**

The value of the receiver can be subtle. It's time to review.

HOW TO KNOW WHAT THE RECEIVER IS

If you want to determine what the value of this is going to be, think about which object is the receiver. In the case of the previous click event, consider that the onclick function has been invoked on the element:

```
document.querySelector('#some-element').onclick = ->
```
⎣_____⎦ ⎣_____⎦
value of expression is the receiver   **the event**

One strategy, then, is to look at the dot in front of wherever the function has been assigned. In general, though, the best way to tell the value of this is to ask yourself, "Who is receiving this event?"

Sometimes you don't want the object that's the receiver of the function. Sometimes you want some other object. That's what the fat arrow is for.

4.5.2   *The fat arrow*

Imagine you now want the text on your HTML element to be changed to "Got clicked" after one second, instead of immediately. To do this, you first attach a click handler and then invoke setTimeout inside it, passing it a function and a number of milliseconds:

```
someElement.onclick = ->
  setTimeout ->
    @innerHTML 'Got clicked'      ◁─┐  When this is invoked, @ will
  , 1000                              refer to the global object.
```

Try that in your browser; it doesn't work. That's because the function being invoked is the one that you gave as an argument to setTimeout.

Take a step away from this specific example for a moment and consider it in a more abstract sense. Think of an object with two properties, one being a single method that returns the object itself:

```
noumenon =                    Object property that
  value: 'noumenon',     ◁─┐  contains string        Object property that
  itself: -> @              └─                    ◁─┐  contains function
```

When you invoke the itself method, it will return the original object. This means you can get the value by first invoking the itself method to get the object back again and then access the property:

```
noumenon.itself().value
# 'noumenon'
```

This example is contrived, but having a method return the object it was called on is a powerful technique (explored in chapter 7). The important thing to consider here is what happens if the function is used somewhere else:

```
detachedFromObject = noumenon.itself

detachedFromObject()
# 'undefined'
```

The value of this is different. It's undefined! The same will happen if you assign the function to the property of another object and make it a method of *that* object:

```
other =
  value: 'other'

other.itself = noumenon.itself

other.itself().value
# 'other'
```

Remember that functions are first-class values? This is the price you have to pay for all that expressive power with dynamic object binding. There's no such thing as a free lunch.

In CoffeeScript, a function never belongs to an object in the same way that methods belong to objects in other object-oriented languages. Instead, a function is bound *dynamically* to the receiving object when invoked. If you pass what you think is a method of an object as a callback function, you're passing a bare-naked first-class function.

If it's still not completely clear, you can experiment with a version of this example on the REPL. First, change the itself method to console.log so you can see what's happening:

```
noumenon.itself = -> console.log @value
```

Now pass the function to setTimeout:

```
setTimeout noumenon.itself, 1000
# 'undefined'
```

As before, the function is being invoked with a different receiver. In the case of setTimout, because it's a global method, the function will be invoked with that global object as the receiver. The question is, with a dynamic receiver object, how do you get a reference to your original object inside a function when it's used as a callback or otherwise called with some different object as the receiver?

USING SCOPE

One way to get a reference to the element that you want is by using function scope. For example, the function that's being invoked by setTimeout is lexically inside the function invoked as the click handler. Closure means that any variables defined in the outer function will be visible to the inner function:

```
someElement.onclick = ->                        Assign this to
  clickedElement = @          ⟵──┤              a variable.
  setTimeout ->
    clickedElement.innerHTML 'Got clicked'   ⟵─┐  Use the variable in the function
  , 1000                                        │  passed to setTimeout.
```

When you assign the @ reference to a variable, the other function defined inside the scope has access to it.

USING THE FAT ARROW

The fat arrow provides a way to keep a lexical reference to this without having to use an intermediate variable such as clickedElement in the previous example. Controlling the value of the receiver is called *function binding*. Using a fat arrow, you can rewrite the previous example:

```
someElement.onclick = ->
  setTimeout =>
    this.innerHTML 'Got clicked'     ⟵─┐  The fat arrow binds
  , 1000                                │  the value of this.
```

The fat arrow causes the function to have `this` bound *lexically* at the point in the code where it appears. This has uses other than handling browse events, which you'll learn more about later, after you've learned more about objects.

So ends the scenic route through binding. From here, you move on to the foundation of CoffeeScript objects: prototypes.

4.6   Prototypes

CoffeeScript is a prototype-based language. Every object (except `null`—you'll learn why later) has a link to another object called its *prototype*. Properties defined on the prototype of an object are also available on the object itself. A prototype-based object system will be unfamiliar to those who're used to the class-based object systems found in most popular programming languages because it supports object creation and inheritance without requiring any classes at all.

In this section you'll learn what it means to create a new object using an existing object as the prototype and how an object inherits properties from its prototype. To understand this, it's important to distinguish inheritance from copying.

4.6.1   Copy

Back when people wore leg warmers, fluorescent clothes, and their hair in a perm, music was distributed on small plastic cartridges called cassettes. Imagine your friend Corey has lent you a cassette he made that contains some of his favorite songs:

```
cassette =
   title: "Awesome songs. To the max!"
   duration: "10:34"
   released: "1988"
   track1: "Safety Dance - Men Without Hats"
   track2: "Funkytown - Lipps, Inc"
   track3: "Electric Avenue - Eddy Grant"
   track4: "We Built This City - Starship"
```

MAKING A COPY

You really like the cassette and decide to create a copy of it:

```
cassetteCopy = {}
for own property, value of cassette
   cassetteCopy[property] = value
```

Your cassette now has all of the tracks from Corey's cassette:

```
cassetteCopy.track3
# "Electric Avenue - Eddy Grant"
```

You give Corey his cassette back and he decides to add another song:

```
cassette.track5 = "Rock Me Amadeus - Falco"
```

Sadly, your copy does not have the new song:

```
cassetteCopy.track5?
# false
```

If only there were a way to have a cassette that would automatically have access to any updates from Corey's cassette. There is—use Corey's cassette as the prototype for your own cassette.

4.6.2 *Object creation*

When you use one object as the prototype of another object, the properties from the prototype aren't copied; instead, they're found via lookup when the property is accessed. Creating an object by using an existing object as the prototype causes the new object to have a permanent link back to the prototype. A copy of an object doesn't have this feature.

The `Object.create` method is one way to create an object using an existing object as its prototype. When a property is accessed on the new object but isn't found, the prototype link is followed and the property is looked for on the prototype object. The property is *inherited* from the prototype.

> **Object.create**
>
> Although the `Object.create` method is part of the fifth edition of the ECMAScript standard, it isn't available in all environments. In particular, versions of Internet Explorer prior to IE9 don't have `Object.create`. A version of `Object.create` that you can use when targeting environments that don't have one built in is found in chapter 11. Exactly what `Object.create` does is also covered in that chapter.

In terms of the cassette, imagine that instead of copying it, you have a small wireless music device that can link itself to Corey's cassette. Once you've linked the device, playing it will cause it to communicate with Corey's cassette and play the tracks on there. Create this device in CoffeeScript:

```
musicDevice = Object.create cassette
```

Now you automatically get updates from Corey's cassette:

```
cassette.track6 = "Sledgehammer - Peter Gabriel"
musicDevice.track6 is "Sledgehammer - Peter Gabriel"
# true
```

The prototype link goes in only one direction. Changing a track directly on `musicDevice` will update it but won't affect the `cassette`:

```
musicDevice.track1 = "Toy Soldiers - Markita"
musicDevice.track1 is "Toy Soldiers - Markita"
# true
```

The original cassette remains unchanged:

```
cassette.track1 is "Safety Dance - Men Without Hats"
# true
```

Figure 4.5   A prototype example

In a similar fashion, adding a new track to musicDevice won't affect cassette:

```
musicDevice.track7 = " Buffalo Stance - Neneh Cherry"
cassette.track7?
# false
```

You can see the dynamic nature of the relationship between objects and their prototypes in figure 4.5. Creating objects from other objects is a simple but powerful mechanism.

4.6.3   *Exercises*

Time to recap what you know about prototypes:

- Create another music device with musicDevice as its prototype.
- Add a new song to Corey's cassette. Can you access it on the new music device? Why?
- Add a new song to musicDevice. Can you access it on the new music device? Why?

4.7   *Behavior*

So far the objects presented have contained only data. When you created an object to hold data about page views, you also created a helper function that acted on the data structure. If a function is going to change an object, there's a very good chance that it should belong to the object. In general, objects should be responsible for their own data. This means the `views` object should own the data it contains and be responsible for manipulating it. As you've learned, a function is called a *method* when it's called against an object. The methods of an object provide the behavior of that object.

In this section you'll learn that creating objects from a prototype can lead to more elegant code. First, consider the page views program from section 4.3.2 and what will happen when you need to extend it.

4.7.1 Refactor

In the first page views program (listing 4.5), there's a single `views` object. Both the `increment` function and the `total` function act on the `views` object by knowing which variable it's assigned to. If you wanted to track views for two different websites, then you could manually create two `views` objects:

```
businessViews = {}
pleasureViews = {}
```

Then you could change `increment` and `total` so that the object they're acting on is passed in as an argument:

```
increment = (recipient, key) ->
  recipient[key] ?= 0
  recipient[key] = recipient[key] + 1

total = (recipient) ->
  sum = 0
  for own page of recipient
    sum = sum + 1
  sum
```

> The recipient argument is the object to use.

Then to add a view to `businessViews`, you'd do this:

```
increment businessViews, '/products/fade-o-meter/enterprise-edition'
```

Now `increment` is modifying the `businessViews` object. To be clear, you should avoid state where possible, as chapter 6 will help you to understand. If you *really* need state, then it's best to contain the state and have the object that owns the state be responsible for changing it. With that in mind, here's a new version of the page views code.

Listing 4.7 Page views revisited

```
views =
  clear: ->
    @pages = {}
  increment: (key) ->
    @pages ?= {}
    @pages[key] ?= 0
    @pages[key] = @pages[key] + 1
  total: ->
    sum = 0
    for own page, count of @pages
      sum = sum + count
    sum
```

> @ is the this reference to the receiving object.

> Initialize the pages property on the specific object on the first call to increment. It's important that a property that keeps state does not live on the prototype. The prototype should contain common behavior.

Now create two view counters:

```
businessViews = Object.create views
personalViews = Object.create views
```

If you increment the value for just one URL on that object 100 times, then the total is 100. But the other object maintains its own state separately. It isn't affected by increments to the first object:

```
for i in [1..100] by 1
  businessViews.increment '/product-details/2454'

businessViews.total()
# 100

personalViews.total()
# 0
```

METHODS

When a function is invoked on an object (when that object is `this`), call it a method. The `views` prototype has three methods: `clear`, `increment`, and `total`.

The `views` prototype has a `clear` method that sets the `pages` property to an empty object. If using existing objects as prototypes creates objects, then existing state on those objects may need to be removed. There are other techniques for managing this, from classes and constructors, which you'll learn about in the next section, to separation of state from behavior with other techniques, which are covered in chapters 6 and 7.

Objects in CoffeeScript are open by default. Having used prototypal inheritance to set up the object relationships, a method can be made available to both of the views objects by updating the prototype. Here's a `pages` method that will return the number of pages that have views against them:

```
views.pagesTotal = ->
  (url for own url of @).length
businessViews.pagesTotal()
```

4.7.2   *Exercise*

Some of the pages on your website aren't interesting and you don't want to track them. Add an `ignore` method to `views` from listing 4.7 that takes the name of a page and adds it to an array of pages that shouldn't be tracked.

4.8   *Classes*

The prototype-based object system in CoffeeScript (and JavaScript) is minimal and low-level, not providing some of the built-in comforts for structuring objects that some other languages have. Although there are *many* techniques for managing objects using prototypes, and you'll learn several of them in upcoming chapters, classes are one well-known technique for managing objects. CoffeeScript has dedicated syntax for creating and using classes on top of the underlying prototype-based object system.

The `clear` method on views is a potential initialization step you may want to do for many objects. The underlying JavaScript uses a constructor function for this purpose. When used with the `new` keyword, a constructor function creates and initializes an object in JavaScript:

```
function Views () {
  this.pages = {};
}
businessViews = new Views();
```

Unfortunately, constructor functions in JavaScript are awkward and confusing. Regardless, if you're creating many of the same sorts of objects, you'll want three features: a simple declarative syntax for defining them, a way to specify a constructor function for initialization, and optimized performance when creating a large number of objects. That's what classes in CoffeeScript give you.

In this section you'll see how to use this syntax to declare classes. You'll also see that objects aren't equal, regardless of whether they were created from the same class. First, how do you declare a class?

4.8.1 Declaration

CoffeeScript provides a class syntax that cleans up some of the awkwardness in JavaScript constructors and handles setting up links to prototype objects. If you were writing a system that was capturing the views for many different sites and wanted to define a class for views, it could be implemented as shown in the following listing.

Listing 4.8   A page views class

```
class Views                                    Class declaration
  constructor: ->            constructor
    @pages = {}              method
  increment: (key) ->
    @pages[key] ?= 0                   increment
    @pages[key] = @pages[key] + 1      method
  total: () ->
    sum = 0
    for own url, count of @pages       total
      sum = sum + count                method
    sum
businessViews = new Views        Creating two objects
personalViews = new Views        using the Views class
```

Comparing listing 4.8 to the prototype-based version from listing 4.7, you'll notice some new keywords: `class`, `constructor`, and `new`.

CLASS DECLARATION

The `class` keyword, followed by a class name, begins the declaration of a class. A class declaration contains methods defining what an object created from the class does. The smallest valid definition of a class is just the `class` keyword with a name:

```
class Empty
```

NEW OPERATOR

Objects can be created from a `class` using the new operator:

```
empty = new Empty
```

CONSTRUCTOR METHOD

The `constructor` method for a class is a function that's called whenever a new object is created from the class. When a new object is created from the `Views` class,

```
newViewsObject = new Views
```

then the constructor is called, in this case assigning an empty object to the `pages` property of the new object.

The example in listing 4.8 is similar to that in listing 4.7. The conceptual difference is that instead of creating an object out of another object, you create an object out of a class. This means you've now learned three ways to create objects in Coffee-Script: ex nihilo, using another object, and using a class.

If you're wondering at this stage how classes and constructors relate to the underlying JavaScript, then try compiling the examples in this section and having a look. The veil will be lifted in chapter 5, where the relationship of CoffeeScript syntax to the JavaScript object model is explored in detail.

4.8.2   *Object identity*

Objects are never equal to each other; an object is equal only to itself:

```
businessViews is personalViews
# false
```

Equality will be true for variables referencing objects only if they refer to the same object:

```
objectReferenceOne = {}
objectReferenceTwo = objectReferenceOne
objectReferenceTwo is objectReferenceOne
# true
```

Two objects created from the same class are not equal:

```
class Black
green = new Black
```

Now `green` is a new `Black` but it is never *the* new `Black`:

```
green is new Black
# false
```

Similarly, `businessViews` and `personalViews` aren't equal because they don't reference the same object:

```
businessViews is personalViews
# false
```

> **Prototypes or classes?**
> It depends. For the page views example, the objects are all going to have the same functionality and they don't need to change while the programming is running. Given that, when the page views example is extended into a full web application later, the first approach will be class-based.

4.8.3 Exercises

Try these exercises to help you understand classes in CoffeeScript:

- Define a class for a `GranTurismo` object with a constructor that takes an `options` object as an argument and assigns all of the options supplied as properties on `@` (`this`).
- Add a `summary` method to the `GranTurismo` class that returns a summary of the options passed to the constructor as a string.

4.9 Putting it together

Listing 4.9 provides the full page view application. To view the current hit count for both personal and business, run the application from the command line:

```
> coffee 4.9.coffee
```

Once the application is running, visit the application homepage at http://127.0.0.1:8080/ in your browser, and you'll see the text "Personal: 0 Business: 0." Now, each time you visit a URL path such as /personal/1 or /business/1 in your browser, the hit will be recorded. Go ahead and visit /personal/1 five times and then visit the application homepage again. You'll see "Personal: 5 Business: 0."

Listing 4.9 Page views web application

```
http = require 'http'

class Views
  constructor: ->
    @pages = {}
  increment: (key) ->
    @pages[key] ?= 0
    @pages[key] = @pages[key] + 1
  total: ->
    sum = 0
    for own url, count of @pages
      sum = sum + count
    sum

businessViews = new Views
personalViews = new Views
```

```
server = http.createServer (request, response) ->
  renderHit = (against) ->
    against.increment request.url
    response.writeHead 200, 'Content Type': 'text/html'
    response.end "recorded"

  if request.url is '/'
    response.writeHead 200, 'Content-Type': 'text/html'
    response.end """
        Personal: #{personalViews.total()}
        Business: #{businessViews.total()}
    """
  else if /\/business\/.*/.test request.url
    renderHit businessViews
  else if /\/personal\/.*/.test request.url
    renderHit personalViews
  else
    response.writeHead 404, 'Content-Type': 'text/html'
    response.end "404"

server.listen 8080, '127.0.0.1'
```

The class syntax used in listing 4.9 isn't the *only* way to write this application. It's simply one approach that you've seen emerge from the CoffeeScript syntax and object system throughout this chapter.

4.10   *Summary*

JavaScript has a powerful object literal syntax that makes objects effective as generic data containers. The power of this literal syntax is evident in the rising popularity of JSON as a data exchange format for web applications. CoffeeScript takes full advantage of this syntax and, if you don't like using curly braces even for object literals, the YAML-style syntax provides an even more succinct alternative.

The prototype-based object model has always been misunderstood in JavaScript. By exploring prototypes first and coming to CoffeeScript's class syntax later as an organizing technique, you have a glimpse into the conceptual elegance of the little-known world of prototype-based object systems.

In the next chapter you'll look deeper into the JavaScript object model and see how CoffeeScript syntax exposes the elegance and expressiveness within, without getting in your way. At the same time you'll learn composition techniques and patterns for both prototype-based and class-based approaches.

Part 2

Composition

Having learned how to use CoffeeScript, you'll now learn how to use CoffeeScript *well*. Using a language well means learning how to effectively compose programs, so this part of the book is about learning to express your programs at a higher level and about learning some more advanced idioms that will make your programs easier to write and to comprehend.

Because learning to do things well requires dealing with challenges, some of the topics covered later in this part will require closer reading, and the examples may require more experimentation. To provide you with context for these topics, some of the listings need to be quite long. Take some time to absorb them.

Composing objects 5

In the previous chapter you traveled the road from object literals to prototypes and then classes. Along the way you started to build an understanding of how objects work in CoffeeScript. Now it's time to reverse course by first defining some classes of your own and then slowly taking them apart to see the objects and prototypes that underpin them. This will give you the complete picture of objects in CoffeeScript.

You'll begin the exploration with classical objects and class inheritance, followed by methods and other class properties and an explanation of the super keyword. Then you'll learn how to modify objects, classes, and prototypes. Finally, this chapter ends by teaching you what mixins are and how to use them. The flexible syntax and object model of CoffeeScript make writing mixins elegant, even though they're not a built-in language feature. First up, classes and classical objects.

5.1   *Being classical*

Although objects in CoffeeScript are fundamentally prototype-based, the prototype-based approach that you learned about in chapter 4 is uncommon in programming languages. The class-based approach, where objects are created *using classes*, is common. So if classes are common, they must be good for something, right? Yes, they are. Classes are natural and convenient for declaring common properties and methods to be shared by multiple objects.

As you saw in the previous chapter, CoffeeScript provides the convenience of classes by providing class syntax on top of objects and prototypes. How does CoffeeScript do that and what are the trade-offs? Read on to find out.

5.1.1   *Raw data*

Imagine that Agtron wants to open an online shop to sell digital cameras. Unsurprisingly, he has asked you to write the program to do that. Figure 5.1 demonstrates the shop homepage that he wants.

Where to start? To sell the cameras, you'll need to know which cameras to sell and how many are in stock. Sample data containing this information has been supplied to you as an object:

```
data =
  X100:
    description: "A really cool camera"
    stock: 5
  X1:
    description: "An awesome camera"
    stock: 6
```

The sample data has information for two cameras, an `X100` and an `X1`. Each camera has a `description` and a `stock` count. Sure, the data could be used in a program without *any* classes, but classes buy you an abstraction by separating your data from your program.

---- **Agtron's Emporium** ----

Figure 5.1   Agtron's shop homepage

5.1.2 *Class abstractions*

To learn why classes are useful, start without *any* abstraction and see what happens. Take the camera data and display each camera as a string suitable for display on the web page:

```
"X100: a camera (5 in stock)"
```

Then create an array of these strings using a comprehension (see section 4.3 if you need a refresher on comprehensions):

```
for own name, info of data
  "#{name}: #{info.description} (#{info.stock} in stock)"

# ["X100: A really cool camera (5 in stock)",
#  "X1: An awesome camera (6 in stock)"]
```

Now imagine that Agtron wants users to purchase cameras by clicking them. Modify the comprehension to create an element in the document, add the camera data, and then add a click handler. Doing this in a web browser looks like the following (note that the following example does not work in your REPL):

```
purchase = (product) ->        ◁——┤ The implementation of the purchase
                                    function isn't important at this point.    Create an element
for own name, info of data                                                    for the camera.
  elem = document.createElement "li"                              ◁———
  elem.innerHTML = "#{name}: #{info.description} (#{info.stock} in stock)"   ◁——
  elem.onclick = purchase name      ◁——
                                         Attach a handler        Put the camera content
                                         for the click event.    into the element.
```

This is getting more complicated: there are more things for your brain to keep track of and more things for you to worry about. Regardless, you can struggle through, so far.

Now suppose Agtron also wants the stock counts to be updated after each purchase request. What will you do? Add some more lines to the comprehension and make it harder to understand? No. As a program grows, instead of piling junk upon junk, you require more abstractions to help you manage things. Time to try classes.

A camera class describes how cameras work. In your program, camera objects are created, rendered onto a web page, and purchased. The following listing shows a `Camera` class with a `constructor` for creating cameras, a `render` method, and a `purchase` method.

Listing 5.1 A simple `Camera` class

```
class Camera
  constructor: (name, info) ->         The constructor function that's
    @name = name                       invoked when a new instance is
    @info = info                       created from the class.          The render method
  render: ->                                                            that displays the
    "#{@name}: #{@info.description} (#{@info.stock} in stock)"          camera as a string.
  purchase: ->          ◁——
                             The actual implementation of the purchase
                             method is omitted in this listing.
```

The new keyword in front of a class name invokes the class `constructor`. When a constructor is invoked with the `new` keyword, an object is created and given to the constructor, where you can access it using the @ symbol. When you `new` a `Camera`,

```
x1 - new Camera 'X1', {
  description: 'An awesome camera', stock: 5
}
```

the object returned has `name` and `info` properties assigned to it by the `constructor`:

```
x1.name
#'X1'
x1.info
#{description: "An awesome camera", stock: 5}
```

The object returned also has the methods, such as `render`, from the class declaration:

```
x1.render()
# "Camera: X1: An Awesome camera (5)"
```

It's worth reiterating at this point that a method in CoffeeScript is really just a property containing a function. Evaluate it and see:

```
x1.render
# [Function]
```

Evaluating a method name without invoking it will produce the function value itself.

> **Private or public?**
>
> Many object-oriented languages divide object methods into those that are private and those that are public (and sometimes other options such as privileged). The Java-Script object model has only public properties. To hide information in JavaScript, you need to use function scope.

You now have a description of how cameras work. How about the other things in the program? The shop is more than cameras. The shop receives all of the camera data and uses it to create all of the camera objects. The `Shop` class is a place to declare the shop behavior. Remember, when you plan to have many objects with the same behavior, a class is a convenient place to describe that behavior

```
class Shop
  constructor: (data) ->
    for name, info of data
      new Camera name, info
```
Class describes behavior

with the sample data that you have:

```
data =
  X100:
    description: "A really cool camera"
    stock: 5
  X1:
    description: "An awesome camera"
    stock: 6
```
Object describes data

Now, create a new shop by invoking the `constructor` with the data:

```
shop = new Shop data
```

You have two instances of the `Camera` class—both created by the `Shop constructor`. What does this look like in the context of a real program? In listing 5.2 the `Camera` and `Shop` classes are fleshed out to implement the first version of the online shop.

IMPORTANT: HOW TO RUN THE LISTINGS
Listings 5.2, 5.3, 5.4, 5.5, 5.8, 5.10, and 5.11 demonstrate different object-based techniques in CoffeeScript using a small client-side program. The final listing, 5.13, is a small server-side program intended to run each of these different listings. To experiment with the code in the listings, invoke listing 5.13 from the command line with the listing number for the client-side program:

```
> coffee 5.13.coffee 5.2
# => Visit http://localhost:8080/ in your browser
```

◁— **Run the server with listing 5.2 as the client script.**

Any changes you make to the listings will be automatically reflected in the client script delivered to the browser. So if you make a change to a client-side script and refresh the browser window, you'll see the result of your changes.

In the next listing the `Shop` class fetches raw JSON (see section 4.4.1) from a remote server and uses it to create cameras. The `http` and `get` functions use some browser APIs that you need not be familiar with here. Experiment with the listing to understand how the application fits together.

Listing 5.2   Agtron's camera shop client application (version 1)

```
http = (method, src, callback) ->
  handler = ->
    if @readyState is 4 and @status is 200
      unless @responseText is null
        callback JSON.parse @responseText

  client = new XMLHttpRequest
  client.onreadystatechange = handler
  client.open method, src
  client.send()
```

http function for making Ajax requests to the server

```
get = (src, callback) ->
  http "GET", src, callback
```

get function for making GET Ajax requests to the server

```
post = (src, callback) ->
  http "POST", src, callback
```

post function for making POST Ajax requests to the server

```
class Camera
  constructor: (name, info) ->
    @name = name
    @info = info
    @view = document.createElement 'div'
    @view.className = "camera"
    document.body.appendChild @view
    @view.onclick = =>
      @purchase()
    @render()
```

Camera class with constructor, render method that writes to the web page, and purchase method

```
render: ->
  @view.innerHTML = "#{@name} (#{@info.stock} stock)"

purchase: ->
  if @info.stock > 0
    post "/json/purchase/camera/#{@name}", (res) =>
      if res.status is "success"
        @info = res.update
        @render()
```

> Camera class with
> constructor, render
> method that writes
> to the web page, and
> purchase method

```
class Shop
  constructor: ->
    get '/json/list/camera', (data) ->
      for own name, info of data
        new Camera name, info
```

> Shop class for initializing
> the application and creating
> all the cameras

```
shop = new Shop
```

In the `Camera` and `Shop` classes, this program has clear descriptions for the behavior of products and shops.

As the program grows, you'll find that you have different classes of similar objects and that you're duplicating methods across different classes. How will you deal with this? One technique is class inheritance.

5.2   *Class inheritance*

In class-based object-oriented languages, the most common technique for organizing classes of objects with some things in common is called *class inheritance*. But Coffee-Script isn't a traditional class-based language. It's a prototype-based language where objects inherit properties from their prototype (see chapter 4 if you need a refresher on prototypes). If CoffeeScript isn't a class-based language, can you do class-based inheritance? Yes, by using the `extends` keyword.

5.2.1   *extends*

Imagine now that Agtron wants to sell more than cameras. He also wants to sell skateboards. Cameras and skateboards are different, so you can't use the same class for both of them. You could copy and paste the `Camera` class, rename a few things to create a `Skateboard` class, and then modify the `Camera` class to add a megapixel count. You could, but you don't. Instead you use `extends`.

DECLARING EXTENDS

Given that cameras and skateboards are different products, you define a `Product` class:

```
class Product
```

Cameras and skateboards can be defined as products by saying their classes *extend* the Product class:

```
class Camera extends Product
class Robot extends Product
class Skateboard extends Product
```

The keyword extends in a class declaration means what it says. If the Product class is declared with a purchase method and the Skateboard class extends it,

```
class Product
  constructor: (name, info) ->
    @name = name
    @info = info

  render: ->
    "#{@name}: #{@info.description} (#{@info.stock} in stock)"

  purchase: ->
    if @info.stock > 0
      post "/json/purchase/camera/#{@name}", (res) =>
        if res.status is "success"
          @info = res.update
          @render()

class Skateboard extends Product
```

constructor from
Camera class

render method
from Camera class

purchase
method from
Camera class

when you new a Skateboard, it has a render method:

```
skateOMatic = new Skateboard "Skate-o-matic", {
  description: "It's a skateboard"
  stock: 1
}

skateOMatic.render()
# Skate-o-matic: "It\'s a skateboard (1 in stock)"
```

Now that you have a Product class, you can modify Camera without affecting skateboards or anything else that extends a product. Add a mexapixels method in the class declaration for Camera:

```
class Camera extends Product
  megapixels: ->
    @info.megapixels || 'Unknown'
```

Use the default operator
(section 2.3.1).

When you create a camera and a skateboard, the camera has a megapixels method but the skateboard does not:

```
x11 = new Camera "x11", {
  description: "The future of photography",
  stock: 4,
  megapixels: 20
}

sk8orama = new Skateboard "Sk8orama", {
  description: "A trendy skateboard",
  stock: 4
}

x11.megapixels?
# true

x11.megapixels()
# 20
```

```
sk8orama.megapixels?
# false
```

If CoffeeScript is not class-based, how does it do class inheritance? It's all in the compiler, and classes in CoffeeScript are just syntax. They are *syntactic sugar* for the prototype-based objects underneath. Something is called syntactic sugar when it makes it a bit easier or *sweeter* for a specific thing in a programming language. Many people, including Scruffy in figure 5.2, have tried to add classes in JavaScript without any syntactic sugar. None of them caught on very much. Without sugar they're unpalatable.

The syntactic sugar CoffeeScript provides for classes makes it easier to write classes in a language that's really prototype-based.

5.2.2   *How does it work?*

At this point you may expect a side-by-side comparison of CoffeeScript class syntax with the compiled JavaScript to show you what's going on. In this case, though, the raw JavaScript actually confuses the matter, so it's too early to think about the compiler. Instead of looking at everything the compiler does, consider a `product` object:

```
product =
  render: ->
  purchase: ->
```

This `product` object has two properties. How do you make lots of them? With a function.

Figure 5.2   Sometimes you need a little sugar.

```
construct = (prototype, name, info) ->          Create a new object with
  object = Object.create prototype              the provided prototype.
  object.name = name            Add some properties
  object.info = info            to the new object.    Return the
  object                                              new object.

clock = construct product, 'clock', stock: 5    Create a product with the name
                                                clock using the construct function.
```

You have two things: a prototypical product and a function that constructs product objects. A class declaration achieves the same thing in a different way:

```
class Product                   The constructor
  constructor: ->
  render: ->                    The description of the
  purchase: ->                  product prototype
```

How does `extends` fit into this picture? Suppose you took the earlier `product` object (not the class) and created a new object from it:

```
camera = Object.create product
camera.megapixels = ->
```

Now if you use `construct` on this `camera` object, you can create other `camera` objects:

```
x11 = construct camera, '', stock: 6
```

This `x11` object inherits from `camera`, which in turn inherits from `product`. The `extends` keyword in a class declaration works in much the same way. It makes the prototype of one class inherit from the prototype for another class. The way that an object inherits from a prototype object that in turn inherits from another prototype is commonly referred to as the *prototype chain*.

In listing 5.3 the client application from listing 5.2 has been enhanced with an inheritance hierarchy using `extends`. To create objects from different classes, the `Shop` constructor has been modified to look at the data source and to `new` the appropriate class. Parts of the full program that are identical to listing 5.2 have been omitted from this listing.

Listing 5.3 Agtron's shop client application with multiple product categories

The http
function is
identical to
listing 5.2
and has
been
omitted
here.

```
# http function omitted - see listing 5.2     The get and post functions are
# get function omitted - see listing 5.2       also identical to listing 5.2 and
# post function omitted - see listing 5.2      have been omitted here.

class Product
  constructor: (name, info) ->
    @name = name
    @info = info
    @view = document.createElement 'div'
    @view.className = "product"            Product
    document.body.appendChild @view        constructor.
    @view.onclick = =>
      @purchase()
    @render()
```

```
  render: ->
    renderInfo = (key,val) ->
      "<div>#{key}: #{val}</div>"
    displayInfo = (renderInfo(key, val) for own key, val of @info)
    @view.innerHTML = "#{@name} #{displayInfo.join ''}"

  purchase: ->
    if @info.stock > 0
      post "/json/purchase/#{@purchaseCategory}/#{@name}", (res) =>
        if res.status is "success"
          @info = res.update
          @render()
```

Product instance methods.

```
class Camera extends Product
  purchaseCategory: 'camera'
  megapixels: -> @info.megapixels || "Unknown"

class Skateboard extends Product
  purchaseCategory: 'skateboard'
  length: -> @info.length || "Unknown"

class Shop
  constructor: ->
    get '/json/list', (data) ->
      for own category of data
        for own name, info of data[category]
          switch category
            when 'camera'
              new Camera name, info
            when 'skateboard'
              new Skateboard name, info
```

Shop constructor creates an instance of the appropriate class based on the data source.

```
shop = new Shop
```

You've now extended a class to share some behavior and keep some other behavior distinct using class inheritance. When working with classes, though, there are times when you have behavior that's related to a class of objects but belongs to the class itself. Declaring these behaviors is simple to do in CoffeeScript. You're about to find out how.

5.3 *Class variables and properties*

So far all of the properties you've defined with classes belong to instances of classes. This means they're properties found on instances of the class:

```
class Product
  render: ->
```
render method defined on class

```
instanceOfProduct = new Product
instanceOfProduct.render
```
render method invoked as property of an instance of the Product class

Some properties don't make sense as instances of the class. Some properties make more sense as properties of the class itself. Imagine all of the products sold in Agtron's shop are faulty and need to be recalled. It's easy to invoke recall on the Product class:

```
Product.recall()
```

It's not so easy to hunt down all of the products ever constructed and invoke `recall` on each one. You might argue that it more accurately reflects the real world for things like product recalls to be much more complicated, but you like simplicity. Class properties can be a simple and useful technique.

> **THESE ARE CLASS METHODS, RIGHT?** Class properties in CoffeeScript can serve similar purposes to class methods in Ruby, Smalltalk, or Objective-C and even static methods in Java or C++.

5.3.1 Usage

Imagine now that Agtron wants a product search feature on his website so that people can find products by name. When a user searches for shark repellant, they should be shown a list of all shark repellant products that Agtron has for sale. The search feature will have an input field where users can enter a search term. Agtron's design for the new homepage is shown in figure 5.3.

In order to find a specific product, you need to keep a reference to each of the product objects. An array of objects does this nicely. Each object in the array has a name property and corresponding value:

```
products = [
    name: "Shark repellant"
  ,
    name: "Duct tape"
]
```

> Notice there are no curly braces in this object definition? Significant indentation has been used instead.

Here's a crude brute-force `find` function for this array:

```
find = (query) ->
  (product for product in products when product.name is query)
```

Use this `find` function by calling it with a product name:

```
find "Duct tape"
# [ { name: 'Duct tape' } ]
```

Figure 5.3 Agtron's shop with product search

The products you already have in the client code for Agtron's shop are objects with name properties, so a similar find function will work. But you do not yet have an array of all the products created. Where should the array of product references go? How about in the Shop constructor?

```
class Shop
  constructor: (data) ->
  products = []
  for own name, info of data
    products.push new Product(name, info)
```

But that assumes that an instance of the Shop class creates *every* instance of Product. Awesome, until somebody news a Product outside of the shop and it's never found. Given that find is *about* products, why not put it on the Product class?

```
Product.find('Pixelmator-X21')
# [ Camera { name="Pixelmator-X21", info={...} } ]
```

The Product class can have a property like an object because it *is* an object.

CLASS METHODS

Any class *is* an object and has properties just like any other object. To specify a class method named find, just assign a function as the find property directly on the class:

```
Product.find = (query) ->
  (product for product in products when product.name is query)
```

For that to work you need somewhere to define the product variable. You don't want an evil global variable; you want a variable that lives with the Product class. You want a class variable.

CLASS VARIABLES

All variables are function-scoped so you're surprised to see what happens when a new variable is assigned in the body of a class declaration:

```
class SecretAgent
  secretWord = "antiquing"         The secretWord variable isn't
                                   defined outside the class body.
secretWord?
# false
```

Class variables are scoped to the class body. The class body has a variable scope like a function (as you'll see later, when compiled to JavaScript the class declaration really *is* a function). They look a little bit like instance properties; be careful to notice the distinction.

CLASS VARIABLES VS. INSTANCE PROPERTIES

Variables always use the = operator, whereas object properties use the : operator:

```
class SecretAgent              Class variable
  secretWord = "antiquing"
  licensedToKill: yes          Instance property
```

Methods can access class variables because they're *inside* the class declaration with them:

```
class SecretAgent
  secretWord = "antiquing"          ◁──┤  Class variable.
  greet: (word) ->
    if word is secretWord           ◁─┐  This method can see the
      "Hello, how are you?"            │  class variable because
bob = new SecretAgent                  └─ it's in the same scope.
bob.greet "antiquing"
# "Hello, how are you?"
```

You now have a place to keep the product variable inside the `Product` class. Unfortunately, that also also makes it invisible to your *Product.find* class method:

```
class Product                  ┌─ Class variable is defined
  products              ◁──────┘  in current scope.
                                                            ┌─ Class variable
Product.find = (query) ->                                   │  isn't visible
  (product for product in products when product.name is query) ◁──┘  outside.
```

The `find` method is not declared *inside* the class. The class body has a function scope, so the `find` method must be defined inside it in order to see the `product` variable. How do you define it *inside* the class body so that all the things related to the class are defined in one place?

5.3.2 *Declaring (to keep things together)*

Inside a constructor, `@` refers to the new object being constructed. Inside an instance method, `@` refers to the instance by default. That much you know. Directly inside the class declaration, `@` refers to the class itself. The `@` keyword is used to define the `find` property on the `Product` class:

```
class Product
  @find = (what) ->              ◁─┐  Directly inside the class
    "#{what} not found"            │  declaration, @ refers to
                                   │  the class.
Product.find "zombie survival kit"
# "zombie survival kit not found"
```

Remember that `@` is dynamic; the object it refers to depends on how the function is invoked. Inside the class body the class body itself has been invoked. Yes, the class body works like a function. It's still too soon to see why, and besides you now have a solution for `Product.find`:

```
class Product                        ┌─ Class variable
  instances = []              ◁──────┘
  @find = (query) ->            ◁─┐  Class method
    (product for product in instances when product.name is query)
  constructor: (name) ->
    instances = instances.concat [@]  ◁─┐  Adding the new instance to the array of instances
    @name = name                         │  using the array concat method (section 2.6.1)
```

Now, by using a class variable and a class method, you have a solution that finds a product:

```
new Product "Green", {}
Product.find 'Green'
# [ { name: 'Green' } ]
```

It's time to tie this back to the overall shop program. A new version of the client application, this time with the `Product.find`, is in listing 5.4. An input field has been added to the HTML document, which provides an interface for users to enter the name of the product they want to find. As with previous listings, some functions and methods that are identical to earlier listings are omitted. The following listing can be run using listing 5.13.

Listing 5.4 Agtron's shop client application with `find`

```
# http, get and post functions omitted - see listing 5.2

class Product
  products = []                                    The products
                                                   class variable.
  @find = (query) ->
    for product in products                        The find class
      product.unmark()                             method invokes
    for product in products when product.name is query    mark and unmark
      product.mark()                               methods that
      product                                      change the view.

  constructor: (name, info) ->
    products.push @
    @name = name
    @info = info
    @view = document.createElement 'div'           The constructor
    @view.className = "product"                    also renders
    document.body.appendChild @view                onto the view.
    @view.onclick = =>
      @purchase()
      @render()
                                                   The render method
  render: ->                                        displays all the keys
    show = ("<div>#{key}: #{val}</div>" for own key, val of @info).join ''   and values of the
    @view.innerHTML = "#{@name} #{show}"           info object.

  purchase: ->                                      The purchase
    if @info.stock > 0                              method sends
      post "/json/purchase/#{@purchaseCategory}/#{@name}", (res) =>   a request
        if res.status is "success"                  and updates
          @info = res.update                        the view via
          @render()                                 render.

  mark: ->                                          The mark and unmark
    @view.style.border = "1px solid black"          methods make the search
                                                    result visible on the view.
  unmark: ->
    @view.style.border = "none"

# class Camera omitted - see listing 5.3
# class Skateboard omitted - see listing 5.3
```

```
class Shop
  constructor: ->
    @view = document.createElement 'input'
    @view.onchange = ->
      Product.find @value
    document.body.appendChild @view
    @render()
    get '/json/list', (data) ->
      for own category of data
        for own name, info of data[category]
          switch category
            when 'camera'
              new Camera name, info
            when 'skateboard'
              new Skateboard name, info

  render: ->
    @view.innerHTML = ""

shop = new Shop
```

The Shop class needs to determine which class to construct based on the data.

Notice that some parts of the program are becoming a bit difficult to follow. The view (which manipulates things displayed in the browser) takes up a lot of room in the program and obscures the other parts of the program. There's a way to move those parts of the code somewhere else where they won't get in the way, and you will learn about it later in the chapter. Before moving on, though, there's one more thing you need to know about class properties.

CLASS PROPERTY INHERITANCE

If a Product class has an existing find method, then a Camera class that extends Product will inherit that existing find method:

```
products = [
    name: "Shark repellant"
  ,
    name: "Duct tape"
]

class Product

Product.find = (query) ->
  (product for product in products when product.name is query)

class Camera extends Product

Camera.find?
# true
```

Add a class property to Product dynamically after Camera has already extended Product. The Camera class doesn't get the class property:

```
class Product

class Camera extends Product

Product.find = (what) -> "#{what} not found"
Product.find?
# true
```

```
Camera.find?
# false
```

The class declaration isn't dynamic. To modify a class at runtime, you need to start thinking in prototypes.

5.3.3   *Exercise*

Write a `Camera.alphabetical` class method that returns an array of all the cameras sorted alphabetically by name.

So far in this chapter you've declared and extended classes and added properties and methods to both instances and classes. In some cases, though, you don't simply want to add behavior—you want to change it. To do this you need to know what happens when you redefine something that you've inherited and how to get back the original after you've redefined it.

5.4   *Overriding and super*

You can change the property of an object any time, just by assigning something to it. What about a class, though? Assigning a new value to a class property works the same as any object:

```
class Human

Human.rights = ['Life', 'Liberty', 'the pursuit of happiness']
Human.rights
# ['Life', 'Liberty', 'the pursuit of happiness']

Human.rights = Human.rights.concat ['To party']
Human.rights
# ['Life', 'Liberty', 'the pursuit of happiness', 'To party']
```

Class methods are just properties on a class. How about instance methods? What happens when you write a class declaration that defines an instance method that's already inherited from another class through `extends`?

5.4.1   *Overriding*

Imagine now that Agtron wants cameras to look different than other products on the shop website. He wants them to have a photo gallery next to their product description. The `Gallery` class has a `constructor` and a `render` method:

```
class Gallery
  constructor: ->
  render: ->
```

Using the `constructor`, a new gallery is created with each new camera:

```
class Camera
  constructor: ->
    @gallery = new Gallery
```

When the camera renders, it will need to invoke the `render` method on the gallery. This means the `Camera` class needs a different `render` method from other products. Put this method inside the class declaration:

```
class Camera extends Product
  render: ->
    @view.innerHTML = """
    #{@name}: #{@info.stock}
    {@gallery.render()}
    """
```

> **A heredoc to output the name and the gallery.
> The gallery output is generated by the render
> method of the gallery object.**

The constructor and the render method have both been overridden:

```
class Camera extends Product
  constructor: (name, info) ->
    @name = name
    @info = info
    @gallery = new Gallery
  render: ->
    @view.innerHTML = """
    #{@name}: #{@info.stock}
    {@gallery.render()}
    """
```

> **Create a gallery from
> the Gallery class.**

> **Get the gallery
> to render.**

To override a method that you got from extending a class, declare a new version in the
new class. Sounds too easy, and it is. What happens when you create some cameras
and try to find them?

```
class Product

Product.find = (query) ->
  (product for product in products when product.name is query)

class Camera extends Product

x1 = new Camera 'X1', {}
Product.find 'X1'
# []
```

The camera was not found! The list of product instances is updated inside the Product
constructor. Once you define a new constructor for the Camera class, the Product constructor won't be invoked when you new a Camera. No Camera instances will be added
to the array. There's a solution to this problem: the super keyword.

5.4.2 *super*

When Camera extends Product, invoking super inside a method invokes the corresponding inherited method. Suppose that the markup on cameras is massive and they
sell at twice the product cost:

```
class Product
  constructor: (name, cost) ->
    @name = name
    @cost = cost
  price: ->
    @cost

class Camera extends Product
  markup = 2

  price: ->
    super()*markup
```

Create a `Camera` and invoke the price method:

```
camera = new Camera 'X10', 10
camera.price()
# 20
```

You can use `super` with any method call, including a constructor. If you haven't overridden a method, then the same inherited method that `super` invokes will be invoked automatically via the prototype. The next listing shows an in-context use of `super` to call the `Product` constructor from the `Camera` constructor. As with other listings in this chapter, you can't run listing 5.5 from the REPL; you need to run it with listing 5.13.

Listing 5.5   Agtron's shop client application with camera gallery

```
# http, get and post functions omitted from this listing

class Gallery
  constructor: (@photos) ->
  render: ->
    images = for photo in @photos
      "<li><img src='#{photo}' alt='sample photo' /></li>"
    "<ul class='gallery'>#{images.join ''}</ul>"

class Product
  constructor: (name, info) ->
    @name = name
    @info = info
    @view = document.createElement 'div'
    @view.className = 'product'
    document.querySelector('.page').appendChild @view
    @render()
  render: ->
    @view.innerHTML = "#{@name}: #{@info.stock}"

class Camera extends Product
  constructor: (name, info) ->
    @gallery = new Gallery info.gallery
    super name, info
    @view.className += ' camera'
  render: ->
    @view.innerHTML = """
      #{@name} (#{@info.stock})
      #{@gallery.render()}
    """

class Shop
  constructor: ->
    @view = document.createElement 'div'
    document.querySelector('.page').appendChild @view
    document.querySelector('.page').className += ' 155'
    @render()
    get '/json/list', (data) ->
      for own category of data
        for own name, info of data[category]
          switch category
```

A Gallery class that only renders some placeholder text.

The Product constructor that the Camera constructor invokes.

The Camera constructor invokes the Product constructor via super.

```
        when 'camera'
          new Camera name, info
        else
          new Product name, info

  render: () ->
    @view.innerHTML = ""

shop = new Shop
```

In listing 5.5 you notice that passing all of the arguments for a constructor through to the super constructor is repetitive. CoffeeScript also provides super as a keyword for this situation:

```
class Gallery

class Camera extends Product
  constructor: (name, info) ->
    @gallery = new Gallery
    super

pixelmatic = new Camera 'The Pixelmatic 5000', {}
pixelmatic.name
# 'The Pixelmatic 5000'
```

Now you know that the CoffeeScript class sugar has been hiding things from you and that syntactic sugar is a language convenience that makes some common expressions easier. When you need to break away from classes, you'll have to dive back down into objects and prototypes, leaving the sugar behind. So, when do you need to break away from classes?

5.5 Modifying prototypes

Remember, there are plain, old objects and prototype links underneath your classes. In this section you'll learn how CoffeeScript's class declarations work by seeing the actual JavaScript they compile to. You'll also learn what you can do to classes and their instances when you start dynamically modifying their prototypes.

5.5.1 How class declarations work

Imagine now that Agtron has extra stock of some products, and he wants to offer special deals on them. If you know beforehand that Agtron is offering special deals on Cameras with the name 'Lacia', then you can handle the special deal in the class declaration:

```
class Camera
  render: ->
    if /'Lacia'/.test @name        If the name of this object
      "Special deal"               looks like 'Lacia', then
                                   it's on special.
```

It's not going to be that easy. Agtron wants to change the special deals dynamically. You don't know in advance what's going to be discounted, so you can't declare it in the class. You'll need to extend the class dynamically. To learn how to extend a class dynamically, you need to learn how classes really work. It's finally time to see the JavaScript that the CoffeeScript compiler creates from a class declaration.

The compiled JavaScript for a CoffeeScript class is shown in the following listing. As always, CoffeeScript is on the left and compiled JavaScript is on the right.

Listing 5.6   CoffeeScript class and compilation to JavaScript

CoffeeScript	JavaScript

```
class Simple
  constructor: ->
    @name = "simple object"

simple = new Simple
```

```
var Simple = (function() {
  function Simple() {
    this.name = 'simple';
  }
  return Simple;
})();

simple = new Simple();
```

Inside a CoffeeScript class you see functions. That explains the variable scope. Coffee-Script classes have a variable scope like functions because they *are* functions. One second, though; where did the constructor go?

CONSTRUCTOR FUNCTIONS

In JavaScript a constructor is a function that creates a new object and links it to a prototype object. In addition to the prototype, all objects have a reference to their constructor function. In JavaScript when you use the `new` keyword in front of a function, an object is created and the function is invoked with the `this` keyword inside the function (known as `@` in CoffeeScript) referring to the new object. In listings 5.6 and 5.7 the CoffeeScript class constructor corresponds to a constructor function in JavaScript.

Raw constructor functions still work in CoffeeScript:

```
SteamShovel = (name) ->                    An ordinary
  @name = name                             function

  steamShovel = new SteamShovel 'Gus'      The function used
  steamShovel.name                         as a constructor
  # 'Gus'

  steamShovel.constructor                  The same function again, accessed via
  # [Function]                             constructor property on an instance
```

Any object created using a function as a constructor has a `constructor` property that references the function. How about methods then? How do they work?

5.5.2   How methods work

The listing that follows shows the compiled JavaScript output for a CoffeeScript class with a constructor and one method.

Listing 5.7 CoffeeScript class, constructor, and method compilation

CoffeeScript
```coffeescript
class SteamShovel
  constructor (name) ->
    @name = name
  speak: ->
    "Hurry up!"

gus = new SteamShovel
gus.speak()
# Hurry up!
```

JavaScript
```javascript
var SteamShovel = (function() {
  function SteamShovel(name) {
    this.name = name;
  }
  SteamShovel.prototype.speak =
    function() {
    return "Hurry up!";
  };
  return SteamShovel;
  };
gus = new SteamShovel();
gus.speak();
```

The object referenced by `SteamShovel.prototype` is the prototypical steam shovel. The `speak` method is created by assigning it as a property on the prototypical steam shovel. You can tell a constructor function which object to use as the prototype for future objects:

```coffeescript
SteamShovel.prototype = {}
```

CoffeeScript classes are syntactic sugar for prototypes and constructor functions. This means you can change properties on the prototype:

```coffeescript
SteamShovel.prototype.grumpy = yes
```

Now all of the objects created using the `SteamShovel` constructor have a `grumpy` property, inherited via the prototype chain:

```coffeescript
gus.grumpy
# true
```

This turns out to be useful for dynamically modifying objects and classes.

5.5.3 *Dynamic classes*

By adding a property to the prototype, you're adding it to all the objects that use it *without touching the class declaration*:

```coffeescript
class Example
example = new Example
Example.prototype.justAdded = -> "just added!"

example.justAdded()
# "just added!"
```

You probably remember doing something similar with raw objects in section 4.6 using `Object.create`. Now you're doing exactly the same thing by accessing the prototype for a whole class of objects by modifying the `prototype` object via the class.

PROTOTYPE SHORTHAND

CoffeeScript has a more convenient shorthand syntax for accessing the prototype using two consecutive colons, so that

```
Example::justAdded = -> "just added!"
```

is equivalent to

```
Example.prototype.justAdded = -> "just added!"
```

Understanding what the CoffeeScript compiler does when you write a class means you're able to modify a class dynamically by modifying the object it uses as the prototype for constructed objects. The next listing demonstrates this in action.

Listing 5.8   Agtron's shop client application with specials

```
# http omitted from this listing
# get omitted from this listing
# post omitted from this listing
class Product
  constructor: (name, info) ->
    @name = name
    @info = info
    @view = document.createElement 'div'
    @view.className = "product #{@category}"
    document.querySelector('.page').appendChild @view
    @view.onclick = =>
      @purchase()
    @render()

  render: ->
    @view.innerHTML = @template()

  purchase: ->
    if @info.stock > 0
      post "/json/purchase/#{@category}/#{@name}", (res) =>
        if res.status is "success"
          @info = res.update
          @render()

  template: =>
    """
    <h2>#{@name}</h2>
    <dl class='info'>
    <dt>Stock</dt>
    <dd>#{@info.stock}</dd>
    <dt>Specials?</dt>
    <dd>#{@specials.join(',') || 'No'}</dd>
    </dl>
    """

class Camera extends Product
  category: 'camera'
  megapixels: -> @info.megapixels || "Unknown"

class Skateboard extends Product
  category: 'skateboard'
  length: -> @info.length || "Unknown"
```

```
class Shop
  constructor: ->
    unless Product::specials?
      Product::specials = []
    @view = document.createElement 'div'
    @render()
    get '/json/list', (data) ->
      for own category of data
        for own name, info of data[category]
          if info.special?
            Product::specials.push info.special
          switch category
            when 'camera'
              new Camera name, info
            when 'skateboard'
              new Skateboard name, info
  render: ->
    @view.innerHTML = ""

shop = new Shop
```

The Shop constructor dynamically adds a property to the Product prototype.

The Shop constructor also adds all the specials to the specials property of the Product prototype.

At this point it's also informative to show an example of the actual JSON data being used. Here's an example of this JSON.

Listing 5.9 Product listings with specials

```
{
  'camera': {
    'Fuji-X100': {
      'description': 'a camera',
      'stock': 5,
      'arrives': 'December 25, 2012 00:00',
      'megapixels': 12.3
    }
  },
  'skateboard': {
    'Powell-Peralta': {
      'description': 'a skateboard',
      'stock': 3,
      'arrives': 'December 25, 2012 00:00',
      'length': '23.3 inches'
    }
  }
}
```

Being JSON, the Shop constructor is able to easily use this data as an object. Remember, JSON is valid syntax for an object in JavaScript and in CoffeeScript. Inside a CoffeeScript program, the data from listing 5.9 can also be represented with significant indentation:

```
products =
  camera:
    'Fuji-X100':
      description: 'a camera'
      stock: 5
```

```
      arrives: 'December 25, 2012 00:00'
      megapixels: 12.3
  skateboard:
    'Powell-Peralta':
      description: 'a skateboard'
      stock: 3
      arrives: 'December 25, 2012 00:00'
        length: '23.3 inches'
```

Through the prototype of a class you're able to modify the properties and behavior of many objects at the same time. This can be done not only with your own classes and objects but also with other objects and classes. Remember, the default for all objects is that they're open to modification. This means you can modify and extend anything, including built-in objects such as the prototypical array.

> **OBJECTS OPEN BY DEFAULT?**   Objects being open means you can change a property on any regular object that you have a reference to. The fifth edition of the ECMAScript standard makes it possible to `freeze` or `seal` an object, preventing it from being modified (see chapter 13).

5.6   *Extending built-ins*

You've seen that classes in CoffeeScript are syntactic sugar. They make working with constructors and prototypes easier. There are constructors for objects other than classes you define. Consider an array, an object, and a string:

```
object = {}
array = []
string = ''
```

Objects, arrays, and strings each have their own constructor functions. Instead of using the literal notation, it's possible, if generally pointless, to create objects, arrays, and strings using constructors:

```
object = new Object
array = new Array
string = new String
```

The prototypes of these objects provide the methods available to all objects, arrays, and strings. In a sense, there's a built-in `Object` class, an `Array` class, and a `String` class. But you now know that classes are really a syntactic convenience in CoffeeScript, so it's more accurate to talk of built-in prototypes and constructor functions.

By modifying built-in prototypes, you can change the behavior of the built-in language. This is a powerful and dangerous technique. In this section you'll learn how you can use it and why it should be treated with caution.

5.6.1   *Built-in constructor prototypes*

The built-in constructors provided to you will depend on the runtime you're using. The constructors you're most likely to encounter are `Object`, `Array`, `String`, `Date`, and `RegExp`.[1] All of these built-in constructors have prototypes that you can modify. For example, consider the `join` method on an array:

```
['yin','yang'].join 'and'
# 'yin and yang'
```

This is a function assigned to the `join` property of the array prototype, meaning that you have access to it and can change it through `Array::join`:

```
Array::join = -> "Array::join was redefined"
['yin','yang'].join 'and'
# "Array::join this was overridden"
```

You can quite easily break built-in code by assigning silly functions to prototypes. That's not all there is to them.

5.6.2 Extending date

Agtron now tells you that he wants to display the date when new stock arrives. This will make the homepage look like figure 5.4.

The stock arrival date is returned in the JSON from the server as a string like this:

```
"October 13, 1975 11:13:00"
```

This is a standard date format that the JavaScript runtime can read.[2] You can create a date from it fairly easily using the built-in `Date` class (otherwise known as the `Date` constructor function):

```
new Date "October 13, 1975 11:13:00"
```

Figure 5.4 Agtron's shop with stock arrival dates

---

[1] A full list of the standard constructors specified by ECMAScript 5 is included in appendix A.
[2] See IETF RFC 1123 http://tools.ietf.org/html/rfc1123.

But Agtron wants it to display how many days from today that is. You think that "how many days from today?" is a question you should be able to ask of any date:

```
productAvailable = new Date "October 13, 1975 11:13:00"
productAvailable.daysFromToday()
```

Because Date is a constructor, you have access to the prototype for all the date objects. Modify the Date prototype and add a daysFromToday method:

```
Date::daysFromToday = ->
  millisecondsInDay = 86400000
  today = new Date
  diff = @ - today
  Math.floor diff/millisecondsInDay
```

Travel back in time and imagine that today is January 20, 2012. How many days until Christmas Day 2012?

```
christmas = new Date "December 25, 2012 00:00"
christmas.daysFromToday()
#339
```

> **December 25, 2012, is in the past, so if you run this example now you will get a negative value.**

A WARNING ABOUT DATES   Because this executes in a web browser, it will use the time on the user's computer. Potential issues with date in a browser, such as time zones and clock drift, are beyond the scope of this chapter and not discussed here.

In the next listing you see how to apply this to the client application for Agtron's shop.

Listing 5.10   Agtron's shop client application with stock arrivals

```
# http omitted
# get omitted
# put omitted

Date::daysFromToday = ->
  millisecondsInDay = 86400000       The daysFromToday
  today = new Date                   method added to the
  diff = @ - today                   built-in Date prototype
  Math.floor diff/millisecondsInDay

class Product
  products = []

  @find = (query) ->
    for product in products
      product.unmark()
    for product in products when product.name is query
      product.mark()
      product

  constructor: (name, info) ->
    products.push @
    @name = name
    @info = info
    @view = document.createElement 'div'
```

```
      @view.className = "product #{@category}"
      document.querySelector('.page').appendChild @view
      @view.onclick = =>
        @purchase()
      @render()

    render: ->
      @view.innerHTML = @template()

    purchase: ->
      if @info.stock > 0
        post "/json/purchase/#{@purchaseCategory}/#{@name}", (res) =>
          if res.status is "success"
            @info = res.update
            @render()

    template: =>
      """
      <h2>#{@name}</h2>
      <dl class='info'>
      <dt>Stock</dt> <dd>#{@info.stock}</dd>
      <dt>New stock arrives in</dt>
      <dd>#{new Date(@info.arrives).daysFromToday()} days</dd>   <⊢
      </dl>
      """

    mark: ->
      @view.style.border = "1px solid black";

    unmark: ->
      @view.style.border = "none";

class Camera extends Product
  category: 'camera'
  megapixels: -> @info.megapixels || "Unknown"

class Skateboard extends Product
  category: 'skateboard'
  length: -> @info.length || "Unknown"

class Shop
  constructor: ->
    unless Product::specials?
      Product::specials = []
    @view = document.createElement 'div'
    @render()
    get '/json/list', (data) ->
      for own category of data
        for own name, info of data[category]
          if info.special?
            Product::specials.push info.special
          switch category
            when 'camera'
              new Camera name, info
            when 'skateboard'
              new Skateboard name, info

  render: ->
    @view = document.createElement 'div'
```

Using the daysFromToday method on an object created with the Date constructor

```
document.querySelector('.page').appendChild @view
@view.innerHTML = """
<form class='search'>
Search: <input id='search' type='text' />
<button id='go'>Go</button>
</form>
"""
@search = document.querySelector '#search'
@go = document.querySelector '#go'
@go.onclick = =>
  Product.find @search.value
  false
@search.onchange = ->
  Product.find @value
  false
```

```
shop = new Shop
```

Extending prototypes is a powerful technique that allows you to change the behavior of any object in CoffeeScript. You have the power. Be careful how you use it.

5.6.3   *Don't modify objects you don't own*

By extending the built-in `Date` object, you're changing it for the entire program. If you're writing a library that other people are going to use, then you're changing things for other people's entire programs. You don't know what those other people are doing in their programs, so extending built-ins has a high potential for breaking other people's code. Modifying built-in prototypes is a bit like breaking into somebody's house and leaving stuff there. This works only if you're Santa Claus.

One alternative to modifying a built-in prototype is to write your own class that extends the built-in and use that instead:

```
class ExtendedDate extends Date
  daysFromToday: ->
    millisecondsInDay = 86400000
    today = new Date
    diff = @ - today
    Math.floor diff/millisecondsInDay
```

You should trade the convenience of extending a built-in for its danger on a case-by-case basis.

You've seen how to declare a class that allows you to create objects from the class. You've also seen how classes are just functions and prototypes when you lift the veil and look underneath. Class convenience comes with some rigidity, meaning you go back to raw prototypes when you need to dynamically extend things. This is an important lesson worth repeating.

THE CLASS SWEET SPOT

If you're mostly creating certain kinds of objects with some extensions, then use classes. They work very well for that. If, however, your problem requires more dynamism than structure, you will need to look outside classes.

What if you had lots of objects that were all quite different but nonetheless had some common behavior?

5.7 Mixins

A *mixin* is a class that contains (mixes together) a combination of methods from other classes. Pure objects and prototypes provide flexibility, and classes provide structure. Mixins are a popular technique in class-based languages to achieve some of the flexibility that prototypes provide while still keeping the structure of classes. Although there's no dedicated syntax for mixins in CoffeeScript, they can be achieved without much fuss. First though, when should you use mixins? When classes become awkward.

5.7.1 Class inheritance can be awkward

Image now that Agtron wants to add news announcements to the shop homepage. This will make the homepage look like figure 5.5.

You consider the classes you have in your system, and it looks like you have a small problem. You have a `Product` class with a `render` method that's used by all the objects whose class definition `extends Product`. Now though, you have a new class, `Announcement`, that certainly isn't a `Product`—it's awkward if you make it extend `Product`:

```
class Announcement
pigsFly = new Announcement
pigsFly.purchase()
# Error
```

Still, you want to reuse the `render` method because it really *is* the same between `Product` and `Announcement`. With your inheritance hat on, you think it might be a good idea to just add another layer to the inheritance hierarchy:

```
class Renderer
class Product extends Renderer
class Camera extends Product

class Announcement extends Renderer
```

Figure 5.5 Agtron's shop with news announcements

Trying to program like that in CoffeeScript is working against the grain. The objects are dynamic and prototype-based at their core. Work with the language.

Rendering is a function that you just happen to invoke on different objects, some of them products and some of them announcements. The function doesn't need to belong to a *particular* class. You can define a render function anywhere in Coffee-Script. The trouble is, when you can define it anywhere, you're spoiled for choice. If you can define it anywhere, where do you actually define it in practice, and how do you keep related functions together? You want collections of related functions that can be used with objects regardless of what class they were created from—if they were created from a class at all! You want mixins.

5.7.2   *Writing a mixin*

The simplest way to write a mixin is by taking advantage of the properties as key-value store objects. Define rendering behavior on a plain, old object:

```coffee
htmlRenderer =
  render: ->
    unless @view?
      @view = document.createElement 'div'
      document.body.appendChild @view
      @view.innerHTML = """
      #{@name}
      #{@info}
      """
```

An object created ex nihilo with a render property referring to a function

To add the `render` method to a class, you modify the class prototype:

```coffee
class Donut
  constructor: (name,info) ->
    @name = name
    @info = info
```

Now add the render method:

```coffee
Donut::render = htmlRenderer.render
```

This works, but it's tedious. Remember, a mixin is a collection of related functions that can be attached as methods to objects. Suppose you have a collection of three functions:

```coffee
dwarves =
  bashful: -> 'Bashful'
  doc: -> 'Doc'
  dopey: -> 'Dopey'
```

To mix dwarves into a `FairyTale` class, you add *all* of the functions to the class prototype:

```coffee
class FairyTale
  for key, value of dwarves
    FairyTale::[key] = value
```

Comprehension of the properties of the dwarves object, adding them to the FairyTale prototype

You want a general solution, though, that will work for `Camera` and looks like so:

```
class Camera
    include @, htmlRenderer
# ReferenceError: include is not defined
```

This is the syntax you want.

You just haven't implemented it yet.

How can you make that work? The `include` function should add all of the properties from the mixin to the class:

```
x1 = new Camera
x1.render()
#renders
```

render method mixed in.

That `include` function is implemented using a comprehension:

```
include = (klass, module) ->
    for key, value of module
        klass::[key] = value
```

This include function copies all the properties from the module argument to the prototype of the klass argument.

Some people prefer to think in terms of classes. A `Mixin` class, from which you can create instances that provide their own `include` method, is shown here.

Listing 5.11 Mixin class

```
class Mixin
    constructor: (methods) ->
        for name, body of methods
            @[name] = body
    include: (klass) ->
        for key, value of @
            klass::[key] = value
```

The include method copies the methods of the current object to the supplied class.

```
htmlRenderer = new Mixin
    render: -> "rendered"
```

Create a mixin.

```
class Camera
    htmlRenderer.include @
```

Include the mixin into the Camera class.

```
leica = new Camera()
```

```
leica.render()
#rendered
```

A Camera instance has a render method added by the mixin.

By comprehending the properties of an existing object and setting them as properties on another object, you're able to mix in behavior from one object to another. Note that the mixin technique you've learned is static. Once the properties have been copied to the `Camera` class, further changes to the `htmlRenderer` object are not seen by `Camera` instances. Mixins created in this way allow you to do a one-time copy of related functions to another object. More sophisticated dynamic programming is demonstrated in later chapters.

5.7.3 *Example: enumerable mixin*

Remember the accumulator from chapter 3 that you used to sum an array of numbers? Accumulating numbers wasn't exciting, but it did demonstrate how to pass a function as an argument to another function:

```
accumulate = (initial, numbers, accumulator) ->
  total = initial or 0
  for number in numbers
    total = accumulator total, number
  total
```

The accumulate
function from
chapter 3

```
sum = (acc, current) -> acc + current
accumulate 0, [5,5,5], sum
# 15
```

The accumulate function takes a sequence of numbers and accumulates the values to a single value. Suppose Agtron wants to know the total stock count of all the products on his site. The Product class had a list of instances:

```
class Product
  instances = []
  constructor: (stock) ->
    instances.push @
    @stock = stock
```

You want to use an accumulator to add up all the stock, but the variable instances is behind the scope of the Product class. You have to accumulate from inside Product:

```
class Product
  instances = []
  constructor: (stock) ->
    instances.push @
    @stock = stock
  stock: ->
    stockAccumulator = (acc, current) -> acc + current.stock
    accumulate(0, instances, stockAccumulator)
```

The Product class now has a reference to an accumulate variable defined somewhere else that isn't really a core part of Product. If instead you create an enumerable mixin, then you'll have a cleaner solution:

```
enumerable =
  accumulate: (initial=0, accumulator, sequence) ->
    total = initial
    for element in sequence
      total = accumulator total, element
    total
```

The enumerable mixin is
just an object containing
the accumulate function
as a property.

Using this enumerable mixin, you can get the stock total:

```
include = (klass, module) ->
  for key, value of module
    klass[key] = value

class Product
  include Product, enumerable
  instances = []
  accumulator = (acc, current) ->
    acc + current.stock
  @stockTotal = -> @accumulate(0, accumulator, instances)
```

Mix in the
enumerable using
the include function.

The Product class knows
the accumulator strategy,
but it doesn't know how
to enumerate.

```
  constructor: (stock) ->
    instances.push @
    @stock = stock
trinkets = new Product 12
valium = new Product 8
laser = new Product 3
Product.stockTotal()
# 23
```

This somewhat contrived example demonstrates how to keep enumeration out of the `Product` class. Enumerating isn't a core concern of a product, so it doesn't really belong there. Having an `enumerable` mixin also means that the accumulator can be used in other places in your program.

5.7.4 *Mixins from null*

You were warned about modifying the prototypes for built-ins. Unfortunately, your colleague Blaine didn't get the memo, and he has modified the prototype for a built-in inside your program. This is what Blaine did:

```
Object::antEater = ->
  "I'm an ant eater!"
```

What happens to the `enumerable` mixin? Not what you want:

```
antFarm = new Product { stock:1 }
antFarm.antEater()
# "I'm an ant eater!"
```

All of the `Product` instances got an `antEater` method. Remember those warnings about the dangers of extending built-in objects such as `Object`? People don't always pay attention to warnings. To avoid getting the new method, you have to guard the comprehension with the `own` keyword (see chapter 4):

```
include = (klass, module) ->
  for own key, value of module          ◁——┤  Add the own keyword to filter out
    klass[key] = value                        properties from the prototype chain.
```

This isn't bulletproof. To guarantee that you don't get properties you don't want, you must explicitly make your mixin an object that's removed from the prototype chain by making it have `null` as the prototype. This is done either by passing `Object.create` the value `null` as the object to create from

```
htmlRenderer = Object.create null
```

or by setting `null` as the prototype if you use a `Mixin` class:

```
class Mixin
  @:: = null
  constructor: (from, to) ->
    for key, val of from
      to[key] = val
```

The `null` value doesn't have any properties and it doesn't have a prototype. If you use it as a prototype, your object won't inherit any properties from the prototype chain.

5.8   *Putting it together*

A mixin is not only useful to solve Agtron's stock counting problem but more generally can be used to clean up some of the aspects of the client program, such as the view, that were embedded in the existing classes without belonging there. In the next listing you see a client program for Agtron's shop demonstrating the use of mixins to clean up the rendering code. Like other listings in this chapter, this is an example designed to run in a browser.

Listing 5.12   Agtron's shop client application

```
server =
  http: (method, src, callback) ->
    handler = ->
      if @readyState is 4 and @status is 200
        unless @responseText is null
          callback JSON.parse @responseText

    client = new XMLHttpRequest
    client.onreadystatechange = handler
    client.open method, src
    client.send()

  get: (src, callback) ->
    @http "GET", src, callback

  post: (src, callback) ->
    @http "POST", src, callback

class View
  @:: = null
  @include = (to, className) =>
    for key, val of @
      to::[key] = val
  @handler = (event, fn) ->
    @node[event] = fn
  @update = ->
    unless @node?
      @node = document.createElement 'div'
      @node.className = @constructor.name.toLowerCase()
      document.querySelector('.page').appendChild @node
    @node.innerHTML = @template()

class Product
  View.include @
  products = []
  @find = (query) ->
    (product for product in products when product.name is query)
  constructor: (@name, @info) ->
    products.push @
    @template = =>
      """
        #{@name}
      """
    @update()
    @handler "onclick", @purchase
```

> The View class, with null as prototype, has only class methods. It knows how to include itself into another object.

> The Product class invokes the include class method of View to use it as a mixin.

> The Product class still retains the template, which it assigns to new products inside the constructor.

```
  purchase: =>
    if @info.stock > 0
      server.post "/json/purchase/#{@category}/#{@name}", (res) =>
        if res.status is "success"
          @info = res.update
          @update()

class Camera extends Product
  category: 'camera'
  megapixels: -> @info.megapixels || "Unknown"

class Skateboard extends Product
  category: 'skateboard'
  length: -> @info.length || "Unknown"

class Shop
  View.include @                                     ◁── The Shop also uses
  constructor: ->                                        the View as a mixin.
    @template = ->                                   ◁── The Shop also still retains the
      "<h1>News: #{@breakingNews}</h1>"                  template. The templates are
                                                          used by the View mixin.
    server.get '/json/news', (news) =>
      @breakingNews = news.breaking
      @update()

    server.get '/json/list', (data) ->
      for own category of data
        for own name, info of data[category]
          switch category
            when 'camera'
              new Camera name, info
            when 'skateboard'
              new Skateboard name, info

shop = new Shop
```

Finally, in this listing you see the server-side component of the shop.

Listing 5.13 Agtron's shop server application

```
http = require 'http'
url = require 'url'
coffee = require 'coffee-script'

data = require('./data').all            │ Load the
news = require('./news').all            │ camera data.

script = "./#{process.argv[2]}.coffee"
client = ""
require('fs').readFile script, 'utf-8', (err, data) ->
  if err then throw err
  client = data

css = ""
require('fs').readFile './client.css', 'utf-8', (err, data) ->    Load the source
  if err then throw err                                           scripts and style
  css = data                                                      sheets ready to
                                                                  serve to clients.
```

```
headers = (res, status, type) ->
  res.writeHead status, 'Content-Type': "text/#{type}"

view = """
<!doctype html>
<head>
<title>Agtron's Cameras</title>
<link rel='stylesheet' href='/css/client.css'></link>
</head>
<body>
<script src='/js/client.js'></script>
</body>
</html>
"""
```

> The page template could be external, but it's small enough to be included here for demonstration purposes.

```
server = http.createServer (req, res) ->
  path = url.parse(req.url).pathname
  if req.method == "POST"
    category = /^\/json\/purchase\/([^/]*)\/([^/]*)$/.exec(path)?[1]
    item = /^\/json\/purchase\/([^/]*)\/([^/]*)$/.exec(path)?[2]
    if category? and item? and data[category][item].stock > 0
      data[category][item].stock -= 1
      headers res, 200, 'json'
      res.write JSON.stringify
        status: 'success',
        update: data[category][item]
    else
      res.write JSON.stringify
        status: 'failure'
    res.end()
    return
  switch path
    when '/json/list'
      headers res, 200, 'json'
      res.end JSON.stringify data
    when '/json/list/camera'
      headers res, 200, 'json'
      cameras = data.camera
      res.end JSON.stringify data.camera
    when '/json/news'
      headers res, 200, 'json'
      res.end JSON.stringify news
    when '/js/client.js'
      headers res, 200, 'javascript'
      writeClientScript = (script) ->
        res.end coffee.compile(script)
      readClientScript writeClientScript
    when '/css/client.css'
      headers res, 200, 'css'
      res.end css
    when '/'
      headers res, 200, 'html'
      res.end view
    else
      if path.match /^\/images\/(.*)\.png$/gi
        fs.readFile ".#{path}", (err, data) ->
```

> If the request is a POST and matches the URL path for a category and product name, then it's a purchase request.

> Use a switch on the url path to determine what resource to serve to a client. This covers the homepage, the client CoffeeScript compiled to JavaScript, the CSS, and the 404 error page.

```
      if err
        headers res, 404, 'image/png'
        res.end()
      else
        headers res, 200, 'image/png'
        res.end data, 'binary'
  else
    headers res, 404, 'html'
    res.end '404'

server.listen 8080, '127.0.0.1', ->
  console.log 'Visit http://localhost:8080/ in your browser'
```

Use a switch on the url path to determine what resource to serve to a client. This covers the homepage, the client CoffeeScript compiled to JavaScript, the CSS, and the 404 error page.

It's quite common for a web framework to be used to create an application such as the one shown in listings 5.12 and 5.13. The web framework usually provides additional tools to help separate the different parts of your program. But developing the entire application from scratch has helped you to explore some common patterns for using classes and prototypes in CoffeeScript.

5.8.1 Exercise

The server-side part of the shop application doesn't use any of the techniques described in this chapter. Write a new version that does use them and compare the two.

5.9 Summary

JavaScript and CoffeeScript are languages with prototype-based objects. JavaScript has always had an uncomfortable relationship with classes. Many people have wanted to add classes to JavaScript; the fourth edition of the ECMAScript specification even proposed adding classes to the language, but that edition was abandoned. With the liberty of making significant syntax changes, CoffeeScript can provide a class syntax that will be familiar to developers from most of the popular class-based object-oriented languages in use today. As you saw in this chapter, the underlying prototype-based model is flexible enough to provide classes.

The choice of whether to use classes at all is up to you. Having learned how they work and by extending them, you've learned more about prototypes. In some later chapters you'll compose objects without classes. Before doing that, though, you'll return to functions and discover techniques borrowed from functional programming in the next chapter.

Composing functions

In contrast to what you learned about objects, you needn't learn any more features to compose programs with functions. Instead, you must learn how to create your own features by putting together functions using the basic function glue that you learned in chapter 3. This principle applies to trivial examples such as defining an average function in terms of sum and divide functions and to nontrivial examples that you'll see in this chapter. To compose programs with functions, you must learn principles and techniques, not features.

Functions have inputs (arguments) and outputs (return values). In that sense, they're like pipes. You need to know not only the different ways of connecting those pipes but also the principles and techniques you need to do so effectively.

In this chapter you'll learn why it's important to break programs into small, clear functions, and how variables and program state can get in the way of doing that effectively. You'll then learn about using functions to create abstractions to make programs smaller and more manageable. Next, you'll learn about some common patterns of abstraction in combinators and, finally, about how function-composition techniques are used to simplify typical CoffeeScript programs that are heavy on callbacks. Before beginning, be aware that this chapter deals with some abstract ideas and techniques that require close attention. With that in mind, first things first—clarity.

6.1 Clarity

A function describes a computational process. It's important that the process that the function describes is represented clearly and accurately. You'll begin with function composition and then look at a specific problem and how to describe it with functions. You'll start with an optimization problem: how can Agtron maximize the profit from his online store when sales figures vary depending on sales prices?

By tracking purchases on his shop website, Agtron has found that when he sets the price for the PhotomakerExtreme (a camera) at $200, he sells (on average) 50 per day. For every $20 that he reduces the price, he sells an additional 10 units per day. Each PhotomakerExtreme costs Agtron $100 from the wholesaler, and it costs $140 per day to run the website.

To solve this problem by composing functions, you'll define functions by describing what they do—using *other* functions.

6.1.1 Functions are descriptions

When you read the body of a function, the intention and meaning should be clear. Suppose your esteemed colleague Mr. Rob Tuse has previously written a function to evaluate the profit for a given `price`:

```
profit = (50+(20/10)*(200-price))*price-(140+(100*(50+((20/10)*(200-price)))))
```

Aside from clues that the words `price` and `profit` afford, can you tell what the function means? Can Rob? Not likely. How do you define `profit` to clearly indicate what it is? Starting by thinking about the relationship. The `profit` for a sale price is the revenue at that price minus the cost at that price:

```
profit = (salePrice) ->
  (revenue salePrice) - (cost salePrice)
```

This `profit` function won't work yet because `revenue` and `cost` aren't defined. The next thing to do, then, is define them:

```
revenue = (salePrice) ->
  (numberSold salePrice) * salePrice

cost = (salePrice) ->
  overhead + (numberSold salePrice) * costPrice
```

These `revenue` and `cost` functions won't work until `overhead`, `numberSold`, and `costPrice` are defined. Define them:

```
overhead = 140
costPrice = 100

numberSold = (salePrice) ->
  50 + 20/10 * (200 - salePrice)
```

> The formula that Agtron worked out for the number of items sold at a given sale price

There's nothing left to define. You have a solution:

```
overhead = 140
costPrice = 100

numberSold = (salePrice) ->
  50 + 20/10 * (200 - salePrice)

revenue = (salePrice) ->
  (numberSold salePrice) * salePrice

cost = (salePrice) ->
  overhead + (numberSold salePrice) * costPrice

profit = (salePrice) ->
  (revenue salePrice) - (cost salePrice)
```

Functions can be defined anywhere, so `numberSold`, `revenue`, and `cost` could be defined inside the `profit` function. When you do this, as shown in the following listing, they're scoped inside the `profit` function, meaning that they're encapsulated.

Listing 6.1   Profit from selling PhotomakerExtreme

```
profit = (salePrice) ->
  overhead = 140
  costPrice = 100
  numberSold = (salePrice) ->
    50 + 20/10 * (200 - salePrice)
  revenue = (salePrice) ->
    (numberSold salePrice) * salePrice
  cost = (salePrice) ->
    overhead + (numberSold salePrice) * costPrice

  (revenue salePrice) - (cost salePrice)
```

> These variables are scoped inside the profit function.

It's easier to comprehend a program with good encapsulation. A program with poor encapsulation is a bit like emptying all the boxes, jars, and packets from your pantry into one big bucket. Good for making soup, but not much good for anything else.

Before continuing, it's time for an important lesson about parentheses.

6.1.2   *Where arguments need parentheses*

Remember that when you're invoking a function with arguments, parentheses are optional:

```
revenue salePrice
revenue(salePrice)
```

> These are effectively the same. The parentheses aren't required.

But parentheses *are* sometimes necessary to indicate where the arguments end. Why? Well, how do you think this expression is evaluated?

```
revenue salePrice - cost salePrice
```

To your eyes this example probably looks like it subtracts the cost at the sale price from the revenue at the sale price. But that's not how the CoffeeScript compiler sees it, and the JavaScript you get might not be what you expect:

```
revenue(salePrice(-(cost(salePrice))));
```

Unfortunately, the CoffeeScript compiler can't read your mind, and the JavaScript it has produced has a syntax error. Parentheses are important to tell the compiler what to do. You should add parentheses for the function invocations:

```
revenue(salePrice) - cost(salePrice)                    ⟵── Parentheses inside
```

Alternatively, you can put the parentheses on the *outside*:

```
(revenue salePrice) - (cost salePrice)                  ⟵── Parentheses outside
```

Whether you prefer the parentheses inside or outside, you should give ambiguous expressions that contain function invocations parentheses to make them unambiguous.

As a program grows, you don't just keep writing more and more functions. Instead, you often modify and adapt the functions you already have.

6.1.3 *Higher-order functions revisited*

In chapter 3 you learned the three basic ways that functions are glued together:

- Invocation through variable reference
- As an argument
- As a return value

In listing 6.1 only the first of these was demonstrated. Next, you'll see the other two types of function glue used for generalizing and for partially applying a function.

Agtron isn't selling just PhotomakerExtreme cameras but other types of cameras too. For those other cameras the overhead, costPrice, and numberSold are different from those for the PhotomakerExtreme. The profit function in listing 6.1 doesn't work for other types of cameras. How can you generalize it to be used for other types?

GENERALIZING A FUNCTION

One way to make the profit function more generally useful is by making overhead, costPrice, and numberSold arguments:

```
profit = (overhead, costPrice, numberSold, salePrice) ->
  revenue = (salePrice) ->
    (numberSold salePrice) * salePrice
  cost = (salePrice) ->
    overhead + (numberSold salePrice) * costPrice

  (revenue salePrice) - (cost salePrice)
```

If the sale price is 100, the overhead is 10, the cost price is 40, and 10 products are sold, then the profit is 590:

```
tenSold = -> 10
profit 10, 40, tenSold, 100
# 590
```

The number sold for a product depends on other values such as the sale price. This is apparent when you use this new function for a photoPro camera and a pixelKing camera.

```
photoProOverhead = 140
photoProCostPrice = 100
photoProNumberSold = (salePrice) -> 50 + 20/10 * (200 - salePrice)
```

How many arguments can you tolerate before your program becomes too hard to understand?

```
profit photoProOverhead, photoProCostPrice, photoProNumberSold, 162
# 7672

pixelKingOverhead = 140
pixelKingCostPrice = 100
pixelKingNumberSold = (salePrice) -> 50 + 20/10 * (200 - salePrice)

profit pixelKingOverhead, pixelKingCostPrice, pixelKingNumberSold, 200
# 14860
```

Flexibility has come at a price. The function now has four arguments, which is unwieldy and a little confusing. Don't wake up one day to realize that all of your functions take nine arguments. Instead of a program made up of functions with more arguments than you can easily comprehend, use another little bit of function glue—the partial application—and return a function.

PARTIAL APPLICATION

The single-argument profit function was a good description of the profit for a given price of a single camera type. Adding more arguments made it more generally useful but obscured the meaning. How can you get a simple, single-argument profit function for different types of cameras?

```
photoProProfit 162
# 7672

pixelKingProfit 200
# 14860
```

How can you make this interface possible?

To make this interface possible, change the profit function to return another function that accepts the single argument:

```
profit = (overhead, costPrice, numberSold) ->
  revenue = (salePrice) ->
    (numberSold salePrice) * salePrice
  cost = (salePrice) ->
    overhead + (numberSold salePrice) * costPrice
  (salePrice) ->
    (revenue salePrice) - (cost salePrice)
```

Take overhead, costPrice, and numberSold as arguments.

Return a function that takes salePrice as an argument.

When invoked, this new profit function *returns* a function that will evaluate to the profit for a specific camera (this time it's a camera called the x1) when *it* is invoked:

```
x1Overhead = 140
x1CostPrice = 100
x1NumberSold = (salePrice) -> 50 + 20/10 * (200 - salePrice)

x1Profit = profit x1Overhead, x1CostPrice, x1NumberSold
x1Profit 162
# 7672
```

This photoProProfit function can be invoked whenever you need it.

Why is this technique called partial application? Because only *some* of the arguments to the function have been provided, so the arguments have been partially applied. In this case the `salePrice` argument hasn't yet been provided and hasn't yet been *applied*.

So far you've been working on defining `profit` without looking at the larger program that it's part of. What program is this `profit` function used for? Agtron is creating a web-based API for his online shop. The API provides information about users and products. Information about a product is accessible from a URL:

```
http://www.agtronsemporium.com/api/product/photomakerExtreme
```

A GET request to the URL for a product responds with information about that product in JSON format:

```
{
  "PhotomakerExtreme": {
    "manufacturer": "Photo Co",
    "stock": 3,
    "cost": 100,
    "base": {
      "price": 200,
      "sold": 50
    },
    "reduction": {
      "discount": 20,
      "additionalSold": 10
    }
  }
}
```

The information about the base price and the reduction will be useful later.

Consider in the next listing the program that Rob Tuse wrote to serve Agtron's API (from listing 6.1). Rob *started* to implement the profit but never finished (perhaps because the program became too difficult to comprehend).

Listing 6.2 How *not* to write a program

```
# Important: Do not write like this

http = require 'http'
url = require 'url'

{users, products} = require './db'

server = http.createServer (req, res) ->
  path = url.parse(req.url).path
  parts = path.split /\//
  switch parts[1]
```

This db dependency is omitted here.

```
    when 'profit'
      res.writeHead 200, 'Content-Type': 'text/plain;charset=utf-8'
      if parts[2] and /^[0-9]+$/gi.test parts[2]
        price - parts[2]
        profit = (50+(20/10)*(200-price))*
        price-(140+(100*(50+((20/10)*(200-price)))))
        res.end (JSON.stringify { profit: profit parts[2] })
      else
        res.end JSON.stringify { profit: 0 }
    when 'user'
      res.writeHead 200, 'Content-Type': 'text/plain;charset=utf-8'
      if req.method is "GET"
        if parts[2] and /^[a-z]+$/gi.test parts[2]
          users.get parts[2], (error, user) ->
            res.end JSON.stringify user, 'utf8'
        else
          users.all (error, users) ->
            res.end JSON.stringify users, 'utf8'
      else if parts[2] and req.method is "POST"
        user = parts[2]
        requestBody = ''
        req.on 'data', (chunk) ->
          requestBody += chunk.toString()
        req.on 'end', ->
          pairs = requestBody.split /&/g
          decodedRequestBody = for pair in pairs
            o = {}
            splitPair = pair.split /\=/g
            o[splitPair[0]] = splitPair[1]
            o
          users.set user, decodedRequestBody, ->
            res.end 'success', 'utf8'
      else
        res.writeHead 404, 'Content-Type': 'text/plain;charset=utf-8'
        res.end '404'
    when 'product'
      res.writeHead 200, 'Content-Type': 'text/plain;charset=utf-8'
      if req.method is "GET"
        products.get parts[2], (product) ->
          res.end JSON.stringify product, 'utf8'
      else if parts[2] and req.method is "POST"
        product = parts[2]
        requestBody = ''
        req.on 'data', (chunk) ->
          requestBody += chunk.toString()
        req.on 'end', ->
          pairs = requestBody.split /&/g
          decodedRequestBody = for pair in pairs
            o = {}
            splitPair = pair.split /\=/g
            o[splitPair[0]] = splitPair[1]
            o
          product.set user, decodedRequestBody, ->
            res.end 'success', 'utf8'
        requestBody = ''
```

> **Part of the program you already addressed**

```
      req.on 'data', (chunk) ->
        requestBody += chunk.toString()
      req.on 'end', ->
        decodedRequestBody = requestBody
        res.end decodedRequestBody, 'utf8'
    else
      res.writeHead 404, 'Content-Type': 'text/plain;charset=utf-8'
      res.end '404'
  else
    res.writeHead 200, 'Content-Type': 'text/html;charset=utf-8'
    res.end 'The API'

server.listen 8080, '127.0.0.1'

# Important: Do not write  like this
```

The server function in listing 6.2 is more than 60 lines long. Ouch! Way too complicated; if you write programs like that, you'll get reactions like those of Scruffy and Agtron in figure 6.1.

Why did Rob write the program like that? He didn't know any better. You do, and you've already started to make the program easier to comprehend with the approach you took for defining `profit`. First, you broke it down by defining it in terms of other small functions. Then you made the solution more generic to work with different products. The original function was hard to follow:

```
profit = (50+(20/10)*(200-price))*price-(140+(100*(50+((20/10)*(200-price)))))
```

Figure 6.1 How not to write programs

Your new version of the same function is more generally useful and explains what it means:

```
profit = (overhead, costPrice, numberSold, salePrice) ->
  revenue = (salePrice) ->
    (numberSold salePrice) * salePrice
  cost = (salePrice) ->
    overhead + (numberSold salePrice) * costPrice

  (revenue salePrice) - (cost salePrice)
```

The overhead, costPrice, numberSold, and salePrice are all values that you either have or can work out using the information you have for a particular product. This will be useful later in this chapter as you continue to make improvements to the original program. First, though, you need to know about *state*.

Gluing existing functions together and building up new functions (and entire programs) are powerful techniques. When you see a programmer staring at the sky proclaiming an epiphany as the result of discovering functional programming, it's usually because of this idea of composing functions (or indeed programs) entirely from other functions. Power requires discipline, particularly where it concerns state. It's time to think about state and why you shouldn't create it where it doesn't already exist.

6.2   *State and mutability*

Just because CoffeeScript allows you to compose functions doesn't mean that *any* program written in CoffeeScript is written in a functional style. A program can have lots of functions and not be written in a functional style. To quote from Chuck Palahniuk's *Fight Club*, "Sticking feathers up your butt does not make you a chicken."

Functional-style programming in CoffeeScript means composing functions. As you'll see in this section, writing programs by composing functions becomes incredibly difficult if the program manages a lot of explicit state. How does state get into a program, and how can you deal with it? The most important thing to remember is that you should *avoid having variables containing state wherever possible*. What does this mean in practice, though? It's time to find out by looking at variables and side effects, objects, and external state.

6.2.1   *Variables, assignment, and side effects*

Variable assignment is at odds with functional programming. Sure, assignment looks harmless enough,

```
state = on
state = off
```

until you discover what happens when you try to glue together functions that assign variables. Consider the numberSold function that evaluates to the number of units sold when invoked with a given sale price:

```
numberSold = (salePrice) ->
  50 + 20/10 * (200 - salePrice)
```
⟵ Again, the formula that Agtron has worked out for the number of items sold at a given sale price

Compare it to a `calculateNumberSold` function that returns the value *and* sets a variable:

```
numberSold = 0
calculateNumberSold = (salePrice) ->
  numberSold = 50 + 20/10 * (200 - salePrice)
```

This assignment is a side effect.

These functions evaluate to the same value, but the `calculateNumberSold` function assigns a value to an outer variable (a variable that's not contained entirely within the function):

```
calculateNumberSold 220
# 10
```

Consider now the `calculateRevenue` function that uses the `numberSold` variable:

```
calculateRevenue = (salePrice) ->
  numberSold * salePrice
```

Suppose you want to show Agtron a graph of the `revenue` for different cameras at different prices. To do this, you start by calculating the revenue for prices between 140 and 145 in a comprehension:

```
for price in [140..145]
  calculateRevenue price
# [1400,1410,1420,1430,1440,1450]
```

Easy—except that the values are wrong and the graph will be wrong. The correct values are [23800,23688,23572,23452,23328,23200]. What went wrong? You forgot to invoke `calculateNumberSold`:

```
for price in [140..145]
  calculateNumberSold price
  calculateRevenue price
# [23800,23688,23572,23425,23328,23200]
```

It's easy to forget in which order functions need to be evaluated. You also need to consider two other factors: other people (such as your good friend Mr. Tuse) and asynchronous programs.

6.2.2 *Local state and shared state*

Suppose `calculateRevenue` requests information from a database or makes a request from a web service. This means that `calculateRevenue` is asynchronous, which you know is very common in CoffeeScript programs. When things are asynchronous, your program looks different, as shown in the following listing.

Listing 6.3 Local state and shared state

```
numberSold = 0

calculateNumberSold = (salePrice) ->
  numberSold = 50 + 20/10 * (200 - salePrice)

calculateRevenue = (salePrice, callback) ->
  callback numberSold * salePrice
```

numberSold is shared state.

```
revenueBetween = (start, finish) ->
  totals = []
  for price in [start..finish]
    calculateNumberSold price
    addToTotals = (result) ->
      totals.push result
    calculateRevenue price, addToTotals
  totals
```

<─┐ **totals is local
  │ (to the function) state.**

```
revenueBetween 140, 145
# [ 23800, 23688, 23572, 23452, 23328, 23200 ]
```

In listing 6.3 the `totals` variable is local to the `revenueBetween` function; other parts of the program can't assign a value to it. On the other hand, `numberSold` is shared by all of the functions in the program because they're all part of the same scope. This can have disastrous consequences.

Now imagine that `calculateRevenue` from listing 6.3 takes some time before it invokes the callback because it has to wait for a database. Approximate this with a `setTimeout` call:

```
oneSecond = 1000
calculateRevenue = (callback) ->
  setTimeout ->
    callback numberSold * salePrice
  , oneSecond
```

You're surprised when you find out what `revenueBetween` returns:

```
revenueBetween 140, 145
# []
```

You kept the totals in an array, assigned values to them, and returned the result. This imperative solution needed things done in a particular order but didn't enforce that order—a move to asynchronous and the solution broke.

There's one instinctive and imperative way to solve this: by adding even more state and going further down the rabbit hole!

```
numberSold = 0
calculateNumberSold = (salePrice) ->
  numberSold = 50 + 20/10 * (200 - salePrice)

calculateRevenue = (salePrice, callback) ->
  callback numberSold * salePrice

revenueBetween = (start, finish, callback) ->
  totals = []
  receivedResponses = 0
  expectedResponses = 0
  for price in [start..finish]
    calculateNumberSold price
    expectedResponses++
    addToTotals = (result) ->
      totals.push result
      receivedResponses++
      if receivedResponses == expectedResponses
        callback totals
    calculateRevenue price, addToTotals
```

Add state by keeping variables for expected and received responses.

Does it work now? Sadly, no. The order of the values will depend on the order in which the callbacks return. Sure, you'll get the revenue values—just not in the order you want!

The problem becomes even worse if some other part of the program changes the value of `numberSold` while an asynchronous part of your program is waiting. Remember, `numberSold` is shared state for several functions.

Can `revenueBetween` get any more intertwined? Indeed it can. Suppose Mr. Tuse modifies the function to also log a message, and for some inexplicable reason changes the value of `numberSold` at the same time:

```
numberSold = 0

calculateNumberSold = (salePrice) ->
  numberSold = 50 + 20/10 * (200 - salePrice)

calculateRevenue = (salePrice, callback) ->
  callback numberSold * salePrice

log = (message) ->
  console.log message
  numberSold = 'uh oh'

revenueBetween = (start, finish, callback) ->
  totals = []
  receivedResponses = 0
  expectedResponses = 0
  for price in [start..finish]
    calculateNumberSold price
    expectedResponses++
    addToTotals = (result) ->
      totals.push result
      receivedResponses++
      if receivedResponses == expectedResponses
        callback totals
      else
        log 'waiting'
    calculateRevenue price, addToTotals
```

For some unknown reason, Rob Tuse has broken your program state.

Now the program produces an array containing `NaN`s:

```
revenueBetween 140, 145
# [ 22400, NaN, NaN, NaN, NaN, NaN ]
```

Should you add more state to fix the problem? No. Please don't. Instead, compose the asynchronous functions, as you'll learn to do later in this chapter. Think about a program with hundreds of functions sharing hundreds of variables. How confident can you be that everything is done in exactly the correct order? How hard is it to test that they are? Avoid having variables containing state wherever possible.

How about object-oriented programming, then? After all, CoffeeScript has objects too. Object-oriented programming encapsulates state in objects. That's a different approach to functional programming. What works in CoffeeScript? Think about those cameras; there used to be `camera` objects back in chapter 5, right? Where did they go?

6.2.3   *Encapsulating state with objects*

One object-based solution uses a `Camera` class with `profit`, and all of the functions that it uses are written as methods:

```
class Camera                              ◁─┐  No instance
  overhead: -> 140                          │  variables
  costPrice: -> 100
  profit: (salePrice) ->
    (@revenue salePrice) - (@cost salePrice)
  numberSold: (salePrice) ->
    50 + 20/10 * (200 - salePrice)
  revenue: (salePrice) ->
    (@numberSold salePrice) * salePrice
   cost: (salePrice) ->
    @overhead() + (@numberSold salePrice) * @costPrice()

phototaka500 = new Camera
phototaka500.profit 162
# 7672
```

Notice that in this case the object `phototaka500` isn't modified after it has been created. No properties are set on the object; it's all method calls, and none of the method calls change any properties on the object. Contrast this with a different approach to the same problem using objects, where methods are called for their side effects instead of for their return values:

```
class Camera                              ◁─┐  profit, revenue, cost, and
  constructor: (@price) ->                  │  price instance variables
  calculateRevenue: ->
    @revenue = (50 + (20 / 10) * (200 - @price)) * @price
  calculateCost: ->
    @cost = 140 + (100 * (50 + ((20 / 10) * (200 - @price))))
  calculateProfit: ->
    @calculateRevenue()
    @calculateCost()
    @profit = @revenue - @cost

phototaka500 = new Camera 162
phototaka500.calculateProfit()
console.log phototaka500.profit
# 7672
```

These two solutions produce the same result. The difference lies in the implementation. The first solution doesn't set any properties on the instance, whereas the second does. Consider for a minute which one is more like the following example that uses variables and shared state:

```
revenue = 0           Variables used to keep state
cost = 0               shared by the functions
sold = 0

calculateRevenue = (salePrice) ->
  revenue = sold * salePrice
```

```
calculateCost = (salePrice) ->
  cost = 140 + sold * 100

calculateNumberSold = (salePrice) ->
  sold = 50 + 20/10 * (200 - salePrice)

calculateProfit = (salePrice) ->
  calculateNumberSold salePrice
  calculateRevenue salePrice
  calculateCost salePrice
  revenue - cost
```

The object approach using *instance variables* is more like the version with shared state kept in variables. This style of programming is called *imperative programming*. All programs written in an imperative style have to answer the question of how to manage the explicit state. In an object-oriented programming style, state is managed by keeping it contained to individual objects. In a functional programming style, the state is essentially managed by not putting it explicitly in the program *at all*.

> **Functional programming and pure functions**
>
> A function that always returns the same value for the same arguments and that has no side effects is called a *pure function*. Because it's very easy to create a non-pure function in CoffeeScript, it's debatable to what extent it can be called a functional programming language. But first-class functions in CoffeeScript mean that, at the least, CoffeeScript supports functional-style programming.

State can't always be avoided; there's still state such as in a database or user interface. You can't keep track of how many users have visited your website unless there's state somewhere. Users can't interact with a completely stateless interface. State exists and your program has to deal with it. The question is, exactly when is state necessary and where should it go?

6.2.4 World state

"Wait a minute," says Scruffy. "It's all well and good to take unnecessary state out of the program, but the real world has state! Without state there's no way to sell cameras because there's no stock count." That's right, Scruffy. There has to be state somewhere; the key is to isolate it and not to share it. In this case, suppose that the stock level is kept in a database. Databases are good at dealing with state. The values in the database are retrieved via callbacks:

```
db.stock 'ijuf', (error, response) ->
  # handling code here
```

This database call could be on the client side or server side. It doesn't matter.

In the next listing you see a comparison between keeping the state in your program and letting the database keep it. When you run this listing, you'll be able to access one version on http://localhost:9091 and the other on http://localhost:9092. Note that this listing uses an external db that's not shown here.

Listing 6.4 State in program or external?

```
http = require 'http'
db = (require './db').stock

stock = 30
serverOne = http.createServer (req, res) ->
  response = switch req.url
    when '/purchase'
      res.writeHead 200, 'Content-Type': 'text/plain;charset=utf8'
      if stock > 0
        stock = stock - 1
        "Purchased! There are #{stock} left."
      else
        'Sorry! no stock left!'
    else
      res.writeHead 404, 'Content-Type': 'text/plain;charset=utf8'
      'Go to /purchase'
  res.end response

serverTwo = http.createServer (req, res) ->
  purchase = (callback) ->
    db.decr 'stock', (error, response) ->
      if error
        callback 0
      else
        callback response

  render = (stock) ->
    res.writeHead 200, 'Content-Type': 'text/plain;charset=utf8'
    response = if stock > 0
      "Purchased! There are #{stock} left."
    else
      'Sorry! no stock left'
    res.end response

  switch req.url
    when '/purchase'
      purchase render
    else
      res.writeHead 404, 'Content-Type': 'text/plain;charset=utf8'
      res.end 'Go to /purchase'

serverOne.listen 9091, '127.0.0.1'
serverTwo.listen 9092, '127.0.0.1'
```

> A server keeping state

> A server using a database to keep state

To put it loosely, state is somebody else's problem. This also applies for state about the client; instead of keeping state about the client inside your application, it should be transferred to your application by the client.

> ### Concurrency?
>
> One problem with shared state is the trouble it creates for concurrent systems. If state depends heavily on things happening in a particular order, then a system where many things are happening at once is a challenge. CoffeeScript programs run on an event loop and only ever do one thing at a time, so the concurrency challenges aren't the same as in a threaded environment. That said, state is still a problem.

Function composition and functional programming in general don't work well when programs have explicit mutable state contained in variables or objects. You've learned that in order to be effective with function composition, you should avoid state in variables and objects wherever possible. When you do avoid state, you can glue functions together explicitly and also create abstractions. Functions can glue other functions together.

6.3 Abstraction

Abstractions can be created from an existing program by carving off small pieces and improving those—removing duplication as you go. In this section you'll continue to improve listing 6.2 by creating abstractions and removing duplication.

6.3.1 Extracting common code

In listing 6.2 much of the duplicated code should have either never happened or been refactored once it became apparent. How does it become apparent? Well, consider what the program actually does.

The API you're creating for Agtron's shop is a thin wrapper for accessing some information in key-value store databases. The databases have two operations, `set` and `get`. The `set` operation takes a key, a value, and a callback function. The `get` operation takes a key and a callback. For example, the user data is loaded from the database in the same way that product data is loaded from the database:

```
users.get parts[2], (error, user) ->
  res.end JSON.stringify user, 'utf8'

products.get parts[2], (product) ->
  res.end JSON.stringify product, 'utf8'
```

There's no meaningful name describing what these sections of the program do, so you start by naming them:

```
loadUserData = (user, callback) ->
  users.get user, (data) ->
    callback data

loadProductData = (product, callback) ->
  products.get product, (data) ->
    callback data
```

If you didn't notice before that the code was repetitive, you definitely notice now. The `saveUserData` and `saveProductData` functions are almost exactly the same.

Instead of having variations of the same basic function appear repeatedly in your program, create an abstraction and eliminate the duplication:

```
makeLoadData = (db) ->
  (entry, callback) ->
    db.get entry, (data) ->
      callback data

makeSaveData = (type) ->
  (entry, value, callback) ->
    db.set entry, value, callback?()
```

> Putting the existential operator in front of a callback prevents an error from occurring if the callback argument is not passed in when the function is invoked. You'll see more about advanced use of the existential operator in the next chapter.

Both of these functions return functions. What are they used for? With these two functions you can create a `loadUserData` function and a `saveUserData` function:

```
loadUserData = makeLoadData 'user'
saveUserData = makeSaveData 'user'
```

You can use the `makeLoadData` function to create a function for `loadAnythingData`, literally:

```
loadAnythingData = makeLoadData 'anything'
```

The `makeLoadData` and `makeSaveData` functions are abstractions that allow you to create individual functions that are useful in specific circumstances. Now look at `makeLoadData` and `makeSaveData`; they're basically the same. Extract the common parts to a single function:

```
makeDbOperator = (db) ->
  (operation) ->
    (entry, value=null, callback) ->
      db[operation] entry, value, (error, data) ->
        callback? error, data
```

This function returns a function that returns a function. When you see an abstraction by itself, it becomes apparent if it's more complicated than it needs to be. You revise `makeDbOperator` to make it simpler:

```
makeDbOperator = (db) ->
  (operation) ->
    (entry, params...) ->
      db[operation] entry, params...
```

When you added global variable assignments to your program, you got an immediate payoff, but it hurt you in the long run. Identifying and writing abstractions is the opposite. A little bit of effort now to create the right abstraction saves you pain in the long run. You can now generate `load` and `save` functions for different data types from this single `makeDbOperator` function:

```
loadProductData = (makeDbOperator 'product') 'get'
saveProductData = (makeDbOperator 'product') 'set'

saveProductData 'photonify1100', 'data for the photonify1100'
loadProductData 'photonify1100'
# 'data for the photonify1100'
```

Writing a program always involves refining the abstractions as you go. When functions are the basic building block, this is done with the same basic function glue: invoking a function, passing a function as an argument, and returning a function.

By refining the abstractions in your program over time, you end up with a program that communicates what it does and that's easier to modify. Even better, it's the start of a library. To develop a really useful library, instead of starting with an idea for a library, extract it from a real project as an abstraction of ideas in that project. In listing 6.5 you can see the new version of the program.

When you run this new version of the program, you can view information about a specific product (such as the x1) by visiting the URL http://localhost:8080/product/x1. To see the profit for that same product at a given price point of 200, visit the URL http://localhost:8080/product/x1/profit?price=200.

The listing that follows is left *deliberately without any annotations*. The purpose of this is to show how far small named functions can go to make a program self-explanatory. Spend a bit more time to pore over this listing and learn how it works.

Listing 6.5 The improved program

```
http = require 'http'
url = require 'url'

{products, users} = require './db'

withCompleteBody = (req, callback) ->
  body = ''
  req.on 'data', (chunk) ->
    body += chunk.toString()
    request.on 'end', -> callback body

paramsAsObject = (params) ->
  pairs = params.split /&/g
  result = {}
  for pair in pairs
    splitPair = pair.split /\=/g
    result[splitPair[0]] = splitPair[1]
  result

header = (response, status, contentType='text/plain;charset=utf-8') ->
  response.writeHead status, 'Content-Type': contentType

httpRequestMatch = (request, method) -> request.method is method
isGet = (request) -> httpRequestMatch request, "GET"
isPost = (request) -> httpRequestMatch request, "POST"

render = (response, content) ->
  header response, 200
  response.end content, 'utf8'

renderAsJson = (response, object) -> render response, JSON.stringify object

notFound = (response) ->
  header response, 404
  response.end 'not found', 'utf8'
```

```
handleProfitRequest = (request, response, price, costPrice, overhead) ->
  valid = (price) -> price and /^[0-9]+$/gi.test price
  if valid price
    renderAsJson response, profit: profit price, costPrice, overhead
  else
    renderAsJson response, profit: 0

makeDbOperator = (db) ->
  (operation) ->
    (entry, params...) ->
      db[operation] entry, params...

makeRequestHandler = (load, save) ->
  rendersIfFound = (response) ->
    (error, data) ->
      if error
        notFound response
      else
        renderAsJson response, data

  (request, response, name) ->
    if isGet request
      load name, rendersIfFound response
    else if isPost request
      withCompleteBody request, ->
        save name, rendersIfFound response
    else
      notFound response

numberSold = (salePrice) ->
  50 + 20/10 * (200 - salePrice)

profit = (salePrice, costPrice, overhead) ->
  revenue = (salePrice) ->
    (numberSold salePrice) * salePrice
  cost = (salePrice) ->
    overhead + (numberSold salePrice) * costPrice
  (revenue salePrice) - (cost salePrice)

loadProductData = (makeDbOperator products) 'get'
saveProductData = (makeDbOperator products) 'set'
loadUserData = (makeDbOperator users) 'get'
saveUserData = (makeDbOperator users) 'set'

handleUserRequest = makeRequestHandler loadUserData, saveUserData
handleProductRequest = makeRequestHandler loadProductData, saveProductData

onProductDataLoaded = (error, data) ->
  price = (parseInt (query.split '=')[1], 10)
  handleProfitRequest request,response,price,data.costPrice,data.overhead

apiServer = (request, response) ->
  path = url.parse(request.url).path
  query = url.parse(request.url).query
  parts = path.split /\//
  switch parts[1]
    when 'user'
      handleUserRequest request, response, parts[2]
    when 'product'if parts.length == 4 and /^profit/.test parts[3]
```

```
      loadProductData parts[2], onProductDataLoaded
    else
      handleProductRequest request, response, parts[2]
  else
    notFound response

server = http.createServer(apiServer).listen 8080, '127.0.0.1'

exports.server = server
```

In terms of the total number of lines, this program is no shorter; it would be possible to make it substantially shorter with different abstractions, but in this case communicating the intention of every part of the program is preferred to brevity. Choose techniques appropriate for your circumstances.

Abstraction isn't always about extracting common code. Sometimes you need to change multiple things in a program at once. Instead of writing it in three places when you obviously don't need to, you can start with the abstraction.

6.3.2 *Adding common code*

Imagine Scruffy calls you at 2:00 a.m. to inform you that the server for Agtron's online store was running so hot that it burst into flames. Sure, nothing that dramatic really happens to you, but consider that your server is having problems because it's using too much processing power, and you learn that the culprit is the database. Your program is making too many requests to the database, so you need to reduce the number of requests it receives. Here are the last 10 lines from the database log:

```
request GET 'All work and no play'
response 'makes Jack a dull boy' (5 ms)
request GET 'All work and no play'
response 'makes Jack a dull boy' (4 ms)
request GET 'All work and no play'
response 'makes Jack a dull boy' (2 ms)
request GET 'All work and no play'
response 'makes Jack a dull boy' (5 ms)
request GET 'All work and no play'
response 'makes Jack a dull boy' (5 ms)
```

That's right; your program is constantly asking the database to fetch the same value. You might imagine that a clever database would cache the responses for you. You might imagine that, but all the while the server is on fire. What can you do?

SPECIFIC CACHE

You recognize that by caching the previous response you can avoid making another request to the database if you need the same value twice in a row. It's tempting to just add caching to the makeDbOperator function, but where do you add it?

```
makeDbOperator = (db) ->
  (operation) ->
    (entry, params...) ->
      db[operation] entry, params...
```

You only want to cache loading of data, not saving of data, and the `makeDbOperator` abstraction doesn't know anything about loading and saving. This is a clear indication that `makeDbOperator` is the wrong place to implement this caching; if it has to know the difference between a load and a save, it has to know too much. The correct place to implement the caching is where you define `loadProductData`:

```
productDataCache = Object.create null
loadProductData = (name, callback) ->
  cachedCall = (makeDbOperator products) 'get'
  if productDataCache.hasOwnProperty name
    console.log 'cache hit'
    console.log productDataCache[name]...
    callback productDataCache[name]...
  else
    cachedCall name, (results...) ->
      productDataCache[name] = results
```

> Remember from the previous chapter that passing null to Object.create means that the created object has null as a prototype and so doesn't inherit any properties you don't want.

What if you need to cache something else in the future? You need a function that can cache *any* function.

GENERAL CACHE

As with previous examples, you can extract such a general function from the specific solution you already have. Note that for simplicity this solution is intended to work by using the first argument as the key and the last argument as the callback:

```
withCachedCallback = (fn) ->
  cache = Object.create null
  (params...) ->
    key = params[0]
    callback = params[params.length - 1]
    if key of cache
      callback cache[key]...
    else
      paramsCopy = params[..]
      paramsCopy[params.length-1] = (params...) ->
        cache[key] = params
        callback params...
      fn paramsCopy...
```

Now you can define a cached `loadProductData` by using `withCachedCallback`:

```
loadProductData = withCachedCallback ((makeDbOperator products) 'get')
```

This function will now cache each response forever. If you want it to cache items for a fixed time, you need to store each cache item with an expiry time:

```
withExpiringCachedCallback = (fn, ttl) ->
  cache = Object.create null
  (params...) ->
    key = params[0]
    callback = params[params.length - 1]
    if cache[key]?.expires > Date.now()
      callback cache[key].entry...
```

```
    else
      paramsCopy = params[..]
      paramsCopy[params.length - 1] = (params...) ->
        console.log params
        cache[key] =
          entry: params
          expires: Date.now() + ttl
        console.log cache[key]
        callback params...
      fn paramsCopy...
```

This caching technique can be applied in a general sense to any function, where it is known as *memoization*.

MEMOIZATION
Caching the evaluation of a function with specific arguments is called memoization. You've seen it used specifically to cache the loading of some data. To reinforce the concept, it's worth also seeing a more abstract numerical example. Though not practical or exciting, memoizing a factorial function is a good way to understand this:

```
factorial = (n) ->
  if n is 0 then 1
  else
    n * (factorial n - 1)
factorial 0
# 1

factorial 4
# 24
factorial 5
# 120
```

$$4 \times 3 \times 2 \times 1$$

$$5 \times 4 \times 3 \times 2 \times 1$$

The value of `factorial 5` is actually the value of `factorial 4` multiplied by 5. This means that once `factorial 4` has been evaluated, then $4 \times 3 \times 2 \times 1$ has already been done once, so `factorial 5` could use the value already worked out instead of working the whole thing out again. Memoization is useful to avoid repeating the same evaluation. There's something else interesting about the definition of `factorial`: it invokes itself. This is called *recursion*, and like memoization it's useful not only for things like factorials but also for problems you actually have.

6.3.3 *Recursion*

Imagine now that the database is having more problems, and half of all requests to the users database result in a timeout. Data is retrieved from the database by invoking `users.get` with a callback function. When the request succeeds, you get data back as the second argument to the callback. You can see this happening by logging to the console:

```
logUserDataFor = (user) ->
  users.get user, (error, data) ->
    if error then console.log 'An error occurred'
    else console.log 'Got the data'
logUserDataFor 'fred'
# 'Got the data'
```

When a timeout occurs, the callback is invoked with an error as the first argument:

```
logUserDataFor 'fred'
# 'An error occurred'
```

Ideally you'd have a database that doesn't suffer frequent timeouts, but suppose the database can't be replaced. The only way to fix the problem is to change the program so that if the database request fails, it will retry until it gets a response. How do you do this? The first retry is easy to write; just put it directly in the callback:

```
logUserDataFor = (user) ->
  users.get user, (error, data) ->
    if error then users.get user, (error, data) ->
      if error then console.log 'An error occurred both times'
      else 'Got the data (on the second attempt)'
    else console.log 'Got the data'
```

How about the second retry or the third, fourth, or tenth retry? You certainly don't want to nest 10 retries (that would be so horrendous that it's not even shown here). Take a look at the alternative:

```
logUserDataFor = (user) ->
  dbRequest = ->                                    ◁─┐  dbRequest is invoked
    users.get user, (error, data) ->                   │  by a callback defined
      if error then dbRequest()                     ◁─┘  inside dbRequest.
      else console.log 'Got the data'
  dbRequest()
```

If the database finally responds the fourth time it's called, you'll see that logged:

```
logUserDataFor 'fred'
# 'An error occurred'
# 'An error occurred'
# 'An error occurred'
# 'Got the data'
```

It's called *recursion* when a function invokes itself, either directly or indirectly. Although the recursive logUserDataFor function works, it's a bit heavy-handed. Instead of trying the request again until the end of time (or the program is terminated), retry a failed database request once every second for the next 5 seconds before giving up:

```
logUserDataFor = (user) ->
  dbRequest = (attempt) ->
    users.get user, (error, data) ->
      if error and attempt < 5
        setTimeout ->
          (dbRequest attempt + 1), 1000
      else console.log 'Got the data'
  dbRequest()
```

That's not the end of your woes. It's not just the users database that suffers timeouts. Suppose that all the databases suffer timeouts, and worse, other services that your program relies on have timeouts too. Instead of writing the same thing repeatedly, create an abstraction that can retry a failed request for any callback-based service:

```
advanceTime = (time, advanceBy) ->
  new Date time*1 + advanceBy

retryFor = (duration, interval) ->
  start = new Date
  retry = (fn, finalCallback) ->
    attempt = new Date
    if attempt < (advanceTime start, duration)
      proxyCallback = (error, data) ->
        if error
          console.log "Error: Retry in #{interval}"
          setTimeout ->
            retry fn, finalCallback
          , interval
        else
          finalCallback error, data
      fn proxyCallback
    else
      console.log "Gave up after #{duration}"
```

This function expects a date and a number to advance the date by. The date is multiplied by 1 so that it is treated as a number to be used for the addition operator.

The retry function invokes itself.

The `retryFor` function returns a function that takes a single function argument and expects to be able to invoke that function attachment with a callback. To use the `retryFor` function to load user data, you first need to create a function that has all other arguments applied except the callback:

```
seconds = (n) ->
  1000*n

getUserData = (user) ->
  (callback) ->
    users.get user, callback

getUserDataForFred = getUserData 'fred'

retryForFiveSeconds = (retryFor (seconds 5), (seconds 1))
retryForFiveSeconds getUserDataForFred, (error, data) ->
  console.log data
```

If the database finally responds after three attempts, then the console output will reflect that:

```
Error: Retry in 1000
Error: Retry in 1000
Error: Retry in 1000
Success
```

With *recursion* you can solve complicated problems with a *small amount of code*. Unfortunately, there's no such thing as a free lunch. A programming language that supports recursive functions must deal with the nature of recursion—it looks infinite.

INFINITE RECURSION, TAIL CALLS, AND THE STACK

Programs that make heavy use of recursion have a problem in JavaScript and CoffeeScript—they can run out of memory. Why? When you invoke a function stack, memory is allocated:

```
memoryEater = ->
memoryEater()
```

> Memory is allocated
> for the function.

Only once the function returns is the memory allocated for it reclaimed. That's a problem with a recursive function because, before returning, a recursive function invokes itself. You can see this in action on the CoffeeScript REPL, which uses the V8 runtime. This will warn you when you've exceeded the maximum call stack size:

```
memoryEater = -> memoryEater()
memoryEater()
# RangeError: Maximum call stack size exceeded
```

The memoryEater function is *infinitely recursive* because it *always* invokes itself. An infinitely recursive function will cause some runtimes to become unresponsive while they continue trying to allocate more and more memory.

A recursive function can run out of memory even without being infinitely recursive. This makes recursive functions a problem because they can run out of stack quite easily. Recursion doesn't *have* to suffer this problem, though; consider the following recursive function:

```
tenThousandCalls = (depth) ->
  if depth < 10000
    (tenThousandCalls depth + 1)
```

Just by looking at it you can tell that it will invoke itself 10,000 times and then complete. If you were a computer, you could figure out before you invoke the function what it's going to do and how much memory you need (or don't need) to allocate. A JavaScript runtime can do the same thing. Where the recursive call is the last expression in the function body (the tail position), then the function is called *tail recursive*. If the runtime recognizes this, it's possible to optimize the amount of memory it allocates. When a runtime can optimize for these types of recursive functions, then it's said to have *tail-call optimization* or *proper tail calls*. Although CoffeeScript programs don't currently have this optimization, it's part of the next edition of the ECMAScript specification.

6.4   *Combinators*

So far you've written functions and created abstractions from those functions. Now that you have abstractions, you can create abstractions from those too. Combinators are abstractions of different ways of putting together functions. Until now, to compose programs using functions you've explicitly glued them together by invocation, through arguments, and as return values.

You don't *have* to do things explicitly—combinators go a step beyond this. What happens when you compose functions without thinking about invocation, arguments, and return values at all?

6.4.1 Compose

Agtron has to pay tax (that's one thing you don't need to imagine). To calculate the tax, you first need to add up the profit for all of the products and then invoke a `tax` function with that value.[1] If you did this imperatively (with commands), you'd make all the individual calculations in sequence:

```
profit = ->

tax = (amount) ->
  amount / 3

netProfit = (products) ->
  profits = (profit product) for product in products
  profits.reduce (acc, p) -> acc + p

netProfitForProducts = netProfit products
taxForProducts = tax netProfitForProducts
```

◁ **Omitted. The profit function appears elsewhere.**

◁ **See the footnote about floating-point arithmetic.**

Imagine now that you also need to evaluate a loyalty discount for a user. To do this imperatively, you first work out the total amount they've spent and then use that value to determine the loyalty category:

```
userSpend = (user) ->
  spend = 100

loyaltyDiscount = (spend) ->
  if spend < 1000 then 0
  else if spend < 5000 then 5
  else if spend < 10000 then 10
  else if spend < 50000 then 20
  else if spend > 50000 then 40

fredSpend = userSpend fred
loyaltyDiscountForFred = loyaltyDiscount fredSpend
```

Function abstraction is about identifying patterns. What's the pattern common to determining tax and determining a loyalty discount? They both invoke one function with an initial value and then invoke a second function with the result from the first function:

```
initialValue = 5
intermediateValue = firstFunction initialValue
finalValue = secondFunction intermediateValue
```

Why is the intermediate value there? It doesn't make the program any clearer. Remove it:

```
initialValue = 5
secondFunction (firstFunction initialValue)
```

---

[1] In practice, the arithmetic operators in JavaScript and CoffeeScript aren't good when working with decimal values because JavaScript's numbers use floating-point arithmetic, which isn't accurate for decimal values. If you need to do arithmetic with decimal values, you should find an appropriate library for decimal arithmetic.

The same applies to calculating the tax. Instead of doing each calculation individually,

```
netProfitForProducts = netProfit products
taxForProducts - tax netProfitForProducts
```

you can put them together:

```
taxForProducts = tax (netProfit products)
```

So far, nothing earth-shattering. Think for a second, though; instead of assigning the result to a variable, what does a function that evaluates the final value look like?

```
taxForProducts = (products) -> tax (netProfit products)
```

You do this often, so you should get to know it properly by learning what it's called. It's called `compose`:

```
compose = (f, g) -> (x) -> f g x
```
⟵ | This looks scary, but it's the classic way to express compose. You'll get used to it, one day.

This little `compose` function lets you join together any two functions:

```
taxForProducts = compose tax, netProfit
loyaltyDiscountForUser = compose loyaltyDiscount, userSpend
```

Naturally, it also works for trivial little cases that you wouldn't really want to do unless you were trying to learn how to compose:

```
addFive = (x) -> x + 5
multiplyByThree = (x) -> x * 3
multiplyByThreeAndThenAddFive = compose addFive, multiplyByThree
multiplyByThreeAndThenAddFive 10
# 35
```
⟵ | The function on the right (the second argument to compose) is evaluated first.

Remember that functions are a bit like pipes. You can explicitly take output from one pipe and use it as the input to another pipe, or you can just connect the pipes together. `Compose` isn't the only way you might want to connect functions together. In figure 6.2 you can see `compose`, as well as the other basic combinators `before`, `after`, and `around` that will be discussed in this section.

First on the menu are `before` and `after`. Dig in.

6.4.2   *Before and after*

Suppose Agtron needs to meet some incredibly bizarre bureaucracy requirements and tells you that you have to log every product that's sold to an external service. You don't have to worry about the service itself, because there's an existing `auditLog` function that does it for you.

There's an existing `sale` function, so you could just chuck an invocation of `auditLog` in there:

```
sale = (user, product) ->
  auditLog "Sold #{product} to #{user}"
  # Some other stuff happens here
```

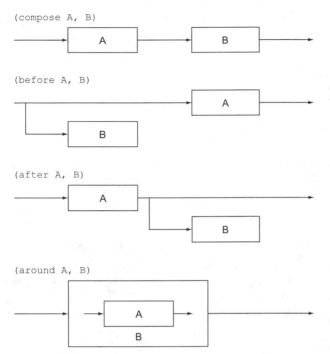

(compose A, B)

(before A, B)

(after A, B)

(around A, B)

Figure 6.2 Visualizing compose, before, after, **and** around

Then Agtron tells you that you also need to log refunds, so you run along and add an auditLog there too:

```
refund = (user, product) ->
  auditLog "Refund for #{product} to #{user}"
  # Some other stuff happens here
```

Then Agtron tells you that you also need to log … you know where this is headed *and* that it will quickly get tedious. What if instead you could add the logging code from the outside so that you could create a new auditedRefund function easily?

```
auditedRefund = withAuditLog refund
```

Or perhaps even assign a new function to the existing refund variable?

```
refund = withAuditLog refund
```

You can do this with the help of before. First, you need to implement it:

```
before = (decoration) ->
  (base) ->
    (params...) ->
      decoration params...
      base params...
```

If you aren't familiar with these dots, they're for rest and spread parameters and they help you deal with an arbitrary number of arguments. You'll learn more about them in the next chapter.

Now you can define the withAuditLog function:

```
withAuditLog = before (params...) ->
  auditLog params...
```

You could also implement `withAuditLog` to use `after` instead of `before`. The difference is only in the order in which the functions are invoked. The definition for `after` is similar to that for `before`:

```
after = (decoration) ->
  (base) ->
    (params...) ->
      result = base params...
      decoration params...
      result
```

The combinators `after` and `before` don't change the behavior of the function that they wrap. When you need to change the return value, or the invocation of the wrapped function, then you need to use `around`.

6.4.3   *Around*

This one is fun. Suppose that the database is changed so that you need to open and close the connection to the database for each operation you do. For every place in the program where you do a set of database operations, you need to put an `openConnection` and a `closeConnection` around them:

```
openConnection()
doSomethingToTheDb()
doSomethingElseToTheDb()
closeConnection()
```

You quickly tire of adding the same two lines of code throughout your program. Worse, sometimes the database fails to open, and you have to graft on a fix for that too:

```
dbConnectionIsOpen = openConnection()
if dbConnectionIsOpen
  doSomethingToTheDb()
  doSomethingElseToTheDb()
  closeConnection()
```

Instead of directly invoking the database open and close functions everywhere, you can use `around`:

```
around = (decoration) ->
  (base) ->
    (params...) ->
      callback = -> base params...
      decoration ([callback].concat params)...
```

A function that's placed around another executes code both before and after it:

```
withOpenDb = around (dbActivity) ->
  openDbConnection()
  dbActivity()
  closeDbConnection()
```

Now you can use `withOpenDb` everywhere:

```
getUserData = withOpenDb (users) ->
  users.get 'user123'
```

Around doesn't just get invoked and discarded: it can control whether or not the function it wraps is invoked *at all*. If openDbConnection evaluates to false when the database fails to open, then the database activity can be skipped:

```
withOpenDb = around (dbActivity) ->
  if openDbConnection()
    dbActivity()
    closeDbConnection()
```

That makes around quite powerful *and dangerous*. It's possible to implement combinators that have even more power (and that are even more dangerous), such as modifying the arguments to the wrapped function and controlling the return value of the created function.

Functions are often used as methods in CoffeeScript, so generic functions that create other functions need to work correctly when those functions are methods. What happens when these combinators are used with methods?

6.4.4   *Working with objects*

The tricky thing about method objects is referencing this (a.k.a. @). Suppose you have a program that controls the movement of a toy robot. The program must start the toy robot engine before making it move. The program also needs to stop the engine once it is done moving the toy robot. This is essentially the same problem as the previous database example, except that in this case, Robot is a class already implemented by Rob Tuse:

```
class Robot
  constructor: (@at=0) ->
  position: ->
    @at
  move: (displacement) ->
    @at += displacement
  startEngine: -> console.log 'start engine'
  stopEngine: -> console.log 'stop engine'
  forward: ->
    @startEngine()
    @move 1
    @stopEngine()
  reverse: ->
    @startEngine()
    @move -1
    @stopEngine()
```

You can see that that's repetitive. Instead of repeating the same code at the start and at the end of all the methods, you could use the existing around function to wrap all of the methods. Unfortunately, everything breaks when you change the Robot class to use the around defined so far:

```
class Robot
  withRunningEngine = around (action) ->
    @startEngine()
    action()
    @stopEngine()
  constructor: (@at=0) ->
  position: ->
    @at
  move: (displacement) ->
    console.log 'move'
    @at += displacement
  startEngine: -> console.log 'start engine'
  stopEngine: -> console.log 'stop engine'
  forward: withRunningEngine ->
    @move 1
  reverse: withRunningEngine ->
    @move -1

bender = new Robot
bender.forward()
bender.forward()
# TypeError: Object #<Object> has no method 'startEngine'
```

It doesn't work because when the function is invoked indirectly, the @ reference is lost. Normally in CoffeeScript you use the fat arrow => to lexically bind the @ reference for a function. In this case, though, you don't want to lexically bind the @, but dynamically bind it.

CALL AND APPLY

Luckily, the Function prototype has two methods, call and apply, that can help you in the rare instances where neither the arrow (->) nor fat arrow (=>) provide what you need. Both call and apply allow you to invoke any function with a specific this bound.

With call you can invoke a function with a specific this and a set number of arguments. Here's a modified example:

```
airplane =
  startEngine: -> 'Engine started!'

withRunningEngine = (first, second) ->
  @startEngine()
  "#{first} then #{second}"

withRunningEngine 'Take-off', 'Fly'
# Object #<Object> has no method 'startEngine'

withRunningEngine.call airplane, 'Take-off', 'Fly'
'Take-off then Fly'
```

With apply you can invoke a function with a specific this and an array of arguments:

```
withRunningEngine.apply airplane, ['Take-off', 'Fly']
'Take-off then Fly'
```

Although the addition of the fat arrow to CoffeeScript removes many of the common uses of call and apply found in JavaScript, there are still occasions, such as now, when you'll find them useful. Using `apply` you can create new versions of `before`, `after`, and `around` that can play nicely with methods. These new versions are shown in the next listing.

Listing 6.6 `Before`, `after`, **and** `around` **with function binding**

```
before = (decoration) ->
  (base) ->
    (params...) ->
      decoration.apply @, params
      base.apply @, params

after  = (decoration) ->
  (base) ->
    (params...) ->
      result = base.apply @, params
      decoration.apply @, params
      result

around = (decoration) ->
  (base) ->
    (params...) ->
      result = undefined
      func = =>
        result = base.apply @, params
      decoration.apply @, ([func].concat params)
      result
```

With this new version of `around`, the robots can move again:

```
bender = new Robot 3
bender.forward()
# start engine
# move
# stop engine
# 4

bender.forward()
# start engine
# move
# stop engine
# 5

bender.reverse()
# start engine
# move
# stop engine
# 4

bender.position()
# 4
```

It takes some time to get used to these programming concepts. At first, it's best to lightly use techniques that you're less familiar with, until you can learn to use them effectively and without creating a mess.

These combinator functions are useful, but so far you've used them only with synchronous things. Much of your program is asynchronous and uses callbacks. Will these techniques work for asynchronous code?

6.4.5   *Asynchronous combinators*

Asynchronous functions that accept callbacks are more difficult to compose than functions that are used purely for their evaluation. So far you've looked at using combinators for a synchronous database and for synchronous robots. The real world isn't so kind. Most of your CoffeeScript programming will be asynchronous.

Consider what happens when multiple asynchronous function calls must be called in order. Start with a fake asynchronous function that requires a callback:

```
forward = (callback) ->
  setTimeout callback, 1000
```

You might have seen this written when the function needs to be called five times in sequence:

```
forward ->
  forward ->
    forward ->
      forward ->
        forward ->
          console.log 'done!'
```

Doing this will get painful very quickly.

The nasty-looking cascade you see here is a common affliction in asynchronous programs. Surely there's a way to defeat this problem by composing functions. To simplify things, consider two standalone asynchronous functions, `start` and `forward`:

```
start = (callback) ->
  console.log 'started'
  setTimeout callback, 200

forward = (callback) ->
  console.log 'moved forward'
  setTimeout callback, 200
```

How do you compose these asynchronous functions? The standard `compose` doesn't work because it expects to use the evaluation of one function as the argument to another:

```
startThenForward = compose forward, start
startThenForward (res) ->
  console.log res
# TypeError: undefined is not a function
```

You need a different `composeAsync` for asynchronous functions. Take a deep breath.

```
composeAsync = (f, g) -> (x) -> g -> f x
```

This async version of compose looks even scarier. Again, though, it's the classic way to express this combinator, so it's best if you learn to get used to it.

This version works, although it's limited to functions that don't take any arguments other than a single callback:

```
startThenForward = composeAsync forward, start
startThenForward ->
  console.log 'done'
# started
# moved forward
# done
```

When the asynchronous functions have arguments other than a callback, things become more interesting. In the next listing you see asynchronous versions of `before` and `after` that Agtron has provided. Take an even deeper breath and then spend some time experimenting with them and dissecting them so that you begin to understand how they work.

Listing 6.7   Asynchronous `before` and `after`

```
beforeAsync = (decoration) ->
  (base) ->
    (params..., callback) ->
      result = undefined
      applyBase = =>
        result = base.apply @, (params.concat callback)
      decoration.apply @, (params.concat applyBase)
      result

afterAsync = (decoration) ->
  (base) ->
    (params..., callback) ->
      decorated = (params...) =>
        decoration.apply @, (params.concat -> (callback.apply @, params))
      base.apply @, (params.concat decorated)
```

There are other ways to deal with resources that are accessed asynchronously, such as treating them as streams of data, as you'll learn about in chapter 9.

Continuations

This concept of passing in the rest of your program as a callback is similar to something called *continuation-passing style*. One of the criticisms of CoffeeScript in its current state is that callbacks all have to be nested. The asynchronous composition techniques presented here and the techniques shown in chapter 9 go a long way to helping solve that problem. Further, in chapter 13 you'll see how JavaScript, and hence CoffeeScript, is evolving to have better language techniques for dealing with asynchronous code.

Later on, over coffee (robots drink coffee too), Agtron tells you what his philosophy professor once told him, "Our understanding of the world often gets tangled up until eventually it becomes one big knot. Philosophy is about teasing out those knots and untangling things so that you have simple explanations of things." The same thing applies to the world of a program. Sometimes things get tangled up. If you pull harder on the knot, you make it worse. If you do surgery on the knot by cutting it, you can break the entire universe. The point is to instead tease out the tangles and make your program less intertwined. The techniques you've seen can help you to tease out some of the knots in your program.

6.5   *Summary*

Function composition is built on just a few basic techniques for gluing functions together. But the simplicity and flexibility of this approach allow you to construct your own programming abstractions. By naming a function, you're growing the programming language yourself. By creating abstractions, you make it easier to construct similar parts of a language without having to write the same program over and over again. You've learned the techniques: keeping programs clear by naming functions, avoiding state, creating abstractions, creating abstractions of abstractions, and then also *using* these techniques to deal with callback functions in asynchronous programs.

In the next chapter you'll look at programming style in CoffeeScript, advanced syntax, and some gotchas.

Style and semantics

This chapter covers

- Rest and spread parameters
- Destructuring assignment
- Dealing with types
- Effective comprehensions
- Fluent interfaces
- Nuances of significant whitespace

In chapter 2 you took a highway drive through the CoffeeScript syntactic landscape. CoffeeScript is a small language, so the drive didn't take you very long. That said, chapter 2 was deliberately fast-paced, and at the speed you were going, some details were necessarily postponed for later. Well, later has arrived.

To understand the full breadth of CoffeeScript programs you'll find in the wild, you need to appreciate some subtler syntactic and semantic aspects of the language that require a bit more care and attention to grasp. These aspects—covered in this chapter—are spread and rest parameters, destructuring assignment, semantic issues around types and dealing with null values, effective use of comprehensions, fluent interfaces, and finally the nuances of dealing with significant indentation. First up, rest and spread parameters.

Team	Points
Wolverines	22
Sabertooths	19
Honey Badgers	11
Mongooses	8
Taipans	4

Figure 7.1 Table of teams ranked by points

7.1 Rest and spread parameters

Imagine you're displaying a table of teams in a competition ordered by the number of points they have (figure 7.1). When a team moves up in the rankings, you highlight the row containing that team.

Suppose you already have a `highlight` function that takes a name, finds it, and highlights it by invoking `color` and `find` functions that have been implemented elsewhere:

```
highlight = (name) ->
  color find(name), 'yellow'
```

Suppose now that your colleague Bobby Tables wants to use the `highlight` function with multiple names. He changes it to work with an array:

```
highlight = (names) ->
  for name in names
    color find(name), 'yellow'
```

Unfortunately, by changing the function Bobby has broken all the other places in your program where `highlight` is invoked with a single name. Sure, this might be little more than a minor inconvenience, but it's an inconvenience that you can avoid entirely by using some syntactic sugar called *rest parameters*.

> **The arguments object**
>
> Experienced JavaScript developers will be familiar with the `arguments` object and the problems it poses by not inheriting from the array prototype. The good news is that rest parameters in CoffeeScript mean that you *never* have to use the `arguments` object again.

7.1.1 Rest

The rest parameter puts multiple function parameters into an array.[1] A rest parameter is a name followed by an ellipsis (three dots), and it can be used to create a better `highlight` function:

```
highlight = (names...) ->
  for name in names
    color find(name), 'yellow'
```

---

[1] If you're familiar with Ruby or Perl, you might be familiar with the splat, which serves the same purpose.

When the `highlight` function is invoked, then `names` is an array containing as many elements as there are arguments:

```
highlight ()                                     ⟵  names will
                                                     be [].      names will be      names will be
highlight 'taipans'                              ⟵              ['taipans'].        ['taipans', 'wolverines',
highlight 'taipans', 'wolverines', 'sabertooths'                              ⟵                      'sabertooths'].
```

Suppose now that you want the `highlight` function to color the first team (identified by the first parameter) gold and color all the other teams (identified by the other parameters) blue. How do you do that? By putting the ellipsis on the second parameter:

```
highlight = (first, rest...) ->
  color find first 'gold'
  for name in rest                             Taipans will be colored gold;
    color find(name), 'blue'                   sabertooths and wolverines
highlight 'taipans', 'sabertooths', 'wolverines'  ⟵  will be colored blue.
```

Using rest parameters, you can convert multiple function parameters into a single array. Using *spread* parameters, you can do the reverse—convert a single array into multiple parameters.

7.1.2 *Spread*

Now that the `highlight` function takes individual arguments, what do you do when you have an array of names? Suppose you have the teams ranked in an array, top team first:

```
teams = ['wolverines', 'sabertooths', 'mongooses']
```

You want to pass the first item (called the *head* of the array) as one parameter and the remaining items (called the *tail*) as the remaining parameters. Doing that manually is clumsy:

```
highlight teams[0], teams[1], teams[2]
```

Your fingers would be sore from typing after a hundred team names or so. The alternative is to *spread* the teams in the array across the function parameters:

```
highlight teams...
```

Compare two different invocations of the `highlight` function:

```
                                   highlight is invoked with the
                                   teams array as the first argument.
highlight teams                ⟵
highlight teams...        ⟵
                                   highlight is invoked with the teams array spread across
                                   as many arguments as there are items in the array.
```

Suppose now that you have an `insert` function that takes a spread, and you want to invoke it from within another function that also takes a spread. Passing the name of the rest parameters directly to `insert` doesn't work:

```
insert = (teams...) ->          For demonstration, this insert function
  teams                         simply returns the names parameter.
```

```
initialize = (teams...) ->
  insert teams
```
                                              | Invoke insert with the name
                                           ⟵ | of the rest parameter.

```
initialize 'wolverines', 'sabertooths', 'mongooses'
# [ [ 'wolverines','sabertooths', 'mongooses' ] ]
```

The rest parameter for `insert` ends up as an array wrapped in an array—definitely not what you wanted. But using the spread you can get the result you need:

```
initialize = (teams...) ->
  insert teams...

initialize 'wolverines', 'sabertooths', 'mongooses'
# [ 'wolverines','sabertooths', 'mongooses' ]
```

Using rest and spread in combination, you can make a flexible and elegant program to highlight the team names in the table. This program appears in the following listing. Note that this listing is intended to run in a web browser; you can use the server from listing 7.5 to achieve that.

Listing 7.1 Competition

```
find = (name) ->
  document.querySelector ".#{name}"
```
The find function uses the native document.querySelector to find elements matching the class name.

```
color = (element, color) ->
  element.style.background = color
```
Set the background color of the element via a style property.

```
insert = (teams...) ->
  root = document.querySelector '.teams'
  for team in teams
    element = document.createElement 'li'
    element.innerHTML = team
    element.className = team
    root.appendChild element
```
Add elements to the page for each team.

```
highlight = (first, rest...) ->
  color find(first), 'gold'
  for name in rest
    color find(name), 'blue'
```
Highlight the first element gold and then the rest blue via a comprehension.

```
initialize = (ranked) ->
  insert ranked...
  first = ranked.slice(0, 1)
  rest = ranked.slice 1
  highlight first, rest...
```
Initialize by inserting the elements and then highlighting.

```
window.onload = ->
  initialize [
    'wolverines'
    'wildcats'
    'mongooses'
  ]
```
Invoke initialize with the array of teams when the browser window loads.

Although rest and spread are only small bits of syntactic sugar (remember, syntactic sugar makes things sweeter), they can make a big difference for code readability, which is a key motivation for many of the syntactic changes that CoffeeScript introduces to JavaScript. Another one of those changes that you haven't yet explored in detail is called *destructuring*.

7.2 Destructuring

Like spread and rest parameters, destructuring assignment allows you to write with a single, terse expression something that would normally require multiple expressions. Think of rest and spread parameters on steroids—destructuring allows you to unpack *any* array or object into variables or arguments.

7.2.1 Arrays

Suppose your program for the competition table needs to keep track of a particular team (such as your favorite team) by making it the active team. Here's a function that Bobby Tables has already written to switch this active team:

```
makeToggler = (active, inactive) ->
  ->
    temporary = active
    active = inactive
    inactive = temporary
    [active, inactive]

toggler = makeToggler 'komodos', 'raptors'

toggler()
# ['raptors', 'komodos']

toggler()
# ['komodos', 'raptors']
```

Notice how three variables are needed to perform the switch.

That doesn't seem very concise, does it? What's the alternative? With destructuring you can do away with so many expressions by assigning values to multiple variables in a single expression:

```
active = 'komodos'
inactive = 'raptors'

[active, inactive] = [inactive, active]

active
# raptors

inactive
# komodos
```

Destructuring assignment swaps the variables.

Rewrite the `toggle` function to use array destructuring:

```
toggler = (a, b) ->
  -> [a,b] = [b,a]

toggle = toggler 'on', 'off'

toggle()
# ['off', 'on']

toggle()
# ['on', 'off']
```

Suppose that in another part of the team competition program you need to relegate the team that finishes last. By using array destructuring you can avoid multiple and confusing array shuffling and variable assignments:

```
relegate = (team) -> "#{team.name} got relegated"

rank = (array..., using) ->
  array.sort (first, second) ->
    first[using] < second[using]

competitors = [
    name: 'wildcats'
    points: 5
  ,
    name: 'bobcats'
    points: 3
]

[first, field..., last] = rank competitors..., 'points'

relegate last
# 'bobcats got relegated'
```

For demonstration, just display the name of the team that got relegated.

Rank an array on a specific property.

You can omit the curly braces in an array of objects only if you comma-separate them and indent with care.

Rank the competitors array on the points property.

This gets you the same result but without shuffling values around multiple variables. That's a good result because every place you shuffle another variable or create a new bit of state is a place where you might introduce an error. This doesn't just apply to arrays—objects can also be destructured.

7.2.2 *Objects*

Imagine that you have some data for all of the teams in the competition. All of the data you need is inside an object, but it's not exactly in the structure you want. Here's the current structure:

```
data =
  team2311:
    name: 'Honey Badgers'
    stats:
      scored: 22
      conceded: 22
      points: 11
  team4326:
    name: 'Mongooses'
    stats:
      scored: 14
      conceded: 19
      points: 8
```

Instead of the current structure, how do you get at the specific parts of the data structure that you need? You might pull the object apart manually:

```
for id, team of data
  name = team.name
  points = team.stats.points
  {
    name: name
    points: points
  }
# [ { name: 'Honey Badgers', points: 11 },
#   { name: 'Mongooses', points: 8 } ]
```

That's no fun. With destructuring you can do it succinctly:

```
for id, team of data
  {name: team.name,  points: team.stats.points}
# [ { name: 'Honey Badgers', points: 11 },
.#   { name: 'Mongooses', points: 8 } ]
```

One place where you see this object destructuring used frequently is at the start of a file in a Node.js program:

```
{pad, trim, dirify} = require 'util'
```

Why? Because the `require` function returns an object, and manually unpacking the object is tedious:

```
util = require 'util'
pad = util.pad
trim = util.trim
dirify = util.dirify
```

Exactly *how* the module system works is covered in detail in chapter 12, but what you can see already is how destructuring is used to remove noise from a program and so helps you to make it simpler.

You're not yet finished with making things simpler, though; CoffeeScript has another bit of syntactic sugar for objects: the object shorthand.

7.2.3 *Object shorthand*

Consider a `competition` module that exposes a `highlight` and an `initialize` method:

```
makeCompetition = ->
  find = ->
    # function body omitted
  color = ->
    # function body omitted
  highlight = ->
    # function body omitted
  initialize = ->
    # function body omitted

  highlight: highlight,
  initialize: initialize

competition = makeCompetition()

# { highlight: [Function], initialize: [Function] }
```

> Expose only the highlight and initialize functions as public by assigning them to properties of the returned object. Remember, you can leave the squigglies (curly braces) off when writing object literals in CoffeeScript.

Here the variable names are the same as the property names on the object, so it's repetitive to write both:

```
highlight = ->
initialize = ->

object =
  highlight: highlight
  initialize: initialize          Repetitive
```

Instead of being repetitive, the object shorthand means you can pack variable values back into an object based on their names:

```
makeCompetition = ->
  find = ->
  color = ->
  highlight = ->
  initialize = -> 'initialized'          Use object shorthand to
                                          export the value of the
  {highlight, initialize}                 variable with the name.

competition = makeCompetition()
competition.initialize()
# 'initialized'
```

The object shorthand also works when specifying parameters. Suppose `makeCompetition` accepts an `options` argument containing the `maxCompetitors` and the `sortOrder`:

```
makeCompetition = (options) ->
  options.max
  options.sort
```

Although an `options` argument saves you from having an unwieldy number of arguments to the function, the end result is often repetitive regardless. You can avoid that by using object destructuring directly in the parameter list. An object in the parameter definition will result in the object properties being destructured to individual named parameters:

```
makeCompetition = ({max, sort}) ->
  {max, sort}
```

This is very handy; you now essentially have named parameters that can be supplied in any order without needing an intermediate `options` parameter:

```
makeCompetition max: 5, sort: ->          The named arguments can
# {max: 5, sort: [Function]}              go in any order and the
                                          effect will be the same.
makeCompetition sort: (->), max: 5
# {max: 5, sort: [Function]}
```

Although this is useful, you should think carefully before using destructuring and make sure you aren't making your program hard to read. These examples and the issue of readability are revisited later in this chapter.

7.2.4 *Array destructuring expansion*

Since CoffeeScript version 1.7, array destructuring also works with expansion. What does that mean? Suppose you have an array of competitors:

```
competitors = [
  { name: 'wildcats', points: 3 }
  { name: 'tigers', points: 1 }
  { name: 'taipans', points: 5 }
]
```

How do you get just the first team and the last team? Prior to CoffeeScript 1.7 you needed to name the first, last, and middle:

```
[first, middle..., last] = competitors
first
# { name: 'wildcats', points: 3 }

last
# { name: 'taipans', points: 5 }
```

Since 1.7, though, you can elide the middle and the result will be the same:

```
[first, ..., last] = competitors
first
# { name: 'wildcats', points: 3 }

last
# { name: 'taipans', points: 5 }
```

This is another small way in which CoffeeScript syntax can help you focus on just the things that matter to you.

7.2.5 *Exercises*

Got the knack for destructuring? Try these exercises to find out:

- Given an array of numbers such as [1,2,3,4,5,6], write a function that uses destructuring and a comprehension to reverse each subsequent pair of numbers in the array so that, for example, [1,2,3,4,5,6] becomes [2,1,4,3,6,5] and [1,2,1,2,1,2] becomes [2,1,2,1,2,1].
- Suppose you've received some JSON containing a phone directory in a format like this:

  ```
  {"A":[{"name":"Andy", "phone":"5551111"},...],"B":[...],...}
  ```

  Write a function that produces the last phone number for a given letter found in the phone directory.

7.2.6 *Putting it together*

Now that you've completed some exercises, it's time to see this new syntax in a program. Rest and spread parameters and destructuring techniques for arrays and objects are demonstrated in the competition program of the following listing. This listing is intended to run in a web browser; you can use the server from listing 7.5 to achieve that.

Listing 7.2   Competition with module pattern

```
makeCompetition = ({max, sort}) ->
  find = (name) ->
    document.querySelector ".#{name}"

  color = (element, color) ->
    element.style.background = color

  insert = (teams...) ->
    root = document.querySelector '.teams'
    for team in teams
      element = document.createElement 'li'
      element.innerHTML = "#{team.name} (#{team.points})"
      element.className = team.name
      root.appendChild element

  highlight = (first, rest...) ->
    color find(first.name), 'gold'
    for team in rest
      color find(team.name), 'blue'

  rank = (unranked) ->
    unranked.sort(sort).slice(0, max)

  initialize = (unranked) ->
    ranked = rank unranked
    insert ranked...
    first = ranked.slice(0, 1)[0]
    rest = ranked.slice 1
    highlight first, rest...

  { initialize }

sortOnPoints = (a, b) ->
  a.points > b.points

window.onload = ->
  competition = makeCompetition(max: 5, sort: sortOnPoints)
  competition.initialize [
    { name: 'wolverines', points: 22 }
    { name: 'wildcats', points: 11 }
    { name: 'mongooses', points: 33 }
    { name: 'raccoons', points: 12 }
    { name: 'badgers', points: 19 }
    { name: 'baboons', points: 16 }
  ]
```

A maker function that returns a competition object. The arguments are named by using object syntax in the function declaration.

Rank the competitors using the sort method on the array prototype.

Return an object with an initialize property and the value of the initialize variable as the value. This is the shorthand syntax for {initialize: initialize}.

The sorting strategy for the teams that will be given to the competition; it sorts on points.

Pass in object as named parameters to the maker function.

CoffeeScript mixes syntax and semantics from JavaScript (both current and future versions) as well as from other programming languages. Some things (such as destructuring) are very useful, whereas other things are (or can be) less useful. Take `null`, for example.

7.3   *No nulls*

When a variable or property is defined but doesn't have a value, then it has the special value `null`. The value `null` is the only value with `typeof null` in CoffeeScript. You might ask what `null` is good for—that's a good question. You see, the `null` value isn't a value you want. Instead, it usually means something has gone wrong. Remember the existential operator used to determine if a variable is either `undefined` or `null`?

```
roundSquare?
# false
```

Well, this existential operator can also be combined with the dot operator and the assignment operator. In this section you'll learn about these additional uses of the existential operator and how they help you live with `null`.

7.3.1 *Null soak*

Imagine you're writing an application that takes information about users and displays it on a web page. The information for a given user is in an object:

```
user =
  name:
    title: 'Mr'
    first: 'Data'
    last: 'Object'
  contact:
    phone:
      home: '555 2234'
      mobile: '555 7766'
    email:
      primary: 'mrdataobject@coffeescriptinaction.com'
```

How do you access the home phone number for this user?

```
user.contact.phone.home
# '555 2234'
```

Suppose that some of the user data is missing or incomplete. For example, consider a user who doesn't have any contact information:

```
user =
  name:
    first: 'Haveno'
    middle: 'Contact'
    last: 'Details'
```

Your program will throw an exception:

```
user.contact.phone.home
# TypeError: cannot read property 'phone' of undefined
```

To avoid this, you *might* wrap the access to the data in a big condition:

```
if user.contact and user.contact.phone and user.contact.phone.home
  user.contact.phone.home
```

Or perhaps you might wrap it in a `try` block:

```
try
  user.contact.phone.home
catch e
  'no contact number'
```

Don't do either. Instead, when rendering information about a user, either display the information or not—don't display an error, null, or undefined. Use the null soak operator (sometimes called the *safe navigation operator*) to soak null values and undefined properties so you don't have to test for them explicitly:

```
user?.contact?.phone?.home
```

This will suppress any errors when accessing the user data. An acceptable time to suppress these errors is when rendering data to a user. For example, suppose you have a render function that uses a heredoc with interpolation to display the phone number somewhere on a website:

```
render = (user) ->
  """
  <html>
  Home phone for #{user.name.first}: #{user.contact.phone.home}
  """
```

Imagine this render function is normally invoked when information about a user is retrieved. Without using the null soak operator, the render function will cause an error when a user property is missing:

```
user =
  name:
    first: 'Donot'
    last: 'Callme'

render user
# TypeError: cannot read property 'phone' of undefined
```

You don't want a render function to show an error to a user when data is missing. Instead, you want to *suppress* internal errors when rendering. Think about it: users don't want to read all your internal errors. Avoid showing errors by using the null soak:

```
render = (user) ->
  """
  <html>
  Home phone for #{user?.name?.first}: #{user?.contact?.phone?.home}
  """

user = null
render user: null
# <html>
# Home phone for undefined: undefined
```

To display something other than undefined, you can use the default operator || to specify a default value:

```
user = null
contact = user?.contact?.phone?.home || 'Not provided'
contact
# Not provided
```

This allows you to present the information you need without an explicit conditional.

NULL SOAK IS NOT FOR ASSIGNMENT

Because null soak is so convenient, it's tempting to use it with assignment:

```
user = {}
user?.contact?.phone?.home = '555 5555'
```

That's a *bad* idea. What's the result of the assignment? Is the value of `user.contact` `.phone.home` now 5? No. The `null` was soaked immediately and `user` doesn't even have a `contact` property:

```
user.contact?
# false
```

Don't use null soak for property assignment. Only use it for *safe access*. Conditional assignment, on the other hand, can be useful and safe for local variables.

7.3.2 *Conditional assignment*

Suppose you want to assign a value to a variable only if it does *not* already contain a value. A simple way to do that is by combining the existential operator with assignment:

```
phone = undefined
phone ?= '555 5555'
phone
# '555 5555'

phone = null
phone ?= '555 1111'
phone
# '555 1111'

phone ?= 'something else'
phone
# '555 1111'
```

Be careful, though; existential assignment isn't for variables that haven't been defined:

```
variableYouNeverDeclared ?= 'something'
# error: the variable "variableYouNeverDeclared" can't be assigned with ?=
    because it has not been declared before
```

In the next listing you once again see the competition rankings program. This time the null soak is used to handle `null` values in the supplied data and when rendering an HTML view. This listing is intended to run in a web browser; you can use the server from listing 7.5 to achieve that.

Listing 7.3   Using null soak in a view

```
makeCompetition = ({max, sort}) ->
  render = (team) ->
    """
    <tr class='#{team?.name||''}'>
    <td>#{team?.name||''}</td>
    <td>#{team?.points||''}</td>
    <td>#{team?.goals?.scored||''}</td>
```

The view is just a lo-fi function called render. Notice how the nulls are soaked in expressions such as team?.goals?.scored and that the default operator is used to output an empty string as the default value.

```
      <td>#{team?.goals?.conceded||''}</td>
      </tr>
      """

  find = (name) ->
    document.querySelector ".#{name}"

  color = (element, color) ->
    element.style.background = color

  insert = (teams...) ->
    root = document.querySelector '.teams'
    for team in teams
      root.innerHTML += render team

  highlight = (first, rest...) ->
    color find(first.name), 'gold'
    for team in rest
      color find(team.name), 'blue'

  rank = (unranked) ->
    unranked.sort(sort).slice(0, max).reverse()

  initialize: (unranked) ->
    ranked = rank unranked
    insert ranked...
    first = ranked.slice(0, 1)[0]
    rest = ranked.slice 1
    highlight first, rest...

sortOnPoints = (a, b) ->
  a.points > b.points

window.onload = ->
  competition = makeCompetition max:5, sort: sortOnPoints
  competition.initialize [
      name: 'wolverines'
      points: 56
      goals:
        scored: 26
        conceded: 8
    ,
      name: 'wildcats'
      points: 53
      goals:
        scored: 32
        conceded: 19
    ,
      name: 'mongooses'
      points: 34
      goals:
        scored: 9
        conceded: 9
    ,
      name: 'raccoons'
      points: 0
  ]
```

The competition is initialized as before except that now the data has information about the goals scored by individual teams.

The raccoons were disqualified so they have zero points and don't have a goals property.

Remember what the type of null is?

```
typeof null
# null
```

There's only one thing with a type of null and it's the null value. As mentioned previously, there are languages with rich and powerful type systems. CoffeeScript isn't one of them, and types, including the null type, can be problematic.

7.4   No types—the duck test

CoffeeScript is dynamically and weakly typed. The most noticeable thing about the typeof operator so far in your CoffeeScript travels should be its absence. When writing programs in CoffeeScript, there's rarely any benefit to be gained from examining types by using the typeof operator. Instead, use a technique called duck typing:

```
class Duck
  walk: ->
  quack: (distance) ->

daffy = new Duck
```

What can you do with a duck? You might put it on a leash and take it for a walk:

```
daffy.walk()
```

If it meets another duck, they might talk to each other:

```
donald = new Duck

donald.quack()
daffy.quack()
```

That's great. Suppose you want to organize a duck race:

```
class DuckRace
  constructor: (@ducks) ->
  go: ->
    duck.walk() for duck in @ducks
```

This DuckRace doesn't know if only ducks are competing. For example, a faster animal such as a hare could enter the race:

```
class Hare
  run: ->
  walk: -> run()

hare = new Hare

race = new DuckRace [hare]
```

That's unfair! How will you prevent non-ducks from entering the race? If you have experience in a strongly typed language, then you might think that the typeof operator will do the trick.

7.4.1 *Don't rely on typeof, instanceof, or constructor*

You want to be strict with entrants to the DuckRace and ensure that they're all real, cer-
tified ducks, and your first thought is to use the typeof operator. Unfortunately, the
typeof operator in CoffeeScript isn't very useful:

```
daffy = new Duck
typeof daffy
# 'object'
```

Almost everything in CoffeeScript is an object, so there's really no point using typeof
here. So, you think that perhaps you can test to see if the object was created from the
Duck class by using the instanceof operator:

```
daffy instanceof Duck
# true
```

Great, that's a duck. Is instanceof the solution? No. What happens when you change
the DuckRace constructor to admit any objects that are instanceof Duck?

```
class DuckRace
  constructor (applicants) ->
    @ducks = d for d in applicants when d instanceof Duck
  go: ->
    duck.walk() for duck in @ducks
```

The race is run. Unfortunately, one of the ducks isn't really a duck. It was a duck, but
it was turned into a snake by an evil warlock:

```
duck = new Duck
ultraDuckMarathon = new DuckRace [duck]

turnIntoSnake = ->
  duck.walk = null
  duck.slither = ->

turnIntoSnake duck
```

◁——┐ **The walk property of this duck
is assigned the value null. It no
longer knows how to walk.**

```
ultraDuckMarathon.go()
# TypeError: Property walk of object #<AsianDuck> is not a function
```

You tried to use a type to solve your problem (via the instanceof operator) and the
result was a type error. Irony.

The instanceof operator doesn't promise anything. It doesn't guarantee that an
object has a particular interface or works a particular way. It doesn't tell you if something is a duck. All it tells you is which class or constructor the object was created with.
In a dynamic language like CoffeeScript, the class or constructor of an object doesn't
guarantee anything about what the object actually does right now. The instanceof
operator is even more brittle because the result will change if you reassign a prototype:

```
class Duck
daffy = new Duck
Duck:: = class Snake

daffy instanceof Duck
# false
```

As a last resort you decide to use the `constructor` property:

```
class Duck
daffy = new Duck
daffy.constructor.name
# Duck
```

That tells you the constructor for the `daffy` object. Again, though, this is a flawed approach in a dynamic language like CoffeeScript. Suppose you create a duck without using a class:

```
duck =
  walk: ->
  quack: ->

daffy = Object.create duck
```

Is `daffy` a duck? It was created from a prototypical duck. If the `constructor.name` is the criteria for being a duck, then `daffy` isn't a duck:

```
daffy.constructor.name
# 'Object'
```

So, with all of the different techniques for constructing and modifying objects in CoffeeScript, it quickly becomes apparent that none of the approaches you try to determine whether something is the correct type are going to work. What's the alternative then? It's called duck typing.

7.4.2 *How to use duck typing*

The principle behind duck typing is that if there's no reliable way in the language to be sure what interface an object implements, then you should rely on the interface itself. Put simply, *if it walks like a duck and quacks like a duck, then it's a duck*:

```
class DuckRace
  duck: (contestant) ->                              If it has a call property,
    contestant.quack?.call and contestant.walk?.call then it can be invoked.
  constructor: (applicants...) ->                    See section 6.4.4.
    @ducks = (applicant for applicant in applicants when @duck applicant)

duck =
  name: 'Daffy'
  quack: ->
  walk: ->

cow =
  name: 'Daisy'
  moo: ->
  walk: ->

race = new DuckRace duck, cow
race.ducks
# [ { name: 'Daffy', quack: [Function], walk: [Function] } ]
```

Without types, how do you have confidence that your program works correctly? You get confidence by writing tests. Good tests for the `DuckRace` class will show how it should be used and demonstrate that it works correctly when used as intended. There's more about testing in chapter 10.

> **Postel's law**
>
> *Be conservative in what you do; be liberal in what you accept from others.*
>
> Duck typing means you're liberal in what you accept. What you accept only has to adhere to an interface.

In listing 7.4 you see a new version of the competition program. This time teams can be added dynamically. The competition organizes a tournament between teams where the winner of each game is determined randomly. Without relying on a type system, any object that can't act like a team for the purposes of the competition is excluded. This listing is intended to run in a web browser; you can use the server from listing 7.5 to achieve that.

Listing 7.4 Competition

```
makeCompetition = ({max, sort}) ->
  POINTS_FOR_WIN = 3
  POINTS_FOR_DRAW = 1
  GOALS_FOR_FORFEIT = 3

  render = (team) ->
  find = (name) ->
  color = (element, color) ->
  insert = (teams...) ->
  highlight = (first, rest...) ->
  rank = (unranked) ->

  competitive = (team) ->
    team?.players is 5 and team?.compete()?

  blankTally = (name) ->
    name: name
    points: 0
    goals:
      scored: 0
      conceded: 0
  roundRobin = (teams) ->
    results = {}
    for teamName, team of teams
      results[teamName] ?= blankTally teamName
      for opponentName, opponent of teams when opponent isnt team
        console.log "#{teamName} #{opponentName}"
        results[opponentName] ?= blankTally opponentName
        if competitive(team) and competitive(opponent)
          # omitted
        else if competitive team
          # omitted
        else if competitive opponent
          # omitted
```

Uppercase constants as convention, but not really constants (see chapter 13 for more on constants and the const keyword in ECMAScript 6).

These functions appear in listing 7.3 and are omitted here for brevity.

Duck type. Determine if a team has enough players and competes.

Provide a blank object to tally scores on.

The roundRobin function loops through the teams and plays them all against each other once.

Code for adding the scores and goals is included in the source. It's omitted here because it's boring and not helpful for understanding the concepts.

```
      results

  run = (teams) ->
    scored = (results for team, results of roundRobin(teams))
    ranked = rank scored
    console.log ranked
    insert ranked...
    first = ranked.slice(0, 1)[0]
    rest = ranked.slice 1
    highlight first, rest...

  { run }

sortOnPoints = (a, b) ->
  a.points > b.points

class Team
  constructor: (@name) ->
  players: 5
  compete: ->
    Math.floor Math.random()*3

window.onload = ->
  competition = makeCompetition(max:5, sort: sortOnPoints)

  disqualified = new Team "Canaries"
  disqualified.compete = null

  bizarros = ->
  bizarros.players = 5
  bizarros.compete = -> 9

  competition.run {
    wolverines : new Team "Wolverines"
    penguins: { players: 5, compete: -> Math.floor Math.random()*3 }
    injured: injured
    sparrows: new Team "Sparrows"
    bizarros: bizarros
  }
```

Convert the object into an array of its values.

The Team class.

A team created with the Team class that doesn't compete. Doesn't meet the interface.

A function with the properties added. Does meet the interface.

A team created with the Team class that does meet the interface.

An object literal that meets the interface.

No typeof is required. Instead, the teams are tested to see whether they have the properties required for something to be considered a team *for the purposes of the competition*. Another function or module elsewhere in the program could have different expectations of what a team is. Types are not built in. Instead, consider the local requirements for objects and use them to determine whether all objects are suitable.

Surely typeof is used sometimes in CoffeeScript?

Yes. The typeof operator is sometimes useful for distinguishing between built-in types. If you're writing library code, you may have good reason to determine if something is typeof function, object, string, or number. For anything else, steer clear of typeof.

Duck typing is a way of thinking. In a dynamic language like CoffeeScript that doesn't enforce types, you don't look at the type but instead look at the actual object you're dealing with. With duck typing you can express programs naturally in CoffeeScript.

Finally, the following listing provides a server that you can use to experiment with the browser code in listings 7.1 through 7.4.

Listing 7.5   The server

```coffee
http = require 'http'
fs = require 'fs'
coffee = require 'coffee-script'

render = (res, head, body) ->
  res.writeHead 200, 'Content-Type': 'text/html'
  res.end """
    <!doctype html>
    <html lang=en>
      <head>
        <meta charset=utf-8>
        <title>Chapter 7</title>
        <style type='text/css'>
        * { font-family: helvetica, arial, sans-serif; }
        body { font-size: 120%; }
        .teams td { padding: 5px; }
        </style>
        #{head}
      </head>
      <body>
        #{body}
      </body>
    </html>
  """

listing = (id) ->
  markup =
    1: """
      <ul class='teams'>
      </ul>"""
    2: """
      <ul class='teams'>
      </ul>"""
    3: """
      <table class='teams'>
        <thead>
          <tr>
            <th>Team</th><th>Points</th><th>Scored</th><th>Conceded</th>
          <tr>
        </thead>
      </table>"""
    4: """
      <table class='teams'>
        <thead>
          <tr>
            <th>Team</th><th>Points</th><th>Scored</th><th>Conceded</th>
```

```coffeescript
            <tr>
          </thead>
        </table>"""
    script =
      1: "<script src='1.js'></script>"
      2: "<script src='2.js'></script>"
      3: "<script src='3.js'></script>"
      4: "<script src='4.js'></script>"

    head: script[id], body: markup[id]

routes = {}

for n in [1..6]
  do ->
    listingNumber = n
    routes["/#{listingNumber}"] = (res) ->
      render res, listing(listingNumber).head, listing(listingNumber).body
    routes["/#{listingNumber}.js"] = (res) ->
      script res, listingNumber

server = http.createServer (req, res) ->
  handler = routes[req.url] or (res) ->
    render res, '', '''
      <ul>
        <li><a href="/1">Listing 7.1</a></li>
        <li><a href="/2">Listing 7.2</a></li>
        <li><a href="/3">Listing 7.3</a></li>
        <li><a href="/4">Listing 7.4</a></li>
      </ul>
    '''
  handler res

script = (res, listing) ->
  res.writeHead 200, 'Content-Type': 'application/javascript'
  fs.readFile "7.#{listing}.coffee", 'utf-8', (e, source) ->
    if e then res.end "/* #{e} */"
    else res.end coffee.compile source

server.listen 8080, '127.0.0.1'
```

So, what else did you zoom through in earlier chapters? Comprehensions! It's now time to revisit comprehensions and explore their use.

7.5   *When to use comprehensions (and when not to)*

Comprehensions provide a natural and powerful syntax for dealing with elements in arrays and properties of objects. You'll recognize this simple comprehension for even numbers:

```coffeescript
evens = (num for num in [1..10] when num%2 == 0)
```

A comprehension is much easier to read than a JavaScript for loop:

```coffeescript
numbers = [1,2,3,4,5,6,7,8,9,10]
evens = []
```

```
for (var i = 0; i !== numbers.length; i++) {
  if(numbers[i]%2 === 0) {
  evens.push(numbers[i]);
}
```

That's not really a fair comparison with JavaScript, though. In recent years it has become more common in JavaScript to use array methods such as map, reduce, and filter instead of for loops:

```
evens = numbers.filter(function(item) {
  return item%2 == 0;
});
```

This works in CoffeeScript too:

```
evens = numbers.filter (item) -> item%2 == 0
```

So, if the array methods work in CoffeeScript, should you use them or should you use comprehensions? How do comprehensions compare to these array methods that JavaScript programmers have become more comfortable with? You'll explore that question in this section, learning where comprehensions are appropriate and where they're not.

> **Careful, the array methods are recent additions**
> New array methods such as map and filter are specified in the fifth edition of the ECMAScript specification. Some older web browsers don't support all features of the fifth edition. A compatibility table for ECMAScript 5 features, such as the new array methods, appears in table 13.2.

7.5.1 *map*

The map method is used to take an array and map it to a different array. Suppose you purchase a book for $10, a toaster for $50, and a printer for $200. The tax rate is 10%. If you have these prices in an array, how do you calculate the tax paid on each item? With a comprehension, you do this:

```
paid = [10, 50, 200]
taxes = (price*0.1 for price in paid)
# [1, 5, 20]
```

In JavaScript this is done with the array map method (Array::map). This technique can be expressed directly in CoffeeScript:

```
taxes = paid.map (item) -> item*0.1
# [1, 5, 20]
```

Which one you use is largely a matter of preference.

7.5.2   *filter*

Suppose you have an array of your friends' addresses, and you want to know which ones live in `'CoffeeVille'`:

```
friends = [
  { name: 'bob', location: 'CoffeeVille' },
  { name: 'tom', location: 'JavaLand' },
  { name: 'sam', location: 'PythonTown' },
  { name: 'jenny', location: 'RubyCity' }
]
```

You can find out with a filter:

```
friends.filter (friend) -> friend.location is 'CoffeeVille'
```

This looks similar when expressed using a comprehension:

```
friend for friend in friends when friend.location is 'CoffeeVille'
```

There's no clear-cut winner. Does this means that comprehensions are overrated? Suppose you have an array of your friends in a variable named `mine`:

```
mine = ['Greg Machine', 'Bronwyn Peters', 'Sylvia Rogers']
```

Consider this to be your set of friends. Now, suppose you spark up a conversation at a party, and you want to know if you have any friends in common with the person you're talking to. Consider the set of their friends to be named `yours`; the solution with a comprehension is elegant:

```
common = (friend for friend in mine when friend in yours)
```

It's no coincidence that this set relationship is elegantly expressed using a comprehension because the syntax for comprehensions is based on a mathematical notation for describing sets. So if you're dealing with sets, comprehensions are a natural fit.

How about the last of the three favorites of JavaScript programmers: `reduce`?

7.5.3   *reduce*

Imagine you're a loan shark—people owe you money. How do you calculate the total amount you're owed? An array of two people who owe you money is easy to add up just by looking at it or by explicitly adding the two values:

```
friends = [
  { name: 'bob', owes: 10 }
  { name: 'sam', owes: 15 }
]
total = friends[0].owes + friends[1].owes
# 25
```

What if you loaned money to a thousand people? You'd use a comprehension:

```
owed = 0
for friend in friends
  owed += friend.owes
```

The built-in `Array::reduce` also works:

```
owing = (initial, friend) ->
  if initial.owers then initial.owes + friend.owes
owed = friends.reduce owing
```

It isn't clear if the comprehension is better. Comprehensions are useful, but they're not the only technique to consider. Comprehensions also have some gotchas you need to be aware of. The first involves functions.

7.5.4 *Defining functions inside comprehensions*

When using comprehensions, you need to be careful about scoping because there's a mistake you can easily make even when you know how comprehensions work.[2] In the snippet that follows, what will be the output of the last line? You might be surprised at the answer; try it on your REPL:

```
people = [ 'bill', 'ted' ]
greetings = {}

for person in people
  greetings[person] = ->
    "My name is #{person}"

greetings.bill()
```

Why does the final expression here evaluate to `'My name is ted'`? You see, functions have access to variables via lexical scope regardless of when they're invoked. Here, there's only one `person` variable in scope. Once the comprehension has run, it will contain the last value assigned to it and not the value it had when the function was declared.

If you *really* need to define a function inside a comprehension and have it access some value from inside the comprehension, then you'll need to create a new lexical scope with another function:

```
people = [ 'bill', 'ted' ]
greetings = {}

for person in people
  do ->
    name = person
    greetings[name] = ->
      "My name is #{name}"

greetings.bill()
# My name is bill
```

> Now the function(s) assigned to greetings[name] will close over the name variables created for each one. Revisit chapter 3 later if you're still not entirely comfortable with closures and how they close over variables.

In contrast, if you use a `forEach` for this example, then you avoid the problem because you're creating a function scope by default:

```
people.forEach (name) -> greetings[name] = "My name is #{name}"
```

---

[2] I made one of these mistakes while preparing the listings for this very chapter.

A comprehension that needs a scope probably shouldn't be a comprehension.

> **A note on generators**
> Future versions of JavaScript (and by extension CoffeeScript) will include something called *generators* (discussed in chapter 13) that will make comprehensions a more powerful general programming tool. Until that day, though, limit comprehensions to expressing set relationships and use more general-purpose programming constructs, such as functions, elsewhere.

The next piece of syntax used often in JavaScript that needs a discussion in relation to CoffeeScript is the fluent interface. Used by many libraries, including the popular jQuery, the fluent interface is a staple of any JavaScript diet.

7.6   *Fluent interfaces*

What's a fluent interface? It's a chain of method calls on a single object:

```
scruffy.eat().sleep().wake()
```

It's a bit like a function composition (chapter 6) except that all the function calls act on a particular object. In this section you'll see why fluent interfaces are useful, how to create them, the issues with indentation and side effects, and finally how to create a fluent wrapper for an object that wasn't designed to have one.

7.6.1   *Why create them?*

Imagine you're helping Scruffy create some animations for an in-browser game called *turt.ly*. He's using an API that Agtron created that allows him to animate the turtle, but he laments that the API is a smidge silly because the class it provides has only four methods: forward, rotate, move, and swap:

```
class Turtle
  forward: (distance) ->
    # moves the turtle distance in the direction it is facing
    this
  rotate: (degrees) ->
    # rotates the turtle 90 degrees clockwise
    this
  move: ({direction, distance}) ->
    # moves the turtle in a given direction
    this
  stop: ->
    # stops the turtle
```

The reason for making the methods evaluate to this is explained later in this section.

The forward method is invoked with an integer that specifies how far forward the turtle should move. The rotate method takes an integer that is the number of degrees that the turtle should rotate *clockwise*—by turning right. To make the turtle walk around a 10 x 10 square, Scruffy has to give it seven commands:

```
turtle = new Turtle
turtle.forward 10
turtle.rotate()
turtle.forward 10
turtle.rotate()
turtle.forward 10
turtle.rotate()
turtle.forward 10
```

When asked about this, Agtron suggests that Scruffy can extend the API by adding a square method to the prototype (see chapter 5):

```
Turtle::square = (size) ->
  @forward size
  @rotate()
  @forward size
  @rotate()
  @forward size
  @rotate()
  @forward size
```

Notice that when adding a square method, you use the @ symbol to invoke a method on the turtle object that the method was invoked on.

Or with brevity:

```
Turtle::square = (size) ->
  for side in [1..4]
    @forward size
    @rotate 90
```

The square method has made making squares easier. But Scruffy still complains that when he wants to draw two squares he has to keep "saying" *turtle*:

```
turtle = new Turtle
turtle.square 4
turtle.forward 8
turtle.square 4
```

He says this is how his math teacher used to talk to him:

> Scruffy, pay attention.
> Scruffy, stop monkeying around.
> Scruffy, go stand outside.
> Scruffy, go to the principal's office.

How can you avoid sounding like Scruffy's math teacher? In JavaScript you might be tempted to use the with statement:

```
turtle = new Turtle();

with(turtle) {
  left();
  forward();
}
```

This example is JavaScript.

But the `with` statement hides variable scope and makes your program ambiguous:

```javascript
address = '123 Turtle Beach Road';
with (turtle) {
  rotate(90);
  address = '55 Dolphin Place';
}
```

**Is that the address variable
or the address property of
the turtle object?**

The `with` statement can make programs confusing. It's been deprecated in JavaScript, and CoffeeScript doesn't have a `with` statement at all. Instead, fluent interfaces provide a solution without the ambiguity. When used with CoffeeScript's significant indentation, though, fluent interfaces do have potential for ambiguity. So before moving on, it's important to understand why that happens and how to avoid it.

7.6.2 *The indentation problem*

In CoffeeScript you need to be careful about indentation when using a fluent interface. If you're not careful, you might get some unexpected results. Imagine for a minute that *you* wrote the CoffeeScript compiler—what would you consider to be the meaning of chained syntax when parentheses are omitted?

```coffeescript
turtle = new Turtle
turtle
.forward 2
.rotate 90
.forward 4
```

**What do you
expect this means?**

Should there be any difference between that and a chained syntax with different indentation?

```coffeescript
turtle
  .forward 2
  .rotate 90
  .forward 4
```

**What do you
expect this means?**

They compile to the same thing. Should they? Much more importantly, versions *before* CoffeeScript 1.7 will compile both of these examples in a way you might not expect. Here's how CoffeeScript 1.6.3 compiles it:

```javascript
turtle.forward(2..rotate(90..forward(4)));
```

**Compiled JavaScript for
the previous examples.**

That will result in the error `Object 90 has no method forward` in JavaScript. With the potential for problems, what style *should* you use with fluent interfaces?

FLUENT INTERFACES WITH PARENTHESES

It's safest to use fluent interfaces *with parentheses and all flush left*:

```coffeescript
turtle = new Turtle
turtle
.forward(2)
.rotate(90)
.forward(4)
```

**Note that compilation will
put it on one line and add
a semicolon at the end.**

That said, indenting method calls in a fluent method call chain is very common in other languages, so you'll frequently see this written so:

```
turtle = new Turtle
turtle
  .forward(2)
  .rotate(90)
  .forward(4)
```

Although the former (flush left) is cleaner (semantically), you should get used to seeing the latter (indented) style. If you're passing an object to a chained method, it's possible to skip the parentheses by indenting arguments:

```
NORTH = 0
turtle = new Turtle
turtle
.move
  direction: NORTH          Invoking the move method with
  distance: 10              an object that has direction and
.stop()                     distance properties
```

This is helpful, and it helps to make the earlier competition examples easier to read:

```
makeCompetition
  max: 5
  sort: ->

makeCompetition
  sort: ->
  max: 5
```

This is useful for object parameters, but in most other cases you should avoid arguments on newlines.

FLUENT INTERFACES WITHOUT PARENTHESES

The minimalist inside you thinks that a fluent interface with parentheses seems wasteful and looks exactly like the equivalent JavaScript:

```
turtle
.forward(3)
.rotate(90)
.forward(1)
```

The good news is that if you're using CoffeeScript 1.7 or later, the compiler will recognize fluent interfaces with parentheses omitted so that the same expression without the parentheses has the same result:

```
turtle
.forward 3
.rotate 90
.forward 1
```

Since CoffeeScript 1.7 the preceding code will compile to the following JavaScript:

```
turtle.forward(2).rotate(90).forward(4);    ◁—— Compiled JavaScript
```

As long as you keep the indentation consistent, you can pick whichever indentation level you prefer, and the compiler will close the parentheses on fluent call chains for you, so the following also works:

```
turtle
  .forward 3
  .rotate 90
  .forward 1
```

You can think of the dot on the newline as closing all and only implicit calls. It does not close other function calls:

```
wait = (duration, callback) ->
  setTimeout callback, duration

wait 5, ->
  turtle
    .forward 10
    .forward 3
```

A dot on a newline does not close the callback function passed to wait.

In CoffeeScript 1.7 the function call and fluent chain compile as follows:

```
wait(5, function() {
  return turtle.forward(1).rotate(90);
});
```

Compiled JavaScript.

Now, back to Scruffy's API work and how a fluent interface makes life easier for him.

7.6.3 *Creating fluent interfaces*

If you're creating an API from scratch, then a fluent interface requires a specific usage of this (a.k.a. @). Remember, inside a method call, @ refers to the current object (the receiver of the method call). Consider what it means to use @ as the final value in a method:

```
class Turtle
  rotate: (degrees) ->
    # rotate the turtle
    @
```

It doesn't matter how the turtle is rotated.

Return the turtle.

Because @ on a line by itself at the end of a function looks a bit lonely, you'll often see the this keyword used instead:

```
class Turtle
  rotate: (degrees) ->
    # rotate the turtle
    this
```

Using this as the final value in a method returns the object that received the method call. So, if you return this, then method calls can be chained:

```
turtle = new Turtle
turtle.rotate(90).rotate(90)
```

If you're creating your own API, you can use this technique to make it fluent. You don't always write the API, though; oftentimes you only use it. For example, Scruffy didn't write the API for the turtle, but he has to use it. How can he use it with a fluent interface?

7.6.4 *Chain*

Not everything that can benefit from a fluent interface actually has one. Many of the APIs provided by web browsers are like this. Take the canvas API, for example. The canvas is covered in more detail in chapter 11, but for now you only need to know that it provides some drawing capabilities to web browsers, a little bit like the turtle:

```
canvas = document.getElementById 'example'
context = canvas.getContext '2d'
context.fillRect 25, 25, 100, 100
context.strokeRect 50, 50, 50, 50
```

Get an element to use as the canvas.

Create a context to draw on.

Fill in a rectangle.

Stroke the outside of the rectangle.

See how you have to repeat the context every time, just like Scruffy had to repeat turtle? Instead of living with that, you can make your own fluent interface out of this nonfluent interface. Remember that with statement from JavaScript? You can declare something roughly similar in CoffeeScript using the apply method on a function:

```
using = (object, fn) -> fn.apply object

using turtle, ->
  @forward 2
  @rotate 90
  @forward 4
```

Close, but not quite the same. You (and Scruffy) really want a fluent interface that chains method calls:

```
chain(turtle)
.forward(2)
.rotate(90)
.forward(4)
```

Before CoffeeScript I.7

```
chain turtle
.forward 2
.rotate 90
.forward 4
```

CoffeeScript I.7 and later

To do this you need to create a chain function that takes an object and returns a fluent interface of the object's methods. This is one of those cases where you need Agtron's help. The implementation of chain that he helps you create and an example of using it are shown in the following listing. If you don't understand exactly how it works, then it's okay to move on and come back to it later.

Listing 7.6 The chain function

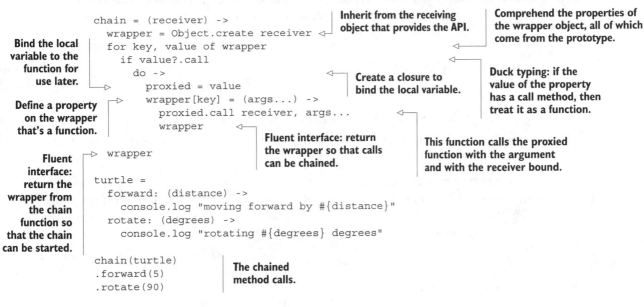

Bind the local variable to the function for use later.

Define a property on the wrapper that's a function.

Fluent interface: return the wrapper from the chain function so that the chain can be started.

```
chain = (receiver) ->
  wrapper = Object.create receiver
  for key, value of wrapper
    if value?.call
      do ->
        proxied = value
        wrapper[key] = (args...) ->
          proxied.call receiver, args...
        wrapper
  wrapper

turtle =
  forward: (distance) ->
    console.log "moving forward by #{distance}"
  rotate: (degrees) ->
    console.log "rotating #{degrees} degrees"

chain(turtle)
.forward(5)
.rotate(90)
```

Inherit from the receiving object that provides the API.

Comprehend the properties of the wrapper object, all of which come from the prototype.

Create a closure to bind the local variable.

Duck typing: if the value of the property has a call method, then treat it as a function.

Fluent interface: return the wrapper so that calls can be chained.

This function calls the proxied function with the argument and with the receiver bound.

The chained method calls.

By providing some syntactic sugar, CoffeeScript can make more-advanced JavaScript techniques a bit more manageable. This sugar doesn't come for free, though; sometimes it can make things ambiguous.

7.7 Ambiguity

Removing parts can make things simpler, but it can also sometimes make them ambiguous. Removing words and symbols from a programming language is no different. To effectively create simple programs, you need to understand where there's potential for ambiguity so that you can avoid it. In CoffeeScript the most common areas where people accidentally create ambiguity are with significant indentation and implicit variable declarations.

7.7.1 Whitespace and indentation

All whitespace looks the same. Lack of visual variety means that you need to take care to make sure programs written in a language with significant indentation aren't ambiguous. You got a hint of this earlier with the turtle:

```
NORTH = 0

turtle
.move
  direction: NORTH
  distance: 10
.stop()
```

When reading this program, it's important to notice that the move method is being invoked with an object that has `direction` and `distance` properties. Now consider a `makeTurtle` function that makes and returns an object:

```
makeTurtle = ->
  move: ->
    # move the turtle
    this
  stop: ->
```

Again, when reading the code you need to pay attention. It's not just an object containing a `stop` property that's returned; it's an object with a `stop` property *and* a move property. How do you avoid this ambiguity?

ADD CHARACTERS TO AVOID AMBIGUITY

Suppose you have a function that returns an array of objects containing information about your friends. It's tempting to leave out all the squiggly braces and end up with something like this:

```
friends = ->
    name: 'Bob'
    address: '12 Bob Street Bobville'
  ,
    name: 'Ralph'
    address: '11 Ralph Parade Ralphtown'
```

Sometimes, though, including the square and squiggly brackets makes it easier to read:

```
friends = ->
  [{
    name: 'Bob'
    address: '12 Bob Street Bobville'
  },
  {
    name: 'Ralph'
    address: '11 Ralph Parade Ralphtown'
  }]
```

This might not seem to be in the spirit of CoffeeScript, but the general rule should be that if you need to look at the compiled JavaScript to figure out if your Coffee-Script syntax is correct, then there's a good chance it's ambiguous. How about those parentheses?

ONLY FUNCTION DECLARATION PARENTHESES HAVE SPACES

When invoking a function, there should be no space before the first parenthesis. No.Space.Ever! Although many syntax questions are a matter of taste, this one is not:

```
clarity = (important) ->
clarity()
```

When declaring, spaces on outside of the parentheses

When invoking, no space before the left parenthesis

When invoking a function, having no parentheses or putting them around the outside works fine:

```
(clarity 10)     ◁─┐  Parentheses outside
clarity 10    ◁─┐  No parentheses
```

But you should never put a space before the parentheses when invoking. It's confusing, broken, and looks too similar to a function being invoked with a callback argument:

```
clarity (10)     ◁─┐  Don't do this          ┌─ The clarity function being invoked with
clarity (x) -> x                    ◁─┘     another (likely a callback) function
```

Finally, a note on subsequent function calls.

ADD PARENTHESES FOR SUBSEQUENT FUNCTION CALLS

Suppose you have three functions, x, y and z, and you invoke them as follows:

```
x y z 4
```

By glancing at it, in what order do you think they're being invoked? Adding parentheses shows you:

```
x(y(z(2)))
```

Even if you got it right this time, it's almost guaranteed that unparenthesized function calls will catch you out in CoffeeScript at least once sometime in the future. To avoid the problem, it's best to add some parentheses any time the expression might be ambiguous. Remember, you shouldn't have to refer to the generated JavaScript to understand what a CoffeeScript program is supposed to do. If it looks ambiguous, then you need to rewrite it. As figure 7.2 shows, you should stick to common language

Figure 7.2 Stick to common language patterns, but be careful of ambiguity.

idioms, but be mindful of anything that might be ambiguous to you later, to the compiler, or to other people who have to work on your program.

One final area for potential confusion is in the way CoffeeScript implicitly declares variables for you.

7.7.2   *Implicit variables*

Remember that variables are declared for you, implicitly, the first time a variable name is used. If a variable name is already defined *anywhere* in the current lexical scope (including outer functions), then that variable is used. This is unlike the var keyword in JavaScript, which will create a variable in the current function scope regardless of whether a variable with the same name exists somewhere in the current lexical scope (such as an outer function). If your programs consist of small modules (as discussed in chapter 12) and you don't have deeply nested lexical scopes, then this implicit variable declaration is unlikely to cause you any pain.

If implicit variables become a problem for you, or if you simply don't like implicit variable declarations, then you can easily get around the absence of shadowing by taking advantage of the fact that function parameters *always* shadow and create local variables with a do expression:

```
x = 5

do (x) ->                   Using a do expression, you can have an
  x = 3                     explicit, local variable that can't clobber
  console.log x             any outer variable when assigned.

console.log x

# 3
# 5
```

This approach gives you a new way of writing a function that has variable names that shadow outer scopes:

```
shadowing = do (x) -> (y) ->
  x = 3
  x + y

shadowing 5
# 8
```

If you use a do expression in this way, then either there must be an outer variable that you want to shadow by assignment inside the do expression or you must assign a value in the parameters for the do expression:

```
do (notPreviouslyDefined) -> notPreviouslyDefined = 9
# ReferenceError: notPreviouslyDefined is not defined

do (notPreviouslyDefined='') -> notPreviouslyDefined = 'It is now'
# 'It is now'
```

Outside the do expression, the variable is still not defined:

```
notPreviouslyDefined
# ReferenceError: notPreviouslyDefined is not defined
```

Unfortunately, the syntax to achieve variables that shadow is a little clunky by Coffee-Script standards. Still, given that function parameters shadow the do expression, you can have local variables and can even approximate a future feature of JavaScript called let that you'll learn about in chapter 13. Until then, that's all there is on syntax.

7.8   *Summary*

CoffeeScript not only simplifies JavaScript's core syntax but also provides some syntactic sugar that can make programs easier to understand. Spread and rest parameters and destructuring provide the means to write concise expressions where long and confusing expressions (and statements) would otherwise be required. The syntax changes that CoffeeScript makes to JavaScript make programming more expressive and succinct.

Although CoffeeScript changes JavaScript's syntax dramatically, it makes only very small changes to JavaScript's semantics. You saw how to make the most natural use of CoffeeScript's dynamic types by learning to use duck typing.

Finally, succinctness of expression is a trade-off, and there is some potential for ambiguity in CoffeeScript. You learned how comprehensions and significant whitespace can be clarified and looked closely at how the common technique of fluent interfaces can be applied in CoffeeScript programs.

Moving on, as expressive and succinct as CoffeeScript is, the syntax and semantics of CoffeeScript have been decided for you. To have full control over the expressive power of the language you use, you need to be able to manipulate the language itself—you need metaprogramming, and that's exactly what the next chapter is about.

Metaprogramming 8

This chapter covers

- Learning about literate CoffeeScript
- Constructing domain-specific languages
- Writing programs that write programs
- Being metacircular: CoffeeScript in CoffeeScript

The term *metaprogramming* is often used to refer to any programming technique sufficiently complicated that you should think thrice before using it. This chapter is *not* about writing complicated programs. Metaprogramming is also often used to refer to the use of metaobjects, where you create objects that create objects. This chapter is not about programming metaobjects—you were already working with metaobjects back in chapter 5. So, then, what is this chapter about?

The most succinct description of metaprogramming is *programs that write programs*. That's what this chapter is about. More importantly, this chapter is about changing the way you think about your programs and the language you write them in. To begin thinking differently, you'll start by swapping programs with program explanations through *literate CoffeeScript*. Next, you'll explore the *creation* of mini-programming languages as domain-specific languages (DSLs). Finally, you'll look at programs that write programs and at how you can change the language you work in by using the CoffeeScript compiler from inside a CoffeeScript program.

8.1 Literate CoffeeScript

In literate programming, as first explained by Donald Knuth,[1] the visible structure of the program source isn't the structure of the executable program. Instead, the visible structure of the program is an explanation of the program in another language. Interspersed code snippets make up the executable program. Inspired by the idea of literate programming, the CoffeeScript compiler supports source files where explanation determines the structure of the source code.

Imagine that Agtron is trying to organize a birthday party for Scruffy. He sends you emails about it, but every time you leave your computer unattended, Scruffy reads your email and finds out what's going on. As a deterrent to Scruffy reading the emails, Agtron wants a simple disguise for all of his emails so that Scruffy will have difficulty reading them. One simple way to disguise messages is by using a cipher called Rot13.

Rot13 is a simple letter-substitution cipher that replaces a letter with the letter 13 letters after it in the alphabet. The built-in string utility for getting character codes can be used. If the character is in the alphabet up to *m*, then add 13 to the character code. If the character is after *m* in the alphabet, then subtract 13 from the character code. Characters can be converted back using the built-in string method. A character is in a specific range regardless of whether it's uppercase or lowercase. Finally, converting a string is done by converting all the characters and joining the results.

With literate CoffeeScript you use the *description* of a program, such as a description of Rot13, as the basis for the program itself. To differentiate them from regular CoffeeScript programs, literate CoffeeScript programs are contained in files with a special extension.

8.1.1 The .litcoffee file extension

Source code contained in a file with a .litcoffee extension is considered a literate CoffeeScript program by the compiler. The key difference between a regular CoffeeScript program and a literate CoffeeScript program is that the comments and the program are reversed. Instead of marking comments with #, you leave the comments raw and indent all of the executable code:

hello.coffee

```
###
Log 'Hello world!' to the console
###

console.log 'Hello World!'
```

hello.litcoffee

```
Log 'Hello world!' to the console

    console.log 'Hello World!'
```

---

[1] Donald Knuth is a computer scientist who is sometimes referred to as the father of the analysis of algorithms. His book *Literate Programming* was published in 1992.

As a further example, consider a literate CoffeeScript program using an excerpt from W. B. Yeats's poem "The Wild Swans at Coole":

```
W B Yeats
The Wild Swans at Coole

The trees are in their autumn beauty,

    trees = [{}, {}]
    for tree in trees
      tree.inAutumnBeauty = yes

The woodland paths are dry,

    paths = [{}, {}, {}]
    for path in paths
      path.dry = yes

Under the October twilight the water
Mirrors a still sky;

    octoberTwilight = {}
    stillSky = {}
    water =
      placeUnder: ->

    water.placeUnder octoberTwilight
    water.mirrors = stillSky

Upon the brimming water among the stones
Are nine-and-fifty swans.

    water.brimming = true
    water.stones = [{}, {}, {}, {}]

    class Swan
      x: 3

    for n in [1..59]
      water.stones.push new Swan
```

By writing the explanation first, you are forced to ponder how well the executable program matches the explanation. In other words, writing the explanation first can change how you think about your program.

Is it *really* literate programming?

Although Donald Knuth's literate programming inspired literate CoffeeScript, important aspects of Knuth's description are missing. That shouldn't discourage you from taking full advantage of it, though.

Literate CoffeeScript files aren't just for exploring poetry. A description of a program can serve as the starting point for creating a literate-style CoffeeScript program. Back to that Rot13 program then, how do you implement that with literate CoffeeScript?

Take the explanation of Rot13 and put it into a .litcoffee file. Then implement the program by putting *indented* program source throughout the explanation. The following listing shows a Rot13 program developed in exactly this way.

Listing 8.1 Literate CoffeeScript Rot13

Explanation of the program is flush left.

Implementation of the program is indented.

```
## Rot13
A simple letter-substitution cipher that replaces a letter
with the letter 13 letters after it in the alphabet.

    charRot13 = (char) ->

The built-in string utility for getting character codes can be used

        charCode = char.charCodeAt(0)

If the character is in the alphabet up to 'm', then
add 13 to the character code

        charCodeRot13 = if charInRange char, 'a', 'm'
          charCode + 13

If the character is after 'm' in the alphabet, then
subtract 13 from the character code

        else if charInRange char, 'n', 'z'
          charCode - 13
        else
          charCode

Characters can be converted back using the built-in string method

        String.fromCharCode charCodeRot13

A character is in a specific range regardless of whether
it's uppercase or lowercase

    charInRange = (char, first, last) ->
      lowerCharCode = char.toLowerCase().charCodeAt(0)
      first.charCodeAt(0) <=  lowerCharCode <= last.charCodeAt(0)

Converting a string is done by converting all the characters
and joining the results

    stringRot13 = (string) ->
      (charRot13 char for char in string).join ''
```

A literate CoffeeScript file is also valid syntax for Markdown. This means that any text formatter that understands Markdown (there are many libraries for generating HTML that understand Markdown) can turn your program into a nicely formatted document.

If you prefer tests (discussed in chapter 10) and self-documenting code over comments, then you might not find the style of literate CoffeeScript to suit your taste for many programs. But even if literate CoffeeScript isn't to your taste, you still share the motivation to write programs that are well explained. That motivation also drives the invention of domain-specific languages.

8.2   *Domain-specific languages*

CoffeeScript is a general-purpose programming language. It may be better suited to some tasks than to others, but the *intention* is that it can be used to solve any programming problem. In contrast, the intention of a DSL is to solve a particular type of problem.

This goes hand in hand with the idea that you should describe your program how you like and then worry about the implementation later. The way you *like* to describe your program may be a natural language such as English, a general-purpose programming language like CoffeeScript, or a more focused DSL designed to solve specific problems.

In this section you'll learn the difference between internal and external DSLs; different techniques for creating internal DSLs using object literals, fluent interfaces, and functions; and finally how to approach the construction of an internal DSL.

8.2.1   *External DSLs*

Imagine for a minute that CSS doesn't exist. How would you use CoffeeScript to style elements in a simple HTML document?

```
<html>
<p>
It is <strong>very</strong> important that you understand this...
</p>
```

Making text contained in a `<strong>` element bold and red could be done by directly manipulating those properties:

```
strongElements = document.getElementsByTagName 'strong'
for strongElement in StrongElements
  strongElement.fontWeight = 'bold'
  strongElement.color = 'red'
```

That would quickly get tedious. You could create a better syntax out of that, perhaps by declaring style rules with objects and then using those objects to style the elements:

```
strongStyle:
  fontWeight: 'bold'
  color: 'red'

strongElements = document.getElementsByTagName 'strong'
for strongElement in StrongElements
  for styleName, styleValue of strongStyle
    strongElement[styleName] = styleValue
```

With the object syntax, you very quickly arrive at syntax very similar to CSS. The limited vocabulary and small number of features make CSS a DSL. Although CSS is an entire language (an *external* DSL), a mini-language with a limited vocabulary is often useful in other contexts where an entire standalone language would be too time-consuming to implement. For those cases, you can create internal DSLs.

8.2.2 Internal DSLs

One well-known example of utilizing a DSL is the popular jQuery framework. Instead of directly using the APIs designed for DOM manipulation, jQuery provides a DSL that simplifies things. Another common use of an internal DSL is in a testing framework. For example, suppose you want to test if an array contains a particular item. Using only the assert module for Node.js works, but you might not find it expressive enough:

```
assert = require 'assert'
haystack = [1..900]
needle = 6
assert needle in haystack
```

The built-in assert module throws an exception when an assertion fails. When it succeeds, as it did here, then there's no output (the output is undefined).

How about testing that a string contains another string?

```
assert 'fundamental'.indexOf('fun') >= 0
```

That works too. But all your tests are phrased in terms of the assertion library, which might not be very comprehensible to you when writing or reading tests. Testing frameworks often hide these things behind a convenient DSL that makes sense in a testing domain:

```
expect('fundamental').to.contain 'fun'
```

This is a minor shift, and for this example it's actually more verbose. So why do it? It makes life easier for users. The more control you have over the language, the more power you have to create with it.

The most common approach to creating DSLs in CoffeeScript comes from JavaScript, and that's to use a fluent interface. You don't have to use a fluent interface, though, because CoffeeScript syntax is sparse.

8.2.3 Object literals

With very little in the way of syntax, CoffeeScript object literals are a useful tool for creating internal DSLs. Imagine Agtron standing next to your desk, coffee in hand. "There's a law," he states, "known as Zawinski's law, that 'Every program attempts to expand until it can read mail.'" If you'll eventually need to write a program that deals with email, you might as well get some practice now.

Consider the format of the exchange between a client and a server using the Simple Mail Transfer Protocol (SMTP). In the following example, client requests are in bold and server responses are in regular-weight font:

```
HELO coffeescriptinaction.com
250 OK
MAIL FROM: scruffy@coffeescriptinaction.com
250 OK - mail from <scruffy@coffeescriptinaction.com>
RCPT TO: agtron@coffeescriptinaction.com
250 OK - Recipient <agtron@coffeescriptinaction.com>
DATA
354 Send data.  End with CRLF.CRLF
Hi Agtron. Just Scruffy testing SMTP.

250 OK QUIT
```

An example of communication between a server and client using SMTP

You *might* implement your SMTP library by emulating the protocol:

```
class Smtp
  constructor: ->
  connect: (host, port=25) ->
  send: (message, callback) ->
```

Would you expect users to adopt this interface?

```
smtp = new Smtp
smtp.connect 'coffeescriptinaction.com'
smtp.send 'MAIL FROM: scruffy@coffeescriptinaction.com', (response) ->
  if response.contains 'OK'
    smtp.send 'RCPT TO: agtron@coffeescriptinaction.com', (response) ->
```

What's the problem with that? For one thing, it looks worse than the raw SMTP. The users of your API don't even care how SMTP works or indeed whether their email is delivered using SMTP at all. Worse, you're forcing users to either flatten your API calls themselves or live in nested callback hell. Not good, but what can you do instead?

Have some empathy and approach the problem as a user. How should it look? How do *you* want to define and send an email?

```
scruffysEmail = new Email
  to: ''
  from: ''
  body: '''

  '''

scruffysEmail.send()
```

This is simpler. Notice how any mention of SMTP is absent? A user doesn't care about how SMTP works; they just want to send an email. It's up to the mail library to determine how to connect to SMTP. Instead of copying the format of the protocol, copy the format that makes sense to people who use your library. Write the program in the language of the user.

The next listing shows this technique in action. This listing requires a dependency called simplesmtp, so if you intend to run it directly, you should first install the dependency:

```
> npm install simplesmtp
```

Once the dependency is installed, you can run the listing.

Listing 8.2   An object literal–based DSL for email (email.coffee)

```
simplesmtp = require 'simplesmtp'          ⟵  A library called simplesmtp is
                                               used to handle SMTP details.
class Email
  SMTP_PORT = 25                               Class variables       Shorthand
  SMTP_SERVER = 'coffeescriptinaction.com'     (chapter 5).          constructor
  constructor: ({@to, @from, @subject, @body}) ->  ⟵                 (chapter 5).
```

```
send: ->
  @client = simplesmtp.connect SMTP_PORT, SMTP_SERVER
  @client.once 'idle', ->
    @client.useEnvelope
      from: @from
      to: @to

  @client.on 'message', ->
    client.write """
    From: #{@from}
    To: #{@to}
    Subject: #{@subject}

    #{@body}

    """
    client.end()
```

> The send method uses simplesmtp to connect, wait until the connection is ready, and then send the message.

Using the library provided by listing 8.2 doesn't require the user to know SMTP:

```
scruffysEmail = new Email
  to: 'agtron@coffeescriptinaction.com'
  from: 'scruffy@coffeescriptinaction.com'
  subject: 'Hi Agtron!'
  body: '''

This is a test email.

  '''
```

> Invoke the constructor with an object literal representing the email to send.

```
scruffysEmail.send()
# { to: 'agtron@coffeescriptinaction.com',
#   from: 'scruffy@coffeescriptinaction.com',
#   subject: 'Hi Agtron!',
#   body: '\nThis is a test email. \n                       ' }
# Error: connect ETIMEDOUT
```

> There is no SMTP server on the domain coffeescriptinaction.com, so this request will fail.

Apart from object literals, what other ways are there to create a DSL in CoffeeScript?

8.2.4 Fluent interfaces

Object literal syntax works well for DSLs in CoffeeScript but not so well in JavaScript because with all the braces ({}) and semicolons (;), JSON tends not to feel very much like a language. This means that object literal DSLs are clunky in JavaScript, so if your CoffeeScript library will be used from inside a JavaScript program (quite likely), you should consider a different approach to your DSL by using a fluent interface (as discussed in chapter 7):

```
scruffysEmail = new Email
scruffysEmail
.to('agtron@coffeescriptinaction.com')
.from('scruffy@coffeescriptinaction.com')
.body '''

Hi Agtron!

'''
```

```
scruffysEmail.send (response) ->
  console.log response
```

An implementation of this fluent-style DSL appears in the following listing.

Listing 8.3   A fluent interface–based DSL for email

```
simplesmtp = require 'simplesmtp'

class Email
  SMTP_PORT = 25
  SMTP_SERVER = 'coffeescriptinaction.com'
  constructor: (options) ->
    ['from', 'to', 'subject', 'body'].forEach (key) =>
      @["_#{key}"] = options?[key]
      @[key] = (newValue) ->
        @["_#{key}"] = newValue
        @

  send: ->
    client = simplesmtp.connect SMTP_PORT, SMTP_SERVER
    client.once 'idle', ->
      client.useEnvelope
        from: @_from
        to: @_to
    client.on 'message', ->
      client.write """
      From: "#{@_from}"
      To: #{@_to}
      Subject: #{@_subject}

      #{@_body}

      """
      client.end()
    @

scruffysEmail = new Email()

scruffysEmail
.to('agtron@coffeescriptinaction.com')
.from('scruffy@coffeescriptinaction.com')
.subject('Hi Agtron!')
.body '''

  This is a test email.

'''

scruffysEmail.send()
```

This constructor makes the fluent interface possible by dynamically adding from, to, subject, and body methods to the instance of Email that's created. Each of these methods sets a corresponding variable on the instance when invoked.

Each dynamically added method must return the current object to enable a fluent interface.

When sending the message, properties on the object that were set by invoking the methods are used.

A fluent interface in action: with an instance of Email, the methods calls can be chained.

Finally, CoffeeScript syntax supports a third way to create nice-looking DSLs.

8.2.5 *Function passing*

The option of omitting parentheses from function calls means that a DSL can be created in CoffeeScript using function composition only (discussed in chapter 6). This has the benefit of allowing a natural-looking DSL made entirely from function names. For example, consider a send function that accepts another function as the parameter:

```
send = (next) ->
  http.send next()

email = ->
```

The syntax is appealing:

```
send email (body 'Hi Agtron') to 'agtron@coffeescriptinaction.com'
```

Unfortunately, a DSL that uses function composition only is generally limited to a single line because of significant indentation. To get multiple lines, you might have to resort to using parentheses and line-continuing backslashes:

```
send email \
(body 'Hi Agtron!')\
(to 'agtron@coffeescriptinaction.com')
```

That makes DSLs based purely on the techniques of function composition a bit clunky in CoffeeScript. That said, there are other ways to use functions for DSLs more effectively, one of which you'll see in the examples that follow.

8.2.6 Constructing a DSL

The lack of syntactic noise in CoffeeScript has meant that people attracted to the notion of writing DSLs have flocked to the language. Here are some examples of domains for which DSLs have been created in CoffeeScript and an accompanying syntax example that's easily implemented in CoffeeScript. Implementing handlers for HTTP requests has been omitted here simply because you have, by now, seen it so many times that it would be rather uninteresting.

HTML

There are three basic ways that programmers deal with HTML from inside their own languages: templates, hooks, and language DSLs that allow them to compose HTML entirely inside their program. One way to compose HTML inside CoffeeScript is with a small DSL:

```
loggedIn = -> true

doctype 5
html ->
    body ->
      ul class: 'info', ->
        li -> 'Logged in' if loggedIn()
```

Here's the HTML generated by this CoffeeScript DSL (with newlines and indentation added for readability):

```
<!DOCTYPE html>
<html>
  <body>
    <ul class='info'>
      <li>Logged in</li>
```

The nice thing about this approach to HTML is that you have the full power of Coffee-Script in your HTML. In the next listing you can see a basic implementation of this HTML DSL that supports a subset of HTML elements.

```
doctype = (variant) ->
  switch variant
    when 5
      "<!DOCTYPE html>"

markup = (wrapper) ->
  (attributes..., descendents) ->
    attributesMarkup = if attributes.length is 1
      ' ' + ("#{name}='#{value}'" for name, value of attributes[0]).join ' '
    else
      ''
    "<#{wrapper}#{attributesMarkup}>#{descendents() || ''}</#{wrapper}>"

html = markup 'html'
body = markup 'body'
ul = markup 'ul'
li = markup 'li'
```

In this example, only a single doctype is supported.

Attributes for the HTML element are contained in all of the parameters except for the last one, which is always reserved for a function containing any nested HTML elements.

The implementation in listing 8.4 supports only a very small subset of elements. But it does demonstrate how well the CoffeeScript syntax can be formed to match your needs. A similar approach can be applied to CSS.

CSS

CSS has traditionally adhered to the principle of least power. Unfortunately, over time least power has turned into insufficient power for many people. The most common approach to tackling the problem has been writing CSS preprocessors such as Less and Sass. CoffeeScript is also a preprocessor, so at a basic level, Sass is to CSS as Coffee-Script is to JavaScript.

An alternative approach to a preprocessor is to embed a DSL in CoffeeScript:

```
emphasis = ->
    fontWeight: 'bold'

css
  'ul':
    emphasis()
  '.x':
    fontSize: '2em'
```

Invoke the css function with the object literal that follows.

The output from this DSL is corresponding CSS:

```
ul {
  font-weight: bold;
}
.x {
  font-size: 2em;
}
```

The need to quote CSS selectors by putting them in strings makes the CoffeeScript DSL more awkward than raw CSS. In the following listing you can see an implementation of a small DSL for CSS.

Listing 8.5 A basic DSL for CSS

```
css = (raw) ->
  hyphenate = (property) ->
    dashThenUpperAsLower = (match, pre, upper) ->
      "#{pre}-#{upper.toLowerCase()}"
    property.replace /([a-z])([A-Z])/g, dashThenUpperAsLower

  output = (for selector, rules of raw              #B
    rules = (for ruleName, ruleValue of rules
      "#{hyphenate ruleName}: #{ruleValue};"
    ).join '\n'
    """
    #{selector} {
      #{rules}
    }
    """
  ).join '\n'
```

> CSS attributes use dashes, but only camel case is possible in CoffeeScript. This function converts camel case property names to hyphenated property names.

The final novel DSL you will look at is an SQL DSL in CoffeeScript.

SQL

With CoffeeScript's liberal syntax, it's tempting to attempt an SQL DSL that looks just like regular SQL by endlessly chaining functions:

```
SELECT '*' FROM 'users' WHERE 'name LIKE "%scruffy%"'
```

But SQL syntax is a little more complicated than you might think, and when you mix that with CoffeeScript's significant indentation, it can get ugly. The simplest way to implement an SQL DSL in CoffeeScript is to use the object literal style:

```
query
  SELECT: '*'
  FROM: 'users'
  WHERE: 'name LIKE "%scruffy%"'
```

Remember, property values can be evaluated at runtime. This can be powerful, but it might make your DSL too permissive:

```
query
  SELECT: '*'
  FROM: 'users'
  WHERE: "name LIKE '%#{session.user.name}%'"
```

What if `session.user.name` contains something that should never appear in an SQL query? Correct handling of SQL connections, databases, and queries is complicated. When you create a DSL, be careful that what you create is appropriate to the *domain*.

Writing internal DSLs not only means bending the language to fit your needs but also means writing programs that target the needs of users, instead of focusing on implementation details that users don't care about. What could be better than a program that's easy to write? A program that you don't have to write at all! How do you achieve this? Instead of writing programs all the time, you write programs that write other programs. There's one program you already use that does this for you—it's called the CoffeeScript compiler.

8.3   How the compiler works

The CoffeeScript compiler is written in CoffeeScript. The first CoffeeScript compiler was written in Ruby, but since version 0.5 the compiler has been implemented in CoffeeScript. That's right, CoffeeScript is compiled using CoffeeScript, something you should spend some time to ponder, as Scruffy does in figure 8.1. The diagram that Scruffy is holding in figure 8.1 is called a Tombstone Diagram (or T-Diagram). If you're interested in exploring compilers outside of this chapter, then you'll likely come across more of them.

Creating the initial compiler for a new language in an existing language and then using the new language to create another compiler that can compile the new language (and the compiler itself!) is known as *bootstrapping* a compiler. You need to know this about the CoffeeScript compiler because you're about to make some changes to it.

Figure 8.1   The CoffeeScript compiler is written in CoffeeScript.

Imagine that one night you're drinking a coffee and relaxing with Scruffy and Agtron. Scruffy jokes that he'd like the function syntax for CoffeeScript to look like lambda calculus:

```
I = (x) -> x
I = λx.x
```

The current CoffeeScript function syntax

The syntax Scruffy wants CoffeeScript to support

Scruffy laments that if only he had real macros in CoffeeScript, he could do what he likes. Agtron pauses, looks at Scruffy, and remarks, "Why don't you just modify Coffee-Script? You could call your custom extension *ScruffyCoffee*."

Use the source

The annotated source code for CoffeeScript is available online. Because CoffeeScript is written in CoffeeScript, you will, by now, be able to read it comfortably:

http://coffeescript.org/documentation/docs/coffee-script.html

To navigate to other parts of the documented source, use the Jump To link at the top right of the online CoffeeScript documentation pages.

In order to make changes to the CoffeeScript compiler, you first need to understand what it does. As with many things in CoffeeScript, you can understand much of this by experimentation on the REPL. At a high level, the CoffeeScript compiler understands the CoffeeScript you provide it by first splitting it into tokens, performing some rewrites on those tokens, and then creating an abstract syntax tree that's a representation of your CoffeeScript program. Figure 8.2 demonstrates the high-level steps that the CoffeeScript 1.6 compiler takes.

To get a basic grasp of this process for CoffeeScript, consider the simple part of the CoffeeScript syntax that Scruffy wants to change: function syntax. The basic expression

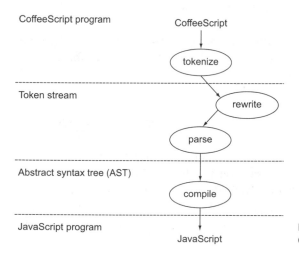

Figure 8.2   The internal CoffeeScript compilation process

that you'll examine in the CoffeeScript compiler is the identity function assigned to a variable I:

```
I = (x) -> x
```

The first thing the compiler must do is convert this string (input stream) to tokens.

Compiler versions

The CoffeeScript compiler version described here is CoffeeScript 1.6.2, so depending on the version of the compiler you have, the results you get when inspecting the compiler may be different (particularly regarding the things that get rewritten). But the general structure of the compiler will be the same, regardless of the version you're using.

8.3.1   Tokenizing

During compilation, the first step is to use a *lexer* to covert the input into an array of tokens known as the token stream. Consider the tokens that the identity function assignment expression produces:

```
coffee = require 'coffee-script'

expression = 'I = (x) -> x'

coffee.tokens expression
#   [[ 'IDENTIFIER', 'I'],
#    [ '=', '='],
#    [ 'PARAM_START', '('],
#    [ 'IDENTIFIER', 'x'],          These tokens have
#    [ 'PARAM_END', ')'],           been modified to
#    [ '->', '->'],                 show only the token
#    [ 'INDENT', 2],                types and values.
#    [ 'IDENTIFIER', 'x'],
#    [ 'OUTDENT', 2],
#    [ 'TERMINATOR', '\n'] ]
```

The lexer has generated tokens that represent the string of CoffeeScript code it was invoked with. Here's a visual representation of how the tokens are broken down:

When tokenizing, it's common for a compiler to ignore some things like comments and specific characters by not generating any tokens for them. Here, whitespace in the middle of the line has been ignored. In addition to skipping characters, the CoffeeScript compiler also modifies the token stream by adding tokens. Notice that the INDENT and OUTDENT tokens don't correspond to any indentation in the original source string. The *rewriter* has added these tokens.

8.3.2 *Rewriting*

The myriad of syntax options in CoffeeScript means that tokenizing and building an abstract syntax tree for everything is a complicated task. Because some of the syntax is mostly convenience, CoffeeScript also has a rewriter that will modify the token stream. The rewriting done by the compiler is described here.

IMPLICIT INDENTATION

One of the things that you've just seen is that the rewriter adds implicit indentation. For example, when you write a function inline, the rewriter assumes that you meant it *with* indentation:

```
I = (x) -> x
```

The [INDENT] in the token stream is placed before the function body:

```
I = (x) ->[INDENT]x
```

Notice that indentation doesn't require a newline. Of course, in practice you always *think* of indentation as being accompanied by a preceding newline because that's the only way you can write it.

NEWLINES

The rewriter also removes some leading and mid-expression newlines:

```
a = 1
b = 2
```

Any important newline, such as one that indicates the end of an expression (a terminator) is preserved:

```
a     =    1      \n      a    =    2       \n
```

IDENTIFIER = NUMBER TERMINATOR IDENTIFIER = NUMBER TERMINATOR

Further rewrites are performed for braces and parentheses.

BRACES AND PARENTHESES

In most places, parentheses and braces are optional. This is convenient but can leave room for some ambiguity. The simplest way for the compiler to deal with these issues is with the rewriter:

```
I = (x) -> x
I 2
```

These common cases where parentheses are implicit and should be added are easy to see:

IDENTIFIER   CALL_START   NUMBER   CALL_END   TERMINATOR

But more complicated examples can be difficult to discern. How do you tokenize this doozy?

```
f ->
  a
.g b, ->
  c
.h a
```

Probably you *don't* tokenize it because you avoid writing code like that. Although you have the option to avoid writing ambiguous code, the compiler doesn't have the same luxury. It must reliably accommodate the different styles, edge cases, and incidentally complex syntax of many programmers. Thus, the full rewriter for braces and parentheses is complicated. Finally, postfix conditionals need some special treatment by the rewriter.

POSTFIX

A postfix conditional such as `play 'football' unless injured` is convenient syntactic sugar but it poses a problem for the compiler, because it reads backwards. To deal with this, the CoffeeScript compiler tags postfix conditionals:

```
play          (      'football'    )      unless    injured        \n
```

IDENTIFIER   CALL_START   STRING   CALL_END   POST_IF   IDENTIFIER   TERMINATOR

Why does the CoffeeScript compiler do all this rewriting? Because rewriting simplifies the next compilation step.

8.3.3 *The abstract syntax tree*

Once the compiler has a token stream, it's ready to use it to create an abstract syntax tree (AST). Whereas the token stream represents the syntax of the program, the AST represents the meaning of the program in terms of the rules of the CoffeeScript grammar. Going back to the simple function expression for which Scruffy wants to provide an alternative syntax, what does the AST for that look like? To get the AST you invoke `coffee.nodes` with either a string of CoffeeScript or a CoffeeScript token stream:

```
coffee = require 'coffee-script'

expression = 'I = (x) -> x'

tokens = coffee.tokens expression

coffee.nodes tokens
# { expressions:
#   [ { variable: [Object],
#       value: [Object],
#       context: undefined,
#       param: undefined,
#       subpattern: undefined } ] }
```

The default string representation of an object on the REPL lacks some details important for understanding what's going on here. By using JSON.stringify and formatting the result, you can better see the AST:

```
console.log JSON.stringify coffee.nodes, null, 2
```

Now you see the AST object for the I = (x) -> x expression:

```
{
  "expressions": [
    {
      "variable": {
        "base": {
          "value": "I"
        },
        "properties": []
      },
      "value": {
        "params": [
          {
            "name": {
              "value": "x"
            }
          }
        ],
        "body": {
          "expressions": [
            {
              "base": {
                "value": "x"
              },
              "properties": []
            }
          ]
        },
        "bound": false
      }
    }
  ]
}
```

Figure 8.3 contains a graphical representation of this AST. It demonstrates a remarkable uniformity and can give new insight into the nature of some expressions. For example, a function is a value with params and a body.

Now that you understand the tokens that are generated from your source code and the AST that's generated from the tokens, you're equipped to modify either (or both) of them to dynamically modify CoffeeScript source inside your CoffeeScript program. What does this mean? It means you can shape your program source to better match your ideas.

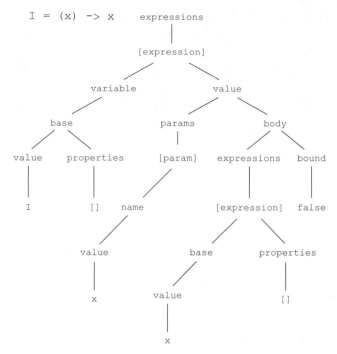

Figure 8.3   An example abstract syntax tree

8.4   *Bending code to your ideas*

To *really* create a language you need to be able to modify the syntax. Although the internal DSL-making potential of CoffeeScript means you can create mini-languages for some tasks, you're still fundamentally constrained to what CoffeeScript syntax accepts.

In order to stretch the language itself, you need to be able to modify it. For a compiled language like CoffeeScript, that means you need to intercept the compiler somehow. To do this you can either work with the compiler at the token or AST stage, or you can place something before or after the compiler. The easiest (though not the most sensible) way to do this is to just preprocess source code using `eval`.

8.4.1   *Can you just eval?*

JavaScript has an `eval` function that takes a string of JavaScript code and executes it in the running program. The string of code is evaluated as if you had written it directly into the program. For example, `var` declarations will go into the current scope. Try it on the Node JavaScript REPL:

```
node> eval('var x = 2');
node> x
node> # 2
```

The use of `eval` is considered dangerous because the code is executed with the privileges of the caller. This means that anything you `eval` can do anything that can be done at the point the `eval` was invoked. The `eval` function is dangerous, but it's certainly interesting.

The CoffeeScript compiler also has an eval method that compiles and evaluates a string of program code. The difference with the eval provided by the CoffeeScript compiler (apart from the fact that it evaluates CoffeeScript) is that by default it sandboxes the code that it evaluates by running it in a separate context. The evaluation of the eval call is the evaluation of the code contained in the string:

```
coffee = require 'coffee-script'
coffee.eval '2'
# 2

evaluation = coffee.eval '2 + 4'
# 6

evaluation
# 6
```

But any variables in the evaled string are only defined in the sandbox:

```
coffee.eval '''
x = 1
y = 2
x + y'''
# 3

x
# Reference Error: x is not defined

y
# Reference Error: y is not defined
```

Still, the CoffeeScript eval allows you to execute arbitrary snippets of CoffeeScript code at runtime. Further, because it's a string that you pass to the eval function, you can generate that string any way you like:

```
coffee = require 'coffee-script'

x = 42
y = coffee.eval "#{x} + 3"

y
# 45
```

This suggests an easy way to get Scruffy's syntax. Use a regular expression to replace his expression with an equivalent function:

```
coffee = require 'coffee-script'

scruffyCode = '''
I = λx.x
'''

coffeeCode = scruffyCode.replace /λ([a-zA-Z]+)[.]([a-zA-Z]+)/g, '($1) -> $2'
identity = coffee.eval coffeeCode
identity 2
#2

hello = identity (name) -> "Hello #{name}"
# [Function]
```

```
hello 'Scruffy'
# 'Hello Scruffy'
```

In the listing that follows, you can see a tiny command-line CoffeeScript program that can execute a .scruffycoffee file using this technique. A .scruffycoffee file is simply a CoffeeScript program that also supports Scruffy's desired λ syntax.

> **Listing 8.6 ScruffyCoffee with `eval` and regular expressions**

```
fs = require 'fs'
coffee = require 'coffee-script'

evalScruffyCoffeeFile = (fileName) ->
  fs.readFile fileName, 'utf-8',(err, source) ->
    coffeeCode = source.replace /λ([a-zA-Z]+)[.]([a-zA-Z]+)/g,'($1) -> $2'
    coffee.eval coffeeCode

fileName = process.argv[2]
unless fileName
  console.log 'No file specified'
  process.exit()
evalScruffyCoffeeFile fileName
```

Manipulating strings often means heavy use of regular expressions. They're powerful and succinct, but for complicated tasks they can become difficult (or impenetrable) for others to read.

Imagine the possibilities when you can evaluate arbitrary snippets of code. Now, stop imagining the possibilities and consider instead your responsibility to write comprehensible programs. Still, the presence of `eval` means you can metaprogram to your heart's content with just a bit of string interpolation. Apart from the dangers, CoffeeScript isn't very well suited for this.

The regular expression and `eval` solution aren't really workable, and the program in listing 8.6 is very limited due to the simplicity of the regular expression. As you try to make the regular expression more complete, you'll realize that you're essentially just poorly reimplementing the CoffeeScript tokenizer for no good reason. Instead, you'll be better off modifying the token stream or the AST.

8.4.2 *Rewriting the token stream*

A slightly less quick-and-dirty way to metaprogram (compared to evaluating strings) is to directly modify the token stream before the AST is generated. By doing that, you're adding your own rewriter to the compilation process. Remember Scruffy's desired syntax?

```
I = λx.x
```

How is it tokenized now?

```
I       =      λx       .       x         \n
⇑       ⇑       ⇑       ⇑       ⇑          ⇑
IDENTIFIER  =  IDENTIFIER  .  IDENTIFIER  TERMINATOR
```

Your rewriter will need to see the λ symbol and know that it needs to rewrite the rest of the expression to a function:

```
coffee = require 'coffee-script'

scruffyCoffee = '''
I = λx.x
'''

tokens = coffee.compile scruffyCoffee

i = 0
while token = tokens[i]
  # handle token
  i++
```

> If the token is a λ, then rewrite expression to a function.

In the next listing you can see a new implementation of ScruffyCoffee that uses a custom rewriter instead of a nasty-looking regular expression.

Listing 8.7   Custom rewriter

```
fs = require 'fs'
coffee = require 'coffee-script'

evalScruffyCoffeeFile = (fileName) ->
  fs.readFile fileName, 'utf-8', (error, scruffyCode) ->
    return if error
    tokens = coffee.tokens scruffyCode

    i = 0
    while token = tokens[i]
      isLambda = token[0] is 'IDENTIFIER' and /^λ[a-zA-Z]+$/.test token[1]
      if isLambda and tokens[i + 1][0] is '.'
        paramStart = ['PARAM_START', '(', {}]
        param = ['IDENTIFIER', token[1].replace(/λ/, ''), {}]
        paramEnd =   ['PARAM_END', ')', {}]
        arrow = ['->', '->', {}]
        indent = ['INDENT', 2, generated: true]
        tokens.splice i, 2, paramStart, param, paramEnd, arrow, indent
        j = i
        while tokens[j][0] isnt 'TERMINATOR'
          j++
        outdent = ['OUTDENT', 2, generated: true]
        tokens.splice j, 0, outdent
        i = i + 3
        continue
      i++
    nodes = coffee.nodes tokens
    javaScript = nodes.compile()
    eval javaScript

fileName = process.argv[2]
process.exit 'No file specified' unless fileName
evalScruffyCoffeeFile fileName
```

> **Loop through all the tokens. When a λ is encountered, the remainder of the tokens that make up the expression must be converted to an equivalent CoffeeScript function, including the correct indent levels.**

Messing around with the token stream is difficult, potentially dangerous, and overall not a whole lot of fun. Luckily, there's a more structured representation of your Coffee-Script program that you can manipulate—the AST.

8.4.3 *Using the abstract syntax tree*

The next option available to you for implementing Scruffy's lambda syntax is to modify the abstract syntax tree in place before generating JavaScript. The AST is excellent for analyzing source code.

MODIFYING PROGRAMS

Imagine it's opposites day and you want addition to replace subtraction (and vice versa) in your CoffeeScript program. How can you swap them? By manipulating the AST! First, use the compiler to generate an AST for the expression 2 + 1:

```
coffee = require 'coffee-script'
nodes = coffee.nodes '2 + 1'
```

The node for this addition expression has an `operator` and `first` and `last` properties representing the left and right sides of the operator, respectively:

```
addition = nodes.expressions[0]
addition.operator
# '+'

addition.first.base.value
# '2'

addition.second.base.value
# '1'
```

When you compile these nodes you get the JavaScript you expect:

```
nodes.compile bare: true
# 'return 2 + 1;'
```

Now, if you change a node, you'll change the compiled output:

```
addition.operator = '-'
nodes.compile bare: true
# 'return 2 - 1'
```

Great! You know how to manipulate the AST, but what can you *actually do* with that?

GENERATING CODE

Imagine you're working in a team and they don't write tests. In the following listing you can see a basic implementation of using the AST to generate files that contain tests for class methods. This same technique could be used dynamically to look at code coverage.

Listing 8.8 Generating method tests via the AST

```
fs = require 'fs'
coffee = require 'coffee-script'

capitalizeFirstLetter = (string) ->
  string.replace /^(.)/, (character) -> character.toUpperCase()

generateTestMethod = (name) ->
  "test#{capitalizeFirstLetter name}: -> assert false"
```

```
walkAst = (node) ->
  generated = "assert = require 'assert'"

  if node.body?.classBody
    className = node.variable.base.value
    methodTests = for expression in node.body.expressions
      if expression.base?.properties
        methodTestBodies = for objectProperties in expression.base.properties
          if objectProperties.value.body?
            generateTestMethod objectProperties.variable.base.value
        methodTestBodies.join '\n\n  '
    methodTestsAsText = methodTests.join('').replace /^\n/, ''
    generated += """
      \n
      class Test#{className}
        #{methodTestsAsText}

      test = new Test#{className}
      for methodName of Test#{className}::
        test[methodName]()
    """

  expressions = node.expressions || []
  if expressions.length isnt 0
    for expression in node.expressions
      generated = walkAst expression
  generated

generateTestStubs = (source) ->
  nodes = coffee.nodes source
  walkAst nodes

generateTestFile = (fileName, callback) ->
  fs.readFile fileName, 'utf-8', (err, source) ->
    if err then callback 'No such file'
    testFileName = fileName.replace '.coffee', '_test.coffee'
    generatedTests = generateTestStubs source
    fs.writeFile "#{testFileName}", generatedTests, callback 'Done'

fileName = process.argv[2]

unless fileName
  console.log 'No file specified'
  process.exit()

generateTestFile fileName, (report) ->
  console.log report
```

Listing 8.8 works on a file containing a class. Consider a file called elephant.coffee containing a class declaration:

```
class Elephant
  walk: ->
    'Walking now'
  forget: ->
    'I never forget'
```

When listing 8.8 is invoked with elephant.coffee, it generates a corresponding test class:

```
> coffee 8.8.coffee elephant.coffee
> # Generated elephant_test.coffee
```

The generated test file contains test stubs for all of the methods on the class:

```
assert = require 'assert'

class TestElephant
  testWalk: -> assert false

  testForget: -> assert false

test = new TestElephant
for methodName of TestElephant::
  test[methodName]()
```

The AST is an excellent source of information about a program. Using the AST and a corresponding grammar is how the CoffeeScript compiler generates your JavaScript program. What's a grammar? Agtron is glad you asked. The *grammar* is the definition for the semantic structure of the language. The grammar determines how the parser interprets the token stream. All 1.x versions of the CoffeeScript compiler use the Jison parser-generator (http://jison.org), so that's a good place to start. If you want a new language, you should probably start from a clean slate. At heart, CoffeeScript is just JavaScript.

8.4.4   *It's just JavaScript*

Amid all the excitement of modifying the CoffeeScript compiler to support whatever syntax takes your fancy on a given day, it's easy to lose sight of the wider ecosystem. You see, it's important that your CoffeeScript programs are still *just JavaScript*. Sure, JavaScript is increasingly becoming a compilation target for a wide range of different languages, but the power of CoffeeScript lies in only doing cleanups and being a small step from JavaScript for those people who want minimal syntax and can live with significant indentation.

Thus, Scruffy's syntax using the λ character is probably not something you'd do in practice. But support for the upcoming JavaScript let syntax (discussed in chapter 13) *is* something that you might want to add:

```
let x = 3
  console.log x
  # 3

console.log x
# ReferenceError: x is not defined
```

Listing 8.9 shows Scruffy's implementation of ScruffyCoffee that supports let by using a rewriter. This listing is invoked with an input file containing a let expression:

```
if true
  let x = 2, y = 2
  console.log 'let expression'
  console.log 'wraps block in closure'
```

The generated JavaScript uses a function closure to approximate a `let`:

```
var ok;

ok = require('assert').ok;

if (true) {
  (function(x, y) {
    console.log('let expression');
    return console.log('wraps block in closure');
  })(2, 2);
}

ok(typeof x === "undefined" || x === null);

ok(typeof y === "undefined" || y === null);
```

Scruffy achieved the function closure by rewriting the token stream so that the `let` expression is replaced with a `do` that has the `let` variables as parameters. Any code at the same level of indentation as the `let` is then scoped inside the `let`:

```
do (x = 2, y = 2) ->
  console.log 'let expression'
  console.log 'wraps block in closure'
```

Scruffy's implementation of `let` is limited. It supports only one `let` per block and it must be the first line. Also, because `let` is a word reserved by the CoffeeScript compiler, Scruffy had to rewrite the raw source before passing it to the tokenizer.

Listing 8.9 Scruffy's `let` implementation using a custom rewriter

```
fs = require 'fs'
coffee = require 'coffee-script'

evalScruffyCoffeeFile = (fileName) ->
  fs.readFile fileName, 'utf-8', (error, scruffyCode) ->
    letReplacedScruffyCode = scruffyCode.replace /\slet\s/, ' $LET '    ◁─── Replace let
    return if error                                                          keyword
    tokens = coffee.tokens letReplacedScruffyCode                            with the
                                                                             string
    i = 0                                                                    $LET.
    consumingLet = false
    waitingForOutdent = false
    while token = tokens[i]
      if token[0] is 'IDENTIFIER' and token[1] is '$LET'
        consumingLet = true                                    If there is a $LET in
        doToken = ['UNARY', 'do', spaced: true]                the token stream,
        tokens.splice i, 1, doToken                            convert it to a do.
      else if consumingLet
        if token[0] is 'CALL_START'
          paramStartToken = ['PARAM_START', '(', spaced: true]     The let variables
          tokens[i + 1][2] = 0                                     are passed in as
          tokens.splice i, 1, paramStartToken                      parameters to
        if token[0] is 'CALL_END'                                  the do.
          paramEndToken = ['PARAM_END', ')', spaced: true]
          functionArrowToken = ['->', '->', spaced: true]
```

The body of the do is indented.

```
      indentToken = ['INDENT', 2, generated: true]
      tokens.splice i, 2, paramEndToken, functionArrowToken, indentToken
      consumingLet = false
      waitingForOutdent = true
    else if waitingForOutdent
      if token[0] is 'OUTDENT' or token[0] is 'TERMINATOR'
        outdentToken = ['OUTDENT', 2, generated: true]
        tokens.splice i, 0, outdentToken
        waitingForOutdent = false
    i++

  nodes = coffee.nodes tokens

  javaScript = nodes.compile()
  eval javaScript

fileName = process.argv[2]
process.exit 'No file specified' unless fileName
    evalScruffyCoffeeFile fileName
```

The next unbalanced outdent must indicate the end of the current block. That's where the do must also be outdented.

As before, modifying the token stream is possible, but it can be risky and is definitely not for the faint of heart. Scruffy achieved his implementation of let by rewriting source before tokenization and by rewriting the token stream, but it would also be possible to manipulate the AST instead of using a token rewriter. It's *your* language, so for your circumstances it might make sense to completely change the syntax. You own the language.

8.5   Summary

Writing programs that write programs is what metaprogramming is all about. In this chapter you saw how literate CoffeeScript works and how it can change the way you think about program source. You then saw how to adapt existing CoffeeScript syntax and create domain-specific languages that provide a closer fit than plain CoffeeScript for certain types of problems. Finally, you saw how to modify CoffeeScript itself from inside a CoffeeScript program.

While learning what works in CoffeeScript, you also saw that CoffeeScript isn't a Lisp. The CoffeeScript compiler is written in CoffeeScript, but it doesn't have a meta-circular evaluator, and the eval function is mostly a distraction. Another way that CoffeeScript is not a Lisp is that it doesn't have macros. That said, there are moves to implement hygienic macros in JavaScript. If you're interested in that, then you should check out the sweet.js project (sweetjs.org). It's also possible to create macros for CoffeeScript, but that's a lesson for another day.

In the next chapter you'll look at how the existing CoffeeScript syntax and semantics work in asynchronous environments.

Composing
the asynchronous

9

> ## *This chapter covers*
> - The limits of processing data synchronously
> - How an event loop works and why you need to think asynchronously
> - Events as data and data as events
> - Event emitters and how to compose event streams

Remember imperative programs? They're a bit like the list of chores that Scruffy's mum used to leave him:

> Clean your room
> Take out the trash
> Do your homework
> No games until you finish your chores!

Scruffy could do the chores in any order, but he couldn't play until the chores were finished. If everything is synchronous, then games just go after chores:

```
chores()
games()
```

You've learned about things that are asynchronous. If Scruffy pays Agtron to do his chores, then he can start his games immediately. Unfortunately, if Agtron never finishes the chores, then Scruffy is in big trouble. You learned that the solution to this in CoffeeScript is to use a callback:

```
chores games
```

This is the equivalent of Scruffy asking Agtron to tell him when the chores are done so that he can start playing games. It's also the programming model used in almost all CoffeeScript programs.

Asynchronous programming changes the way that programs are structured. Further, not only are all programs in CoffeeScript asynchronous, but they also run on a single event loop. This presents unique challenges when you're writing programs.

In this chapter you'll start by processing some data synchronously and see how far you can get before a synchronous approach breaks down. Then you'll see how to write programs using an asynchronous approach and learn how to manage the challenges that asynchronous programming presents.

9.1   Data processing

All programs need to deal with data: reading data in, processing (usually), and writing data out. Although the most common way to read, process, and write is synchronously, the synchronous approach quickly breaks down in a CoffeeScript program due to the nature of the event loop. In this section you'll find out exactly why it breaks down and what you can do about it.

Imagine Agtron and Scruffy are organizing the World Volcano Mogul Skiing Championship. You're working with them to display the names of competitors, one per second, on electronic billboards placed strategically across the volcano tops. The names must be displayed in alphabetical order, but they're supplied in random order in a file called competitors with each line containing one competitor in the format *Competitor number: Last name, First name*:

```
0212: Turnbill, Geralyn
0055: Spielvogel, Cierra
0072: Renyer, Connie
0011: Engholm, Ciara
0088: Gitting, Estrella
```

The entire file contains 1,500 names. To sort the names, you'll first need to read the file into an array. Suppose you're using Node.js to do this, and that, without knowing any better, you're doing it synchronously. What happens?

9.1.1   Reading

It's possible to read a file synchronously in Node.js and then convert the response to an array:

```
fs = require 'fs'
raw = fs.readFileSync 'competitors', 'utf-8'
competitors = raw.split /\n/
```

But the standard approach is to read the file asynchronously and pass in a callback that's invoked when the file is read:

```
readFile = (file, callback) ->
  fs.readFile file, 'utf-8', (error, response) ->
    throw error if error
    callback response
```

Reading files asynchronously is the standard approach because doing things synchronously can have disastrous consequences, as you'll soon see.

A function to get an array of the competitors asynchronously invokes the `readFile` function with another callback function that converts the response to an array:

```
readFileAsArray = (file, callback) ->          ←─┤ Takes file to read
  asArray = (data, delimiter) ->                   │ and callback
    callback data.split(delimiter)    Splits string
  readFile(file, asArray)             on delimiter  ←─┤ Invokes readFile with
                                                       │ file and strategy
```

This function can be invoked with a callback that prints the resulting array:

```
readFileAsArray 'competitors', (result) ->
  console.log result
# ['0212: Turnbill, Geralyn'
# '0055: Spielvogel, Cierra'
# '0072: Renyer, Connie'
# '0011: Engholm, Ciara'
# '0088: Gitting, Estrella']
```

The asynchronous version might seem a bit inside out. So why bother doing things asynchronously? To appreciate this technique, try processing the data from the file.

9.1.2 Sorting

`Array::prototype` has a built-in `sort` method. When invoked with no arguments, the array is sorted in lexicographical order—like a dictionary:

```
[4,3,4,7,6].sort()
# [3,4,4,6,7]

['aardvark', 'zebra', 'porcupine'].sort()
# ['aardvark', 'porcupine', 'zebra']
```

Suppose you have the array of competitors assigned to a `competitors` variable:

```
competitors.sort()
# ['0011: Engholm, Ciara',
#  '0055: Spielvogel, Cierra',
#  '0072: Renyer, Connie',
#  '0088: Gitting, Estrella',
#  '0212: Turnbill, Geralyn']
```

You don't just want the competitors sorted lexicographically, though; you want them sorted lexicographically *by their last name.*

> ### Array::sort is destructive
>
> Note that `sort` is *destructive*. The original array is sorted *in place* and returned:
>
> ```
> sortedCompetitors = competitors.sort()
> sortedCompetitors is competitors
> # true
> ```
>
> Being destructive means that the built-in `sort` isn't well suited to function composition (discussed in chapter 6).

SORT COMPARATOR

To sort the competitors by last name, you first need a function that can compare competitors on their last name. This function takes two competitor names, determines their last names, and returns `-1` if the first competitor should come first or `1` if the second competitor should come first:

```
compareOnLastName = (competitors...) ->
  lastName = (s) ->                                        Get the last name.
    s.split(/\s/g)[1]
  if lastName(competitors[0]) > lastName(competitors[1])   Compare the
    1                                                        strings on the
  else                                                       last name.
    -1

compareOnLastName "0212: Turnbill, Geralyn", "0072: Renyer, Connie"
# 1
```

When you invoke `sort` with `compareOnLastName`, the array is sorted, ordering the elements:

```
competitors.sort compareOnLastName
# ["0011: Engholm, Ciara"
#  "0088: Gitting, Estrella"
#  "0072: Renyer, Connie"
#  "0455: Spielvogel, Cierra"
#  "0212: Turnbill, Geralyn"]
```

This sorting is synchronous. There's no callback—no way to say "go off and sort this array and let me know when it's done." It works, though, and a program that reads the competitors file, sorts the competitors on last name, and serves the sorted array wrapped in JSON ready to be used for the billboards is provided in the following listing.

Listing 9.1 Displaying names sorted on a field inefficiently

```
fs = require 'fs'
http = require 'http'

readFile = (file, strategy) ->
  fs.readFile file, 'utf-8', (error, response) ->
    throw error if error
    strategy response
```

```
readFileAsArray = (file, delimiter, callback) ->
  asArray = (data) ->
    callback data.split(delimiter).slice(0,-1)
  readFile(file, asArray)
```
Reads a file into an array by splitting on delimiter

```
compareOnLastName = (a,b) ->
  lastName = (s) ->
    s.split(/\s+/g)[1].replace /,/, ','
  if !a or !b
    1
  else if lastName(a) >= lastName(b)
    1
  else
    -1
```
Splits the competitor strings and compares

```
sortedCompetitorsFromFile = (fileName, callback) ->
  newline = /\n/gi
  readFileAsArray fileName, newline, (array) ->
    callback array.sort(compareOnLastName)
```
Reads the file as lines and passes sorted lines to callback

```
makeServer = ->
  responseData = ''
  server = http.createServer (request, response) ->
    response.writeHead 200, 'Content-Type': 'text/html'
    response.end JSON.stringify responseData
  server.listen 8888, '127.0.0.1'
  (data) ->
    responseData = data
```
Uses closure to keep data

```
main = (fileName) ->
  server = makeServer()

  loadData = ->
    console.log 'Loading data'
    sortedCompetitorsFromFile fileName, (data) ->
      console.log 'Data loaded'
      server data

  loadData()
  fs.watchFile fileName, loadData
```
loadData is invoked immediately and passed to file watcher

```
if process.argv[2]
  main process.argv[2]
  console.log "starting server on port 8888"
else
  console.log "usage: coffee 9.1.coffee [file]"
```
Deals with program arguments

Running the application with the competitors file containing 1,500 competitors serves the resulting JSON at http://localhost:8888/:

```
> coffee listing.91.coffee competitors.txt
Loading data
Starting server on port 8888
Data loaded
```

If you visit this page in a web browser, you'll see that the performance is fine. Nothing to worry about; the array is being sorted synchronously but it's not hurting the program—not yet anyway. It's tempting early on to assume that you only need to think asynchronous when reading things like files and network resources, but you soon find out that this is wrong. Read on.

9.1.3 *Performance*

Imagine now that Scruffy informs you there are not 1,500 competitors as anticipated but actually 150,000 competitors. He also says that he's using the program you wrote, and it takes a long time to sort the 150,000 competitors. The application freezes for several seconds each time it loads data. You need to figure out what's going on.

TIMING PROGRAMS

A crude but effective way to get a simple measurement of the time it takes for part of a program to execute is by using the built-in `Date` objects. To evaluate the time difference between two `Date` objects, you use subtraction:

```
begin = new Date          Create two objects
end = new Date            from Date class
difference = begin - end               Subtract earlier date
                                       from later date
```

With this, you can change the `loadData` function from listing 9.1 to show how long it takes to load data:

```
loadData = ->
  start = new Date()
  console.log 'Loading and processing data'
  sortedCompetitorsFromFile fileName, (data) ->
    elapsed = new Date() - start
    console.log "Data loaded in #{elapsed/1000} seconds"
    server data
```

It takes less than one-tenth of a second for 1,500 competitors, but for 150,000 competitors it takes 35 seconds! This is not simply due to sorting. Look how long it takes to sort an array of 150,000 numbers:

```
random = (size) -> Math.floor Math.random()*size           Generating an array of
random150000 = (random(150000) for number in [1..150000])  150,000 random numbers

begin = new Date
random150000.sort()
end = new Date              50 milliseconds (time
console.log end - begin     will vary on different
# 50                        computers)
```

The built-in `Array::sort` can sort 150,000 random numbers in milliseconds, not seconds like your competitor sorting. The slow sorting is caused by the comparison function. Why? Because the `compareOnLastName` function is slow. When the array is sorted, every item might need to be compared to every other item! That's more comparisons than you want to see written down, quite apart from the effect it has on the performance of your program. To avoid this problem, your first thought is to optimize the sorting to be fast enough.

9.1.4 *Decorate, sort, undecorate*

It's always faster to do nothing than to do something. Consider what the *something* is that happens inside the `compareOnLastName` function:

```
compareOnLastName = (a,b) ->
  lastName = (s) ->
    s.split(/\s+/g)[1].replace /,/, ''
  if !a or !b
    1
  else if lastName(a) >= lastName(b)
    1
  else
    -1
```

Last name occurs after the first space.

Return 1 if either last name is missing.

Two last names are extracted for each comparison, which is expensive and unnecessary because the last name only needs to be determined *once* for each competitor. That can be done before any sorting occurs. A technique known as *decorate-sort-undecorate*, which uses this idea, is demonstrated here.

Listing 9.2 Decorate-sort-undecorate

```
decorateSortUndecorate = (array, sortRule) ->
  decorate = (array) ->
    {original: item, sortOn: sortRule item} for item in array

  undecorate = (array) ->
    item.original for item in array

  comparator = (left, right) ->
    if left.sortOn > right.sortOn
      1
    else
      -1

  decorated = decorate array
  sorted = decorated.sort comparator
  undecorate sorted
```

Convert the array of strings to an array of objects.

Inverse of the decorate function.

Sort using the sortOn property of the object created by the decorate function.

Decorate the array. **Run the sort.** **Undecorate the sorted array.**

The `decorate` function invoked with an array of strings containing competitor names returns an object with a `sortOn` property. This property contains the string used to compare the competitor to other competitors:

```
lastName = (s) -> s.split(/\s+/g)[1].replace /,/, ''
sortRule = (name) -> lastName name
decorate = (array) ->
  {original: item, sortOn: sortRule item} for item in array

decorate ['0011: Engholm, Ciara']
# [{original: '0011: Engholm, Ciara', sortOn: 'Engholm'}]
```

The `undecorate` function does the reverse. It takes an object created by `decorate` and returns the original string:

```
undecorate = (array) ->
  item.original for item in array

undecorate [{original: '0011: Engholm, Ciara', sortOn: 'Engholm'}]
# ['0011: Engholm, Ciara']
```

Now you can sort the array much faster. An example comparison between the performance with and without decorate-sort-decorate appears in table 9.1. Although actual results will vary significantly across different environments and computers, the decorate-sort-undecorate version is always substantially faster because it does less work.

Table 9.1 Performance improvement of decorate-sort-undecorate

Number of entries	Decorate-sort-undecorate	Original version
500	0.003 seconds	1.575 seconds
3,000	0.024 seconds	4.866 seconds
150,000	0.116 seconds	18.138 seconds

Decorate-sort-undecorate is a useful technique. Eliminating repeated computation of the same thing makes the array sorting perform fast enough to be acceptable without making the program freeze for a long time. It's just barely avoiding the problem, but sometimes avoiding the problem is exactly the right approach.

You can't always avoid the problem, though. CoffeeScript programs run on an event loop, and an event loop does only one thing at a time.

9.2 *Event loops*

CoffeeScript programs, whether on Node.js or in a web browser, are executed on a single-threaded event loop where only one thing ever happens at a time. If you try to make something happen (like evaluating a CoffeeScript expression) while something else is happening, then the new thing will have to wait until the first thing is finished. To keep your CoffeeScript program from locking up, you need to adopt particular asynchronous programming techniques that are suited to a single-threaded event loop. In this section you'll learn how to do that.

Imagine that your billboard code was so successful that Joe from Million Corporation phones you to say he wants to use it for the Intergalactic Volcano Mogul Skiing Championships. He says there are approximately 1.5 million names. A decorate-sort-undecorate version of the application with these 1.5 million names makes your program unresponsive:

```
Loading and processing data
Starting server on port 8888
Data loaded in 5.482 seconds
```

Agtron happens to be walking past (his timing is impeccable). He looks at what you're doing, smiles, and asks if he can show you something. He shows you what's happening while your program is sorting all those competitors by adding a `setInterval` intended to log to the console once per second:

```
start = new Date()
setInterval ->
  console.log "Clock tick after #{(new Date()-start)/1000} seconds"
, 1000
```

You expect to see a *clock tick* each second, but that's *not* what happens:

```
Loading and processing data
Starting server on port 8888
Data loaded in 4.636 seconds
Clock tick at 4.643 seconds
Clock tick at 4.643 seconds
```

The program does only *one thing at a time*. If it spends 5 seconds sorting an array, then nothing else happens during those 5 seconds—the event loop experiences a blackout. Then, once the event loop is free, you see two events that have been waiting to be handled occur immediately one after the other.

9.2.1 *Events and blackouts*

When something happens that the event loop needs to handle, then the event loop receives an event. For example, when you evaluated the `setInterval` call with a function and a delay of 1,000 milliseconds, you were requesting that an event occur on the event loop in 1,000 milliseconds and for the function you supplied to be invoked as the handler for the event:

```
setInterval ->
  console.log "Clock tick after #{(new Date()-start)/1000} seconds"
, 1000
```

Similarly, when you request a file to be read asynchronously, you're asking the file to be read outside of the event loop and for an event to be triggered on the event loop once the file has been read. Again, the function you supply is the handler that will be invoked when the event occurs:

```
fs.readFile 'myFile.txt', (err, data) ->
  console.log 'invoked as the handler when the event occurs'
```

Because an asynchronous file read occurs outside of the event loop, the time it takes for the response to come back doesn't affect the event loop. Other events can be handled and other computations can be done until the response comes back. In figure 9.1 you can see other events being handled as they arrive on the event loop while asynchronous requests are requested and the results are awaited.

An event loop like the one in figure 9.1 is in good shape because nothing is blocking it. If it takes 2 seconds to get a response for a request back from a web service somewhere on the other side of the world, that doesn't matter because it's happening asynchronously. The program will carry on doing other things until the response

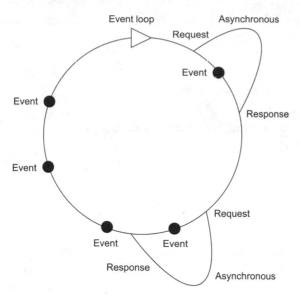

Figure 9.1   Asynchronous I/O doesn't block the event loop.

comes back, at which point the response is added to the event queue and processed at the next available time.

What does an event loop in poor shape look like? Well, if a program spends a lot of time processing something synchronously, such as sorting a list of a million or more competitors, the event loop will be blocked for a long time and the program will experience a blackout while it waits for the synchronous operation to complete before doing anything else. That's exactly what happens if you try to read a massive file synchronously,

```
dataForMyMassiveFile = fs.readFileSync 'myMassiveFile.mpg'
```

or when you try to synchronously sort a million competitors by their last name. In figure 9.2 you see an event loop in a poor state with a synchronous, blocking operation

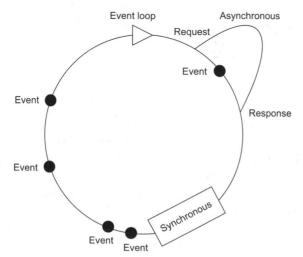

Figure 9.2   Blocking the event loop stops the world.

on the event loop. Notice how nothing else happens during the synchronous block and how two events that have had to wait for it to complete are handled shortly after.

The event loop is the wrong place to do heavy processing. You can get away with sorting 15,000 competitors if you do it efficiently and infrequently, but you won't get away with sorting millions of competitors. A program on the event loop must respond quickly to incoming events. If it spends all the time processing things, that defeats the purpose. Besides, some things aren't just large—they're infinite.

9.2.2 *Infinite time*

How do you deal with a data source that never ends? Think about how you kept track of the most popular pages on a website in chapter 3. You didn't try to load all of the data; after all, that would be impossible because the data never finishes. Trying to load it all at once is effectively the same as doing this:

```
loop 0
```

Not desirable. In figure 9.3 you can see Agtron and Scruffy play out what might happen if Agtron ran on an event loop.

The solution when you have a source of data that doesn't end (like a list of names that keeps getting new names added to it) is to treat it as a source of events. This is what event emitters are used for.

Figure 9.3 Don't block the event loop—unless you like to wait.

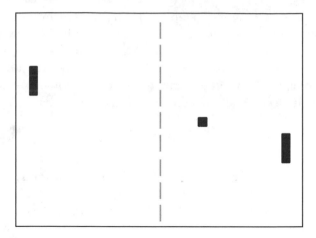

Figure 9.4   In your version of Pong, the user controls the paddle with the keyboard.

9.3   *Event emitters*

Website traffic is data that comes from users. Users are an excellent place to start looking at event emitters. Imagine that you're building a browser-based version of the 1972 classic Atari game Pong, as shown in figure 9.4. In this game the users control the movement of the paddles up and down on the screen to hit the ball back and forth across the screen.

User data doesn't stop until the game stops, so it's effectively infinite. How is it processed?

9.3.1   *User events*

Anything that's done asynchronously on the event loop (like reading a file) causes an event to be triggered when it's done. There's another important type of event that you don't request (not directly anyway) but that you definitely want to listen to and handle. That type of event is the user event.

How do you handle user events in a CoffeeScript program? By attaching a handler to them. For example, start by attaching an event handler for keydown events:

```
UP = 38                                    38 and 40 are the keycodes for the up
DOWN = 40                                  and down arrow keys, respectively.

paddle =
  up: ->                                   This paddle is for demonstration
  down: ->                                 only; it does nothing.

document.onkeydown = (event) ->
  switch event.keyCode                     Assign a handler function to
    when UP then paddle.up()               be invoked when a keydown
    when DOWN then paddle.down()           event occurs.
```

What does this have to do with reading data? Consider this sequence of keydown events that occurred during a game of Pong:

```
UP, DOWN, DOWN, DOWN, UP, DOWN, UP, UP, UP
```

It's an array. It's just that at the start of the game you don't have any of the data, and at the end of the game you have all the data. You don't wait until all the keydown event data arrives before doing anything—that wouldn't make for a very fun game. You process data as it arrives. The same can apply to any source of data; it can be treated as a source of events.

9.3.2 *Data as events*

If you treat a data source as a source of events, you can read and process *parts* of it asynchronously as each part arrives. Remember that blocking the event loop causes other events to queue up, as happened when your program spent almost 5 seconds waiting for some data to be loaded and processed:

```
Loading and processing data
Starting server on port 8888
Data loaded in 4.636 seconds
Clock tick at 4.643 seconds
Clock tick at 4.643 seconds
```

What does the data actually look like, though? Compare it to the keydown data from the game of Pong:

```
# competitor data
["0011: Engholm, Ciara", "0088: Gitting, Estrella", "0072: Renyer, Connie"]

# keypress data
[UP, DOWN, DOWN, DOWN, UP, DOWN, UP, UP, UP]
```

They're both arrays. So, if a source of events (an event emitter) can produce an array, then you can use one to produce the competitor data. What does it look like if the source of the competitor data is an event emitter? Consider a function that takes a callback as a parameter that it invokes once per second with the value 'A competitor'. New data is produced and passed to the callback asynchronously:

```
ONE_SECOND = 1000

start = new Date()
competitorEmitter = (callback) ->
  setInterval ->
    callback 'A competitor'
  , ONE_SECOND

receiver = (data) ->
  now = new Date()
  elapsed = now - start
  console.log "#{data} received after #{elapsed/ONE_SECOND} seconds"

competitorEmitter receiver

# A competitor received after 0.995 seconds
# A competitor received after 1.995 seconds
# A competitor received after 2.995 seconds
# A competitor received after 3.995 seconds
```

This can also be wrapped up into a `DataEmitter` class:

```coffeescript
class DataEmitter
  constructor: (interval) ->
    @listeners = []
    setInterval ->
      listener() for listener in listeners
    , interval
  ondata: (listener) ->
    listeners.push listener

emitter = new DataEmitter 1.5*ONE_SECOND

emitter.ondata ->
  console.log "Service responds at #{difference()} seconds past minute"
```

A fake DataEmitter class for emitting events on a schedule

This event emitter is a fake, but it helps to show what an event emitter does. In Node.js there's an `EventEmitter` class in the core `events` module.

9.3.3   *Using event emitters in Node.js*

The `EventEmitter` in the core Node.js `events` module is a JavaScript class that you can extend in your own CoffeeScript program:

```coffeescript
{EventEmitter} = require 'events'

class CompetitorEmitter extends EventEmitter
```

If the `CompetitorEmitter` is going to emit competitors as it reads them, then it doesn't make sense for it to load the entire competitors source file in one go. Instead, it should open the source file as a stream using `createReadStream` from the Node.js core `fs` module:

```coffeescript
fs = require 'fs'

sourceStream = fs.createReadStream 'competitors.txt'
```

The `createReadStream` method returns a `Stream`, which extends `EventEmitter`. It allows a file to be read in chunks instead of waiting to load the whole file.

The following listing contains a `CompetitorsEmitter` that reads the competitors file and emits arrays of competitors while the file is being read.

Listing 9.3   Sort competitors from stream

```coffeescript
fs = require 'fs'
{EventEmitter} = require 'events'

ONE_SECOND = 1000

lastName = (s) ->
  try
    s.split(/\s+/g)[1].replace /,/, ','
  catch e
    ''

undecorate = (array) ->
  item.original for item in array
```

```
class CompetitorsEmitter extends EventEmitter
  validCompetitor = (string) ->
    /^[0-9]+:\s[a-zA-Z],\s[a-zA-Z]\n/.test string
```
Check that competitor names have the expected format.

```
  lines = (data) ->
    chunk = data.split /\n/
    first = chunk[0]
    last = chunk[chunk.length-1]
    {chunk, first, last}
```
Read the lines from the data provided.

```
  insertionSort = (array, items) ->
    insertAt = 0
    for item in items
      toInsert = original: item, sortOn: lastName(item)
      for existing in array
        if toInsert.lastName > existing.lastName
          insertAt++
      array.splice insertAt, 0, toInsert
```
Sort the competitors by inserting them in the correct order as they are received.

Read the file as a stream and then read the line from each chunk of the stream received.

```
  constructor: (source) ->
    @competitors = []
    stream = fs.createReadStream source, {flags: 'r', encoding: 'utf-8'}
    stream.on 'data', (data) =>
      {chunk, first, last} = lines data
      if not validCompetitor last
        @remainder = last
        chunk.pop()
      if not validCompetitor first
        chunk[0] = @remainder + first
      insertionSort @competitors, chunk
      @emit 'data', @competitors

path = require 'path'
if !fs.existsSync 'competitors.15000.txt'
  console.error 'Error: File competitors.15000.txt not found'
  process.exit()

competitors = new CompetitorsEmitter 'competitors.15000.txt'
competitors.on 'data', (competitors) ->
    console.log "There are #{competitors.length} competitors"

start = new Date()
setInterval ->
  now = new Date()
  console.log "Tick at #{(now - start)/ONE_SECOND}"
, ONE_SECOND/10
```

When the program in listing 9.3 is executed, the events generated by setInterval aren't forced to wait long for the event loop. Note that for this program to run, you'll need a competitors.15000.txt file in the same format as the previous competitors files:

```
> coffee 9.3.coffee
There are 1468 competitors
There are 2937 competitors
There are 4406 competitors
Tick at 0.121
...
```

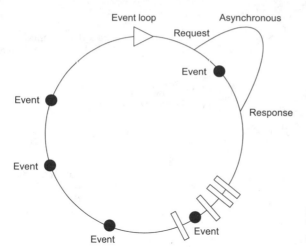

Figure 9.5   Don't wait forever. Treat input as a series of events and process it as it arrives.

Now that the data is being loaded as a stream and sorted as it arrives, the processing is broken up into multiple blocks. This means that the event loop isn't blocked for a long, continuous time. Instead, the event loop is blocked for multiple smaller chunks of time, as shown in figure 9.5 and by comparison to figure 9.3.

There's only one event loop, and *the event loop is the wrong place to do data processing*. It's reasonable to do some processing to generate responses to events, but anything that you expect will take time should be done offline or handled outside of the event loop.

> **Where should data processing be done?**
> If your application needs to process something that you know will take a long time, then it simply has to be done outside the event loop. Send the processing somewhere else (to another program) with a callback so that it can be done asynchronously, with your program being notified when it's done.

How does the solution in listing 9.4 perform with a list of 1.5 million names? It doesn't block the event loop for 5 seconds, but it does take *minutes* to complete (try to execute it and go make yourself a coffee while you wait). Despite the slow performance, by treating the data source as an event emitter you're able to process the entire list without blocking the event loop. The same approach works in reverse—just as data can be treated as events, so can events be treated as data.

9.3.4   *Events as data*

Suppose now that the competitor data also contains the fastest time for each competitor on a particular ski run:

```
0212: Turnbill, Geralyn, '12:13'
0055: Spielvogel, Cierra, '11:55'
0072: Renyer, Connie, '11:33'
0011: Engholm, Ciara, '14:10'
```

You receive a call from Joe, who says that he wants to display only competitors who have a best time faster than 12:00. It's tempting to modify the existing code to add the condition:

```
for item in chunk
  insertAt = 0
  if scoreBetterThan item, '12:00'
    toInsert = { original: item, sortOn: lastName(item) }
    for competitor in @competitors
      if toInsert.lastName > competitor.lastName
        insertAt++
    @competitors.splice insertAt, 0, toInsert
```

Wait a minute! What happens when Joe asks you to show only competitors with names starting with *J* or those with competitor numbers starting with 02? Remember that the data is really an array. It's being loaded asynchronously, but it's still an array. If it were an array of data, you wouldn't write a big `for` loop with a bunch of conditionals. Instead, you'd use array methods such as `filter`. What would that look like?

```
fasterThan = (n) ->
  (z) ->
    z.time < n

lastNameStartsWith = (letter) ->
  (s) -> competitor.lastName[0] is letter

result = \
competitors
.filter(fasterThan '12:00')
.filter(lastNameStartsWith 'a')
```

How you'd like to be able to filter events

If the data is really an array, then that's how you'd like to process it. The problem is that you don't actually have the array—not yet anyway. Think about it, though; you don't need to process *any* of the data until the values are needed somewhere else in the program. The manipulations that will be done on the data when it's actually needed can be defined up front, before any of the data is available. Treating a series of asynchronous events as an array is an abstraction—one that makes it easier to compose events in familiar ways.

9.4 Event composition

In this section you'll see how to hide the plumbing of an event emitter to make it easier to compose events. This starts by learning to be lazy.

9.4.1 Lazy data handling

The data that you have now and the data that you'll have as the result of a series of events isn't as different as you might think. In a sense, the difference is that an array is an expression of the value:

```
['Geralyn Turnbull', 'Connie Renyer']
```

Whereas the data that you don't have yet is like a function that returns the data:

```
-> ['Geralyn Turnbull', 'Connie Renyer']
```

The first expression is the data itself; the second returns the data when invoked. This makes a good starting place on the road to composing asynchronous events.

Imagine that you need to do more with the list of names than just display them; imagine that you want to put them into a phone book like the one from chapter 4:

```
phoneNumbers = [
  { name: 'hannibal', number: '555-5551', relationship: 'friend' }
  { name: 'darth', number: '555-5552', relationship: 'colleague' }
  { name: 'hal_9000', number: 'disconnected', relationship: 'friend' }
  { name: 'freddy', number: '555-5554', relationship: 'friend' }
  { name: 'T-800', number: '555-5555', relationship: 'colleague' }
]
```

To get an array containing only friends, you either use a comprehension with a when clause or the Array::filter method. In this case, use filter:

```
relationshipIs = (relationship) ->
  (item) -> item.relationship is relationship

phoneNumbers
.filter(relationshipIs 'friend')
```

Suppose, though, that you don't have the data but a function that returns the data:

```
getPhoneNumbers = -> phoneNumbers
```

You'll remember writing fluent interfaces in chapter 7. Here goes another one; suppose you call it withResultOf:

```
withResultOf(getPhoneNumbers)
.filter(relationshipIs 'friend')
```

The withResultOf function will need to return an object that has a filter method:

```
withResultOf = (fn) ->
  filter: ->
```

At some point in the program, you'll need the actual data itself. Call this method that returns the data evaluate:

```
withResultOf = (fn) ->
  runInOrder = []
  {
    filter: (filterFn) ->
      runInOrder.push (data) -> item for item in data when filterFn item
      @                              <--┐
    evaluate: ->                        │  Returning "this" to
      data = fn()                       │  allow chaining for
      for processFn in runInOrder       │  the fluent interface
        processFn data
  }
```

By now, this is a familiar pattern: some imperative code hidden behind a largely functional interface:

```
withResultOf(getPhoneNumbers)
.filter(relationshipIs 'friend')
.evaluate()

# [
#   { name: 'hannibal', number: '555-5551', relationship: 'friend' },
#   { name: 'hal_9000', number: 'disconnected', relationship: 'friend' },
#   { name: 'freddy', number: '555-5554', relationship: 'friend' }
# ]
```

But you don't have to evaluate it immediately. You might want to call it later or pass it to another function. This is *lazy* because the computation is defined early, but the evaluation occurs only when `evaluate` is invoked. This is very different from just determining the computation later on.

Just like a function, this event stream filter is now first-class. For example, one of your work colleagues wants to sync live with your business contacts. You can easily send him a filtered event stream:

```
withResultOf(getPhoneNumbers)
.filter(relationshipIs 'business')
```

When he wants to use it, he evaluates it and gets the values up to now, filtered:

```
suppliedContacts.evaluate()
```

That technique works for data streams or functions that actually return the values. But when you look at your event-driven program, the functions don't return the values at all; they invoke a callback with the return value:

```
fs.readFile, 'filename', callback
```

So, how can you extend `withResultOf` to work for asynchronous functions that invoke callbacks?

9.4.2 *Lazy event handling*

Consider again the data for the phone book. This time it's not returned by a function but instead passed as an argument to a callback:

```
phonebookData = (callback) ->
  callback [
    { name: 'hannibal', number: '555-5551', relationship: 'friend' }
    { name: 'darth', number: '555-5552', relationship: 'colleague' }
    { name: 'hal_9000', number: 'disconnected', relationship: 'friend' }
    { name: 'freddy', number: '555-5554', relationship: 'friend' }
    { name: 'T-800', number: '555-5555', relationship: 'colleague' }
  ]
```

If the phone book is an event emitter, then it's still callback-driven, except that the callback is called repeatedly as new data arrives:

```
phonebook.on 'data', callback
```

The sequence of values produced by an event emitter is an array; you just don't have all of the values yet. Think of the array of keyboard commands that were produced during the running game of Pong—it was also produced by an event emitter (a user):

```
[ UP, DOWN, DOWN, DOWN, UP, DOWN, UP, UP, UP ]
```

An event emitter generating the phone book doesn't change what the data looks like. Instead of letting the source of the data dictate how you use it, decide on the interface you want first, and then figure out how to make it work.

9.4.3   *Composing event streams*

Suppose the phone book information is arriving asynchronously, with each subsequent chunk arriving as it becomes available. The source of the data is an event emitter named `phonebookEmitter` that may or may not stop producing more events. Now suppose that you want to filter the phone book to just friends. The interface that you want is one that matches what you use for an array:

```
phonebook = \
withEvents(phonebookEmitter)
.filter(relationship 'friend')
```

You start by trying this on a different source of events so that you can control what's happening. Create your own event emitter that emits numbers:

```
{EventEmitter} = require 'events'

even = (number) -> number%2 is 0

emitter = new EventEmitter
evenNumberEvents = withEvents(emitter, 'number').filter(even)

emitter.emit 'number', 2
emitter.emit 'number', 5
```

When `evaluate` is invoked, you expect to get an array containing only the even numbers:

```
evenNumberEvents.evaluate()
# [2]
```

If more events occur, then invoking `evaluate` again will show the even numbers up to that point:

```
emitter.emit 'number', 4
emitter.emit 'number', 3

evenNumberEvents.evaluate()
# [2,4]
```

The expression for the filtered events is like a function expression:

```
withEvents(emitter, 'number').filter(even)
```

It can be passed around inside a program without being evaluated. So how do you implement it? In the next listing you see a working phone book application with filtering capabilities. Note that this listing reads a file called phone_numbers.csv that looks like this:

```
hannibal,555-5551,friend
darth,555-5552,colleague
hal_9000,disconnected,friend
freddy,555-5554,friend
T-800,555-5555,colleague
dolly,555-3322,associate
```

This phone_numbers.csv file is included with the book's downloadable content.

Listing 9.4 Phone book with data loaded from event stream

```
fs = require 'fs'
{EventEmitter} = require 'events'

withEvents = (emitter, event) ->
  pipeline = []
  data = []

  reset = ->                          Reset the event
    pipeline = []                     "log" when started.

  run = ->
    result = data
    for processor in pipeline
      if processor.filter?            Process all the filters
        result = result.filter processor.filter    and maps against
      else if processor.map?          the event log.
        result = result.map processor.map
    result

  emitter.on event, (datum) ->        Add event listeners
    data.push datum                   to the emitter.

  filter: (filter) ->
    pipeline.push {filter: filter}
    @
  map: (map) ->                       Create the fluent
    pipeline.push {map: map}          interface by returning
    @                                 @ in the methods.
  evaluate: ->
    result = run()
    reset()
    result

class CSVRowEmitter extends EventEmitter    Extend EventEmitter
                                            to emit rows from a
  valid = (row) ->                          file in CSV format.
    /[^,]+,[^,]+,[^,]+/.test row

  constructor: (source) ->
    @remainder = ''
    @numbers = []
    stream = fs.createReadStream source, {flags: 'r', encoding: 'utf-8'}
    stream.on 'data', (data) =>
      chunk = data.split /\n/
```

```
      firstRow = chunk[0]
      lastRow = chunk[chunk.length-1]
      if not valid firstRow and @remainder
        chunk[0] = @remainder + firstRow
      if not valid lastRow
        @remainder = lastRow
        chunk.pop()
      else @remainder = ''

      @emit('row', row) for row in chunk when valid row
class PhoneBook
  asObject = (row) ->
    [name, number, relationship] = row.split ','
    { name, number, relationship }

  asString = (data) ->
    "#{data.name}: #{data.number} (#{data.relationship})"

  print = (s) ->
    s.join '\n'

  relationshipIs = (relationship) ->
    (data) -> data.relationship is relationship

  nameIs = (name) ->
    (data) -> data.name is name

  constructor: (sourceCsv) ->
    csv = new CSVRowEmitter sourceCsv
    @numbers = withEvents(csv, 'row')

  list: (relationship) ->
    evaluated = \
    if relationship
      @numbers
      .map(asObject)
      .filter(relationshipIs relationship)
      .evaluate()
    else
      @numbers
      .map(asObject)
      .evaluate()

    print(asString data for data in evaluated)

  get: (name) ->
    evaluated = \
    @numbers
    .map(asObject)
    .filter(nameIs name)
    .evaluate()

    print(asString data for data in evaluated)

console.log "Phonebook. Commands are get, list and exit."

process.stdin.setEncoding 'utf8'
stdin = process.openStdin()

phonebook = new PhoneBook 'phone_numbers.csv'
```

Things that operate on a phone book belong in the PhoneBook class.

Use the fluent interface created.

```
stdin.on 'data', (chunk) ->
  args = chunk.split ' '
  command = args[0].trim()
  name = relationship = args[1].trim() if args[1]
  console.log switch command
    when 'get'
      phonebook.get name
    when 'list'
      phonebook.list relationship
    when 'exit'
      process.exit 1
    else 'Unknown command'
```

Read input from the console.

The same technique works for other sources of events. Using the `withEvents` function, you can map and filter user events, such as keyboard interaction.

9.4.4   *Client side*

It's time to look at that game of Pong again, because the same technique that worked for a data stream works for user input data. The paddles in a game of Pong are moved up and down the screen based on keyboard presses performed by the players. Suppose the game of Pong will run in a browser and that the HTML structure is as follows:

```
<!DOCTYPE html>
<html dir="ltr" lang="en-US">
  <head>
    <meta http-equiv="Content-Type" content="text/html; charset=utf-8">
    <title>Pong</title>
  </head>
  <body>
    <div id="pong"></div>
  </body>
  <script src="9.5.js"></script>
</html>
```

Attaching a handler to keyboard events means that the data supplied by the keyboard (the key presses) is received:

```
document.on 'keypress', (event) ->
  console.log 'The keyboard was pressed'
```

Sure, you could write an entire program inside the keypress handler, but that will eventually lead to event handler spaghetti. In the next listing you see the paddle-controlling code for Pong implemented by treating the key presses as a stream of event data. Compile this listing and use it with the sample HTML shown previously to experiment.

Listing 9.5   Controlling paddles in a web browser

```
withEvents = (emitter, event) ->
  pipeline = []
  data = []

  reset = ->
    pipeline = []
```

```
run = ->
  result = data
  for processor in pipeline
    if processor.filter?
      result = result.filter processor.filter
    else if processor.map?
      result = result.map processor.map
  result

emitter.on event, (datum) ->
  data.push datum

filter: (filter) ->
  pipeline.push {filter: filter}
  @
map: (map) ->
  pipeline.push {map: map}
  @
drain: (fn) ->
  emitter.on event, (datum) ->
    result = run()
    data = []
    fn result
evaluate: ->
  result = run()
  reset()
  result
```

A drain runs each event through the filters and maps and invokes a callback.

```
UP = 38
DOWN = 40
Q = 81
A = 65
```

Some variables (uppercase to indicate constants) that map the keycode supplied by an event to the key on the keyboard that was pressed.

```
doc =
  on: (event, fn) ->
    old = document["on#{event}"] || ->
    document["on#{event}"] = (e) ->
      old e
      fn e
```

A thin wrapper around the document used to attach listeners to keyboard events.

```
class Paddle

  constructor: (@top=0, @left=0) ->
    @render()

  move: (displacement) ->
    @top += displacement*5
    @paddle.style.top = @top + 'px'
```

Moves the graphical paddle on the screen.

```
  render: ->
    @paddle = document.createElement 'div'
    @paddle.className = 'paddle'
    @paddle.style.backgroundColor = 'black'
    @paddle.style.position = 'absolute'
    @paddle.style.top = "#{@top}px"
    @paddle.style.left = "#{@left}px"
    @paddle.style.width = '20px'
    @paddle.style.height = '100px'
    document.querySelector('#pong').appendChild @paddle
```

Creates a graphical paddle on the screen.

```
displacement = ([up,down]) ->
  (event) ->
    switch event.keyCode
      when up then -1
      when down then 1
      else 0
move = (paddle) ->
  (moves) ->
    for displacement in moves
      paddle.move displacement
keys = (expected) ->
  (pressed) ->
    pressed.keyCode in expected
paddle1 = new Paddle 0,0
paddle1.keys = [Q,A]

paddle2 = new Paddle 0,200
paddle2.keys = [UP,DOWN]

withEvents(doc, 'keydown')
.filter(keys paddle1.keys)
.map(displacement paddle1.keys)
.drain(move paddle1)

withEvents(doc, 'keydown')
.filter(keys paddle2.keys)
.map(displacement paddle2.keys)
.drain(move paddle2)
```

Paddle 1 is controlled by Q and A keys; paddle 2 is controlled by up- and down-arrow keys.

The core movement logic becomes clear.

There are other ways to structure this (perhaps without a paddle class), but it's important to see how the program is broken up into small composable units even though it's handling multiple users. Regardless of the source of events, this technique helps you to manage event streams. With first-class functions and a terse syntax for both functions and objects, CoffeeScript makes it possible to write readable code.

9.4.5 *Multiple event sources*

That works for a single source of events, but what happens when you have multiple sources of events? Suppose you have two sources of data:

```
source1 = [13,14,15]
source2 = [23,24,25]
```

For arrays, to zip them means to create a new array by interleaving the two arrays together, like a zipper:

```
zip = (a, b) ->
  zipped = []
  while a.length or b.length
    do ->
      fromA = a.pop()
      fromB = b.pop()
      if fromB then zipped.push fromB
      if fromB then zipped.push fromA
  zipped.reverse()
```

```
zip source1, source2
# [13,23,14,24,15,25]
```

Streams of events, when treated as arrays, can be zipped together in the same way. With two event streams where the source order doesn't matter, zipping them together as they arrive is done in the same way as two arrays are zipped together.

9.5   *Summary*

In this chapter you started by processing data synchronously and quickly learned how you are guaranteed that heavy processing, no matter how well optimized, will eventually break your program if you try to do it all synchronously on the event loop. That wasn't the end of the story, though, and you later learned that large or infinite data could be handled effectively as event streams.

You also learned that changing the way you looked at events and treating them as streams made them easier to compose. Because all CoffeeScript programs run on an event loop with callbacks and event handlers, if you repeatedly add more and more event handlers and scatter related program code in unrelated parts of a program, you'll quickly find your program to be incomprehensible. By thinking of event emitters as sources of data, you can apply familiar techniques such as mapping and filtering to help make them more manageable.

When writing all of this code, how do you know it does what it's supposed to do? In the next chapter you'll learn about test-driven development and how to ensure your CoffeeScript programs are well tested.

Part 3

Applications

Learning how to use CoffeeScript and how to use it well is not enough. It's necessary, but it's not sufficient. Why? Because the applications you write using CoffeeScript exist in a real world with practical considerations beyond the language itself. This part of the book prepares you for writing robust and maintainable applications in CoffeeScript both today and in the future.

Because this part explores topics that are ancillary to CoffeeScript, it takes the time to also teach the underlying concepts in those topics. Depending on your familiarity with the focus of each chapter, you should adapt your reading style accordingly.

Driving with tests 10

This chapter covers

- Understanding unit tests
- Dealing effectively with dependencies inside tests
- How to test asynchronous programs
- How to test behavior
- Test suites and how to automate your test suite

> I saw the best minds of my generation destroyed by madness.
>
> From *Howl* by Allen Ginsberg

You have to solve harder problems in CoffeeScript today than most people had to solve in JavaScript in the early days. Back then, JavaScript was used to enhance browser applications. Today you're writing entire applications in CoffeeScript. Writing more of the program means dealing with more of the problems. Writing tests for your programs can help with these problems and save you from losing your mind. Writing the tests *first*, before writing the programs, is a technique referred to as *test-driven development*.

If you've never done it before, test-driven development can feel uncomfortable, like having your pants on backwards. Be patient and give it some time, though; it might take a while to adjust. If you've done test-driven development before but not in CoffeeScript, you'll be pleasantly surprised at how easy some of the techniques are.

This chapter presents and encourages a test-driven approach to development and leads you through the creation of your own tiny test framework. In practice, it's more likely you'd use an existing test framework, but your understanding will be deeper if you go through the steps to build a tiny framework. The techniques for writing unit tests, dealing with dependencies, testing asynchronous callback-driven code, and structuring tests can be applied in other ways. First of all, why are tests important and why do you need automated tests? Why can't you just test manually?

10.1   No tests? Disaster awaits

One time-honored approach to testing JavaScript applications is to test everything manually. Manual tests are important, but a testing strategy that uses only manual tests doesn't work. You've seen it many times before. It's not sufficient, it doesn't scale, and it's expensive because you need the real application and real humans to do all of it. Humans are *really* expensive, and you don't need to spend all their valuable time doing something the computer can do.

Manual testing is more difficult in the long run. If it's too difficult, you'll decide not to do the tests, and before you know it, *there are no tests*.

WHAT HAPPENS WHEN YOU DON'T WRITE TESTS?

Imagine you've written all of the tracking code for Agtron's site. It tells him how many visitors his shop gets. Yesterday he had more than 100,000 visitors. You have no idea how he managed to get that much traffic to his website, but it's awesome nonetheless. Even better, your application and the accompanying tracking application, both written entirely in CoffeeScript, are performing nicely. No hiccups. As the sun sets before the weekend, you get a phone call from Agtron asking you to change the tracking program to add tracking of mouse movements for every user. Beer in hand on a Friday evening, you deftly implement a solution. On your way out the door, you go live to the production servers. Job done.

You awake in the night to the sound of your phone ringing. Something is wrong. The tracking program isn't tracking *any* users. It occurs to you to debug the client-side program on the live server to see if you can find the problem there. When you load it up, though, you remember that the code on the production server has been compressed to make it download faster. It's a big sea of unreadable code similar to this:

```
((function(){var a,b,c=function(a,b){return function(){return
a.apply(b,arguments)}};b=require("http"),a=function(){function
a(a,b){this.options=a,this.http=b,this.controller=c(this.controller,this),thi
s.pages=[]}return a.prototype.start=function(a){return
this.server=this.http.createServer(this.controller),this.server.listen(this.o
ptions.port,a)},a.prototype.stop=function(){return
this.server.close()},a.prototype.controller=function(a,b){return
this.increment(a.url),b.writeHead(200,{"Content-Type":"text/
html"}),b.write(""),b.end()},a.prototype.increment=function(a){var
```

```
b,c;return(c=(b=this.pages)[a])==null&&(b[a]=0),this.pages[a]=this.pages[a]+1
},a.prototype.total=function(){var a,b,c,d;c=0,d=this.pages;for(b in
d)a=d[b],c+=a;return c},a}(),exports.Tracking=a})).call(this);
```

You have no chance of debugging it. In a panic, your brain compiles a knee-jerk list of inappropriate reactions:

- Buy a one-way ticket to Tibet and live in a monastery on a mountaintop collecting sticks for the rest of your life.
- Give up on programming and move into management.
- Stop using CoffeeScript and go back to using only JavaScript.

Settle yourself. Instead, you decide to roll back the changes and deploy the last-known working version of the tracking program. There will be time to figure out what was wrong with the changes first thing in the morning.

The next morning, sitting at your desk and clutching your morning coffee, you're on the phone with Agtron discussing what went wrong.

"How come the tests didn't catch this problem?"

"The thing about the tests," you reply, "is that there are no tests."

Silence.

This story might have a happy ending. More likely it doesn't. Instead of following it through, imagine a world where you have tests for everything the program does. Tests that you can run every time you make a change (or even when you don't make a change) to make sure that the program is working as it should. That sounds better than a late-night panic when things go wrong. To live in that world, you need to learn how to write tests.

10.2 How to write tests

Ask your dentist which teeth you should brush. The answer will be "only the ones you want to keep." It's the same with tests—test only the parts of the program that you want to work. There are three basic steps:

1. Write a test.
2. Watch it fail.
3. Change the program to make the test pass.

This sequence begins with *writing a test*. How do you write a test?

FRAMEWORKS Although it's common to use a *kitchen-sink-included* testing framework to write tests, these frameworks aren't necessary to learn *how* to test. By learning to write tests without a testing framework, you'll understand the principles behind testing frameworks.

A test can be just a stated requirement for what the program should do. A simple requirement for something the tracking application should do is this:

It should record each product the user clicks on.

If this test is translated into something that can be executed (a test program), then it can be run automatically against the real program every time a change is made. Tests that are run automatically provide frequent feedback that the program does what it should. Without tests, there's only *hope* that the program will do what it should. The broken tracking application showed you that hope isn't an effective long-term testing strategy. How do you write a test for the requirement?

To learn how to test effectively, you need to learn about assertions, how to write them for the smallest parts (units) of your program, how to repeatedly write them as you develop your program, and how to get reliable feedback to tell you whether your assertions hold or not. The first step is understanding assertions.

10.2.1 *Assertions*

For a moment, forget about how you'll implement the tracking application. Imagine that it's already written and that as part of your work you have a `totalVisits` variable that tells you how many visits have been recorded. The test would follow along these lines:

```
initial = totalVisits
# Somehow visit the homepage
# Assert that the totalVisits has increased by one
```

There are two parts of this that you don't yet know how to write in CoffeeScript: write a program that visits the homepage (like a real user), and assert that the number of visits has increased afterward. You'll learn assertions first.

An *assertion* is a statement about the value of an expression. It either passes or fails. CoffeeScript doesn't have assertions built-in, but Node.js has a built-in assert module that you can use. To use the `assert` module you `require` it:

```
assert = require 'assert'
# { [Function: ok] …
```

Then you invoke one of the assert methods, such as `assert.ok`, which tests whether an expression is truthy. If the assertion succeeds, it evaluates to `undefined`:

```
assert.ok 4 is 4
# undefined
```

If the assertion fails, an exception is thrown:

```
assert.ok 4 == 5
# AssertionError: false == true
```

Tests *describe* something the program does. The description is an important part of the test. One way to put a description in a test is by wrapping it in a function assigned to a variable named after the description:

```
do assert4Equals4 = ->
  assert.ok 4 == 4
```
Use the do -> to invoke the test function immediately.

Another useful assertion method is `assert.equal`, which takes two arguments and throws an exception if the arguments aren't equal:

```
do assert4Equals4 = ->
  assert.equal 4, 4
```

Although obviously fake, this small test demonstrates a very basic *unit test*. A test to see if a small unit of your program does what it should do is a unit test.

10.2.2 *How to unit test*

In order to understand the mechanics of writing tests, it's worthwhile to take only a small part of an application and implement it using a test-driven approach. Suppose that as part of the dashboard for Agtron's tracking application, you need to highlight the most popular product. To highlight it you must add a class attribute to a DOM element in a web page. Consider the following HTML fragment:

```
<html>
<div class="product special">X12</div>
```

The `<div>` has two classes: `product` and `special`. You want some way to add a third class of `popular` so that it becomes

```
<html>
<div class="product special popular">X12</div>
```

Putting aside manipulation of HTML elements for a moment, this problem is about adding words to a string. When you're writing this individual unit of code, the requirement is this:

> *It should add a word to a space-separated string of words.*

Follow the steps. Write a test; watch it fail; make it pass.

WRITE A TEST

Create a file called word_utils.spec.coffee and put the following failing test inside:

```
assert = require 'assert'              ⟵┤ Require the built-in
                                          assert module.
do addWordShouldAddOneWord = ->                The input value    The value
  input = "product special"           ⟵┤      for addWord.       that addWord
  expectedOutput = "product special popular"              ⟵┐     should return.
  actualOutput = addWord input, "popular"                       ⟵┐ The value
  assert.equal expectedOutput, actualOutput  ⟵┐ Assert that the    that addWord
                                                Assert that the    actually returned.
                                                actual and expected
                                                values are equal.
```

WATCH IT FAIL

There's no `addWord` function yet, so this test should throw an error, and throwing an error counts as a failure. It does throw an error:

```
> coffee word_utils.spec.coffee
ReferenceError: addWord is not defined
```

Create a file called word_utils.coffee and `require` it in the test file:

```
assert = require 'assert'
{addWord} = require './word_utils'

do addWordShouldAddOneWord = ->
  input = "ultra mega"
  expectedOutput = "ultra mega ok"
  actualOutput = addWord input, "ok"
  assert.equal expectedOutput, actualOutput
```

Require the implementation from inside the test.

MAKE IT PASS

Implement the `addWord` function to make the test pass. The word_utils.coffee file initially exports an empty `addWord` function:

```
addWord = (existing, addition) -> # not implemented
exports.addWord = addWord
```

In practice you'd now continue to implement a working solution. This time, though, pause for a moment and think, what would happen if you ran the test now? It should fail because the `addWord` function returns `undefined`. To make sure the program is currently working how you think it's working, you run the test:

```
> coffee word_utils.spec.coffee
AssertionError: "ultra mega ok" == "undefined"
```

It fails exactly as you expected it to. *That's good.* You now implement a working `addWord` function:

```
addWord = (text, word) ->
  "#{text} #{word}"
```

You run the test and it passes:

```
> coffee word_utils.spec.coffee
# No output
```

The common.js assertions return `undefined` when there's no failure, so there's no console output when this test passes.

You've just done test-driven development. You wrote the test; you watched it fail; you implemented the solution to make it pass. By writing the test first, you know that you have a test for that specific part of your program. Yes, it's possible that the test is wrong. No, having tests isn't a guarantee that the program never does anything wrong. What you can guarantee, though, is that if you don't write tests you'll have much less confidence that your program does what it should.

You repeat the process as you write the program. Like the cliché, you *lather, rinse, repeat*. If you have a new requirement, write a new test.

10.2.3 *Rinse and repeat*

The most popular product doesn't stay the most popular forever. You need to be able to remove the highlight from an element once it's no longer the most popular. Removing the class `popular` from

```
<html>
<div class="product special popular"></div>
```

results in

```
<html>
<div class="product special"></div>
```

This requirement can be written like this:

> *It should remove a word from a space-separated string of words.*

Same thing again. Write a test; watch it fail; make it pass.

WRITE A TEST

A test for a function that removes a word is as follows:

```
assert = require 'assert'
{addWord, removeWord} = require './word_utils'

do removeWordShouldRemoveOneWord = ->
  input = "product special"
  expectedOutput = "product"
  actualOutput = removeWord input, "special"
  assert.equal expectedOutput, actualOutput
```

Before you've implemented any solution, the test fails as expected. The first implementation of removeWords uses the replace method on a string to replace the word with an empty string:

```
removeWord = (text, word) ->
  text.replace word, ''
```

Remember to export the new function from the word_utils file:

```
exports.removeWord = removeWord
```

You now have an implementation. Does the test now pass or does it still fail?

WATCH IT FAIL

Run the test:

```
> coffee word_utils.spec.coffee
# AssertionError: "product" == "product "
```

These strings aren't equal. Note the whitespace on the end of the second string.

The test fails because the whitespace is different.

MAKE IT PASS

To make the test pass, you try again with another solution using a regular expression to remove any whitespace left behind:

```
removeWord = (text, word) ->
  replaced = text.replace word, ''
  replaced.replace(/^\s\s*/, '').replace(/\s\s*$/, '')
```

Remove the word.

Remove any leading or trailing whitespace.

Now the test passes:

```
> coffee word_utils.spec.coffee
# No output
```

Agtron, peering over your shoulder, asks if he can try something. Agreeing, you hand him the keyboard. You anticipate that Agtron is going to show you how to improve your test. He changes the test to run against multiple input values:

```coffee
do removeWordShouldRemoveOneWord = ->
  tests = [
    initial: "product special"
    replace: "special"
    expected: "product"
  ,
    initial: "product special"
    replace: "spec"
    expected: "product special"
  ]

  for test in tests
    actual = removeWord(test.initial, test.replace)
    assert.equal actual, test.expected
```

**An array of
two test cases**

**A for...in loop to
execute the array
of test cases**

The test fails:

```
> coffee word_utils.spec.coffee
#AssertionError: "product ial" == "product special"
```

Agtron hasn't just shown you how to improve the test; he's shown you that the test was insufficient. You need a better `removeWord` function. In chapter 3 you learned to split a string of words into an array of words. With this technique, you have a new solution:

```coffee
removeWord = (text, toRemove) ->
  words = text.split /\s/
  (word for word in words when word isnt toRemove).join ' '
```

You now have a passing test:

```
> coffee word_utils.spec.coffee
# No output
```

This example is trivial and only tests a very small simple function. The process is important, though, and it's always the same, as you've just seen.

Until now you've used a three-step process that included watching the test fail. You might consider this step as implied, making the process two steps:

1 Write a failing test for a single unit of code.
2 Write code that passes the test.

The important thing is that the test is written first. It's also very different from how you wrote the broken tracking application, which was solution first, test second. Actually, the tracking application never got to the second part, so there was no feedback about whether the application worked as it should. Test feedback matters.

10.2.4 *Feedback*

Currently, when a test passes you're blandly greeted with empty console output:

```
> coffee word_utils.spec.coffee
>
```

Empty console output

It would be useful to see feedback for each test stating whether it passed or failed. The following listing contains the tests for addWord and removeWord and a fact function that runs a test wrapped inside a try...catch.

Listing 10.1   Add and remove word

```
assert = require 'assert'

{addWord, removeWord} = require './word_utils'

fact = (description, fn) ->
  try
    fn()
    console.log "#{description}: OK"
  catch e
    console.error "#{description}: \n#{e.stack}"
    throw e

fact "addWord adds a word", ->
  input = "product special"
  expectedOutput = "product special popular"
  actualOutput = addWord input, "popular"

  assert.equal expectedOutput, actualOutput

fact "removeWord removes a word and surrounding whitespace", ->
  tests = [
    initial: "product special"
    replace: "special"
    expected: "product"
  ,
    initial: "product special"
    replace: "spec"
    expected: "product special"
  ]

  for {initial, replace, expected} in tests
    assert.equal removeWord(initial, replace), expected
```

A destructuring require from the two functions exported from word_utils.

The fact function takes two arguments: a string description of the test and the function that's to be tested. It wraps the test function call inside a try...catch, passing the test if no exception occurs and failing the test if an exception does occur.

Running this file outputs the description of each fact along with the result:

```
> coffee word_utils.spec.coffee
addWord adds a word: OK
removeWord removes a word and surrounding whitespace: OK
```

The addWord and removeWord functions are general solutions to part of a more specific problem of adding a class to a <div>. What would have happened had you dove straight in and written an addWord implementation like this?

```
addClass = (selector, newClass) ->
  element = document.querySelector selector
  if element.className?
    element.className = "#{element.className} #{newClass}"
  else
    element.className = newClass
```

Try to write a test for it:

```
fact "addClass adds a class to an element using a selector", ->
  addClass '#a .b', 'popular'
  actualClass = document.querySelector(selector).className
  assert.equals 'product special popular', actualClass
```

This is actually asserting the result of a side effect. That smells.

Notice that the test asserts something on the document. This is only *indirectly* testing the addClass function. Worse, if the document ever changes the way it works, you'll need to update both the function and the test. No thanks.

The addClass function depends on the presence of a document to work. In other words, document is a dependency. How do you deal effectively with dependencies in a test?

10.3   *Dependencies*

When you write a test, the part of the program you're testing is the *system under test.* Anything that you're not testing but that the system under tests *uses* is a dependency.

Imagine a car. To test if the battery is working, a device called an *ammeter,* which tests if the battery is producing electricity, is used. The car needs electricity to start and to power accessories such as the radio. A battery that's removed from the car can still be tested with an ammeter. Not the radio, though; if the battery is removed, then the radio won't turn on, preventing it from being tested. How do you test the radio without the battery? Well, the radio doesn't need the battery *specifically* but only some equivalent source of electricity.

The same principle applies to components in a program. When you test part of a program, the dependencies don't need to be the real thing, just something that's equivalent as far as the test is concerned. In this section you'll learn why testing programs with dependencies is a challenge, how you can isolate those dependencies, and how to deal with them by using *test doubles.*

10.3.1   *Why dependencies make testing difficult*

Remember the task at hand: rewrite the tracking application using a test-driven approach. One part of the application is a dashboard that Agtron uses to see what's happening on his web shop: how many visitors there are, what they're looking at, and things like that. Imagine you're writing a test for part of the dashboard that extracts some data obtained via an HTTP service that returns JSON:

```
fact "data is parsed correctly", ->
  extractData 'support', (res) ->
    assert.equals res.status, 'online'
```

A simplified example of data from the HTTP service contains just one property and value:

```
{ status: 'online' }
```

You implement `extractData` to take a callback and pass it as the callback to `http.get`:

```
http = require 'http'
extractData = (topic, callback) ->
  options =
    host: 'www.agtronsemporium.com'
    port: 80
    path: "/service/#{topic}"

  http.get(options, (res) ->
    callback res.something
  ).on 'error', (e) ->
    console.log e
```

This works well until the day you crash the website. When www.agtronsemporium.com crashes, you're no longer able to get data from it. This causes the `extractData` function to fail because `http.get` doesn't work.

Imagine you're working on the program during this time when the HTTP service is down:

```
> AssertionError: "undefined" == "online"
```

This is a problem. Whenever the external site is down, you have no way to verify that the program is working correctly, even at the unit level. Unit tests shouldn't break when a dependency (in this case the external site) is unavailable. To make sure that unit tests work all the time, you need something that does the job of an HTTP service that isn't an HTTP service. You need something that won't break like an egg on your face. A thing that does the job during a test is a test double.

10.3.2 *Test doubles*

There are many terms for things that replace dependencies during a test (such as spies, mocks, and stubs). In this chapter *test double* or just *double* is used as a general term for something that replaces a dependency in a test. A double is like the stunt double for an actor or the friend who brought their jumper cables around that time your car battery was dead. When the real thing isn't suitable, you use a double.

In a minute you'll see how to create a double, but suppose for now you already have one; how do you get it into the program during the tests? By injecting it.

INJECTION

Picking up the actor metaphor again, consider a scene where an actor has to do a stunt:

```
class Actor
  soliloquy: ->
    'To be or not to be...'          An example
  stunt: ->                          Actor class.
    'My arm! Call an ambulance.'
scene = ->
  imaStarr = new Actor              The scene depends
  imaStarr.soliloquy()              on the actor.
  imaStarr.stunt()
  'Scene completed'
```

A test for this scene asserts that it returns the value `'Scene completed'`:

```
fact 'The scene is completed', ->
  assert.equals scene(), 'Scene completed'
```

The scene itself obtains the actor, so a test for this scene has no way to replace the actor with a double. If instead the scene is provided with the actor, then replacing the actor with a double becomes possible:

```
scene = (actor) ->
  actor.soliloquy()
  actor.stunt()
  'Scene completed'
```

Now you can replace the actor with a double by passing it in as an argument. The double will need to be convincing, though. It's no good having a double that doesn't know how to `soliloquy` because the scene won't work if it doesn't. So how do you create a test double that works?

> **FRAMEWORKS**   If you use a test framework, it will likely provide some standard ways to create test doubles. But as with assertions, you don't need a testing framework to learn how to use doubles. In some languages it's very difficult to create a double without a framework, but in CoffeeScript it's quite easy. This is because objects are like an all-night café—always open.

CREATING A DOUBLE FROM SCRATCH

During the scene, the actor does a `soliloquy` and a `stunt`—both methods of the actor object. A double that takes the place of the actor during the scene without ruining it needs to know how to do (or pretend to do) things that the actor has to do. Create a double that can `soliloquy` and `stunt` using an object literal:

```
actorDouble =
  soliloquy: ->
  stunt: ->
```

The scene completes successfully with this `actorDouble` in place of the actor:

```
scene = (actor) ->
  actor.soliloquy()
  actor.stunt()
  'Scene completed'

fact 'The scene is completed', ->
  actorDouble =
    soliloquy: ->
    stunt: ->
  assert.equal scene(actorDouble), 'Scene completed'
# The scene is completed: OK
```

This technique of providing dependencies to part of a program is called *dependency injection*. Creating doubles in this way to pass them in as arguments is straightforward, if at times a little inconvenient, in CoffeeScript.

Consider the `extractData` function that contains a dependency on `http`. Any tests against it will suffer the same difficulties that the tests for `scene` had:

```
http = require 'http'

extractData = (topic, callback) ->
  options =
    host: 'www.agtronsemporium.com'
    port: 80
    path: "/data/#{topic}"

  http.get(options, (res) ->
    callback res
  ).on 'error', (e) ->
    console.log e
```

Spot the dependency.

As you can see, the `http` dependency makes testing very difficult because it breaks all the tests any time the external site is offline. You can solve this with an `http` double. The double must know how to act like the real thing, so by looking at `extractData` you can see that the double must have a `get` method and an `on` method:

```
http =
  get: (options, callback) ->
    callback 'canned response'
    @
  on: (event, callback) ->
    # do nothing
```

Return the current object to create a fluent interface (see chapter 7).

To the `extractData` function, this `http` double will look just like a real `http`. In duck-typing terms (chapter 7), it walks like an `http` and quacks like an `http`, so it's an `http`.

Having the double is only half the story; it also needs to be injected during the test. In order to allow this, the `extractData` function must be changed to allow the dependency to be injected:

```
http = require 'http'

extractData = (topic, http, callback) ->
  options =
    host: 'www.agtronsemporium.com'
    port: 80
    path: "/data/#{topic}"

  http.get(options, (res) ->
    callback res.something
  ).on 'error', (e) ->
    console.log e
```

Now that http is being injected, you can remove this old 'http' require.

The http object injected.

The http object used.

Now the tests can be written such that they don't break every time something goes wrong in the real world.

Injecting dependencies in this way isn't the only option; dependencies can be isolated to specific locations in the program so that they can be avoided as much as possible in other, easily testable units of the program.

CREATING A DOUBLE WITH PROTOTYPES

Sometimes you need a double for an object with lots of properties, but only one of those properties needs to be replaced inside the test. Consider this `Form` class, which has a dependency on the global `window` object present in all web browsers:

```
class Form
  reloader = ->
    window.location.reload()
```

A real `window` object in a web browser has many properties:

```
window =
  location:
    href: ''
    reload: ->
  closed: false
  screen:
    top: 0
    left: 0
  # hundreds of other properties not shown here
```

At the moment it doesn't matter what any of the methods do, so they've been left empty.

A real `window` object in a web browser has more than 200 properties. It would take a very long time to create a suitable double to use inside the test. Instead of writing a double from scratch, you can use `Object.create` to create a double with the real thing as a prototype and then override just the parts you need to. For the `Form` class you need to override the `reload` method:

```
windowDouble = Object.create window
windowDouble.location.reload = ->
```

This saves some time in creating a double to inject during testing. Change the `Form` class to accept an injected window in the constructor:

```
class Form
  constructor: (@window) ->
  reloader: ->
    @window.location.reload()
```

ISOLATION

The `extractData` function does too much. It fetches and extracts the data when really it should just extract the data. Breaking out the fetching of data into a separate function removes the dependency that `extractData` has on `http`. This means that tests for `extractData` don't need to even know about `http`, let alone create a double:

```
fetchData (http, callback) ->
  options =
    host: 'www.agtronscameras.com'
    port: 80
    path: "/data/#{topic}"

  http.get(options, (res) ->
    callback res
  ).on 'error', (e) ->
    console.log e
```

```
extractData = (data) ->
  console.log data

fetchAndExtractData = ->
  fetchData http, extractData
```

The next listing shows the final version of the tests with dependencies avoided where possible and injected where necessary.

Listing 10.2   Testing with a double

```
assert = require 'assert'

fact = (description, fn) ->
  try
    fn()
    console.log "#{description}: OK"
  catch e
    console.log "#{description}: \n#{e.stack}"

http =
  get: (options, callback) ->
    callback "canned response"
    @
  on: (event, callback) ->

fetch = (topic, http, callback) ->
  options =
    host: 'www.agtronscameras.com'
    port: 80
    path: "/data/#{topic}"

  http.get(options, (result) ->
    callback result
  ).on 'error', (e) ->
    console.log e

parse = (data) ->
  "parsed canned response"

fact "data is parsed correctly", ->
  parsed = parse 'canned response'
  assert.equal parsed, "parsed canned response"

fact "data is fetched correctly", ->
  fetch "a-topic", http,  (result) ->
    assert.equal result, "canned response"
```

> The http double to be used by tests

> Very simple parse function shown to demonstrate it tested in isolation from fetch

When you isolate dependencies and inject them only into places where you absolutely need them, the program is easier to reason about and easier to test. Dependency injection can lead to a particular problem, though. In a world where everything is injected, all you see is things being injected. What does this mean and how can you avoid it?

10.3.3 *Avoiding dependency injection hell*

Imagine you're writing part of the dashboard for Agtron's tracking application that displays the number of visits for a particular user. As part of this, you have a `visits` function with three dependencies: a database, an HTTP service, and a user.

Suppose this `visits` function looks up the user in the database and then uses that information to get the number of hits for the user from the HTTP service:

```
visits = (database, http, user) ->
  http.hitsFor database.userIdFor(user.name)
```

Suppose you then find out that some users have requested their data be kept private and that information be available only in a `permissions` file. You add another argument:

```
visits = (database, http, user, permissions) ->
  if permissions.allowDataFor user
    http.hitsFor database.userIdFor(user.name)
  else
    'private'
```

With more and more dependencies, you can see that this will get more and more unwieldy. An options object passed in as an argument (see chapter 4) is a common solution to the problem of having too many arguments:

```
visits = (dependencies) ->
  if dependencies.permissions.allowDataFor user
    dependencies.http.hitsFor dependencies.database.userIdFor(user.name)
  else
    'private'
```

That's different . . . and worse! The function is now *harder* to understand.

Think about it; most of the time you don't need all of those options. If you partially apply the function (discussed in chapter 6) and create a new function that has fewer arguments, then you can make it more manageable. Instead of having lots of dependencies,

```
visits = (database, http, user, permissions) ->
  if permissions.allowDataFor user
    http.hitsFor database.userIdFor(user.name)
  else
    'private
```

make a `makeVisits` function that fixes the `user` and `permissions` arguments to `visits`:

```
makeVisitsForUser = (database, http) ->
  (user, permissions) ->
    visits database, http, user, permissions
```

This function would typically be used dynamically, but an example of using it for a single known user, by explicitly passing in a user and permissions, is as follows:

```
database = new Database          database and http created from a class. It's likely that these wouldn't
http = new Http                  be created using classes; the classes are used here as examples.

visitsForUser = makeVisitsForUser bob, permissions    ←┤ Getting a two-argument
                                                         function as visitsForBob.
```

The resulting `visitsForBob` function can then be used:

```
bob = new User
permissionsForBob = new Permissions

visitsForUser bob, permissionsForBob
```

Examples of how user and permissions might be created.

◁── **Invoke the visitsForUser function to get the visits for bob.**

Cute, you think, but how is it useful in a test? Imagine you have two tests that use the `visits` function. Each of them creates doubles for `database`, `http`, `user`, and `permissions`:

```
fact 'Visits not shown when permissions are private', ->
  database = databaseDouble
  http = httpDouble
  user = userDouble
  permissions = new Permissions
  assert.equal visits(database, http, user, permissions), 'private'

fact 'Returns visits for user', ->
  database = databaseDouble
  http = httpDouble
  user = userDouble
  permissions = new Permissions
  assert.equal visits(database, http, user, permissions), 'private'
```

Notice that the dependencies are essentially the same in both cases. If the program has already been structured to have the `makeVisitsForUser` function, then dealing with the dependencies in the test is easier:

```
database = databaseDouble
http = httpDouble
visitsForUser = makeVisitsForUser database, http

fact !Visits not returned when permissions are private', ->
  user = new User
  privatePermissions = new Permissions private: true
  assert.equal visitsForUser(user, privatePermissions), 'private'

fact 'Visits returned for user', ->
  user = new User
  privatePermissions = new Permissions private: true
  assert.equal visitsForBob(database, http), 'private'
```

This change looks minor at a small scale (and it is), but as a program grows, if it has been composed with functions, then you can avoid some messy dependency situations that are otherwise difficult to solve.

In this section you've learned to deal with program dependencies when writing unit tests. The general approach is to create a test double that takes the place of the dependency during the test. You've also seen the different ways to get doubles where you need them during tests. By forcing yourself to write programs that allow dependencies to be replaced by doubles during tests, your programs will be easier to maintain. That's an added benefit that you'll appreciate on another day.

What else do you need to know about testing? This is CoffeeScript, so your applications almost always run in an event-driven environment. One of the things you'll have to deal with in an event-driven environment is the tension between asynchronous code and the desire to structure tests synchronously.

10.4 Testing the asynchronous

CoffeeScript programs, usually run in the browser or on Node.js, are usually event driven, and I/O is almost always asynchronous. Why is this a problem? Well, consider the following test structure:

```
fact 'the tracking application tracks a user mouse click', ->
  options = {}
  tracking = new Tracking options, http
  tracking.start ->
  fred.visit '/page/1'
  assert.equal tracking.total(), 1
```

The start method of the tracking object expects a callback function that will be invoked when it's finished. But the test invokes the visit method of the fred object and asserts the result of invoking the total method on the tracking object immediately, without bothering to wait for the start method to finish. If the start method hasn't finished by the time the assertion occurs, the test will fail.

There are three related techniques for dealing with asynchronous I/O in tests: live with it, remove it, or expect it.

10.4.1 Live with it

One technique for testing asynchronous programs is to just reflect the asynchronous nature in your tests. To do this, add assertions as part of a callback to the function you're testing:

```
fact 'the tracking application tracks a user mouse click', ->
  options = {}
  tracking = new Tracking options, http
  tracking.start ->
    assert.equal tracking.total(), 0
    fred = new User serverOptions, http
    fred.visit '/page/1', ->
      fred.clickMouse ->
        assert.equal tracking.total(), 1
      tracking.stop()
```

> The remainder of the test is passed as the callback to the start method of the tracking object.

Leaving the callback in the test for the start method works well for a while. But what if the start method has some external dependency? What if the start method performs some potentially error-prone network I/O?

10.4.2 Remove it

There are two types of functions that accept callbacks. One uses I/O and the other one doesn't. *Don't do any I/O in a unit test.* Remember the http double?

```
http =
  get: (options, callback) ->
    callback()
    @
  on: (event, callback) ->
    # do nothing
```

The get method takes a callback as an argument but it isn't asynchronous; it's invoked immediately. It's unlike a real http where the callback is invoked only after a network request has successfully returned. This means the http double has removed the dependency on the external HTTP service whenever it's used in place of the real http. If you pass in an http double as a dependency to the tracking object, then you're removing the external dependency from the test:

```
fact 'the tracking application tracks a user mouse click', ->
  options = {}
  http =
    get: (options, callback) ->
      callback()
      @
    on: (event, callback) ->
    # do nothing

  tracking = new Tracking options, http
  tracking.start ->
  fred.visit '/page/1'
  assert.equal tracking.total(), 1
```

Perhaps you don't really need an http double at all. Instead, you can create a double of a method that *uses* it. Replace the start method with a double:

```
fact 'the tracking application tracks a user mouse click', ->
  tracking = new Tracking options, http
  tracking.start = (callback) ->
    callback()

  fred.visit '/page/1'
  assert.equal tracking.total(), 1
```

This example oversimplifies the scenario, but you can clearly see that instead of a double for an object, you essentially have a double for a function. This is often referred to as a *method stub*, but you can think of it like any other double.

10.4.3 *Expect it*

Suppose you're testing a program that talks to a database via this http object. You don't really care about the response you get back asynchronously from the database. What you *do* care about is that you made the correct call to it. If the correct call was made, you trust the database to do the right thing. After all, a database that doesn't store things when you tell it to is probably not a database worth having.

Consider the `http` module; you might *expect* a particular method to be called with specific parameters. A simple way to test that the call happened is to remember it in the test, using a variable:

```
fact 'http service should be accessed', ->
  getWasCalled = false
  http =
    get: ->
      getWasCalled = true
  invokeTheThingThatGets()
  assert.ok getWasCalled
```

Local variable to remember whether the get method was called.

The http double changes the value of the local variable when the get method is invoked.

Invoking this function should call the get method of the http double.

Assert that the get method was called by checking the local variable.

Using lexical scope, you can store information about whether the `get` method has been invoked on `http`. It's a simple technique for testing whether a dependency has been called.

The full unit tests for the `Tracking` class are shown in listing 10.3. This listing makes use of the `fact` function from listing 10.1 extracted into a separate file as follows:

```
exports.fact = (description, fn) ->
  try
    fn()
    console.log "#{description}: OK"
  catch e
    console.error "#{description}: "
    throw e
```

Also note that the module being tested (listing 10.4) is also required at the top of the test.

Listing 10.3 Test for the `Tracking` class

```
assert = require 'assert'
{fact} = require './fact'
{Tracking} = require './10.4'

fact 'controller responds with 200 header and empty body', ->
  request =  url: '/some/url'

  response =
    write: (body) ->
      @body = body
    writeHead: (status) ->
      @status = status
    end: ->
      @ended = true

  tracking = new Tracking
  for view in [1..10]
    tracking.controller request, response

  assert.equal response.status, 200
  assert.equal response.body, ''
  assert.ok response.ended
  assert.equal tracking.pages['/some/url'], 10
```

Fact function from module

Tracking class from module

HTTP response double

Checks response

```
fact 'increments once for each key', ->
  tracking = new Tracking
  tracking.increment 'a/page' for i in [1..100]     Increments some
  tracking.increment 'another/page'                 different page counts

  assert.equal tracking.pages['a/page'], 100        Tests that page counts
  assert.equal tracking.total(), 101                are as expected

fact 'starts and stops server', ->
  http =
    createServer: ->
      @created = true
      listen: =>                                    http
        @listening = true                           double
      close: =>
        @listening = false

  tracking = new Tracking {}, http
  tracking.start()                                  Tests that server
                                                    starts and stops
  assert.ok http.listening                          correctly

  tracking.stop()
  assert.ok not http.listening
```

The Tracking class is shown in the next listing.

Listing 10.4 The `Tracking` class

```
http = require 'http'

class Tracking
  constructor: (@options, @http) ->
    @pages = []                                     Initialized pages
  start: (callback) ->
    @server = @http.createServer @controller        Creates the server, passes
    @server.listen @options.port, callback          controller to it, and then starts it
  stop: ->
    @server.close()                                 Closes the server
  controller: (request, response) =>
    @increment request.url
    response.writeHead 200, 'Content-Type': 'text/html'   Handles responses
    response.write ''                                      that arrive, invoking
    response.end()                                         increment
  increment: (key) ->
    @pages[key] ?= 0                                Increases the
    @pages[key] = @pages[key] + 1                  relevant page count
  total: ->
    sum = 0
    for page, count of @pages                      Totals the counts
      sum = sum + count                            for all pages
    sum

exports.Tracking = Tracking                         ◁── Exports
                                                        Tracking class
```

10.4.4 *Exercise*

Write a small expectation library that makes the following possible:

```
fact 'http service should be accessed', ->
  httpDouble = double http
  tracking = new Tracking {}, httpDouble
  assert.ok httpDouble.listen.called == true
```

Assertions, unit tests, dependencies, expectations, and dealing with the asynchronous are important, but remember why you started down this path in the first place. You want to write real programs with evidence that they do what they're supposed to do. This means you started with a test for what the program *does*.

10.5 *System tests*

You started with a requirement:

> *It should record each product the user clicks on.*

This is a system requirement. System tests are often *functional tests* because they test the functionality of the whole system. Functional tests are *not* related to functional programming, so you might find the term *system test* less confusing.

To learn how to test-drive the development of a program, you looked only at small components of the overall tracking system. This was necessary for you to understand how things work but was somewhat artificial. In practice you'd implement only the components required to get a passing test for a single system requirement.

The good news is that you now have the pieces of the test-driven development puzzle you need to start with a system requirement, write a test for it, and continue to write the code to meet that requirement:

```
fact 'the tracking application tracks a single mouse click', ->
  tracking.start ->
    assert.equals tracking.total, 0
    userVisitsPageAndClicks()
    assert.equals tracking.total, 1
```

You know that the asynchronous part of the tracking program has been reflected in the test, with the remainder of the test being passed to the start method. You also know that userVisitsPageAndClicks is going to create a double for a user because having a real user for your test isn't practical; you'd need to kidnap one and keep them locked in your basement. The following listing demonstrates this slightly differently as a full working example.

Listing 10.5   System test for tracking application

```
assert = require 'assert'
{fact} = require './fact'
http = require 'http'

{Tracking} = require './10.4'
{User} = require './10.6'
```

```
SERVER_OPTIONS =              Server config options—uppercase by
  host: 'localhost'           convention but not real constants.
  port: 8080

fact 'the tracking application tracks a user mouse click', ->
  tracking = new Tracking SERVER_OPTIONS, http

  tracking.start ->
    assert.equal tracking.total(), 0
    fred = new User SERVER_OPTIONS, http
    fred.visitPage '/some/url', ->          Assert the tracking total inside
     fred.clickMouse ->                     the callback to the asynchronous
        assert.equal tracking.total(), 1    user mouse click.
        tracking.stop()
```

The User class used in listing 10.5 is shown in the next listing. This class provides a
user that can interact inside the tests. Think of it like a test double for a real person. It
simulates what happens when a real person visits the site.

Listing 10.6 The User class

```
class User
  constructor: (@options, @http) ->        Constructor shorthand
  visitPage: (url, callback) ->            (chapter 5).
    @options.path = url
    @options.method = 'GET'
    callback()
  clickMouse: (callback) ->                For testing, the user
    request = @http.request @options, (request, response) ->   just needs to create
      callback()                           the necessary http
    request.end()                          request.

exports.User = User
```

It's time to put all of these tests together and create a test suite.

10.6   Test suites

You have tests. Some of them are unit tests. Some of them are system tests. The total
set of all the tests for the application belong together in a test suite.

All of the tests you have are executable, but to execute them you have to run each
of them individually. Suppose you have your tests in three files. To test if the program
is working correctly, you'll need to execute all three files from the command line:

```
> coffee test1.coffee
# OK

> coffee test2.coffee
# OK

> coffee test3.coffee
# Fail
```

If you have to run all of the tests individually, then the chances that you *actually will*
run them all the time is rather small. To get the full value of the tests, they need to be

easy to run—all at once. In this section you'll learn how to create a test suite for your tests that makes it easy to run them all at once. This involves removing some repetition with test setups and teardowns, making it easier to run the tests with a single command, and making the tests run for you, automatically. First up, setups and teardowns.

10.6.1 *Setups and teardowns*

It's very likely that you have several tests that require a "bunch of the same stuff" to be in place before they run. Suppose you have three that all require an `http` double. You might start writing the first test like this:

```
fact 'this test uses a http double', ->
  http =
    get: (options, callback) ->
      callback()
      @
    on: (event, callback) ->
      # do nothing
```

When you write the second test, you don't want to replicate the code for `http double`, so you move it outside the `fact`:

```
httpPrototype =
  get: (options, callback) ->
    callback()
    @
  on: (event, callback) ->
    # do nothing
fact 'this test uses a http double', ->
  http = Object.create httpPrototype

fact 'this test also uses a http double', ->
  http = Object.create httpPrototype
```

Even that is tedious. What you really want is to define some setup that's done either before all of your tests or before each of your tests. By now you know that functions are good for this sort of thing. For example, you can extract the double creation into a `createHttp` function to run before each test:

```
createHttp = ->
  http =
    get: (options, callback) ->
      callback()
      @
    on: (event, callback) ->
      # do nothing
  http
fact 'this test uses a http double' ->
  http = createHttp()
  # the rest of the test goes here
```

If you have to create 10 doubles, you'll have to call 10 different setup functions. No thanks. The simplest way to handle setup for groups of tests is to take advantage of function scope. If you have three tests that use an `http` double, put them in a single scope:

```
do ->
  http = {}
  setup = ->                                    ◁─┐
    http =                                        │
      get: (options, callback) ->                 │
        callback()                                │
        @                                         │
      on: (event, callback) ->                    │   Setup function in
        # do nothing                              │   the do -> scope
                                                  │   is available to all
  fact 'this test uses a http double' ->          │   facts contained
    setup()                                  ◁───┤
    # the rest of the test goes here              │
                                                  │
  fact 'this test also uses a http double' ->     │
    setup()                                  ◁───┘
    # the rest of the test goes here
```

Similarly, when each test is finished, you might need to clean up after yourself by extracting the cleanup work to a `teardown` function that's invoked after each test.

With setups and teardowns, you've tidied things up inside test files. How about multiple test files—how do you deal with those?

10.6.2 *Test helpers and runners*

You still have to run your test files individually. To test three modules, you must invoke three test files:

```
> coffee word_utils.spec.coffee
# OK

> coffee tracking.spec.coffee
# OK

> coffee another.spec.coffee
# OK
```

This is annoying. When there's only one file to test, it's almost bearable, but what about when there are 10, 100, or 1,000 test files? To be confident that you'll actually go to the bother of running the tests, they need to all be invoked with a single command.

TEST HELPERS

You have a new dependency problem in your tests. Everywhere you look, there are `require` statements that grab different parts of the program and do scaffolding in order to get a sufficient environment in place so that your tests will run. This is annoying to do multiple times. Don't let the machines mock you.

A test helper provides a single place to put all of the things that the tests need to run. The test helper for the tracking application tests is in the listing that follows.

Listing 10.7   The test helper

```
dependencies =
  'Tracking': '../tracking'
  'User': '../user'
  'fact': '../fact'
```
Keep a hash of dependencies required during tests.

```
for dependency, path of dependencies
  exports[dependency] = require(path)[dependency]
```
Export them all from the test helper.

To run the test files together, you can write another *test runner* file that finds all of the tests and runs them.

TEST RUNNERS

You want all your tests to run with a single command, a test command reminiscent of the ring of power in *The Lord of The Rings*:

> One command to rule them all, one command to find them, one command
> to bring them all and in the darkness bind them.

You get the idea.

A simple test runner just finds test files in a specific directory based on their filenamcs and executes their contents as CoffeeScript. This test runner can also inject `require` dependencies into a file by munging the file source to put additional `require` expressions at the top of the file before they're run. This is a somewhat unsophisticated and brutish approach, but in the absence of a test framework or a more elegant solution, it works. The following listing shows such a test runner.

Listing 10.8   The test runner

```
fs = require 'fs'
coffee = require 'coffee-script'

test = (file) ->
  fs.readFile file, 'utf-8', (err, data) ->
    it = """
      {fact} = require './fact'
      assert = require 'assert'
      #{data}
    """
    coffee.run it, filename: file

spec = (file) ->
  /[^.]*\.spec\.coffee$/.test file

fs.readdir '.', (err, files) ->
  for file in files
    test file if spec file
```

The test file source has some requires inserted at the top, and then the resulting source is run. This saves you from having to put these specific requires at the top of every file.

Run all the test files in the current directory that have a filename ending with .spec.coffee.

Injecting modules into the source code of a test before passing it to the runtime makes you slightly uneasy, but it works and can make writing tests a bit easier. Making it easier to write tests means you'll be more likely to actually write them, keeping the rest of the program cleaner. Although different test frameworks will have other ways to provide these conveniences for you, the reasons behind them are the same.

What does the setup of the program look like after all this is done? The file and directory structure for the tracking application should now be rearranged to look like this:

```
├──tracking/
│    ├── test.coffee          ⟵  The test runner
│    ├── spec/                    from listing 10.8
│    │    ├── tracking.spec.coffee
│    │    ├── 2.spec.coffee       Test files; copy the contents of
│    │    ├── 3.spec.coffee       listing 10.3 to tracking.spec.coffee
│    ├── src/
│    │    ├── tracking.coffee     Program file; copy the contents
│    │    ├── 2.coffee            of listing 10.4 to tracking.coffee
│    │    ├── 3.coffee
```

Move the test (or spec) files to a spec folder and the program source files to an src folder, keeping them clearly separated. When you do this, you'll also need to update any require paths.

When the test.coffee file is executed, all of the tests in the test directory run and report the result:

```
> coffee test.coffee
```

Instead of invoking it using the `coffee` command, you can change test.coffee into an executable script, allowing the tests to be run without invoking `coffee` directly on the command line:

```
> ./test
```

An executable script is easier to integrate with other programs. Be sure to make the script executable. The exact method of doing this depends on the platform you're running on. Here is a simple shell script for *nix-based systems that assumes Coffee-Script is installed:

```
#!/bin/bash
set -eu

TEST_DIR=$(dirname "$0")        A simple bash script for
                                running a CoffeeScript
main () {                       program in test.coffee
  coffee test.coffee
}

main "$@"
```

It's nice that you can run all the tests with a single command. What would be even nicer, though, is if you didn't have to remember to run them at all.

10.6.3 *Watchers*

The final piece of the test suite puzzle is getting tests to run automatically when a file is changed. This way, you wouldn't even need to run the single command that executes the tests. Instead, you can start the watcher. The watcher script here is called autotest because it runs the tests automatically:

```
> ./autotest
```

Then start writing tests. If you write a failing test in the file test1.spec.coffee,

```
fact 'True should equal false', ->
  assert.equal true, false
```

then you'll see a message on the command line:

```
> True should equal false
> Assertion Error: true != false
> at spec/1.spec.coffee
```

An example autotest script is shown in the next listing. This file needs to be executable.

Listing 10.9   The watcher

```
#!/usr/bin/env coffee                    ⊲─── Specify that this shell
                                              script is CoffeeScript.
coffee = require 'coffee-script'
fs     = require 'fs'

SPEC_PATH = './spec/'      Define some paths to use everywhere in the program. These are uppercase
SRC_PATH = './src/'        by convention only; there are no real constants in CoffeeScript.

test = (file) ->
  fs.readFile SPEC_PATH + file, 'utf-8', (err, data) ->
    it = """
      {fact} = require '../fact'
      assert = require 'assert'
      #{data}
    """
    coffee.run it, filename: SPEC_PATH + file    ⊲─── Add the file path back to
                                                      coffee.run so it knows where to
spec = (file) ->                                      look for requires inside the file.
  if /#/.test file then false
  else /\.spec\.coffee$/.test file

tests = ->
  fs.readdir SPEC_PATH, (err, files) ->
    for file in files
      test file if spec file

fs.watch SPEC_PATH, (event, filename) ->        Watch the specifications and
  tests()                                        the program source. Rerun all
                                                 the tests if any files change in
fs.watch SRC_PATH, (event, filename) ->          either of them.
  tests()
```

This autotest runs as a script in a *nix environment (such as your MacBook or your Linux or BSD server). Consult a local expert for how to create a version for your operating system.

The test script and watch script provided here read only a single directory. In practice you might need to monitor all of the subdirectories as well. But it's just as likely

Figure 10.1   Tests are evidence that your program works.

that you'll be using an existing testing framework. Having seen how the testing stack goes together, though, you're in a better position to work with an existing testing framework. You know how to use a test framework because you've written one. That's right: in this chapter you've written your own test framework. It wasn't that difficult!

By writing (or using) a test framework, you've made it easier to write tests. If it's easier to write tests, it's more likely that you actually *will* write tests and, as a result, actually have evidence that your program behaves the way it's supposed to. Evidence is good. Scruffy and Agtron wouldn't trust your untested software any more than they would trust the untested medicine in figure 10.1.

You get the message. Write tests.

10.7   Summary

You've learned how to test programs. Actually, by writing tests without a test framework, you've written your own tiny test framework. That was surprisingly easy to do in CoffeeScript, wasn't it? This was valuable in showing you how the fundamental principles work. When you have to use a testing framework, you'll understand the basic principles behind it. A testing framework provides easier ways to do some of the tasks outlined in this chapter. Although which test framework you use often comes down to personal choice, popular test frameworks worth exploring are Jasmine, Mocha, and node-unit, all of which can be found in the Node.js package manager, npm.

Why go to all this trouble writing tests? Surely this program is small enough that it doesn't need any tests. You're familiar with the phrase, "famous last words"? If you don't have any tests, then there's a very good chance that one day you'll become unglued. It's quite possible that when you do become unglued, you will do some heroics and save the day all by yourself. Or perhaps by sheer brilliance or determination you don't need the tests. The tests are boring—until one day they fail. Then they're priceless.

The next chapter is about creating user interfaces for web browsers: what the rules are, when to break them, and how the strengths of CoffeeScript can help with some of the challenges unique to user interfaces.

In the browser

This chapter covers

- Building browser-based programs
- Creating polyfills for cross-browser compatibility
- Building retained- and immediate-mode interfaces
- Structuring browser-based programs

A web browser can be a hostile environment in which to run a program, but Coffee-Script can help you keep your browser-based applications manageable. It's not the individual features of CoffeeScript that help you in a browser. Instead, it's the focus on simplicity and clarity of expression and semantics that help you to keep your sanity in the world of web browsers, which can at times seem insane. That said, although the benefit of CoffeeScript in a browser is in how you use it to structure programs, it's still important to learn the challenges of the browser environment that your CoffeeScript programs live in.

In this chapter you'll learn how to write browser-based programs in CoffeeScript that run on multiple, often incompatible, browsers. To get there you'll learn how to deliver your CoffeeScript to a browser, how to deal with browsers that don't support the features you need, how to create user interfaces using retained- and immediate-mode techniques, how to create animations, and how to manage the structure of your program and how fast it runs. It's time to get started.

11.1 Getting started

Imagine Agtron has a few servers that frequently run out of both CPU and network bandwidth. This causes his online shop to temporarily go offline, and Agtron loses money. If only Agtron had a web-based dashboard to show him the status of his servers (in real time), then he could prevent the shop from being offline.

Your mission, should you choose to accept it, is to create a real-time dashboard for Agtron. In figure 11.1 you see Agtron's back-of-the-envelope drawing of how he wants the dashboard to look when viewing the status for a single server. It looks a bit like a heart-rate monitor found in a hospital.

This is going to be a browser-based dashboard, so you start with the basic HTML in the following listing.

Listing 11.1 The basic HTML page

```html
<!DOCTYPE html>
<html dir='ltr' lang='en-US'>
  <head>
    <meta http-equiv='Content-Type' content='text/html; charset=utf-8'>
    <title>Radiator</title>
    <style type="text/css">
    html, body { padding: 0; margin:0; }
    </style>
    <script src='status.js'></script>          ◁——  This status.js file is compiled
  </head>                                             from the CoffeeScript in listings
  <body>                                              that appear later in this chapter.
    <div id='status'></div>
  </body>
</html>
```

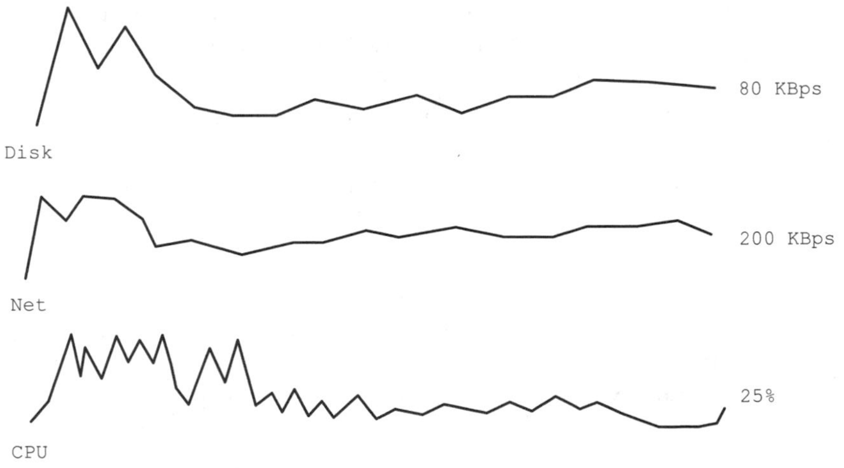

Figure 11.1   Agtron's dashboard

The script referenced by `<script src='status.js'></script>` is a JavaScript file, but your browser-based program will be written in CoffeeScript. How do you deliver your CoffeeScript program to a browser?

11.1.1 *Manual compilation*

The first option you have is to use the manual command-line CoffeeScript compiler. But that will quickly become tedious if you have to invoke the compiler every time you change your program. Suppose the program is contained in the file status.coffee:

```
> coffee -c status.coffee
```

You don't want to manually recompile again and again. There are other options; one of them is to send CoffeeScript straight to the browser.

11.1.2 *Browser compilation*

Browsers execute JavaScript, not CoffeeScript. But because CoffeeScript is implemented *in CoffeeScript*, a compiled version of CoffeeScript can run in the browser and compile CoffeeScript for you on the fly. Read the previous sentence again. Let it sink in.

Once you're ready, you can compile CoffeeScript in a browser by first including a browser-specific version of CoffeeScript:

```
<script src='http://coffeescript.org/extras/coffee-script.js'></script>
```

Once your HTML document has that, you can include a CoffeeScript source file:

```
<script type='text/coffeescript' src='status.coffee'></script>
```

Web browsers don't recognize the `text/coffeescript` script *type*, but by including CoffeeScript in the browser, the CoffeeScript compiler can turn your CoffeeScript source files into JavaScript on the fly. How does it do this? It loads the source of your CoffeeScript program, compiles it, and then tells the browser to evaluate the compiled JavaScript.

That sounds too good to be true! Unfortunately it is. Sending CoffeeScript directly to the browser comes with a performance disadvantage because every time the browser loads your program, it has to first load the CoffeeScript, then compile the program, and *then* run it. Regardless, you don't want to compile your CoffeeScript manually. You need a third alternative.

11.1.3 *Automatic compilation*

Manual compilation is not only annoying; it can hurt your interface. To develop good user interfaces, it helps to have frequent and direct feedback from the working interface. If you have to manually compile every time, you'll lose your flow.

To keep the immediacy when writing CoffeeScript programs for web browsers, use the `-w` (watch) compiler argument to automatically recompile every time you save a change to a file. Invoke the compiler with the watch option and the filenames you want to compile:

```
> coffee -c -w status.coffee
```

Each time you save a change, you're notified that the compiler has run:

```
# 21:52:16 - compiled status.coffee
# 21:52:57 - compiled status.coffee
# 21:53:00 - compiled status.coffee
```

Now that you're happily compiling away (or not), it's time to get back to the task of building Agtron's dashboard.

11.2 *Communicating with the outside world*

Before you can display any data about Agtron's servers, you need to get that data from somewhere. Suppose Agtron has already implemented a data server that collects information from all of the servers he wants to monitor and serves them up for you over HTTP as JSON. Agtron's back-of-the-envelope network diagram is shown in figure 11.2.

Your CoffeeScript program is entirely browser-based, so you'll need to understand the different techniques for loading data from a server from inside a browser. In this section you'll learn three techniques: XMLHttpRequest, dynamic script insertion, and WebSocket.

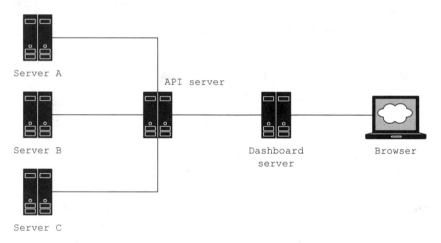

Figure 11.2   Agtron's servers

11.2.1 *Using XMLHttpRequest*

One technique you've seen for fetching data over the web in a browser-based program is to use the XMLHttpRequest object (discussed in chapter 5). Here, you wrap it in an http function:

```
http = (method, src, callback) ->
  handler = ->
    if @readyState is 4 and @status is 200
      unless @responseText is null
        callback JSON.parse @responseText

  client = new XMLHttpRequest
  client.onreadystatechange = handler
```

```
    client.open method, src
    client.send()

get = (src, callback) ->
  http "GET", src, callback
```

Unfortunately, there's a catch with using `XMLHttpRequest`. For security reasons, it works only if the data you're loading is on the same domain as your browser-based application. Suppose that in your case the dashboard is on one particular domain at http://www.agtronsemporium.com, and the data server is on a different domain at http://www.agtronsapi.com. How do you load data from a different domain?

11.2.2 *Dynamic script insertion*

An alternative technique to `XMLHttpRequest` that works across different domains is to take advantage of the browser's ability to dynamically load and execute new `<script>`s at any time. You might call this *hot code loading* because program code is being loaded while the program is running (while it's *hot*). To load an external script dynamically into the application, you dynamically insert a `script` element with the desired `src` attribute:

```
window.serverStatusCallback = (status) ->
  console.log status

head = document.querySelector 'head'
script = document.createElement 'script'
script.src = 'http://www.agtronsapi.com/server-status.js'
head.appendChild script
```

If the `server-status` script that's loaded has the data wrapped in the appropriate callback, as follows, then the status will be logged to the console:

```
window.serverStatusCallback({
  'server 1': {
    'cpu': 22,
    'network': {
      'in': 2343,
      'out' 3344
    }
  }
});
```

But that will only load the data once, and Agtron wants to leave the application running and see the information about his servers update over time. A simple approach to getting regular data updates is to just ask for the data periodically.

> **HOW TO RUN THE LISTINGS**   The remaining listings in this chapter are client-side and require a server to run. The downloadable code includes a server.coffee file that can be used to experiment with the listings. Run server.coffee from the command line and visit http://localhost:8080/ to start experimenting.

In the following listing, you see the techniques described in this section used in a first version of the dashboard program that repeatedly polls Agtron's servers to get the most recent data. Instead of displaying a graph, this first version simply displays the current numerical value as text.

Listing 11.2   The status updating script

```
window.onload = ->
  status = document.querySelector '#status'

  render = (buffer) ->
    status.style.color = 'green'
    status.style.fontSize = '120px'
    status.innerHTML = buffer[buffer.length-1]

  nextCallbackId = do ->
    callbackId = 0
    -> callbackId = callbackId + 1

  nextCallbackName = ->
    "callback#{nextCallbackId()}"

  fetch = (src, callback) ->
    head = document.querySelector 'head'
    script = document.createElement 'script'
    ajaxCallbackName = nextCallbackName()
    window[ajaxCallbackName] = (data) ->
      callback data
    script.src = src + "?callback=#{ajaxCallbackName}"
    head.appendChild script

  seconds = (n) ->
    1000*n

  framesPerSecond = (n) ->
    (seconds 1)/n

  makeUpdater = (buffer = []) ->
    bufferRenderer = (json) ->
      buffer.push (JSON.parse json).hits
      render buffer

    ->
      window.setInterval ->
        fetch '/feed.json', bufferRenderer
      , framesPerSecond 20

  updater = makeUpdater()
  updater()
```

The window.onload event is fired when the browser window has loaded, by which time it's ready to execute the program. For simplicity in this first version of the program, the entire thing is declared inside the function assigned to window.onload.

This render function simply updates the page with the most recent values.

Some dynamic script insertion used to fetch data.

This makeUpdater function returns a function that will, in turn, return a function that creates an updater.

A Request to feed.json returns JSON containing the number of hits.

But as with most things in browser-based programs, there's a catch. Although some code (such as JSON data for Agtron's servers) is safe to hot load,

```
{
  'servers': [
    {
      'name': 'tolimas'
      'cpu': 22,
      'network': {
        'in': 2343,
```

```
      'out' 3344
    }
  }
]
}
```

other code can be unsafe, and unsafe code (be it malicious or clumsy) inserted into a hot program can have disastrous effects. Imagine dynamically inserting a script that overrides the built-in `map` method (chapter 5) on the `Array` prototype. All of your arrays will break!

```
Array::map = -> null        ◁── Suppose this line
                                is hot-loaded.

[9,8,7,6].map (item) -> item*2    ◁── Any use of map will
# null                                now return null.
```

If you load source code into your program, there's a chance that source code will do something that you don't want it to. It's possible to sandbox code in a browser as you learned to do on the server (in chapter 8), but the only safe rule to follow in a web browser is to *load source code only from sources you trust*.

You trust Agtron's data server to only return objects and not to override any prototypes or do anything else nasty to you. If you only poll it for new information periodically, as in listing 11.2, will you be getting data updates often enough? Surely there's some way to get updates in real time.

11.2.3 *Going real time with WebSocket*

If the data server could inform your dashboard application when there was new data, then you wouldn't need to poll. When the server informs the client in this way, the server is said to *push* data to the client. To achieve this, you need to open something called a WebSocket connection between the server and your dashboard.

To experiment with and learn about WebSocket, it's useful to have a local server that will push some data down a WebSocket connection so that you can play with it. You see a very basic Node.js-powered CoffeeScript program that pushes random data down a WebSocket connection in the following listing.

Listing 11.3   A random-number socket emitter

```
{EventEmitter} = require 'events'
WebSocketServer = (require 'websocket').server    ◁── The websocket protocol
                                                      handling here is
                                                      provided by a library.
seconds = (n) -> n*1000

emitRandomNumbers = (emitter, event, interval) ->
  setInterval ->
    emitter.emit event, Math.floor Math.random()*100
  , interval

source = new EventEmitter
emitRandomNumbers source, 'update', seconds(4)
```

```
attachSocketServer = (server) ->
  socketServer = new WebSocketServer httpServer: server
  socketServer.on 'request', (request) ->
    connection = request.accept 'graph', request.origin
    source.on 'update', (data) ->
      connection.sendUTF JSON.stringify data
```

> A function that will
> attach a socket
> server to an existing
> HTTP server.

```
exports.attachSocketServer = attachSocketServer
```

Before WebSocket, web browsers didn't have any standard way to have data pushed to them. Instead, various tricks were cobbled together to get real-time effects in browsers. Recently, work to standardize the WebSocket protocol (http://tools.ietf.org/html/rfc6455) has made life easier for you, and you can open a connection without much fuss:

```
socket = new WebSocket 'ws://www.agtronsapi.com/server-data-socket'
```

As with most things in a browser, `WebSocket` is event driven, so you must listen for events:

```
socket.onmessage = (message) -> console.log "Received message #{message}"
```

The server is now responsible for *pushing* the data to the client instead of the client having to ask the server for new data. This is a browser-based program, though, so there must be a catch. Indeed there is.

WebSocket is a new technology, so you can't be sure that any given browser will support it. Cross-browser compatibility is something you must always be aware of when building browser-based programs. Such programs have to work in multiple different browsers—browsers that may not support the same features.

11.3 *Cross-browser compatibility*

Imagine now that Scruffy tells you he received an email from his 106-year-old great-grandmother telling you that the dashboard doesn't work for her. You're not sure why Scruffy's 106-year-old great-grandmother needs to use Agtron's dashboard, but apparently she does. When you ask what she sees when she opens the dashboard, she tells you it's a blank screen. Why does she see a blank screen?

The problem is that Scruffy's elderly great-grandmother is using an elderly browser. Suppose this browser is called *Browser X*. When you obtain a copy of Browser X and use it to view the dashboard, you quickly see that there's an error when it executes `document.querySelector`:

```
document.querySelector '#status'
# document.querySelector is not a function
```

Your browser-based program has to run on many different browsers. Each browser may or may not support a particular browser feature that you use in your program (even when those features are standardized). Special objects that belong to the browser called *host objects* provide some of those features. You've already encountered the `XMLHttpRequest` and `document` host objects.

> **Feature detection**
>
> The technique demonstrated in this section is called *feature detection* because it checks to see whether a runtime has a specific feature and defines it if it does not. A contrasting approach is to detect the runtime instead of the feature. Detecting the runtime proves to be ultimately unmaintainable and isn't recommended except in rare cases where a runtime is completely broken.

Web browsers define host objects such as the `document` object. They might not be defined outside of a browser, such as on the REPL:

```
document?
# false
```

Host objects are part of the Document Object Model (DOM) and can differ wildly across browsers. Although the behavior of *some* host objects is standardized, you should anticipate that different browsers will behave differently. More importantly, host objects don't behave like regular objects. They might *look* like regular objects, but they're not. *Don't expect host objects to work like regular objects.*

> **The Document Object Model**
>
> The convention, or model, that defines how your browser-based application interacts with host objects that belong to the document loaded by the web browser is called the *Document Object Model (DOM)*. Objects provided by the document are called *DOM objects*, and *all* DOM objects are host objects. DOM objects, such as `document`, are often a source of frustration.

How do you deal with incompatibilities in the host objects of different browsers? By using polyfills.

11.3.1 Polyfilling host objects

A *polyfill* is a function or group of functions that makes a smooth surface on which your main program can be written, without having to worry about the inconsistencies. It comes from *polyfilla* (also known as *spackling paste*)—a product that's used to fill in gaps and cracks on a wall to create a smooth surface, just like Scruffy and Agtron are doing in figure 11.3. A polyfill in a web browser works the same way—filling in the gaps and cracks between the different browsers.

   Your first polyfill is for the `document.querySelector` that doesn't work in Browser X. You use the method to find an element using an ID, so a reasonable first polyfill for your needs relies on `document.getElementById`. The trick is to define the method only if it doesn't already exist:

```
document.querySelector ?= (selector) ->
  (document.getElementById (selector.replace /^#/gi, ''))
```

Define document .querySelector only if it doesn't already exist.

Figure 11.3　Scruffy and Agtron using a polyfill

But suppose that once you've defined `querySelector`, another programmer (such as Scruffy) comes along and, quite reasonably, expects it to work according to the specification. What happens when Scruffy tries to use your polyfill to find an element using the class name?

```
<ul class='pages'>
  <li></li>
  <li class='active'>Home</li>
  <li>About</li>
  <li>Contact</li>
</ul>
```

Your polyfill fails silently and returns `null` as if nothing were wrong:

```
document.querySelector '.links .active'
# null
```

Suppose, though, that you don't have time to implement (or even read) the entire specification. Change your polyfill to throw an exception if it's used for something that you know it doesn't support:

```
document.querySelector ?= (selector) ->
  if /^#/.test selector
    (document.getElementById (selector.replace /^#/gi, ''))
  else
    throw new Error 'Not supported by this implementation'
```

This polyfill throws an exception if it doesn't implement what you try to use it for.

Now at least other programmers are warned that your polyfill doesn't implement the specification (assuming that they didn't read your tests to discover that already). If needed, they can override your implementation with a more complete one.

It's not just host objects that are inconsistent across browsers, though—some language features aren't implemented by all browsers. In fact, the absence of things like `Array.map` in older browsers was one of the early motivations for creating CoffeeScript.

11.3.2 Polyfilling language features

Each browser moves at a different pace. One browser might implement a new feature of JavaScript while it's still just ideas, whereas another browser may implement the same feature years after it's standardized.

For example, take a language feature that you're familiar with—being able to create a new object with an existing object as the prototype using `Object.create`. It's easy to take this feature for granted, but unfortunately, when you test your program in Browser X, you discover that it isn't defined. What do you do? Polyfill:

```
Object.create ?= (prototype) ->
  F = ->
  F.prototype = prototype
  new F()
```

Define this polyfill only if it doesn't exist.

Declare a function to be used as the constructor for the new object.

Set the prototype for the constructor to be the prototype parameter.

Create and return a new instance by new-ing the constructor function F.

Job done, right? Not quite. Agtron later informs you that your polyfill doesn't implement the entire specification (you know, the one you didn't have time to read). There's actually a second parameter (see chapter 13). To prevent people from getting nasty surprises when they use your polyfill, you take the approach of throwing an exception if the polyfill is used for part of the specification that it doesn't implement:

```
Object.create ?= (prototype, extensions) ->
  if extensions
    throw new Error 'Not supported by this implementation'
  else
    F = ->
    F.prototype = prototype
    new F()
```

Throw an exception if this method is invoked with a second parameter.

Not all language features can be fixed with a polyfill in this way. Any language feature that requires syntax can't be polyfilled at runtime. Writing a polyfill for language syntax would be like building a house out of wallpaper. Changing syntax means compilation. Back to Agtron's dashboard—how will you create those graphs that Agtron wants? More generally, how will you create the user interface?

11.4 Creating a user interface

There are two styles of managing your drawing in a web browser: *retained mode* and *immediate mode*. Although web browsers have traditionally used a retained mode, some recent APIs such as `canvas` are immediate mode. The difference between retained and immediate mode isn't crucial to your understanding of CoffeeScript, but understanding it will help you write better CoffeeScript programs in the browser. It's time to learn both.

11.4.1 *Retained mode with the DOM*

In retained mode, what you draw to the view, such as a graph, can be directly modified and manipulated after it has been drawn. Inside a browser, the DOM is a retained-mode API. You can both assign a value to the innerHTML property of a DOM element *and* get the current value:

```
number = document.querySelector '#status'
number.innerHTML = 55

number.innerHTML
# 55
```

That's the essence of retained mode. Information persists and can be retrieved.

How do you take this retained-mode API and display a chart for Agtron? Well, a line chart like the one Agtron wants is a bit too involved to start with when working with the DOM, so instead Agtron suggests that you start with a bar chart of 20 bars:

```
for number, index in values
  measurement[index].style.height = 55
```

A program that displays a bar chart of the last 20 values obtained (by setting the heights of 20 DOM elements) is shown in the following listing. Some sections of the listing are the same as, or similar to, sections of listing 11.2.

Listing 11.4   Drawing a bar chart with DOM elements

```
window.onload = ->
  status = document.querySelector '#status'

  ensureBars = (number) ->
    unless (document.querySelectorAll '.bar').length >= number
      for n in [0..number]
        bar = document.createElement 'div'
        bar.className = 'bar'
        bar.style.width = '60px'
        bar.style.position = 'absolute'
        bar.style.bottom = '0'
        bar.style.background = 'green'
        bar.style.color = 'white'
        bar.style.left = "#{60*n}px"
        status.appendChild bar

  render = (buffer) ->
    ensureBars 20
    bars = document.querySelectorAll '.bar'
    for bar, index in bars
      bar.style.height = "#{buffer[index]}px"
      bar.innerHTML = buffer[index] || 0
```

> **The ensureBars function renders the last 20 values in the buffer as bars.**

```
nextCallbackId = do ->
  callbackId = 0
  -> callbackId = callbackId + 1

nextCallbackName = ->
  "callback#{nextCallbackId()}"

fetch = (src, callback) ->
  head = document.querySelector 'head'
  script = document.createElement 'script'
  ajaxCallbackName = nextCallbackName()
  window[ajaxCallbackName] = (data) ->
    callback data
  script.src = src + "?callback=#{ajaxCallbackName}"
  head.appendChild script

seconds = (n) ->
  1000*n

framesPerSecond = (n) ->
  (seconds 1)/n

makeUpdater = (buffer = []) ->
  bufferRenderer = (json) ->
    buffer.push (JSON.parse json).hits
    if buffer.length is 22 then buffer.shift()
    render buffer

  ->
    window.setInterval ->
      fetch '/feed.json', bufferRenderer      ⟵┐  A request to feed.json
    , framesPerSecond 1                           returns JSON containing
                                                  the number of hits.
updater = makeUpdater()
updater()
```

Agtron wants a line chart. How do you draw a line chart? Drawing a line chart using regular DOM elements wouldn't be much fun, so instead you'll draw the line chart using something called *canvas* that involves immediate-mode techniques.

11.4.2 *Immediate mode with HTML5 canvas*

In immediate mode, the view is only a buffer, and what you draw to it has no life outside of that buffer. There's no way to get elements back out of the buffer, so you never directly access or manipulate them. The HTML5 feature called *canvas* provides an immediate-mode API for browser-based drawing.

For now, assume that the standard canvas interface is supported everywhere you need it to be—if it isn't, you can write a polyfill for it later. To create a canvas, you create a new canvas element, append it to the existing status element (see listing 11.1), and then create a context inside the new element:

```
graph = document.createElement 'canvas'
graph.width = '800'
graph.height = '600'
```

```
graph.id = 'graph'
document.querySelector('#status').appendChild graph
```

> The new element to hold the graph is appended to the status element.

```
context = canvas.getContext '2d'
```

> Create a '2d' (two-dimensional) context on the element.

To draw a graph, you'll also use some other parts of the `canvas` API: `beginPath`, `lineTo`, and `stroke`. With those you can now draw a line. The basic mechanism is simple; you use coordinates to create a path on the canvas and then `stroke` or `fill` that path:

```
context.beginPath()
context.lineTo 0,0
context.lineTo 1,10
context.stroke()
```

> Begin a new path.

> This path starts at 0,0. That's the top left.

> Make a line to 1,10.

> Stroke the path, drawing the border.

With the graph data in an array, you convert it to a graph on a canvas with `beginPath`, `lineTo`, and `stroke`:

```
createGraph = (element) ->
  graph = document.createElement 'canvas'
  graph.width = '800'
  graph.height = '600'
  graph.id = 'graph'
  element.appendChild graph
  graph

getClearedContext = (element) ->
  element.width = element.width
  element.getContext()

drawLineGraph = (element, graphData, horizontalScale) ->
  context = element.
  context.beginPath()
  for y, x in graphData
    context.lineTo x*horizontalScale, y
  context.stroke()

status = document.querySelector '#status'
drawLineGraph getClearedContext(status), [110,160,350,100,260,240], 100
```

This will draw a simple line graph on the canvas like the one in figure 11.4.

Drawing with `canvas` is easy! This immediate mode is puzzling, though; if the canvas doesn't remember anything, then how do you know what you drew last time? How

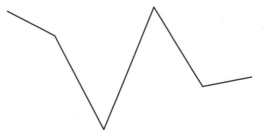

Figure 11.4 Drawing a simple line graph on a canvas

can you animate without knowing where you start? The trick with immediate mode is to not need to.

One of the hallmarks of immediate-mode UIs is a single `render` function that draws *everything* to the screen. Suppose your UI contains a graph and a title. Define a render function as drawing a graph and a title:

```
render = ->
  drawGraph()
  drawTitle()
```

You haven't yet defined `drawTitle`, but that's okay; the `render` function doesn't have to care about how `drawTitle` is implemented.

The next listing contains a program for rendering a line graph using `canvas`. This program has some parts in common with listing 11.4. Compare the retained- and immediate-mode approaches by comparing the listings.

Listing 11.5 Drawing a line chart with HTML5 `canvas`

```
window.onload = ->
  status = document.querySelector '#status'
  status.style.width = '640px'
  status.style.height = '480px'
  canvas = document.createElement 'canvas'
  canvas.width = '640'
  canvas.height = '480'
  status.appendChild canvas
  context = canvas.getContext '2d'

  drawTitle = (title) ->
    context.font = 'italic 20px sans-serif'
    context.fillText title

  drawGraph = (buffer) ->
    canvas.width = canvas.width           ◁─┐  Setting the width of the canvas
    context.fillStyle = 'black'              │  will clear it, so it's used here on
    context.clearRect 0, 0, 640, 480         │  each render to remove anything
    context.fillRect 0, 0, 640, 480          │  currently on the canvas.
    context.lineWidth = 2
    context.strokeStyle = '#5AB946'
    context.beginPath()
    prev = 0
    for y, x in buffer
      unless y is prev
        context.lineTo 0 + x*10, 100 + y
      prev = y
    context.stroke()

  render = (buffer) ->
    drawGraph buffer
    drawTitle 'Server Dashboard'

  nextCallbackId = do ->
    callbackId = 0
    -> callbackId = callbackId + 1
```

```
nextCallbackName = ->
  "callback#{nextCallbackId()}"

fetch = (src, callback) ->
  head = document.querySelector 'head'
  script = document.createElement 'script'
  ajaxCallbackName = nextCallbackName()
  window[ajaxCallbackName] = (data) ->
    callback data
  script.src = src + "?callback=#{ajaxCallbackName}"
  head.appendChild script

seconds = (n) ->
  1000*n

framesPerSecond = (n) ->
  (seconds 1)/n

makeUpdater = (buffer = []) ->
  bufferRenderer = (json) ->
    buffer.push (JSON.parse json).hits
    if buffer.length is 22 then buffer.shift()
    render buffer

  ->
    window.setInterval ->
      fetch '/feed.json', bufferRenderer
    , framesPerSecond 1
updater = makeUpdater()
updater()
```

The programs in listings 11.4 and 11.5 both update several times per second. The constantly changing data makes the graphs look like they're moving. This movement is stuttered, but the feeling of movement is there nonetheless.

Animation can be a subtle and nuanced thing, but the realization that you don't need to explicitly request animation to make something appear animated is an important one when considering immediate-mode graphics. You want to create smooth animations, though. How do you do that?

11.5 *Creating animations*

The time-honored way to animate in a browser is to use `setInterval` or `setTimeout` to repeatedly change some property of a DOM object over time. Suppose you have a reference named bar to a DOM object that you want to animate:

```
seconds = (n) -> n*1000
setInterval bar.height, seconds 1
```

In a retained-mode API like the DOM, you directly manipulate the property on the object. How the object is rendered is taken care of by the retained-mode API. This is in contrast to an immediate-mode API like `canvas` where you do the rendering yourself.

This section explores animations in retained and immediate mode. It also explores the question of how to keep animations smooth in the single-threaded event-loop environment of a web browser.

11.5.1 *Retained mode*

To animate DOM objects in retained mode you repeatedly change a `style` property. Suppose you want to animate the bar on a bar chart so that instead of changing from a height of 20 to a height of 40 instantaneously (as with listing 11.4), it animates the change smoothly over one second.

TWEENS   The creation of animation between two states is called a *tween*.

A single bar in your bar chart is drawn as a single DOM element, and the height is set as a `style` property:

```
bar.style.height = 20
```

To animate this to a height of 40 in one second, use `setInterval` and increase the height by 1 pixel until the element reaches the target height:

```
bar = document.querySelector '#bar'          ◁┐ This solution is in
targetHeight = 65                             │ an imperative style.
interval = setInterval ->
  currentHeight = bar.style.height.replace /px/, ''    ◁┐
  if currentHeight >= targetHeight                      │ Using the current
    clearInterval interval                              │ height to set the
  else                                                  │ new height is
    bar.style.height currentHeight + 1 + 'px'          ◁┘ retained mode.
, 100
```

A named abstraction adds some clarity:

```
animateStyleInPixels = (element, propertyName, targetValue) ->
  interval = setInterval ->
    currentValue = element.style[propertyName].replace /px/, ''
    if currentValue >= targetValue
      clearInterval interval
    else
      bar.style[propertyName] = currentValue + 1 + 'px'
  , 100

bar = document.querySelector '.bar'
animateStyleInPixels bar, 'height', 65
```

That's all there is to basic animation in retained mode. Instead of moving things to their destinations immediately, you animate (tween) them from the start state to the end state. How does animation in immediate mode look different?

11.5.2 *Immediate mode*

Immediate-mode animation is like a flipbook or cell-based animation with each frame being a standalone static image. By rapidly flipping through the frames (the pages of the flipbook), you create the appearance of movement. When the frames change faster than the human eye can detect, the animation appears smooth. In the next listing, you see a program for a 30-frames-per-second immediate-mode graph.

Listing 11.6 Animating an immediate-mode line graph

```
window.onload = ->
  graph = document.querySelector '#status'
  graph.width = window.innerWidth
  graph.height = window.innerHeight
  context = graph.getContext '2d'

  render = (buffer) ->
    context.fillStyle = 'black'
    context.clearRect 0, 0, graph.width, graph.height
    context.fillRect 0, 0, graph.width, graph.height
    context.lineWidth = 5
    context.strokeStyle = '#5AB946'
    context.beginPath()
    prev = 0
    for y, x in buffer()
      unless y is prev
        context.lineTo 0 + x, 100 + y
      prev = y
    context.stroke()

  seconds = (n) ->
    1000*n

  framesPerSecond = (n) ->
    (seconds 1)/n

  buffer = []

  nextCallbackId = do ->
    callbackId = 0
    -> callbackId = callbackId + 1

  nextCallbackName = ->
    "callback#{nextCallbackId()}"

  fetch = (src, callback) ->
    head = document.querySelector 'head'
    script = document.createElement 'script'
    ajaxCallbackName = nextCallbackName()
    window[ajaxCallbackName] = (data) ->
      callback data
    script.src = src + "?callback=#{ajaxCallbackName}"
    head.appendChild script

  window.setInterval ->
    fetch '/feed.json', (json) ->
      render ->
        buffer.push (JSON.parse json).hits
        if buffer.length is graph.width then buffer.shift()
        buffer
  , framesPerSecond 30
```

> A render function that draws everything is a classic example of immediate mode.

Agtron points out that the solution in listing 11.6 works fine if data is being received frequently. If it's not being received frequently, you need to consider buffering and interpolation. That, however, is a lesson for another day. The final thing to consider with your browser-based program is how to put it together.

11.6 Structuring programs

Depending on the nature or circumstances of the problem (or the people solving the problem), an immediate-mode API can be inappropriate. Suppose that you must work with canvas, but you really need a retained-mode API. What can you do? Use the powerful design technique called wishful thinking.

11.6.1 Abstraction and APIs

Write your program *as if you already had the retained-mode API* that you want, and then implement it. Suppose you want a fluent retained-mode API that can draw a circle and then move the circle around. You call the API Cézanne after the famous French artist Paul Cézanne:

```
scene = Cézanne
.createScene('#scene')
.size(400, 400)

circle = scene
.createCircle()
.radius(10)
.color(Cézanne.RawUmber)
.position(20, 20)

circle.animatePosition 360, 360, 2
```

This looks *very* different from the canvas API. If you need an API like Cézanne but you start with raw canvas, then every single line that you write moves you farther from the API that you want. It's tempting to think that because you're not writing a library for other people to use, you don't need to create a nice, readable API. The opposite is true. Unless your program is throwaway (some are!), then write the API today that you will be happy to use in six months' time.

So, how do you implement an API like Cézanne on an immediate-mode API? The following listing shows an implementation of a retained-mode Cézanne API that can draw and animate circles.

Listing 11.7 A retained-mode circle-drawing API for canvas called Cézanne

```
Cézanne = do ->

  seconds = (n) -> n*1000
  framesPerSecond = 30
  tickInterval = seconds(1)/framesPerSecond

  circlePrototype =
    radius: (radius) ->
      @radius = radius
      this
    color: (hex) ->
      @hex = hex
      this
    position: (x, y) ->
      @x = x
      @y = y
      @context.beginPath()
```

```
      @context.fillStyle = @color
      @context.arc @x, @y, @radius, (Math.PI/180)*360, 0, true
      @context.closePath()
      @context.fill()
      this
    animatePosition: (x, y, duration) ->
      @frames ?= []
      frameCount = Math.ceil seconds(duration)/tickInterval
      for n in [1..frameCount]
        if n is frameCount
          do =>
            frame = n
            @frames.unshift =>
              @position x, y
        else
          do =>
            frame = n
            @frames.unshift =>
              @position x/frameCount*frame, y/frameCount*frame

scenePrototype =
  clear: ->
    @canvas.width = @width
  size: (width, height) ->
    @width = width
    @height = height
    @canvas.width = width
    @canvas.height = height
    this
  addElement: (element) ->
    @elements ?= []
    @elements.push element
    element.context = @context
  startClock: ->
    clockTick = =>
      @clear()
      for element in @elements
        frame = element.frames.pop()
        frame?()
    @clockInterval = window.setInterval clockTick, tickInterval

  createCircle: ->
    circle = Object.create circlePrototype
    @addElement circle
    circle

RawUmber: '#826644'
Viridian: '#40826d'

createScene: (selector) ->
  scene = Object.create scenePrototype
  node = document.querySelector selector
  scene.canvas = document.createElement 'canvas'
  scene.context = scene.canvas.getContext '2d'
  node.appendChild scene.canvas
  scene.startClock()
  scene
```

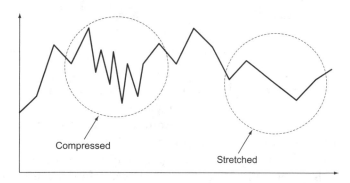

**Figure 11.5 Some
setInterval inaccuracy
is making the graph
inaccurate.**

The animations provided by the implementation of Cézanne shown in listing 11.7 aren't very smooth. What's wrong with them? They don't deal with time effectively. Whatever your choice of API, you'll have to deal with time. Time is always a concern.

11.6.2 Dealing with time

The problem with setTimeout and setInterval is that they aren't guaranteed to be accurate. In chapter 9 you saw that you could block the event loop by executing a long-running process. This is a problem for any program, but it's *visibly* bad for your animations. Figure 11.5 shows what happens when the event loop is blocked for something time-critical like drawing a graph.

If you block the event loop for 5 seconds, then instead of the animations you want, you'll get incorrect (and often surprising) animations. The same problem happens for any time-sensitive drawing inside a browser. Remember, the browser provides you with a single event loop—anything that happens on the event loop can impact time-based rendering.

The issue of timeout accuracy has more subtle implications. Although you'll notice if your event loop is blocked for a second, you won't normally notice if your event loop is blocked for 50 milliseconds. For an animation, even a 50-millisecond inaccuracy can make it look terrible. For something time-critical like a game, accuracy of the timing and animations is essential.

One tactic for getting around this is called *drift compensation*:

```
synchronisedInterval = (fn, t, maxDrift) ->
  drift = null
  previous = null
  compensate = 5
  reset = (hard = false) ->
    drift = 0 if hard
    previous = Date.now()
    if drift > maxDrift
      setTimeout runner, (t - compensate)
    else
      setTimeout runner, t
  runner = ->
    current = Date.now()
```

> **The compensation is achieved by resetting the timeout, accounting for the difference between the expected previous timeout and the actual timeout.**

```
    drift += current - previous - t
    previous = current
    fn()
    reset()
  reset true
```

If you have 100 timeouts running and you're trying to do drift compensation for all of them, then you might notice the browser performance starting to degrade. One solution in cases where you need to synchronize many events is to have a single *world* interval that synchronizes all the other events in the program to it.

Understanding different techniques for drawing, animation, and timing is essential to writing effective browser applications. Although programming for browser-based user interfaces is a topic too big to cover fully here, you have learned the core concepts you need to start building interfaces in CoffeeScript today.

11.7   *Summary*

In this chapter you learned about writing CoffeeScript programs in a web browser and the unique challenges that browser incompatibilities, animations, and timing present to you as a developer.

In the next chapter you'll see how to put together the various server and client components of your CoffeeScript application in a reliable and repeatable way with modules and builds.

Modules and builds

12

This chapter covers

- Modular applications with the Node.js module system
- Automated builds
- How to make modules work in a web browser
- Releasing your modular application to the world

It's unlikely that you'll only ever write programs that are contained entirely in a single file. Instead, a typical application consists of many files, often written by many people, and, as a result, one big file won't cut it. Breaking a program into many files makes each file easier to manage but also means you need some way to manage multiple files. Together, the files make up your program.

Individually, the part of the program contained in a single file is called a module. For example, you're by now very familiar with `fs`, the filesystem module:

```
fs = require 'fs'
```

What you're not yet familiar with is creating your own modules. That's what you'll learn in this chapter: how to create and use server-side modules for Node.js, how to build those modules into a complete application using *Cake*, how to run your tests against that built application, and how to use the same approach to modules in a web browser. Finally, you'll learn how to deploy your program for the world to see. First up, modules.

12.1   Server-side modules (on Node.js)

JavaScript doesn't have modules. To clarify: the JavaScript *language* doesn't define a standard module system. The modules that you've used so far in your Node.js-based programs have been Node.js modules.

Imagine you're working on an application to power Agtron's blog (depending on your opinion of blogs, you might also need to imagine that it's 2004 to make the picture more vivid). The application needs to display a list of Agtron's blog posts on the homepage. Each item in the list links to a page containing the content of the blog post. Figure 12.1 shows examples of the two page types in a browser.

Agtron has some blog posts already written and has supplied them to you as text files. The first line of each file contains the title of the post, and the rest of the file contains the content. Consider this example in a file named my-trip-to-the-zoo.txt:

```
# -- my-trip-to-the-zoo.txt --

My trip to the zoo

I went to the Zoo. There were animals.
```

Scruffy already has written an early version of the application. It's contained entirely in a single file called application.coffee. Imagine that as you work with Scruffy on the application, the file gets bigger and bigger until it becomes a seething mess of intertwined code. Madness ensues.

Alright, madness might not ensue, but it remains true that keeping all the different parts of the program in a single file can prevent you from keeping them apart *in your head*. You agree with Scruffy to split the application into multiple smaller files divided by the natural boundaries of the application. The structure you agree on with Scruffy appears in the following listing.

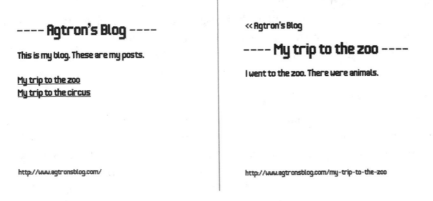

Figure 12.1   Agtron's blog in a web browser

Listing 12.1   File and directory structure for your blog application

```
|
├── app                                        ◁──── The application    The root directory
|   ├── controllers                 ◁─────          directory          for the project
|   |   ├── blog.coffee
|   |   ├── controller.coffee
|   |   └── static.coffee                      Application has
|   ├── load.coffee                            models, views,
|   ├── models                      ◁─────     and controllers
|   |   ├── model.coffee
|   |   └── post.coffee
|   ├── server.coffee
|   └── views                       ◁─────
|       ├── list.coffee
|       ├── post.coffee
|       └── view.coffee
├── content                         ◁──── The content directory,
|   ├── my-trip-to-the-circus.txt         containing the blog posts
|   └── my-trip-to-the-zoo.txt
```

The structure in listing 12.1 suits your current needs. Other solutions are possible (such as generating a static website from Agtron's content), but the one in listing 12.1 is what you chose.

When an application is divided into multiple parts, or *modules,* there must be a way to join the modules together. That's done using a *module system.* At a high level, the module system provides a way for one part of the system to use parts of the program from another module, like in figure 12.2.

How do you use this module system? By creating files to be the modules and then joining them together with require and exports.

In this section, you'll learn to create, require, and export modules, why module names are not filenames, and how the module cache works. Finally, you'll see several listings presenting a complete program made up of multiple modules. First, you'll examine creating and requiring modules.

12.1.1 *Creating and requiring*

The first problem you and Scruffy encounter is that the Blog class extends the Controller class. When both classes are in the application.coffee file, everything works fine:

```
class Controller

class Blog extends Controller
```

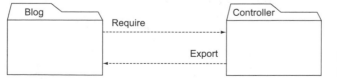

Figure 12.2   The structure of modules

There are no errors when compiling:

```
coffee -c application.coffee
```

But once you split those classes into separate files according to listing 12.1, then blog.coffee doesn't compile:

```
# -- blog.coffee --

class Blog extends Controller
```

You get a reference error:

```
coffee -c blog.coffee
# ReferenceError: Controller is not defined
```

You need some way for one file in your application to load other files. The built-in Node.js module system can do that. It's a good place to start looking at modules. To use the parts of the application contained in controller.coffee from inside blog.coffee, you `require` it with the module system:

```
require './controller'
```

When you `require './controller'`, the module loader finds the controller.coffee file relative to the current directory, loads it, and evaluates it. To load a local file, you can also use `../.`, which looks in the parent directory. This works the same as file paths on your command line.

Using `require` is only half the equation, though; blog.coffee still won't compile:

```
# -- blog.coffee -

require './controller'

class Blog extends Controller
```

You still get a reference error:

```
coffee -c blog.coffee
# ReferenceError: Controller is not defined
```

To use the `Controller` class inside the blog file, you first need to `export` it from the controller file.

12.1.2 *Exporting*

To make a property available to other modules via `require`, you assign it to `exports` inside the module. You do that at the end of the file:

```
# -- controller.coffee -

class Controller

exports.Controller = Controller
```

Now you can require the `controller` module and access the `Controller` property it assigned to exports:

```
# -- blog.coffee --
controller = require './controller'
class Blog extends controller.Controller
```

The idiomatic way to write `require` in CoffeeScript uses destructuring assignment (see chapter 7) on the object returned, avoiding the repetitiveness of unpacking properties from the controller:

```
# -- blog.coffee --
{Controller} = require './controller'     ◁─┐  Destructure the Controller
                                              property from the
class Blog extends Controller                 controller module.
```

Now you have a local variable `Controller` in blog.coffee that references the `Controller` class from controller.coffee.

Camel case for exports

Although variable naming can be a matter of taste, all of the standard libraries for JavaScript, whether in the browser or not, use camel case for naming all functions, methods, and properties. Thus, in the interests of being a good module citizen, you should *always* use camel case for anything you export from a module. So, instead of `exports.myproperty`, it should be `exports.myProperty` or `exports.myClass` if you're exporting a class. In view of this, you might also choose to use camel case for all variables. It's up to you.

In summary, to keep different parts of the application in different files, you need to export from one file and require in the other. Suppose you have a module_a.coffee file and a module_b.coffee file in the same directory:

module_a.coffee

```
w = 3
x = {a: 1}

exports.y = x
```

module_b.coffee

```
z = require('./module_a').y

# z == {a: 1}
```

The calls to `require` don't have any file extensions. Why not?

12.1.3 *No file extensions*

So far, all of the calls to `require` haven't included any of the .coffee file extensions. What happens if you create a `require` statement *with* a file extension?

```
{Controller} = require './controller.coffee'
```

The program runs just fine when invoked as CoffeeScript from the command line. Was there any reason to leave off the file extensions?

```
> coffee blog.coffee
# application is running successfully at http://localhost:8080
```

If you first compile the blog.coffee file and then run it, everything breaks:

```
> coffee -c blog.coffee
> node blog.js
controller.coffee:2
class Controller
^^^^^

...
SyntaxError: Unexpected reserved word
```

Never put the file extension in a require statement. A JavaScript program can't require a CoffeeScript file without loading the CoffeeScript compiler first. If you leave file extensions *out*, however, then your compiled JavaScript modules can load other compiled JavaScript modules, instead of trying to load CoffeeScript files. The source for a module is in a file, but you don't think of it as requiring the file itself but as requiring the module it contains. There's another good reason for thinking this way: modules are cached.

12.1.4 *The module cache*

Modules can be loaded by specifying the location of a file, but they're not loaded from source each time they're required. Modules are cached, meaning that the second, third, or other subsequent load of the same file in your application will *not* evaluate the file again. Instead, loading any module again anywhere else in the application will return the *same object* with the same properties assigned to exports the first time the file was evaluated.

Why does this matter? Suppose you want to keep track of all the posts created inside your post module:

```
class Post
  posts = []
  constructor: (@title, @body) ->
    posts.push @
  @all: -> posts

exports.Post = Post
```

It doesn't matter how many times you require it; the same object will be returned by the require method:

```
{Post} = require './post'

aPost = new Post 'A Post', 'Some content'
anotherPost = new Post 'Another Post', 'Some more content'
Post.all().length
# 2
```

When you `require` the same module again (in the same REPL session or program), you get a reference to the same object, even if you assign it to a different name:

```
TheSamePost = require('./post').Post

aThirdPost = new Post 'Three', 'Content three'
TheSamePost.all().length
# 3

Post.all().length
# 3
```

If this isn't the behavior you want, then you'll need to wrap the export in a function in order to create a new scope every time it's `required`:

```
makePost = ->
  class Post
    posts = []
    constructor: (@title, @body) ->
      posts.push @
    @all: -> posts

  {Post}

exports.makePost = makePost
```

This `makePost` function now returns a different `Post` class each time it's evaluated:

```
{Post} = require('./post').makePost()
new Post 'A post', 'Some content'

Other = require ('./post').makePost().Post

Post.all().length
# 1

Other.all().length
# 0
```

In summary, be mindful that modules are loaded only once from source and then cached. This has implications for testing because often when running tests you'll want a clean state before each test. If you have a module that maintains some internal state, then you might find it difficult to test. It's best not to keep state in a module.

That's all there is to requiring local modules. Prefix the path to the module with either `./` or `../` and then specify the location of the file containing the module. A require that doesn't prefix the path with either of those will cause the module loader to look for a built-in or packaged module.[1]

For the modules you do create, what does it look like when they're all together?

---

[1] Creating built-in and packaged modules is outside the scope of this book.

12.1.5 *Putting it together*

You work with Scruffy on the blog application until you have just enough to show Agtron. Although there are both tests and application code, only the application code appears in listings 12.2 through 12.10. These listings demonstrate an ordinary application made up of multiple modules connected together with exports and require. The first one, listing 12.2, shows server.coffee, which is the entry point to the application:

```
> coffee server.coffee
```

The server requires the built-in Node.js module http and some local modules.

Listing 12.2 server.coffee

```
http = require 'http'
{load} = require './load'
{Blog} = require './controllers'

load './content'

server = new http.Server()
server.listen '8080', 'localhost'

blog = new Blog server
```

In the next listing you see load.coffee, which takes all the content files listed in the content directory and creates posts from them. Because the server.coffee file requires load, the load.coffee file will be evaluated when server.coffee is evaluated.

Listing 12.3 load.coffee

```
fs = require 'fs'
{Post} = require './models/post'

load = (dir) ->
  fs.readdir dir, (err, files) ->
    for file in files when /.*[.]md$/.test file
      fs.readFile "#{dir}/#{file}", 'utf-8', (err, data) ->
        [title, content...] = data.split '\n'
        new Post title, content.join '\n'

exports.load = load
```

> Read all the files with extension .md in the supplied directory and create Post objects from each one.

The next listing shows the Controller class. This controller can handle incoming HTTP requests and respond as desired. It invokes a method on a particular view in order to generate the body of the response.

Listing 12.4 controllers/controller.coffee

```
class Controller
  routes = {}

  @route = (path, method) ->
    routes[path] = method
```

```coffee
constructor: (server) ->
  server.on 'request', (req, res) =>
    path = require('url').parse(request.url).pathname
    handlers = []
    for route, handler of routes
      if new RegExp("^#{route}$").test(path)
        handlers.push
          handler: handler
          matches: path.match(new RegExp("^#{route}$"))
    method = handlers[0]?.handler || 'default'
    res.end @[method](req, res, handlers[0]?.matches.slice(1)...)
```

> The controller constructor attaches its handler to the provided server. This handler looks at incoming requests and decides how the response is created.

```coffee
render: (view) ->
  @response.writeHead 200, 'Content-Type': 'text/html'
  @response.end view.render()
```

> The render method writes headers and then the response body by rendering the provided view.

```coffee
default: (@request, @response) ->
  @render render: -> 'unknown'
```

> A default request handler for when no handler is found to render a response.

```coffee
exports.Controller = Controller
```

In the next listing you see the Blog class that inherits from the Controller class. This inheritance is a by-product of your chosen design and isn't necessary when you have only a single blog controller. But it does help to demonstrate real-world use of modules. To have Blog inherit from Controller, the blog module needs to first load the controller module.

Listing 12.5   controllers/blog.coffee

```coffee
fs = require 'fs'
{Controller} = require './controller'
{Post} = require '../models'
{views} = require '../views'

class Blog extends Controller

  @route '/', 'index'
  index: (@request, @response) =>
    @posts = Post.all()
    @render views 'list', @posts

  @route '/([a-zA-Z0-9-]+)', 'show'
  show: (@request, @response, id) =>
    @post = Post.get id
    if @post
      @render views 'post', @post
    else ''
```

> These look like annotations but they're just a method call on @ that specifies a URL to match and the name of a method to use when rendering a response to a request that matches the URL.

```coffee
exports.Blog = Blog
```

There is also a base Model class from which other models can inherit. It appears in the listing that follows.

```
class Model
  dirify: (s) -> s.toLowerCase().replace /[^a-zA-Z0-9-]/gi, '-'

exports.Model = Model
```

This Model class has only a utility method to convert a post title into a path suitable for use in a URL.

The Post class appears in the next listing. It inherits from the base Model class, and it has to require the model module. This Post class knows how to get an individual post, how to get all of the posts, and how to purge all the posts.

Listing 12.7 models/post.coffee

```
{Model} = require './model'

class Post extends Model
  posts = []
  constructor: (@title, @body) ->
    throw 'requires title' unless @title
    super
    @slug = @dirify @title
    posts.push @

  @all: -> posts

  @get: (slug) -> (post for post in posts when post.slug is slug)[0]

  @purge = ->
    posts = []

exports.Post = Post
```

Constructor calls the superconstructor and creates a slug (used for the URL) from the title.

Removes all posts from the internal array.

This Post class assumes post titles are unique. One day this may change, but for now it does the job.

In the following listing you see the base View class. This View class contains a basic HTML document that can be used to render a response. In a larger program, it's likely that you'd use a template system. In this small example, though, a simple interpolated multiline string does just enough to serve as a template.

Listing 12.8 views/view.coffee

```
class View
  render: ->
    'Lost?'

  wrap: (content) ->
    """
    <!DOCTYPE html>
    <html dir='ltr' lang='en-US'>
    <head>
    <meta http-equiv='Content-Type' content='text/html; charset=utf-8'>
    <title>Agtron's blog</title>
    #{content}
    """

exports.View = View
```

Only a single (very simple) page template is required so far. Keeping it here is sufficient. If the application grows, you'll need to look for another solution.

The next listing shows the `List` class that inherits from `View`. This `List` class is used to render a list of posts.

Listing 12.9   views/list.coffee

```coffee
{View} = require './view'

class List extends View
  constructor: (@posts) ->
  render: ->
    all = (for post in @posts
      "<li><a href='#{post.slug}'>#{post.title}</a></li>"
    ).join ''
    @wrap """
    <ul>#{all}</ul>
    """
```

> Again, a view that renders a template stored in a variable.

```coffee
exports.List = List
```

Finally, the `Post` class appears in the next listing. It also inherits from the `View` class. This `Post` class is used to render the title and body of an individual post.

Listing 12.10   views/post.coffee

```coffee
{View} = require './view'

class Post extends View
  constructor: (@post) ->
  render: ->
    @wrap """
    <h1>#{@post.title}</h1>
    <div class='content'>
    #{@post.body}
    </div>
    """
```

> Shorthand constructor that only sets a post property. The function body is empty.

> Again, a view that renders a template stored in a variable.

```coffee
exports.Post = Post
```

That was a lot of listings. All of these modules are probably overkill for a site as simple as the one you're creating. That's deliberate. The preceding listings present a working Model-View-Controller (a technique for breaking a program into different parts). Whether or not you're familiar with Model-View-Controller isn't important here. What is important is that you've seen a reasonably sized application built from modules. By examining them, you've seen examples from a real program of how `require` and `exports` work.

So far it's been all individual modules, but sometimes you'll want to include a whole group of modules. In that case you'll need a module index.

12.1.6 *Indexes*

When you have many modules, it's easier to load several of them together instead of loading them all individually. Node.js supports module indexes to help you with this.[2] An index file is the module you get back when you require a directory.

Suppose you have a set of modules that you keep under a directory named utils:

```
├── utils/
│    ├── string.coffee
│    ├── array.coffee
│    ├── statistics.coffee
```

If you want to use several of those utility modules from another module, having to do multiple require statements is tedious:

```
{trim, pad} = require 'utils/string'
{remove} = require 'utils/array'
{chebyshev} = require 'utils/stats'
```

To avoid that tedium, create an intermediary index file from which you can load all of the other modules. An index file goes in the same directory as the other modules and does both require and exports for each of them:

```
exports.string = require '.utils/string'
exports.array = require '.utils/array'
exports.stats = require '.utils/stats'
```

Now when you require the utils/index module, you can destructure the object returned by require in a single line:

```
{string:{trim,pad},array:{remove},stats:{chebyshev}} = require './utils/index'
```

This creates trim, pad, remove, and chebyshev variables in the local module that reference the properties of the same name exported from the string, array, and stats modules via the index module. To make things a bit easier, the Node.js module system knows to look for an index file implicitly when a directory name is supplied:

```
{string:{trim,pad},array:{remove},stats:{chebyshev}} = require './utils'
```

The module system has allowed your program to still run correctly after it has been broken into individual files. Remember, though, that your CoffeeScript program doesn't actually run as CoffeeScript. It compiles to JavaScript and runs as JavaScript. Once your program gets bigger, it becomes impractical to individually compile all of the source files to JavaScript and then run it. Although the command-line CoffeeScript compiler is capable of compiling multiple files, your build eventually becomes too complicated to do it all manually each time, especially if things need to be done in a particular order. You need an automated build.

---

[2] You can also create Node.js packages with npm, but again, that's beyond the scope of this book.

> **How about packages?**
>
> You'll notice that you've been installing Node.js programs (and modules) by using npm. This is because npm is how you install external modules, manage those modules, and also package your own modules so that they can be installed using npm. Although npm is an important part of the Node.js ecosystem, a deep exploration of it is beyond the scope of this book. The official npm documentation is available via https://npmjs.org/ and is a good place to start exploring npm.

12.2 Build automation with Cake

Imagine you've been working with Scruffy and running your build manually all day. Each time you wanted to compile the CoffeeScript application, you just ran the compiler from the command line:

```
> coffee -c -o compiled app
```

⊲ **The -o option to coffee lets you specify the output directory for the compiled files.**

Running the application was fairly easy:

```
> node compiled/server.js
```

Running the tests was also fairly easy:

```
> node compiled/tests.js
```

You've only had to remember two things—easy when there's one application, but not so easy when there are lots of applications. Imagine you're asked to work on another program that you've never seen before. Here's the directory structure:

```
├── lib
│   ├── highball.coffee
│   ├── cocktail.coffee
│   ├── julep.coffee
├── app
│   ├── punch.coffee
│   ├── fizz.coffee
│   ├── flip.coffee
├── vendor
│   ├── mug.coffee
│   ├── beaker.coffee
│   ├── teacup.coffee
├── resources
│   ├── reference.csv
```

How do you compile *that* program? Perhaps there's some documentation somewhere that tells you how to build it; it might even be up to date, perhaps not. For an application that lives in a single file, the build just means compiling a single file:

```
> coffee -c single_file_application.coffee
```

Figure 12.3   A build that nobody understands often results in disaster.

For a larger application, though, it's not so easy. All the CoffeeScript files need to be compiled. The compiled files might need to go into a specific directory, and some other files may need to go in there with them. For a large application, the build can be complicated. Instead of doing it manually each time, the build itself should be a CoffeeScript program. Otherwise, there's a good chance you'll end up creating complicated software with a complicated build process that nobody can understand—similar to what Scruffy experiences in figure 12.3.

Keep your build simple. A simple build written in CoffeeScript can be made with something called *Cake*. In this section you'll learn about Cake and how to use it to create tasks for your build and for your tests. You'll also learn about task dependencies.

12.2.1 *Cake and build tasks*

The tool provided by CoffeeScript for writing builds is called Cake. It's similar to the Unix utility Make and the Ruby utility Rake. It's smaller than either of those and provides fewer features. That said, Make is one of the most widely used build utilities, so if you're already familiar with it, you may prefer to use that. Either way, read on to learn how Cake works.

Imagine you agree with Scruffy to make life easier on yourselves (and anybody else who needs to build your application) by writing the build using Cake. When you have CoffeeScript installed, it's simple to get started using Cake by placing a file named

Cakefile in the root directory of your project. Once you have the Cakefile, you invoke cake from the command line. Your Cakefile is currently empty, so the cake command doesn't do anything interesting:

```
> cake
```

For Cake to do something, you need to put one or more tasks in your Cakefile. In Cake, a task is a function that takes the name of the task, the description of the task, and a function that's the task itself as the three arguments:

```
task 'build', 'Compile all the CoffeeScript', ->
  console.log 'Not implemented yet'
```

> **Task names should contain only letters, dots, and colons. Cake doesn't currently support spaces in task names.**

When you run cake with no arguments, it displays a list of all the tasks in the Cakefile. Right now you have only a single build task, so that's what it shows you:

```
> cake
cake build          # Compile all the CoffeeScript
```

You can run a specific task by putting the name of the task as the argument to cake:

```
> cake build
Not implemented yet
```

The task isn't very useful yet. Here's a build task that compiles the CoffeeScript files in the application, puts the compiled JavaScript into a compiled folder, and logs Build complete to the console when it's finished:

```
{spawn} = require 'child_process'

task 'build', 'Compile all the CoffeeScript', ->
  coffee = spawn 'coffee', ['-c', '-o', "compiled/app", "app"]
  coffee.on 'exit', (code) ->
    console.log 'Build complete'
```

> **spawn is part of the Node.js core libraries. It allows you to spawn a different process. In this case you're spawning the CoffeeScript compiler and passing the same arguments you'd pass to it on the command line.**

> **Some familiar event-driven code. When the compiler is done, the task logs "Build complete" to the console.**

Now when you invoke cake build, the build is executed:

```
> cake build
# Build complete
```

The compiled JavaScript files for all of your CoffeeScript files are now in the compiled folder:

```
├── app
│   ├── controllers
│   │   ├── blog.coffee
│   │   ├── controller.coffee
```

> **The source CoffeeScript files**

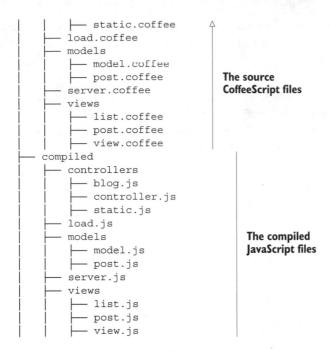

```
|   |   ├── static.coffee
|   ├── load.coffee
|   ├── models
|   |   ├── model.coffee
|   |   ├── post.coffee          The source
|   ├── server.coffee           CoffeeScript files
|   ├── views
|   |   ├── list.coffee
|   |   ├── post.coffee
|   |   ├── view.coffee
├── compiled
|   ├── controllers
|   |   ├── blog.js
|   |   ├── controller.js
|   |   ├── static.js
|   ├── load.js
|   ├── models
|   |   ├── model.js             The compiled
|   |   ├── post.js             JavaScript files
|   ├── server.js
|   ├── views
|   |   ├── list.js
|   |   ├── post.js
|   |   ├── view.js
```

If you create and maintain a build task for every project you have, then you'll always be able to build each of them with a single command. Even better, by going to the project directory and running cake without any arguments, you'll be able to see all of the build tasks that have been written for that project.

Now, with a working build for the application, Scruffy is getting impatient to write a program that deploys the application to the server. You agree—deploying manually gets tiring after the first few times. Not so fast, though; is the compiled application actually working as it's designed to? How can you be sure?

12.2.2 Test tasks

Suppose that you've been running all of the tests for the blog application manually. The application is small, so it hasn't bothered you too much to run each test from the command line as you work. Imagine that late in the afternoon, right before leaving for the day, you run the build, copy the application to the production server, and launch it. Everything breaks. You ran the build but you forgot to run the full test suite. Some of your work in progress broke another part of the application. You've just launched something that doesn't work. You quickly undo the changes on the server and launch an older, working version of the software.

Releasing a broken application into production is stressful. To prevent that from happening, every single build should also run the tests to make sure the application is working. Add a test task to the Cakefile:

```
task 'test', 'Run all the tests', ->
  console.log 'No tests'
```

The tests are in a spec directory inside your project:

```
├── Cakefile
├── app
│   ├── # application files are here
├── spec
│   ├── # test files are here
```

To write a task that will run these tests, it's best to look at the tests to see what you're dealing with.

A SPECIFICATION

Suppose you already have tests for the Post class. Those tests appear here.

Listing 12.11 A specification for the Post class

```
{describe, it} = require 'chromic'
{Post} = require '../../app/models/post'

describe 'Post', ->
  post = new Post 'A post', 'with contents'
  another = new Post 'Another post', 'with contents'

  it 'should return all posts', ->
    Post.all().length.shouldBe 2

  it 'should return a specific post', ->
    Post.get(post.slug).shouldBe 'a-post'
```

A small testing module called chromic has been used.

Notice that the test has to require the module it's testing.

USING CHROMIC   Listing 12.11 uses a testing module called chromic that was created just for this book. The complete source code for this small testing framework is provided in the downloadable code. Alternatively, you can install it using npm install chromic.

You need a Cake task to run tests such as the one in listing 12.11.

A TASK TO RUN THE TESTS

To run the tests against the compiled version of the application, the test task will need to perform these steps:

1   Delete any existing compiled files.
2   Compile the application.
3   Compile the tests.
4   Run the tests.

The test task appears in the next listing. Because the application and tests are both compiled before the tests are run, the body of the build task has been extracted to a function.

Listing 12.12   Part of a Cakefile with `build` and `test` tasks

```
# See listing 12.19 for the complete Cakefile this is part of
```

Compile function that takes a directory from which it should compile files.

```
compile (directory) = ->
  coffee = spawn 'coffee', ['-c', '-o', "compiled/#{directory}", directory]

coffee.on 'exit', (code) ->
  console.log 'Build complete'

clean = (path, callback) ->
  exec "rm -rf #{path}", -> callback?()
```
A clean function that deletes a directory.

```
forAllSpecsIn = (dir, fn) ->
  execFile 'find', [ dir ], (err, stdout, stderr) ->
    fileList = stdout.split '\n'
    for file in fileList
      fn file if /_spec.js$/.test file
```
Invoke a function for all the _spec.js files in a directory.

```
runSpecs = (folder) ->
  forAllSpecsIn folder, (file) ->
    require "./#{file}"
```
Run the specs by passing a function that requires a test to forAllSpecsIn.

```
task 'build', 'Compile the application', ->
  clean 'compiled', ->
    compile 'app', ->
      'Build complete'
```
The build task cleans and then compiles.

```
task 'test' , 'Run the tests', ->
  clean 'compiled', ->
    compile 'app', ->
      compile 'spec', ->
        runSpecs 'compiled', ->
          console.log 'Tests complete'
```
The test task cleans and compiles the app, then cleans and compiles the tests, and then runs the tests.

You now have a `build` task and a `test` task. There's a small amount of duplication, but extracting the `compile` function helped.

In some cases you want an entire task to execute before another task; you need to create a task dependency.

12.2.3 Task dependencies

Good news! Cake doesn't get task dependencies *wrong*. The bad news is that it doesn't actually provide task dependencies for you, so you get no help. But there's an `invoke` function that calls one task from another, so you can start by using that:

```
task 'build', ->
task 'test', -> invoke 'build'
```

This will make the `test` task invoke the `build` task before it runs, but it doesn't check to see if the `build` task has already been invoked. Suppose in your Cakefile you have three tasks: `deploy`, `build`, and `test`:

```
task 'build', ->
  console.log 'built'
```

```
task 'test', ->
  invoke 'build'

task 'deploy', ->
  invoke 'build'
  invoke 'test'
```

The `deploy` task should do a deployment only if the `build` and `test` tasks both complete successfully, and the `test` task requires a completed build to run, so that should run only if the `build` task is completed. Unfortunately, if you use the tasks as defined previously, then the `build` task will be invoked twice when you deploy:

```
> cake deploy
# built
# built
```

`invoke` does *only* what it says in the name: invokes the other task. It doesn't care if the other task has been run once, twice, or 100 times. Because Cake doesn't provide any way to tell a task to run only once each time, you have to do it yourself, with a variable. This isn't pretty, but it works:

```
built = false

task 'build', ->
  return if built
  built = true
```

> **If built is true, then the task has already been run.**

Now you're automating your build with Cake. Depending on how complicated your build is, you might need to dive into some of the more advanced Node.js libraries for doing things like spawning, forking, and executing external processes. The official Node.js documentation is the best place to get up-to-date information on those.

Now it's time to look at how the modules and builds you've gotten used to can be applied to those parts of your application that run on the client. It's time for the client side. After all, it's quite likely that the client side is the majority of your application.

12.3 Client-side modules (in a web browser)

Imagine now that Agtron wants to add comments to his blog and have them updated and visible immediately without users having to refresh the page. To achieve this you'll need part of the application to run on the client. This is commonly referred to as a *thick client*.

Scruffy has board meetings all day for the rest of the week but agrees to modify the server-side application so that it will serve up all the data for the comments as JSON and also to modify the application to serve the JavaScript files that will be your client-side application. *You don't have to worry about how Scruffy is going to achieve that.* Later that day you receive an email from Scruffy telling you to put the client-side scripts into the app folder:

```
├── Cakefile
│   ├── app
│   │   ├── # application files are here
│   ├── client
│   │   ├── # Put your files here (Scruffy)
│   ├── spec
│   │   ├── # test files are here
```

Put the client and spec directories in the same directory as the app directory.

When you move the application to run on the client in a web browser, how will you organize it into modules? Web browsers don't understand modules. Two options come to mind:

- Return to the dark ages and just develop your entire application in a single file.
- Find a way to get modules to work on the client.

You've been spoiled with modules in Node.js and you don't want to return to the Dark Ages. Given that you're already familiar with Node.js modules, it's worth investigating how you can get the same thing to work for your program on the client.

12.3.1 *Making modules work in a browser*

If web browsers don't support modules,[3] then how are you going to keep your program modular? One technique you've used in the past is to have a top-level object with a hierarchy of properties on it. Individual modules are then just properties on that top-level object.

For example, you *might* build your client-side application by putting everything on a global app object, mirroring the directory structure you had on the server:

```
@app.controllers = do ->
  controller = do ->
  blog = do ->
```

In this case, your entire application can be clobbered if somebody can get source code into the application:

```
@app = loadSomeNefariousProgram()
```

That's not the biggest problem, though. The biggest problem is that if you don't enforce modularity with an actual module system, then the chances of you actually writing modular code are diminished. You need a module system that works on the client, but you'll need to implement it yourself. The module system that you've used on the server has worked well, so it makes sense to make the same thing work on the client.

How do you implement modules on the client? First, you pretend that they already work and start to write your client-side program accordingly, using the powerful design technique called wishful thinking. Once you have something that uses modules on the client, you'll know what you need to implement to make them work.

---

[3] There are no modules in the fifth edition of the ECMAScript specification. See chapter 13 for a discussion of modules in upcoming editions of ECMAScript.

REQUIREMENTS

Suppose you're adding the comment functionality to the application and you need to `require` the `comments` module from inside the `main` module. You write these two modules in separate files:

```
# -- main.coffee --
{Comments} = require 'comments'

# <rest of module omitted>

# -- comments.coffee --
class Comments

# <rest of module omitted>

exports.Comments = Comments
```

Loading many script files in a web browser is slow, so the first thing you do is write a Cake task that compiles these modules into a single `application.coffee` file:

```
task 'concatenate', 'Compile multiple CoffeeScript files', ->
```

But even when this file contains both modules, they still can't see each other. Note that the `main` module appeared first, but the order could be different, depending on how you concatenate the files:

```
(function() {
  var Comments;
  Comments = (function() {
    function Comments() {}
    return Comments;
  })();
  exports.Comments = Comments;
}).call(this);
```
The result of compiling **main.coffee**

```
(function() {
  var Comments;
  Comments = require('comments').Comments;
}).call(this);
```
The result of compiling **comments.coffee**

This won't work in any browser. In order to allow modules to `require` other modules, you need to write your own module system or use an existing solution.

> **Client-side module solutions**
> There are many alternatives and they differ per platform. The solution presented here is along the same lines as Stitch; see https://github.com/sstephenson/stitch/.

If you write your own module system, then you'll have to change how your Coffee-Script program is compiled. That's not so scary after chapter 8, so you decide to write your own—with a little help from Agtron.

12.3.2   *How to write a module system*

For modules to work when they're all contained in a single file, there must be some way to define a module and to tell it how to do require and exports. On the server, a module was defined implicitly by just having a file. On the client, however, the individual files will be concatenated to a single file, with each module declared and passed to a defmodule function, as shown in the following JavaScript example:

```
defmodule({'main': function (require, exports) {
  var Comments = require('./comments').Comments;
}});

defmodule({'comments': function (require, exports) {
  var Comments;
  Comments = (function() {
    function Comments() {}
  return Comments;
  })();

  exports.Comments = Comments;
}});
```

Each module is passed to a defmodule function. This allows the modules to be loaded as required and to have require and exports defined in their scope by being passed in as arguments. This might remind you of dependency injection from chapter 10.

> **AMD modules?**
>
> Another technique for defining modules is Asynchronous Module Definitions (AMD). AMD uses a define function that accepts a module name, its dependencies, and the module definition. In AMD, an object returned from the function contains the properties that are exported from the module. Because the setup is similar to what you just implemented, when you encounter AMD modules in the wild, you'll understand the basic premise behind them.

At this point you get a little help from Agtron. He writes tests and produces the solution shown in the following listing. It's very likely that in practice you'll use an existing library to provide modules on the client, and many of them will use techniques similar to the following listing. It's always useful to understand how things work, though, so take some time to explore the solution.

Listing 12.13   require and defmodule for the browser (lib/modules.coffee)

```
do ->
  modules = {}
  cache = {}
  @require = (raw_name) ->
    name = raw_name.replace /[^a-z]/gi, ''
    return cache[name].exports if cache[name]
    if modules[name]
      module = exports: {}
      cache[name] = module
      modules[name]((name) ->
        require name
      , module.exports)
      module.exports
```

Wrap it in a do -> to keep variables private.

Assign a require method to the current object. When this script is executed in a browser, the current object will be the global object. In a browser, that's generally the window object.

```
      else throw "No such module #{name}"

   @defmodule = (bundle) ->                          ◁─┐  Assign a defmodule method
     for own key of bundle                              │  to the global object
       modules[key] = bundle[key]
```

So how does it work? When you load a module, the require invocations trigger other modules to be evaluated, which in turn will cause any require invocations in that module to be evaluated. The application will need to load one module that will load all of the others. The overall structure of the compiled output will have a single require call at the end to invoke this module:

```
defmodule('comments': function(require, exports) {
  class Comments
  exports.Comments = Comments;
});

defmodule('main': function(require, exports) {
  var Comments = require('./comments').Comments;
});

require './main'
```

You now have to write the Cake task that compiles your CoffeeScript modules from separate files into a single JavaScript file that includes the module library from listing 12.13 and wraps each module in a defmodule. This Cake task appears in the next listing. This task is suitable for compiling your small project. If your project becomes large (thousands of modules), then you might need to revisit it.

Listing 12.14 Cake task for client-side modules

```
task 'build:client', 'build client side stuff with modules', ->    │ lib/modules.coffee
  compiler = require 'coffee-script'                                │ contains the code
  modules = fs.readFileSync "lib/modules.coffee", "utf-8"    ◁──────┘ from listing 12.13.

  modules = compiler.compile modules, bare: true    ◁─────┐  CoffeeScript is compiled
  files = fs.readdirSync 'client'                          │  bare, meaning that there's
  source = (for file in files when /\.coffee$/.test file   │  no outer function wrapper.
    module = file.replace /\.coffee/, ''
    fileSource = fs.readFileSync "client/#{file}", "utf-8"    ◁───┐ Because this is in the
                                                                  │ build where you don't
    """                                                           │ care about blocking,
    defmodule({#{module}: function (require, exports) {            │ readFileSync is acceptable.
      #{compiler.compile(fileSource, bare: true)}
    }});
    """                                  All of the modules are
  ).join '\n\n'     ◁───────────────────│  concatenated with a simple join.

  out = modules + '\n\n' + source                                  ┌ Write the entire
  fs.writeFileSync 'compiled/app/client/application.js'    ◁───────┘ compiled
                                                                     application to
                                                                     application.js.
```

The actual file output is the compiled CoffeeScript wrapped in the defmodule call.

Now you're able to use the same module system that you use on the server for your client-side application as well. There are other techniques for client-side programs, but the principles are always the same. Moreover, the modules system used in Node.js, which is based on common.js, is the closest thing to a de facto standard until ECMAScript standardizes modules (and browser makers implement them).

12.3.3 *Tests*

Client-side modules can be tested the same way as server-side modules. All of the testing techniques you learned in chapter 10 (such as dependency injection) apply to modules whether on the server or on the client. In the following listing you can see the test for the client-side `Comments` module.

Listing 12.15 Comments specification (spec/comments_spec.coffee)

```coffee
{describe, it} = require 'chromic'

{Comments} = require '../../app/client/comments'

describe 'Comments', ->
  it 'should post a comment to the server', ->
    requested = false
    httpRequest = (url) -> requested = url
    comments = new Comments 'http://the-url', {}, httpRequest
    comment = 'Hey Agtron. Nice site.'
    comments.post comment
    requested.shouldBe "http://the-url/comments?insert=#{comment}"

  it 'should fetch the comments when constructed', ->
    requested = false
    httpRequest = (url) -> requested = url
    comments = new Comments 'http://the-url', {}, httpRequest
    requested.shouldBe "http://the-url/comments"

  it 'should bind to event on the element', ->
    comments = new Comments 'http://the-url', {}, ->
    element =
      querySelector: -> element
      value: 'A comment from Scruffy'

    comments.bind element, 'post'
    postReceived = false
    comments.post = (comment) -> postReceived = comment
    element.onpost()
    postReceived.shouldBe element.value

  it 'should render comments to the page as a list', ->
    out = innerHTML: (content) -> renderedContent = content
    comments = new Comments 'http://the-url', out, ->
    comments.render '["One", "Two", "Three"]'
    out.innerHTML.shouldBe "<ul><li>One</li><li>Two</li><li>Three</li></ul>"
```

The next listing contains the `Comments` module.

Listing 12.16 The `Comments` module (client/comments.coffee)

```coffee
class Comments
  constructor: (@url, @out, @httpRequest) ->
    @httpRequest "#{@url}/comments", @render
```

```
post: (comment) ->
  @httpRequest "#{@url}/comments?insert=#{comment}", @render
bind: (element, event) ->
  comment = element.querySelector 'textarea'
  element["on#{event}"] = =>
    @post comment.value
    false
render: (data) =>
  inLi = (text) -> "<li>#{text}</li>"
  if data isnt ''
    comments = JSON.parse data
    if comments.map?
      formatted = comments.map(inLi).join ''
      @out.innerHTML = "<ul>#{formatted}</ul>"
```

```
exports.Comments = Comments
```

With a build and tests for the server and client components of the application in place, it's now time to learn how to deploy it.

12.4 *Application deployment*

You have your application broken into modules both on the server and on the client. You also have a build that compiles all your CoffeeScript modules, makes them work for the browser, *and* runs all of your tests in order to make sure the program behaves as it should. What's left is deployment to a server for the world to behold. In this section you'll learn why you always deploy the compiled JavaScript (and not CoffeeScript) and how to package up a version of your compiled application ready to be deployed to a server.

Right now, to run your compiled application, you pass the main application file, server.js, to Node:

```
> node compiled/app/server.js
```

That runs the application locally, but to run the application on a *remote server,* you first need to get it onto the server. Once it's there, the application needs to know how to run on that server. A simple deployment follows these steps:

1 Create the artifact and manifest.
2 Upload and extract the artifact and manifest.
3 Stop the old version of the application.
4 Start the new version of the application.

If you're deploying to multiple servers, then the deployment process will be more complicated, but the basic concepts remain the same. In this section you're at step 1, where you'll create a version of your application, an artifact, that is ready for deployment, as well as a manifest that will give the application information it needs to run on the environment you deploy it to.

12.4.1 *Creating an artifact (something that's easy to deploy)*

First, you need to create something that will be sent to the server and become the program that runs there. That something is called an *artifact*.

Given that you have a compiled version of the application already, you can create an artifact from the compiled program. From Cake, the Node.js execFile command allows you to call out to an external program that can compress the compiled program and put it in a single file ready to be deployed:

> **Execute the command-line program tar to create the artifact. If your operating system doesn't have a tar command, then consult the relevant documentation and use an equivalent program.**

```
createArtifact = (path, version, callback) ->
  execFile "tar", ["-cvf", "artifact.#{version}.tar", path], (e, d) ->
    callback()

task 'artifact', 'build the artifact', ->
  version = fs.readFileSync './VERSION', 'utf-8'
  createArtifact 'compiled', version, ->
    console.log "done. artifact.#{version}.tar generated"
```

> **The build version is kept in a file. As before, in a build it's generally acceptable to use synchronous file loads if the build can't run at all without those files.**

When you run cake artifact, a file containing all of the compiled files is created. Create a file called VERSION in the same directory as the Cakefile and put the number 1 in it. Now when you invoke cake with the artifact task, it will use this version number when generating the artifact:

```
> cake artifact
# done. artifact.1.tar generated
```

How about the manifest? Why do you need one and how do you create it?

12.4.2 *Creating a manifest (something that tells your artifact where it is)*

Consider that in development you run the application on localhost on port 8080. Looking at listing 12.2, you notice that this value is hardcoded:

```
server.listen '8080', 'localhost'
```

In production this might need to be something else:

```
server.listen '80, 'agtronsblog.com'
```

This is just one example of something that's likely to change when you run the application on another environment, such as the production environment.

WHICH ENVIRONMENT IS THIS?

The application doesn't magically know which environment it's running in. You have to tell it by using an *environment variable*. Inside a Node.js application, you can access environment variables through process.env. The environment variable you'll use is called NODE_ENV and is either set for you by the environment you're running on or is set by you when your program is started on the command line. Suppose it's already set; *here's how not to use the NODE_ENV environment variable:*

```
if process.env.NODE_ENV is 'production'
  server.listen '80', 'agtronsblog.com'
else if process.env.NODE_ENV is 'development'
  server.listen '8080', 'localhost'
```

> **Don't do this everywhere in your program; it would be a maintenance nightmare later down the track.**

Instead of using NODE_ENV in many parts of your program, you should read it once and keep all of the environment information in a single place. That's what a manifest, or *environment config*, does. So how do you load one?

LOADING AN ENVIRONMENT CONFIG

The application needs to know how to run on the environment it's deployed to. This information is provided in the manifest.

> **Using Node.js on Windows?**
>
> Some of the listings in this chapter won't work as is on all operating systems (such as Windows). They're designed to run on Unix-like operating systems. For other operating systems you'll need to call out to other commands in order to achieve the same results. That said, the techniques demonstrated here all still apply, so you can still follow along.

Write the configuration as a "plain-old object" and expose it as a module. A server.coffee file that uses a configuration loaded from a local `config` module appears in the following listing.

Listing 12.17   The blog application (server.coffee)

```
http = require 'http'
{load} = require './load'
{Blog} = require './controllers'

load './content'

config = require('./config')[process.env.NODE_ENV]    ◁─┐  Require the config file and
                                                           get the export that matches
server = new http.Server()                                 the current environment.
server.listen config.port, config.host

blog = new Blog server
```

The local `config` module appears in the next listing. There's a configuration for the development and production environments. Any other environments you have (such as testing or staging environments) should also be defined in this file.

Listing 12.18   The blog application configuration file (config.coffee)

```
config =
  development:
    host: 'localhost'
    port: '8080'
  production:
    host: 'agtronsblog.com'
    port: '80'
```

```
for key, value of config
  exports[key] = value
```

Your application is now ready to run in a specific environment with a particular configuration. So how does the environment variable get set?

DEFINING THE ENVIRONMENT

You can define the environment where the program is invoked. Define the environment to be *development*

```
> NODE_ENV=development node compiled/server.js
```

or to be *production*

```
> NODE_ENV=production node compiled/server.js
```

Now that it can run on different environments, the application is ready to be deployed.

DEPLOYING TO A REMOTE SERVER

The process for getting the application running on a remote server can vary depending on the target, but the basic steps remain the same. Here are the steps again:

1 Create the artifact and manifest.
2 Upload and extract the artifact and manifest.
3 Stop the old version of the application.
4 Start the new version of the application.

Now you're at step 2 where you'll upload the artifact that you created and extract it so that it's ready to run. You can write a Cake task to perform steps 1 and 2 for the production environment defined in the `config`:

```
task 'production:deploy', 'deploy the application to production' ->
  VERSION = fs.readFileSync('./VERSION', 'utf-8')
  SERVER = require('./app/config').production.host
  clean 'compiled', ->
    compile 'app', ->
      copy 'content', 'compiled', ->
        createArtifact 'compiled', VERSION, ->
      execFile 'scp', [
        "artifact.#{VERSION}.tar",
        "#{SERVER}:~/."
      ], (err, data) ->
          console.log "Uploaded artifact #{VERSION} to #{SERVER}"
```

For a production server, steps 3 and 4 will depend on exactly how the application is being run on the environment, so the remaining steps are not presented here.

Continuing on, it's now time to look at the entire build and examine the Cakefile that builds the entire application. Any projects you have in the future are likely to have a similar folder structure and can borrow heavily from the final Cakefile that appears in listing 12.19.

12.5   The final Cakefile

After writing all these individual Cake tasks, it's useful to look now at the entire Cakefile and see where there's room for improvement.

12.5.1   Tidying up

The Cakefile in listing 12.19 contains all of the build tasks that you created while developing the blog application. Running `cake` on the command line will show you which tasks are defined:

```
> cake
cake clean                      # delete existing build
cake build                      # run the build
cake test                       # run the tests
cake development:start          # start the application locally
```

Note that any functions used by the build but not defined as tasks have been moved to a separate module that's loaded by the Cakefile.

Listing 12.19   The Cakefile for the blog application (Cakefile)

```
s = require 'fs'
{exec, execFile} = require 'child_process'

buildUtilities = require './build_utilities'      ◁— Load the utilities.

{
clean,
compile,
copy,
createArtifact,
runSpecs,
runApp
} = buildUtilities.fromDir './'

VERSION = fs.readFileSync('./VERSION', 'utf-8')   ◁——┐

task 'clean', 'delete existing build', ->
  execFile "npm", ["install"], ->
    clean "compiled"

task 'build', 'run the build', ->
  clean 'compiled', ->
    compile 'app', ->
      copy 'content', 'compiled', ->
        createArtifact 'compiled', VERSION, ->
          console.log 'Build complete'

task 'test' , 'run the tests', ->
  clean 'compiled', ->
    compile 'app', ->
      compile 'spec', ->
        runSpecs 'compiled', ->
          console.log 'Tests complete'
```

Get the current desired build version. You'll need a VERSION file containing a number in the same directory as the Cakefile for this to work.

Remove old files.

A full build requires other tasks and functions to be run in sequence. Callbacks are used for this.

A test run requires a build but not an artifact.

```
task "development:start", "start on development", ->          Starting on development
  runApp 'development'                                        simply executes Node.

SERVER = require('./app/config').production.host             A sample config file is provided
                                                             in the downloadable code.
deploy = ->
  console.log "Deploy..."
  tarOptions = ["-cvf","artifact.#{VERSION}.tar","compiled"]
  execFile "tar", tarOptions,(err, data) ->
    console.log '1. Created artifact'
    execFile 'scp', [
      "artifact.#{VERSION}.tar",
      "#{SERVER}:~/."
    ], (err, data) ->
      console.log '2. Uploaded artifact'
      exec """
      ssh #{SERVER} 'cd ~/;
      rm -rf compiled;                                        Details of the SSH
      tar -xvf artifact.#{VERSION}.tar;                       command used
      cd ~/compiled;                                          are omitted here
      NODE_ENV=production nohup node app/server.js &' &       for brevity.
      """, (err, data) ->
        console.log '3. Started server'
        console.log 'Done'

task "production:deploy", "deploys the app to production", ->
  clean 'compiled', ->
    compile 'app', ->
      copy 'content', 'compiled', ->
        createArtifact 'compiled', VERSION, ->
          deploy()
```

The Cakefile in listing 12.19 would have been large and difficult to read if all of the functions called from the build tasks were included. Instead, those functions are in another file called build_utilities.coffee, which appears in the following listing.

Listing 12.20 Build utilities (build_utilities.coffee)

```
fs = require 'fs'                                             The Node.js module
{spawn, exec, execFile, fork} = require 'child_process'      for external processes
                                                             is required.
clientCompiled = false

forAllSpecsIn = (dir, fn) ->
  execFile 'find', [ dir ], (err, stdout, stderr) ->         Look at a directory
    fileList = stdout.split '\n'                              of files and execFile
    for file in fileList                                     each one.
      fn file if /_spec.js$/.test file

compileClient = (callback) ->
  return callback() if clientCompiled
  clientCompiled = true                                      Compile the client-
  compiler = require 'coffee-script'                         side modules to work
  modules = fs.readFileSync "lib/modules.coffee", "utf-8"    on the client and
  modules = compiler.compile modules, bare: true             concatenate them.
  files = fs.readdirSync 'client'
```

```
  fs.mkdirSync "compiled/app/client"
  source = (for file in files when /\.coffee$/.test file
    module = file.replace /\.coffee/, ''
    fileSource = fs.readFileSync "client/#{file}", "utf-8"
    fs.writeFileSync "compiled/app/client/#{module}.js",
        compiler.compile fileSource
    """
    defmodule({#{module}: function (require, exports) {
      #{compiler.compile(fileSource, bare: true)}
    }});
    """
  ).join '\n\n'

  out = modules + '\n\n' + source
  fs.writeFileSync 'compiled/app/client/application.js', out

  callback?()

exports.fromDir = (root) ->

  return unless root

  compile = (path, callback) ->
    coffee = spawn 'coffee', ['-c', '-o', "#{root}compiled/#{path}", path]

    coffee.on 'exit', (code, s) ->
      if code is 0 then compileClient callback
      else console.log 'error compiling'

    coffee.on 'message', (data) ->
      console.log data

  createArtifact = (path, version, callback) ->
    execFile "tar", ["-cvf", "artifact.#{version}.tar", path], (e, d) ->
      callback?()

  runSpecs = (folder) ->
    forAllSpecsIn "#{root}#{folder}", (file) ->
      require "./#{file}"

  clean = (path, callback) ->
    exec "rm -r #{root}#{path}", (err) -> callback?()

  copy = (src, dst, callback) ->
    exec "cp -R #{root}#{src} #{root}#{dst}/.", ->
      callback?()

  runApp = (env) ->
    exec 'NODE_ENV=#{env} node compiled/app/server.js &', ->
      console.log "Running..."

  {clean, compile, copy, createArtifact, runSpecs, runApp}
```

> **Compile the client-side modules to work on the client and concatenate them.**

> **Create the build artifact.**

The Cakefile is complete, but you can see a callback waterfall in some of the tasks—where asynchronous operations that must happen in sequence lead you to deeply nested callbacks:

```
task 'build', 'run the build', ->
  clean 'compiled', ->
    compile 'app', ->
```

```
copy 'content', 'compiled', ->
  createArtifact 'compiled', VERSION, ->
    console.log 'Build complete'
```

Compare this to a roughly equivalent section of a Makefile:

```
build: artifact

artifact: clean compile copy
    tar -cvf artifact.tar compiled
```

Cake is a simple tool, and in some instances you may be better off using a dedicated build tool. That said, CoffeeScript provides powerful syntactic techniques, so you could roll your own fluent interface:

```
task 'build', 'run the build', ->
  clean('compiled')
  .then(compile 'app')
  .then(copy 'content', 'compiled')
  .then(createArtifact 'compiled', VERSION)
  .then(-> console.log 'done')
  .run()
```

Or perhaps you could implement your own function to handle dependencies:

```
task 'build', 'run the build', depends ['clean', 'compile', 'copy'], ->
```

Or you could implement your own syntax by extending the CoffeeScript compiler (see chapter 8). Many things are possible, but for now, it's time to recap.

12.6 *Summary*

In this chapter you learned how to structure a simple application into discrete modules on the server and on the client and then how to build, test, and release it.

That marks the end of your discovery of the current world of CoffeeScript, but it doesn't mark the end of your journey. Your journey continues into the future, where in the next chapter you'll look at where JavaScript is headed and at how CoffeeScript fits into that picture.

ECMAScript and
the future of CoffeeScript

13

This chapter covers

- CoffeeScript and the future of JavaScript
- Features in ECMAScript 5 you can use today
- Upcoming features in ECMAScript 6
- Source maps for debugging

Whatever your opinion of JavaScript (and regardless of whether learning Coffee-Script has changed it), you should count on it being around for a long time—long enough, at least, that it will probably outlast your career as a programmer. For that reason it's important to look at what the future holds for JavaScript and how it will affect CoffeeScript.

In this chapter you'll look at the evolving relationship between CoffeeScript and JavaScript and why your understanding of CoffeeScript applies not only to Java-Script today but also to the JavaScript of tomorrow. You'll see how JavaScript versions relate to different editions of the ECMAScript specification that documents the evolving JavaScript standard. Lastly, this chapter discusses one of the most important tool-related aspects of the JavaScript ecosystem: how to debug Coffee-Script programs with source maps. Before looking at the future, though, where are you now?

13.1 CoffeeScript in the context of JavaScript

When talking about language versions, it's important to first have a broad overview. Table 13.1 shows a timeline of major versions of the ECMAScript specification.

Table 13.1 An ECMAScript timeline

Edition	Date published	Examples of new features
1	June 1997	
2	June 1998	
3	December 1999	Regular expressions Improved string handling Exception handling
4	*Abandoned*	
5	December 2009	Strict mode Native JSON support New object methods Property descriptors
6	*In progress*	Rest and spread parameters Template strings Default parameters Destructuring assignment Function syntax Classes

The fifth and sixth editions of the ECMAScript specification are most relevant to Coffee-Script. Some of the features introduced by these editions are instantly recognizable from CoffeeScript, others are vaguely familiar, and some are brand new. All of them are explored in this chapter.

> ### JavaScript, ECMAScript? Which is it?
> ECMAScript is the name of the language standardized by the ECMA-262 specification by Ecma International. JavaScript is a dialect of ECMAScript (and a trademark of Oracle Corporation), but it's the name used by almost everybody when referring to the language. In this chapter, ECMAScript is used when referring to the ECMA-262 specification.

13.1.1 A better JavaScript through CoffeeScript

JavaScript is the host for CoffeeScript. The word *host* conjures up images of human parasites like worms and bedbugs. In the case of CoffeeScript, though, JavaScript benefits from the relationship. One of the ways that JavaScript benefits is by taking some of the features in CoffeeScript and adding them to future versions of JavaScript.

Imagine you're working with Scruffy on a library to automatically fetch form values and synchronize them with a server. In this listing you can see the initial program that Scruffy has called *Formulaic*.

Listing 13.1 Formulaic form bindings

```coffeescript
class Formulaic
  constructor: (@root, @selector, @http) ->
    @subscribers = []
    @fields = @extractFields()
    @startPolling()

  extractFields: ->
    element = @root.querySelector @selector
    fields = element.getElementsByTagName 'input'
    extracted = {}
    for field in fields
      extracted[field.name] = field.value
    extracted

  startPolling: ->
    diff = =>
      for own key, value of @extractFields()
        if @fields[key] isnt value
          @fields[key] = value
          @notify()
    setInterval diff, 100

  subscribe: (subscriber) ->
    @subscribers.push subscriber

  notify: ->
    subscriber() for subscriber in @subscribers
```

How do you use the `Formulaic` class from listing 13.1? Consider the following HTML document:

```html
<!doctype html>
<html>
<form id='contact-details'>
<input type='text' name='first-name'>
<input type='text' name='last-name'>
<input type='text' name='email'>
```

You `new` a `Formulaic` instance by passing the `document` and the selector for the form:

```coffeescript
new Formulaic document, '#contact-details'
```

Agtron tells you that extending and improving Formulaic will require you to learn some ECMAScript 5 *and* some ECMAScript 6 features. Sounds good! Time to get started.

13.1.2 *Future JavaScript features that CoffeeScript has today*

Some of the features coming in future versions of ECMAScript are already present in CoffeeScript in one form or another. This means that even if the names of these features sound only vaguely familiar, you already know and use rest and spread parameters, template strings, default parameters, and destructuring assignment. Because you already know them, it's best to get them out of the way before moving on to the interesting stuff.

REST AND SPREAD

The rest and spread operators proposed for ECMAScript 6 work the same way as the ones you're familiar with in CoffeeScript (aside from some syntactical differences). Here's the CoffeeScript syntax you're familiar with:

```
rest = (a, b, r...) -> r
rest 1,2,3,4,5,6,7
# [3,4,5,6,7]

spread = [1,2,3,4,5,6,7]
rest spread
# [3,4,5,6,7]
```

In JavaScript with ECMAScript 6 it looks similar, but the ellipsis goes on the front of the variable name:

```
rest = function (a, b, ...r) {  return r; }
rest(1,2,3,4,5,6,7);
# [3,4,5,6,7]
```
ECMAScript 6 example

The ECMAScript 6 specification also has string interpolation.

TEMPLATE STRINGS

In CoffeeScript you use string interpolation to insert values into strings without having to manually concatenate them:

```
word = 'interpolation'

"Just like string #{word}"
# Just like string interpolation
```

What's the alternative in JavaScript today? Concatenating strings with the + operator:

```
"Just like string " + word
```

Imagine trying to create an HTML template with concatenation instead of interpolation:

```
"""
<html>
<title>#{title}</title>
<body>
<h1>#{ heading}</h1>

#{content}
"""
```

ECMAScript 6 will have *template strings* that provide the string interpolation you know and love, but with different syntax:

```
var word = 'interpolation';
`Just like string ${word}.`
# Just like string interpolation.
```
ECMAScript 6 example

Template strings are multiline (like heredocs) and will support custom substitution functions. In CoffeeScript the back tick ` is already used to put raw JavaScript in your CoffeeScript programs, so the JavaScript template string syntax won't work in CoffeeScript.

ARROW FUNCTION SYNTAX

JavaScript syntax benefits from CoffeeScript. One inspiration that JavaScript will take from CoffeeScript is arrows instead of the `function` keyword. The ECMAScript 6 standard does not specify the single-arrow function but it does have the fat arrow:

```
let square = (x) => x * x          ⟵── ECMAScript 6 example
```

You would be forgiven for mistaking that for CoffeeScript. That's because it was *inspired* by CoffeeScript syntax—the relationship between CoffeeScript and ECMAScript is *symbiotic*.

That's it for the familiar things. How about all the unfamiliar features that you need to know about to stay in the game? To begin with, what's in ECMAScript 5 that a CoffeeScripter needs to find out about?

13.2 ECMAScript 5

Released in December 2009, the primary focus for the changes in ECMAScript 5 was to improve robustness for the language and, as a result, for runtimes and programs. The key features to be aware of are native JSON support, strict mode, property descriptors, and changes to the `Object` object. The best way to learn them is to try them, which means your runtime needs to support them.

13.2.1 Runtime support

It's easy to play with the ECMAScript 5 features discussed in this section; simply fire up the CoffeeScript REPL. All of these features are supported in the V8 JavaScript engine that powers Node.js, your REPL, and all of your server-side CoffeeScript programs. Unfortunately, the same does not hold true for all of your browser-based programs. Some browsers don't support all of these features, so if you need to support those browsers, you have to either avoid those features or use a polyfill (as discussed in chapter 11) where possible.

> **Polyfills**
>
> If you find yourself stuck writing programs for a browser that doesn't support the ECMAScript 5 feature that you want, you will need to polyfill. Sometimes you need to polyfill things you might think are essential, such as JSON.

The ECMAScript features supported by a particular browser depend on which version of which JavaScript runtime it uses. When writing programs, however, it's usually browser versions that are discussed. So that's what we'll discuss now. Table 13.2 shows which versions of major browsers support the ECMAScript 5 features that are discussed in this section.

Table 13.2   Support for ECMAScript 5 in some popular browsers

Feature	IE8	IE9	IE10	FF 4+	Sf 6+	Ch 7+
`Object.create`	No	Yes	Yes	Yes	Yes	Yes
Object property descriptors	No	Yes	Yes	Yes	Yes	Yes
New array methods (e.g., `map`)	No	Yes	Yes	Yes	Yes	Yes
Strict mode	No	No	Yes*	Yes	Yes	Yes
Native JSON	Yes	Yes	Yes	Yes	Yes	Yes

IE = Internet Explorer; FF = Firefox; Sf = Safari; Ch = Chrome
* = Known bugs in implementation

When you target a browser older than the ones in table 13.2 (Internet Explorer 7, Safari 5, or Firefox 3.5, for example), there's a good chance that it won't support the ECMAScript 5 features you want to use. In that case, it's best to consult the documentation for that browser.

So, what are these features and, more importantly, how will they be useful for your programs (such as Formulaic)?

13.2.2   *Object.create*

You know that `Object.create` produces a new object with an existing object as the prototype. What you might not know is that `Object.create` also has a second parameter, an object of property names and descriptors:

```
homer =
  'first-name': 'Homer'
  'last-name': 'Simpson'

homerTwo = Object.create homer,
  clone:
    value: true
    writable: false
  'middle-name':
    value: 'Clone'
    writable: false

homerTwo.clone
# true
```

If your CoffeeScript program is running in an environment without a native `Object.create`, then objects won't support property descriptors and any polyfill for `Object.create` won't have the second parameter.

13.2.3   *JSON*

ECMAScript 5 introduced the global `JSON` object and the `JSON.stringify` and `JSON.parse` methods. What do they do, and why can't you just use JSON directly in your programs? After all, valid JSON is a valid JavaScript object.

Consider the Formulaic program. So far it's not particularly useful because it doesn't send the form information anywhere. How do you implement a sync method in Formulaic that communicates with an external server? The sync method should post all of the form data to a specific URL by invoking the http.post method:

```
sync: ->
  throw new Error 'No transport' unless @http? and @url?
  data = extractFields
  @http.post @url, JSON.stringify(@)
```

What does invoking JSON.stringify do? It turns an object into a string.

STRINGIFY

To turn an object into a valid JSON string, use JSON.stringify:

```
fred = {firstName: 'Fred', lastName: 'Flintstone'}
JSON.stringify fred
# '{"firstName":"Fred","lastName":"Flintstone"}'
```

However, when you use JSON.stringify on a Formulaic instance you're really only interested in the field values, but you get much more:

```
{
    "root":{
        "location":{},
        "contact-form":{
            "0":{},
            "1":{},
        }
    },
    "selector":".contact-form",
    "subscribers":[],
    "fields":{
        "search":""
    }
}
```

Worse, some other objects will not JSON.stringify at all. For example, try it on the REPL with the global object:

```
JSON.stringify @
# TypeError: Converting circular structure to JSON
```

What can you do? Formulaic is *your* class, so surely you can tell it how to turn itself into JSON? Indeed, you can. Even better, you can tell JSON.stringify about it.

CONVERTING TO JSON

If an object has a toJSON method, then JSON.stringify will invoke it and use it as the value to stringify:

```
class Formulaic
  toJSON: -> "message": "Determine your own JSON representation"

formulaic = new Formulaic
JSON.stringify formulaic
# '{"message":"Determine your own JSON representation"}'
```

That takes care of sending the form information to the server. How about getting the form back? Suppose the server responds to a POST with updated JSON for the object:

```
sync: ->
  throw new Error 'No transport' unless @http? and @url?
  @http.post @url, JSON.stringify(@extractFields()), (response) ->
    @fields = JSON.parse response
```

What does invoking `JSON.parse` do?

PARSE

The `JSON.parse` method converts a string of JSON to an object. If you need to polyfill `JSON.parse`, you can do it dangerously with an `eval`:

```
JSON.parse ?= (json) ->
  eval json

barney = JSON.parse '{"firstName":"Barney","lastName":"Rubble"}'"
barney.lastName
# "Rubble"
```

Be warned: `eval` is evil. When you `eval` code, it can do anything, so you should never `eval` code you don't trust. The ECMAScript 5 specification adds a native `JSON.parse` over `eval` (for safety reasons) and over other techniques for parsing JSON (for performance reasons).

The native JSON support is the most immediately applicable solution for Formulaic. How does Formulaic send form data back to the server and what format does it use? In the next listing you see an extended version of Formulaic that uses native JSON support.

Listing 13.2   Formulaic with server sync

```
class Formulaic
  constructor: (@root, @selector, @http) ->
    @subscribers = []
    @fields = @extractFields()
    @startPolling()

  extractFields: ->
    element = @root.querySelector @selector
    fields = element.getElementsByTagName 'input'
    extracted = {}
    for field in fields
      extracted[field.name] = field.value
    extracted

  update: =>
    for own key, value of @extractFields()
      if @fields[key] isnt value
        @fields[key] = value
        @notify()

  startPolling: ->
    setInterval @update, 100

  subscribe: (subscriber) ->
    @subscribers.push subscriber
```

```
  notify: ->
    subscriber() for subscriber in @subscribers

  sync: ->
    throw new Error 'No transport' unless @http? and @url?
    @http.post @url, JSON.stringify(@extractFields()), (response) ->
      @fields = JSON.parse response

exports.Formulaic = Formulaic
```

The Formulaic program in listing 13.2 is far from finished. For one thing, it fetches data from the server but doesn't actually put any changes it receives back into the visible form that the user edits. To do that, you need some new features of the `Object` object.

13.2.4 *Property descriptors*

The new problem Agtron has given you and Scruffy is to improve Formulaic so that a change from the server is reflected in the form. This means that a change to the object representing the form needs to trigger an update in the form:

```
form = new Formulaic document, '#contact-details'
form.fields['first-name'] = 'Tyrone'
```

You *could* get Formulaic to poll the field properties. You could, but you don't have to. Why? Well, *until now* you've treated all object properties as having just a name and a value:

```
form.fields =
  'first-name': 'Fred'
```

```
         ⇡               ⇡
       name            value
```

With ECMAScript 5, though, properties don't have just names and values; they also have *descriptors*. The property descriptors are `value`, `get`, `set`, `configurable`, `enumerable`, and `writable`. The `get` and `set` descriptors are commonly known as getters and setters.

GETTERS AND SETTERS

Consider the `'first-name'` property of `form.fields`. Until now, when a property value is changed, that's the full extent of it, and you'd better like it. With a `set` property descriptor, though, you can create a property *and* define what happens when a new value is assigned to it! One way to do that is with `Object.defineProperty`:

```
Object.defineProperty form.fields, 'first-name',
  set: (newValue) => @root.getElementsByName('first-name')[0].value = newValue
```

For Formulaic, a `get` property descriptor means you don't need to poll the form fields for changes. Instead, you can define a function that gets the latest value from the form field any time the object property is accessed:

```
Object.defineProperty form.fields, 'first-name',
  set: (newValue) => @updateView 'first-name', newValue
  get: => @updateField 'first-name'
```

In the following listing you see a new version of Formulaic using getters and setters.

Listing 13.3   Using getters and setters

```coffeescript
class Formulaic
  "use strict"
  constructor: (@root, @selector, @http) ->
    @fields = {}
    @subscribers = []
    @extractFields()

  bind: (field) ->
    Object.defineProperty @fields, field.name,
      set: (newValue) =>
        field.value = newValue
        @sync()
      get: ->
        field.value
      enumerable: true

    updateField = =>
      @fields[field.name] = field.value

    updateField()
    field.addEventListener 'input', updateField

  documentFields: ->
    element = @root.querySelector @selector
    element.getElementsByTagName 'input'

  extractFields: ->
    @bind field for field in @documentFields()

  sync: ->
    throw new Error 'No transport' unless @http?
    if @url?
      @http.post @url, JSON.stringify(@fields), (response) =>
        @fields = JSON.parse response

exports.Formulaic = Formulaic
```

"use strict" is discussed later in this section.

Now what? Agtron wants to know what happens when the form is considered *complete* and should no longer be changed. How will you stop the `Formulaic` instance from being modified?

PREVENTING CHANGES

Suppose now that the form also contains a unique identifier for a user. This user ID should never change. Unfortunately, regular object properties can be changed by anybody who has a reference to the object.

With property descriptors, you can create properties that can't be changed:

```coffeescript
class User

user = Object.create User.prototype,
  id:
    value: 'u58440329'
    enumerable: true
    writable: false
    configurable: false
```

```
name:
  value: 'Robert'
```

Due to the `writable` descriptor being `false`, attempts to change this property have no effect:

```
user.id = '0'
user.id
# u58440329
```

Also, due to the `enumerable` descriptor being `false`, the property doesn't appear in a comprehension:

```
property for property of user
# [ 'name' ]
```

Finally, due to the `configurable` descriptor being `false`, the property can't be made writable or enumerable again:

```
Object.defineProperty user, id, writable: true
# Cannot redefine property: id
```

Using `Object.defineProperty` gets tedious when you need to add or change multiple properties, but some other methods new to the `Object` object make it easier.

FREEZING, SEALING, AND PREVENTING EXTENSIONS

To make working with multiple descriptors at the same time easier, some other methods have been added. First, with `Object.freeze` you can stop any properties on `form.fields` from being modified. Suppose your form contains a user object; to stop it from being modified, you freeze it:

```
user =
  name: 'Robert'

Object.freeze user
```

Now none of the properties are `writable` or `configurable` and no new properties can be added:

```
user.name = 'Janet'
user.name
# 'Robert'

user.address = '10 Elephant Parade'
user.address?
# false

Object.defineProperty user, 'phone', value: '555 4312'
# Cannot define property:phone, object is not extensible.
```

That's all well and good. How do they apply to Formulaic?

13.2.5 *Putting it together*

To answer Agtron's question of locking the form when it's complete, Scruffy wants to change Formulaic to use `Object.freeze` so that all of the fields on an instance can be frozen:

```
form = new Formulaic, '#form'
Object.freeze form

form.fields.user.id = 'u2344999'
form.fields.user.id
# 'u2344999'
```

It's not working! Why not? Because *freezing an object is shallow*—it only freezes the properties and doesn't work recursively to freeze properties of objects that are properties. You must either be careful to freeze the object containing the actual properties you want to be frozen (as you'll see in listing 13.4) or recursively freeze everything in the object to achieve a deep freeze. A typical implementation of a deep freeze follows:

```
deepFreeze = (o) ->
  Object.freeze o
  for own propKey of o
    prop = o[propKey]
    if typeof prop != 'object' || Object.isFrozen prop
      continue
    deepFreeze prop
```

> ## Freezing doesn't follow the prototype chain
> Although a frozen object is itself immutable, other objects on its prototype chain may not be. If you're creating mixins or constant objects and you really want them to be isolated, use `null` as the prototype first and then freeze the object.

That's enough time in the deep freeze; what about the other methods, `Object.seal` and `Object.preventExtensions`? They're similar to `Object.freeze`, but they're less restrictive about what can be changed in the object afterward. In table 13.3 you can see the different levels of restriction that these methods place on the objects they're invoked with.

Table 13.3 How `seal`, `freeze`, and `preventExtensions` affect an object

Method	Property action			
	Add	Delete	Edit value	Edit descriptor
freeze	No	No	No	No
seal	No	No	Yes	No
preventExtensions	No	Yes	Yes	Yes

You can test whether an object is frozen, sealed, or has had extensions prevented by using `Object.isFrozen`, `Object.isSealed`, and `Object.isExtensible`, respectively.

There's a problem when you try to freeze the `form.fields` property of a Formulaic instance because the properties on that are all getters and setters—the values are stored somewhere else and the Formulaic instance is only acting as a proxy for the fields. A solution to this appears in the next listing.

Listing 13.4   Formulaic with disabled fields

```
class Formulaic
  "use strict"
  constructor: (@root, @selector, @http) ->
    @fields = {}
    @extractFields()

  bind: (field) ->
    Object.defineProperty @fields, field.name,
      set: (newValue) =>
        field.value = newValue
        @sync()
      get: ->
        field.value
      enumerable: true
      configurable: true

    updateField = =>
      @fields[field.name] = field.value

    updateField()
    field.addEventListener 'input', updateField

  disable: ->
    for key, value of @fields
      Object.defineProperty @fields, key, { value }
    for field in @documentFields()
      field.disabled = true

    Object.freeze @fields

  documentFields: ->
    element = @root.querySelector @selector
    element.getElementsByTagName 'input'

  extractFields: ->
    @bind field for field in @documentFields()

  sync: ->
    throw new Error 'No transport' unless @http?
    if @url?
      @http.post @url, JSON.stringify(@fields), (response) =>
        @fields = JSON.parse response

exports.Formulaic = Formulaic
```

> "use strict" is covered later in this section.

The final part of ECMAScript 5 that you need to know about is strict mode. Notice that both listings 13.3 and 13.4 included something called "use strict" in them. What does it do and why might you want to include it?

13.2.6 *Strict mode*

When most of your JavaScript programs are written in CoffeeScript, it can be easy to forget JavaScript's problems. CoffeeScript protects you from some JavaScript follies, so the "use strict" pragma added in ECMAScript 5 doesn't appear in your programs often. But it's still important to understand how it relates to CoffeeScript.

Strict mode forbids some things in JavaScript that are dangerous; if you use them, you'll get an error. For example, with strict mode, using an undeclared global variable in JavaScript will cause a ReferenceError:

```
failsStrictMode = function() {
  "use strict";
  undeclaredVariable = 3;
};

failsStrictMode()
// Reference Error
```

ECMAScript 5 example

Of course, implicit variable declaration in CoffeeScript means that you won't see this error in CoffeeScript programs.

As you can see in the previous example, to enable strict mode you add the pragma "use strict" to some scope in your program. Any violations of strict mode inside that scope will cause an error.

The CoffeeScript compiler won't compile your program into something that breaks strict mode, but it won't complain if you break strict mode yourself. So when you *run* the following compiled program, the runtime will throw a syntax error:

```
"use strict"

failsStrict =
  duplicateKey: 1
  "duplicateKey": 2
```

There's nothing to stop you from adding the "use strict" pragma to your Coffee-Script program if you want to ensure that your programs adhere to strict mode.

That's enough for ECMAScript 5. It's time to look into the future a little bit and see what ECMAScript 6 has in store for you.

13.3 *ECMAScript 6*

> **IMPORTANT** The ECMAScript 6 specification is still a work in progress. Any of the features discussed here may change before they're finalized.

ECMAScript 6 is more ambitious than ECMAScript 5. In fact, at the time of writing, it's still at least a year from being finalized and probably years from being widely supported. Still, these things have a habit of changing while you aren't looking, so it's best to keep aware of the changes that are coming. Besides, some of them can already be used.

There are some specific features you can expect in ECMAScript 6 that have current or future relevance to CoffeeScript, and they're covered in this section: modules, const, let, sets, maps, proxies, comprehensions, iterators, and generators.

To try these features from the CoffeeScript REPL, you'll need two things. First, you'll need a recent version of Node.js. To see which version you have, pass `--version` to Node.js.

```
> node --version
```

The features described in this section require the version to be 0.10.24 or newer. If you have an older version, you should upgrade your version of Node.js.

The second thing you'll need to do to try the new features on the CoffeeScript REPL is to pass arguments to Node.js when you start the CoffeeScript REPL telling it to enable the new features. When invoking the CoffeeScript REPL, these options are passed individually as flags. For example, to enable proxies you set the `harmony-proxy` flag:

```
> coffee -i --nodejs --harmony-proxies
```

What if you want to use all of the new features? Well, Harmony was the name given early on to a large set of features that were intended for the next version of the ECMAScript specification. You can enable all of these Harmony features in Coffee-Script/node.js/V8 with a single `harmony` flag:

```
> coffee -i --nodejs --harmony
```

To try the CoffeeScript code snippets for the features in this section, you should invoke the REPL with `harmony` enabled.

The first feature worth mentioning—in part because it's a point of contention—is the module system.

13.3.1 Modules

JavaScript wasn't designed with a module system, so when people needed modules for client-side programs they invented their own. Now there are many different module systems, so almost everybody is a traveler in a foreign country—carrying their module adapters everywhere they go so they can plug things in.

Until ECMAScript 6 standardizes modules, you'll need to use some other module system. One approach, outlined in chapter 12, is to use the Node.js module syntax for both server and client modules and compile them out for the client (where they aren't supported) using a build step.

In the long term, JavaScript needs a standardized module system for the sake of interoperability. The module system that's proposed for ECMAScript 6 is similar to the Node.js module system. But the keyword `module` is already used by Node.js to refer to the current module, so something will have to change:

```
module Formulaic
  export Formulaic
```

CoffeeScript that can compile to module-supporting ECMAScript 6

Then elsewhere you import...from:

```
module QuoteApplication
  import { Formulaic } from Formulaic
```
**CoffeeScript that can compile to
module-supporting ECMAScript 6**

Your CoffeeScript program has a compilation step, so regardless of the module system your CoffeeScript program uses today, the JavaScript that it generates can use a different module system tomorrow. Because the module system is one of the most likely areas that can still change, it's easier to move on to more defined areas such as const and let.

13.3.2   *const and let*

The variable-scoping rules catch out many programmers new to JavaScript. One of the reasons for this is that it has a syntax similar to C and Java but very different scoping rules. In order to provide some of the naming rules that people expect to find in JavaScript, two new keywords, const and let, are being added in ECMAScript 6. You'll notice that you almost use their semantics already.

CONST

Many CoffeeScript programs have a few variables that are written in uppercase:

```
ONE_SECOND = 1000

setInterval ->
  rocket.forward()
, ONE_SECOND
```

Why name this variable in uppercase? In JavaScript it's really just tradition handed down from programming languages with a C heritage. It's meant to indicate that the value shouldn't be changed. The problem is that it *can* be changed:

```
ONE_SECOND = 0
```

Suppose your program needs to get some information about the environment it's running in, such as whether it's in production or development mode:

```
MODE = 'development'
```

Because the MODE variable can be changed by any other part of the program, there's some potential for your program to break:

```
const MODE = 'development';
MODE = 5;
# TypeError: redeclaration of const MODE
```
ECMAScript 6

> ### Everything is immutable?
> If you take a functional approach to your CoffeeScript programs, then you might already treat most (if not all) of your variables as being constant. If you're brave, then you modify the compilation of your CoffeeScript programs to turn all of your var declarations into const declarations.

The keyword `const` is a reserved word in the CoffeeScript compiler, but as of Coffee-Script 1.6 `const` itself is not supported.

LET

Variables in CoffeeScript are always function scoped. What if you don't want a name to be scoped to a function? Consider a trivial example with a comprehension inside a function:

```
number = 4
double = (numbers) -> number * 2 for number in numbers
double [3,4,5,6]

number              | The value of this outer variable has
# 6               <─┘ been changed by the comprehension.
```

Comprehensions in CoffeeScript have side effects. The names used are variables and so they use the same scoping rules and implicit declaration as any other variables in CoffeeScript. The ECMAScript 6 `let` expression is designed for names that should *only* apply to a block of code, just like the comprehension shown previously:

```
if (something) {
  let x = 3;          ECMAScript 6
}
```

If you don't like comprehensions to have side effects, you can see how that could be useful. How can you use it in CoffeeScript? Well, the brevity and flexibility of Coffee-Script's syntax mean that you can approximate `let` with a simple `do ->` form:

```
number = 5
do (number=0) -> number for number in numbers
```

Function parameters always *shadow*, so there's no way to assign a value to the `number` variable. This means you can rewrite the earlier example so that the comprehension doesn't clobber the outer variable:

```
number = 4
double = do (number=0) ->
  (numbers) -> number * 2 for number in numbers
double [3,4,5,6]
number
# 4
```

CoffeeScript favors simplicity. Sometimes when you think you need a specific new feature, there's an easy way to achieve the result you want without it. It's possible to write entire CoffeeScript programs that use only parameters and never use variables.

Remember, `const` and `let` are reserved words in the CoffeeScript compiler, so you can't use them. How about something you can use? How about some more objects?

13.3.3 *Sets, Maps, and WeakMaps*

Objects are useful as key-value pairs, but they're not dedicated for use as key-value stores. This can lead to problems such as properties on the prototype chain being included in comprehensions unless the own keyword is used. ECMAScript 6 specifies several dedicated APIs better optimized for some cases where you'd otherwise use a plain object. These are Set, Map, and WeakMap.

SET

A Set is just an ordered list of unique elements—a bit like a shopping list. Try it on a harmony-enabled REPL; use coffee -i --nodejs –harmony:

```
shopping = new Set()

shopping.has 'eggs'
# false

shopping.add 'milk'
shopping.has 'milk'
# true

shopping.delete 'milk'
shopping.has 'milk'
# false
```

On to the Map; how does it differ? Well, in the analogy format you remember from high school English tests, Set is to Array as Map is to Object.

MAP

A Map is *dedicated* to storing key-value pairs. Aren't objects already good at that? Yes, but a Map allows *any* value (not just a string) to be used as a key:

```
map = new Map

harold = name: 'Harold'
map.set harold, age: 50

map.get harold
# {age: 50}
```

Be mindful that when you use an object as a key, only the actual object can be used to get from a Map instance, not just any old object that *looks* the same:

```
map.get {name: 'Harold'}
# undefined
```

Unfortunately, a Map can be a problem because it can eat memory. Sounds dangerous— what does it mean?

WEAKMAP

In addition to Map there's also a WeakMap. A WeakMap is a Map that is *not* enumerable. The reason it's not enumerable is so that objects referenced by it can be garbage collected if the only reference to the object is in the WeakMap instance itself:

```
stackOfPapers =
  paperOnGladiators:
    text:
      "Gladiators, it seems, were fat."
```

```
papersMap = new WeakMap
papersMap.add stackOfPapers.paperOnGladiators

delete stackOfPapers.paperOnGladiators
```

When that's implemented using a WeakMap, then deleting the paperOnGladiators from the stackOfPapers allows it to be garbage collected. But if it were implemented using a regular Map, then deleting the object wouldn't make it available for garbage collection because the Map has a strong reference to the deleted paper. You can see how a Map could lead to object hoarding and a massive amount of uncollected garbage in some instances.

These features may not be setting your hair on fire. They're very useful for solving some specific problems, but they don't really expand your universe as a programmer. That's about to change, because it's time to explore proxies.

13.3.4 *Proxies*

With proxies you can give revocable access to an object. How is that useful? Imagine you're a superhero. What happens when the bad guys take you to their secret hideout? They blindfold you so that you don't know how to get there. In other words, they take you to the hideout without giving you any *reference* to it:

```
class SecretHideout
hideout = new SecretHideout()
proxy = new Proxy hideout, {}
```

Just as you can't lead the police to a hideout you can't find, there's no way you can touch a proxied object because your reference is to the proxy, not the original object:

```
proxy.policeAssault = true

hideout.policeAssault
# false
```

More importantly, a proxy can capture *any* call to the object behind the proxy by defining a handler object that defines a get and set for any property accessed on the proxy. In the case of Formulaic, a form can be placed behind a proxy handler. The handler must have get and set methods that specify what happens when a property on the proxied object is accessed or modified:

```
form = document.getElementById '#the-form'
handler =
  get: -> 'property access intercepted by proxy'
  set: -> 'property modify intercepted by proxy'
proxiedForm = new Proxy form, handler

proxiedForm.name
# 'property access intercepted by proxy'

proxiedForm.phone = '555 9988'
# 'property modify intercepted by proxy'
```

This is useful for Formulaic. The existing implementation extracts all of the fields and creates an intermediate representation of the form. With ECMAScript 6, instead of this intermediate representation your program can use a proxy. In listing 13.5 you can see Proxy and Map used to create a new version of Formulaic. In order for this program to work, it will need to execute in a runtime that supports proxies. For that reason, this listing throws an error if proxies are not supported.

Listing 13.5   Formulaic using `Proxy`

```coffeescript
throw new Error 'Proxy required' unless Proxy?

class Formulaic

  constructor: (@root, @selector, @http, @url) ->
    @source = @root.querySelector @selector
    @handler =
      get: (target, property) ->
        target[property]?.value
      set: (target, property, value) =>
        if @valid property then @sync()
    @fields = new Proxy @source, @handler

  valid: (property) ->
    property isnt ''

  addField: (field, value) ->
    throw new Error "Can't append to DOM" unless @source.appendChild?

    newField = @root.createElement 'input'
    newField.value = value
    @source.appendChild newField

  sync: ->
    throw new Error 'No HTTP specified' unless @http? and @url?

    @http.post @url, JSON.stringify(@source), (response) =>   #B
      for field, fieldResponse of JSON.parse response
        if field of @source
          @source[field].value = fieldResponse.value
        else
          @addField field, fieldResponse.value
```

The advantage of a Proxy approach is that it provides a way to unify an interface:

```coffeescript
form = new Formulaic document, '#form', http, 'http://agtron.co/formulaic/1'

form.fields.login = 'scruffy1234'
```

You *only* change properties on an instance of the Formulaic class, but the underlying implementation can be communicating with the server and updating the view for you. In fact, the proxy can do *anything* in response to a get or set. Listing 13.5 shows one other use for proxies, by validating the field value to ensure empty strings are not used.

The fun doesn't stop at proxies, though. Another exciting feature proposed for ECMAScript 6 is the addition of iterators, generators, and the concept of yield, which combine to finally give comprehensions real power.

13.3.5 *Comprehensions, iterators, and generators*

Comprehensions, iterators, and generators in ECMAScript 6 will be familiar to Python programmers. Why do they matter? Event streams. You'll remember (from chapter 9) that composing programs with event streams is problematic. To improve these programs, you developed a fluent interface for asynchronous streams of events that abstracted away some of the complexity, giving you a cleaner programming model to work with. The combination of comprehensions, iterators, and generators can provide the same power at a different syntactic level.

First, though, you need to see how JavaScript is getting comprehensions very much like the ones you already know in CoffeeScript.

COMPREHENSIONS

ECMAScript 6 has array comprehensions similar to those you're familiar with in CoffeeScript:

```
double = function(n) {
  return n * 2;
};
numbers = [2,3,5,4,2];
var doubled = [double number for each (number in numbers)];
```
ECMAScript 6

The only syntactic difference from CoffeeScript is some brackets and parentheses:

```
double (n) ->
  n * 2
numbers = [2,3,5,4,2]
doubled = double number for number in numbers
```

Array comprehensions are nice, but they're certainly no earth-shattering new feature. You might have noticed that in CoffeeScript too; the comprehensions are nice, but they're fairly limited. That changes once iterators and generators are introduced; comprehensions become very powerful.

Consider some keyboard-handling code for a computer game. When the user presses the up-arrow, down-arrow, left-arrow, left-arrow, and down-arrow keys, then the data your program ultimately receives is an array (just like in chapter 9):

```
[UP, DOWN, LEFT, LEFT, DOWN]
```

Unfortunately, there's a catch with this array—you don't have it yet. When the game starts, you haven't received any events, so you can't use a comprehension on it because a comprehension works on values—not on values you'll get later.

What if you *could* use a comprehension for these keyboard commands? What if comprehensions worked with arrays that you don't have yet? With iterators and generators they do!

ITERATORS

So, what's an iterator? Think of it as an object with a `next` method:

```
keyCommandIterator -
  next: ->
    if Math.floor Math.random()*10 > 5
      UP
    else
      DOWN
```

An iterator that uses Math.random() to return either UP or DOWN

```
keyCommandIterator.next()
# UP
keyCommandIterator.next()
# UP
```

To use this iterator in ECMAScript 6, you need to declare it as an `iterator` property on the prototype of your object. In CoffeeScript, that means putting it in the class declaration:

```
class KeyboardEvents
  iterator: keyCommandIterator
```

You iterate over an instance of `KeyboardEvents` with an ECMAScript 6 comprehension:

```
scruffysKeyboard = new KeyboardEvents
for event of scruffysKeyboard
  console.log scruffysKeyboard
```

```
# UP
# UP
# DOWN
```

This will run until you terminate it.

Now the potential for comprehensions starts to become apparent, but if you have a sweet tooth, it might not seem like very much sugar yet. Just making comprehensions work with objects that have a `next` method isn't enough. That's good, because it doesn't end there. Comprehensions in ECMAScript 6 will also work with a new sort of function: a generator.

GENERATORS

Comprehensions with objects and iterators work, but they're a bit cumbersome. Suppose you don't have a keyboard event object and a dedicated iterator. Instead, you just have a function that produces a value:

```
UP = 1
DOWN = -1
keyboardEvents = ->
  if Math.floor Math.random()*10 > 5
    UP
  else
    DOWN
```

Wouldn't it be nice if there were some way to express a function that could work like an iterator on an object? You'd need some special syntax for a function that could give control back to the invoking function without being finished. There's such a thing proposed for ECMAScript 6 called a *generator function*. Instead of being evaluated and returning a value, a generator function *yields* values.

In order to support this new feature, ECMAScript 6 had to add new syntax to indicate that a function is a generator:

ECMAScript 6

```
const UP = 1;
const DOWN = -1;

function* keyboardEventGenerator () {
  for (;;) {
    if(Math.floor(Math.random()*10) > 5) {
      yield UP;
    }
    else {
      yield DOWN;
    }
  }
}
```

The new function* syntax indicates that the function being defined is a generator and should contain yield statements.

CoffeeScript will need to add new syntax to support the `yield` keyword for generators. One option is the starred arrow `->*`:

```
keyboardEventGenerator = ->*
  while true
    if Math.floor Math.random()*10 > 5
      yield UP
    else
      yield DOWN
```

At the time of writing, the actual syntax hasn't been decided and CoffeeScript doesn't currently support generators. Both the ECMAScript 6 specification and the CoffeeScript syntax to deal with it are still evolving.

A generator is like a function, but instead of just being evaluated, it can *suspend execution and resume later.* Being able to yield in the middle of a function means that the generator and the function that uses it work together. With regular functions, a function invocation always completes before the calling function resumes. In contrast, with generators, the calling function gets control back *many times.* That's why generator functions are sometimes known as *co-routines* in languages where the equivalents of functions are known as *routines.*

Will these generators be useful in CoffeeScript? Absolutely. They'll be useful in all those places where you've either ended up with event-emitter spaghetti code or have created your own abstraction to deal with them. Generators and comprehensions will give you more syntactic flexibility.

Language features in JavaScript are nice, but in the ever-expanding JavaScript universe, new languages are being invented almost daily. The rising popularity of compile-to-JavaScript languages (like CoffeeScript) means that runtimes need to find better ways to support them. One of the ways that JavaScript runtimes are starting to do this is with *source maps.*

13.4   Source maps for debugging

Debugging CoffeeScript by looking at the compiled JavaScript is difficult. An error in a running JavaScript program is easy to understand if the program was written in JavaScript but not so easy if the program was transpiled from another language such as CoffeeScript. So how do you use a debugger on a CoffeeScript program?

13.4.1   Why source maps?

You don't really need the debugger to work, right? When you develop everything by writing a test first (see chapter 11), and your code doesn't work, you can change a test or write a new test to see what's happening. There's some degree of truth in that, but it's not practical. Even if you tend not to use it much, one day you'll need the debugger and you don't want to be presented with the compiled JavaScript version of your program.

Imagine a browser-based program you wrote—a program, any program, it doesn't matter which one. Imagine now that you wrote this program in a file called (ingeniously) program.coffee. What do you see if the program throws an exception? You see text something like so:

```
Reference Error: x is not defined        -- program.js 23
```

This is telling you that your program has thrown a reference error in line 23 of program.js. That's nice, except that you didn't write any program.js because you wrote your program in CoffeeScript! So what's the problem?

The problem is not that CoffeeScript is compiled. There are many compiled languages with good debuggers. The problem is that the JavaScript runtime has no knowledge of your original CoffeeScript source, so it has no way to show you where the problem is in your original source. That changes with source maps. Source maps allow the CoffeeScript compiler to tell the JavaScript runtime how source lines in the JavaScript correspond to source lines in the original CoffeeScript source.

13.4.2   Getting started with source maps

To try CoffeeScript with source maps, you'll need both a runtime that supports them and a CoffeeScript compiler that can create a source map. Right now, that means a CoffeeScript compiler version greater than 1.6 and a recent version of your web browser that supports source maps.[1] Before long, source maps will be supported by more runtimes.

To understand what they do, here's a trivial program you can whet your source-maps appetite on:

```coffeescript
double = (array) ->
  throw new Error 'Using source maps'       ◁─┤  A deliberate error that you
  item * 2 for item in array                     expect to see thrown when
                                                  the program executes
double [1,2,3,4]
```

---

[1] Consult the documentation for your browser to determine if it supports source maps and how you can enable them.

Suppose the program is contained in a file called sourcemaps.coffee. You're familiar with the standard way to compile:

```
> coffee sourcemaps.coffee
```

To generate a corresponding *map* file, you pass the -m or --map flag:

```
> coffee --map sourcemaps.coffee
```

The source map won't make much sense because it's not intended to be human readable. It's a JSON file containing information that the runtime can use to map from the compiled JavaScript program to your original CoffeeScript source:

```
{
  "version":3,
  "file":" sourcemaps.coffee",
  "sources":[
    "sourcemaps.coffee"
  ],
  "names":[],
  "mappings":"AAAC;;;EAAA,MAAA,GAAS,SAAA,CAAA,KAAA,CAAA;;;MAAW,2BAAqB,aAArB,
    aAAA,CAAA,KAAA,CAAA;QAAa,OAAQ;oBAArB,IAAA,CAAA,CAAA,CAAO;;;;;EAC3B,OAAO,
    IAAP,CAAY,MAAA,CAAO,CAAA;AAAA,IAAC,CAAD;AAAA,IAAG,CAAH;AAAA,IAAK,CAAL;
    AAAA,IAAO,CAAP;AAAA,EAAA,CAAP,CAAZ;EACA,KAAA,CAAM,GAAA,CAAI,KAAJ,CAAU,
    mBAAV,CAAN"
}
```

To use the source map, the runtime needs to be told where to find it. To tell the runtime where to find the source map, either put a comment in the compiled JavaScript or set an *X-SourceMap* header if the file is served over HTTP. You add a comment to the file like this:

```
echo '\n//@ sourceMappingURL=sourcemaps.js.map' >> sourcemaps.js
```

Now, consider that 'Using source maps' error that your program throws—how does it appear? When you run the program in an environment that doesn't understand source maps, you'll see the error reported in the compiled JavaScript file:

```
Uncaught Error: Using source maps
double -- sourcemap.js:5
```

That's not very useful. An exception in compiled JavaScript when you're writing your program in CoffeeScript is difficult to comprehend. In contrast, with source maps you'll see the error reported in your original CoffeeScript program:

```
Uncaught Error: Using source maps
double -- sourcemaps.coffee:2
```

It gets better. Not only will you see errors on appropriate lines, but you'll also be able to harness the full power of your favorite IDE on your CoffeeScript program. Stepping through and setting breakpoints will be done in your CoffeeScript source, and not in the generated JavaScript.

Enabling source maps in your browser

As with most configuration options, each browser will have a slightly different way of enabling source maps. As an example, Chrome 27 allows you to enable source maps via a check box in the settings for the developer tools. Consult the documentation for the relevant version of the browser (or other runtime) you're using for details on how to enable source maps.

It's still early days for source maps, so you'll need to consult the documentation for your individual runtime to get them working. If you like to use the debugger, you can already see that it's a useful tool.

The future will include JavaScript, but it's not all JavaScript. Every day there are more languages that compile to JavaScript. Source maps go just that little bit further to opening up the JavaScript language to embrace them.

13.5 *Summary*

In this chapter you looked at the language ecosystem around CoffeeScript. Specifically, you saw how CoffeeScript not only benefits from advancements in the ECMAScript specification but also contributes to them. Your deeper understanding of both current and future language features will ultimately make you a better CoffeeScript programmer.

As a CoffeeScript programmer, you also need tools like source maps. Support for those is emerging rapidly on runtimes, so by starting today you'll be prepared for tomorrow (which will arrive sooner than you think). Regardless of whether you're ultimately writing JavaScript, CoffeeScript, or a mixture of both, you'll be better off for learning what the future holds. After all, learning and using are, to borrow a phrase from Scruffy's high school English teacher, inexorably intertwined.

appendix A
Reserved words

The CoffeeScript compiler maintains a list of reserved words that will break compilation if you use them as variable names in a program.

For CoffeeScript 1.6.3 the reserved words list appears in table A.1.

Table A.1 CoffeeScript compiler 1.6.3 reserved words

case	implements	instanceof	super
default	interface	return	undefined
function	package	throw	then
var	private	break	unless
void	protected	continue	until
with	public	debugger	loop
const	static	if	of
let	yield	else	by
enum	true	switch	when
export	false	for	and
import	null	while	or
native	this	do	is
__hasProp	new	try	isnt
__extends	delete	catch	not
__slice	typeof	finally	yes
__bind	in	class	no
__indexOf	arguments	extends	on
	eval		off

Some of the reserved words in CoffeeScript are reserved because the compiler uses them in the generated JavaScript. Others are reserved because they're reserved words in the ECMAScript specification, as shown in tables A.2 and A.3.

Table A.2   Reserved words in the fifth edition of the ECMAScript specification

break	return	with	new
do	void	default	var
instanceof	continue	if	catch
typeof	for	throw	finally
case	switch	delete	debugger
else	while	in	function
try	this		

There are some words that are reserved for future editions of the ECMAScript specification, as shown in table A.3. Some of them, such as `class`, also have meaning in Coffee-Script. Don't use them as identifiers.

Table A.3   Words reserved for future editions of the ECMAScript specification

class	export	interface	private
enum	import	package	public
extends	implements	protected	const
super	let	static	yield

There are some built-in constructors that you should treat as reserved. If you redefine them, you'll most likely break your programs:

`Object, Function, Array, String, Boolean, Number, Date, RegExp, Error, EvalError, RangeError, ReferenceError, SyntaxError, TypeError, URIError`

There are other global objects and value properties that you've encountered:

`Math, JSON, Infinity, NaN`

Finally, there are some global functions:

`eval, parseInt, parseFloat, isNaN, isFinite, decodeURI, decodeURIComponent, encodeURI, encodeURIComponent`

appendix B
Answers to exercises

About the exercises

These exercises are provided for you to practice using CoffeeScript and also to spend some time reflecting on CoffeeScript. These two activities are an essential component of learning a new programming language. Attempting the exercises is more important than looking at the solutions.

Exercise 2.3.3

```
torch = price: 21
umbrella = {}
combinedCost = (torch.price || 0) + (umbrella.price || 0)
# 21
```

Exercise 2.4.4

```
animal = "crocodile"
collective = switch animal
  when "antelope" then "herd"
  when "baboon" then "rumpus"
  when "badger" then "cete"
  when "cobra" then "quiver"
  when "crocodile" then "bask"
# bask
```

Exercise 2.5.3

```
animal = "cobra"
collective = switch animal
  when "antelope" then "herd"
  when "baboon" then "rumpus"
  when "badger" then "cete"
  when "cobra" then "quiver"
  when "crocodile" then "bask"
"The collective of #{animal} is #{collective}"
# The collective of cobra is quiver
```

Exercise 2.6.5

```
animals = 'baboons badgers antelopes cobras crocodiles'

result - for animal in animals.split " "
  collective = switch animal
    when "antelopes" then "herd"
    when "baboons" then "rumpus"
    when "badgers" then "cete"
    when "cobras" then "quiver"
    when "crocodiles" then "bask"
  "A #{collective} of #{animal}"
```

Exercises 3.1.5

```
countWords = (text) ->
  words = text.split /[\s,]/
  significantWords = (word for word in words when word.length > 3)
  significantWords.length

everyOtherWord = (text) ->
  words = text.split /[\s,]/
  takeOther = for word, index in words
    if index % 2 then ""
    else word
  takeOther.join(" ").replace /\s\s/gi, " "
```

Exercises 3.3.4

```
http = require 'http'
fs = require 'fs'

sourceFile = 'attendees'
fileContents = 'File not read yet.'

readSourceFile = ->
  fs.readFile sourceFile, 'utf-8', (error, data) ->
    if error
      console.log error
    else
      fileContents = data

fs.watchFile sourceFile, readSourceFile

countWords = (text) ->
  text.split(/,/gi).length

readSourceFile sourceFile

server = http.createServer (request, response) ->
  response.end "#{countWords(fileContents)}"

server.listen 8080, '127.0.0.1'
```

Exercises 3.4.4

```
accumulate = (initial, items, accumulator) ->
  total = initial
  for item in items
    total = accumulator total, item
  total
```

```
sumFractions = (fractions) ->
  accumulator = (lhs, rhs) ->
    if lhs is '0/0'
      rhs
    else if rhs is '0/0'
      lhs
    else
      lhsSplit = lhs.split /\//gi
      rhsSplit = rhs.split /\//gi
      lhsNumer = 1*lhsSplit[0]
      lhsDenom = 1*lhsSplit[1]
      rhsNumer = 1*rhsSplit[0]
      rhsDenom = 1*rhsSplit[1]
      if lhsDenom isnt rhsDenom
        commonDenom = lhsDenom*rhsDenom
      else
        commonDenom = lhsDenom

      sumNumer = lhsNumer*(commonDenom/lhsDenom) + rhsNumer*(commonDenom/
    rhsDenom)
      "#{sumNumer}/#{commonDenom}"

  accumulate '0/0', fractions, accumulator
console.log sumFractions ['2/6', '1/4']
# '14/24'
```

And the keep function:

```
keep = (arr, cond) ->
  item for item in arr when cond item
```

Exercises 4.2.3

Adding edit to listing 4.2:

```
phonebook =
  numbers:
    hannibal: '555-5551'
    darth: '555-5552'
    hal9000: 'disconnected'
    freddy: '555-5554'
    'T-800': '555-5555'
  list: ->
    "#{name}: #{number}" for name, number of @numbers
  add: (name, number) ->
    if not (name of @numbers)
      @numbers[name] = number
    else
      "#{name} already exists"
  edit: (name, number) ->
    if name of @numbers
      @numbers[name] = number
    else
      "#{name} not found"
  get: (name) ->
    if name of @numbers
      "#{name}: #{@numbers[name]}"
```

```
    else
       "#{name} not found"

console.log "Phonebook. Commands are add, get, edit, list, and exit."

process.stdin.setEncoding 'utf8'
stdin = process.openStdin()

stdin.on 'data', (chunk) ->
  args = chunk.split ' '
  command = args[0].trim()
  name = args[1].trim() if args[1]
  number = args[2].trim() if args[2]
  switch command
    when 'add'
      res = phonebook.add(name, number) if name and number
      console.log res
    when 'get'
      console.log phonebook.get(name) if name
    when 'edit'
      console.log phonebook.edit(name, number) if name and number
    when 'list'
      console.log phonebook.list()
    when 'exit'
      process.exit 1
```

Setting properties on an object:

```
css = (element, styles) ->
  element.style ?= {}
  for key, value of styles
    element.style[key] = value

class Element
div = new Element
css div, width: 10

div.style.width
# 10
```

Exercise 4.6.3

The original music device is

```
cassette =
  title: "Awesome songs. To the max!"
  duration: "10:34"
  released: "1988"
  track1: "Safety Dance - Men Without Hats"
  track2: "Funkytown - Lipps, Inc"
  track3: "Electric Avenue - Eddy Grant"
  track4: "We built this city - Starship"
```

The music device was created from it:

```
musicDevice = Object.create cassette
```

Creating another one from the first is the same:

```
secondMusicDevice = Object.create musicDevice
```

Changes to either the original cassette or the music device will be visible on the second music device:

```
cassette.track5 = "Hello - Lionel Richie"

secondMusicDevice.track5
# "Hello - Lionel Richie"

musicDevice.track6 = "Mickey - Toni Basil"

secondMusicDevice.track6
# "Mickey - Toni Basil"
```

Multiple prototype references like this are called the *prototype chain*. You'll learn more about it in chapter 5.

Exercise 4.7.2

```
views =
  excluded: []
  pages: {}
  clear: ->
    @pages = {}
  increment: (key) ->
   unless key in @excluded
     @pages[key] ?= 0
     @pages[key] = @pages[key] + 1
  ignore: (page) ->
     @excluded = @excluded.concat page
  total: ->
    sum = 0
    for own page, count of @pages
      sum = sum + count
    sum
```

Exercises 4.8.3

```
class GranTurismo
  constructor: (options) ->
    @options = options
  summary: ->
    ("#{key}: #{value}" for key, value of @options).join "\n"

options =
  wheels: 'phat'
  dice: 'fluffy'

scruffysGranTurismo = new GranTurismo options

scruffysGranTurismo.summary()
# wheels: phat
# dice: fluffy
```

The constructor could use the shorthand for arguments:

```
class GranTurismo
  constructor: (@options) ->
    summary: ->
      ("#{key}: #{value}" for key, value of @options).join "\n"
```

This is equivalent to the first version.

Exercise 5.3.3

Here are `Product` and `Camera` classes based on listing 5.4 with an alphabetical class method added to the Camera class:

```
class Product
# any implementation of Product

class Camera extends Product
  cameras = []
  @alphabetical = ->
    cameras.sort (a, b) -> a.name > b.name
  constructor: ->
    all.push @
    super
```

The Camera class can keep an array of all instances for `alphabetical` just as the `Product` class kept an array of products for `find`. The `Camera` constructor uses `super` to ensure the `Product` constructor is also invoked so that `Product.find` doesn't break.

Exercise 5.8.1

Applying some basic class techniques to the server-side application helps to increase clarity:

```
fs = require 'fs'
http = require 'http'
url = require 'url'
coffee = require 'coffee-script'

class ShopServer
  constructor: (@host, @port, @shopData, @shopNews) ->
    @css = ''
    fs.readFile './client.css', 'utf-8', (err, data) =>
      if err then throw err
      @css = data

  readClientScript: (callback) ->
    script = "./client.coffee"
    fs.readFile script, 'utf-8', (err, data) ->
      if err then throw err
      callback data

  headers: (res, status, type) ->
    res.writeHead status, 'Content-Type': "text/#{type}"

  renderView: ->
    """
    <!doctype html>
    <head>
    <title>Agtron's Emporium</title>
    <link rel='stylesheet' href='/css/client.css' />
    </head>
    <body>
    <div class='page'>
    <h1>----Agtron&#8217;s Emporium----</h1>
    <script src='/js/client.js'></script>
```

```coffeescript
      </div>
      </body>
      </html>
      """

  handleClientJs: (path, req, res) ->
    @headers res, 200, 'javascript'
    writeClientScript = (script) ->
      res.end coffee.compile(script)
    @readClientScript writeClientScript

  handleClientCss: (path, req, res) ->
      @headers res, 200, 'css'
      res.end @css

  handleImage: (path, req, res) ->
    fs.readFile ".#{path}", (err, data) =>
      if err
        @headers res, 404, 'image/png'
        res.end()
      else
        @headers res, 200, 'image/png'
        res.end data, 'binary'

  handleJson: (path, req, res) ->
    switch path
      when '/json/list'
        @headers res, 200, 'json'
        res.end JSON.stringify(@shopData)
      when '/json/list/camera'
        @headers res, 200, 'json'
        camera = @shopData.camera
        res.end JSON.stringify(camera)
      when '/json/news'
        @headers res, 200, 'json'
        res.end JSON.stringify(@shopNews)
      else
        @headers res, 404, 'json'
        res.end JSON.stringify(status: 404)

  handlePost: (path, req, res) ->
    category = /^\/json\/purchase\/([^/]*)\/([^/]*)$/.exec(path)?[1]
    item = /^\/json\/purchase\/([^/]*)\/([^/]*)$/.exec(path)?[2]
    if category? and item? and data[category][item].stock > 0
      data[category][item].stock -= 1
      @headers res, 200, 'json'
      res.write JSON.stringify
        status: 'success',
        update: data[category][item]
    else
      res.write JSON.stringify
        status: 'failure'
    res.end()

  handleGet: (path, req, res) ->
    if path is '/'
      @headers res, 200, 'html'
      res.end @renderView()
```

```
      else if path.match /\/json/
        @handleJson path, req, res
      else if path is '/js/client.js'
        @handleClientJs path, req, res
      else if path is '/css/client.css'
        @handleClientCss path, req, res
      else if path.match /^\/images\/(.*)\.png$/gi
        @handleImage path, req, res
      else
        @headers res, 404, 'html'
        res.end '404'

  start: ->
    @httpServer = http.createServer (req, res) =>
      path = url.parse(req.url).pathname
      if req.method == "POST"
        @handlePost path, req, res
      else
        @handleGet path, req, res

    @httpServer.listen @port, @host, =>
      console.log "Running at #{@host}:#{@port}"

  stop: ->
    @httpServer?.close()

data = require('./data').all
news = require('./news').all
shopServer = new ShopServer '127.0.0.1', 9999, data, news

shopServer.start()
```

There are some further opportunities in the preceding program for encapsulation, but for a program of little over 100 lines you'd likely find any more to be overkill.

Exercises 7.2.5

Your first thought might be to do something like this:

```
swapPairs = (array) ->
  for index in array by 2
    [first, second] = array[index-1..index]
    [second, first]
```

This is close, but you'll end up with an array of arrays:

```
swapPairs([3,4,3,4,3,4])
# [ [ 4, 3 ], [ 4, 3 ], [ 4, 3 ] ]

swapPairs([1,2,3,4,5,6])
# [ [ 2, 1 ], [ 4, 3 ], [ 6, 5 ] ]
```

Solve this by using the array concat method with rest:

```
swapPairs = (array) ->
  reversedPairs = for index in array by 2
    [first, second] = array[index-1..index]
    [second, first]
  [].concat reversedPairs...
```

```
swapPairs([3,4,3,4,3,4])
# [ 4, 3, 4, 3, 4, 3 ]

swapPairs([1,2,3,4,5,6])
# [ 2, 1, 4, 3, 6, 5 ]
```

For the second exercise, use a combination of rest, array, and object destructuring:

```
phoneDirectory =
  A: [
      name: 'Abe'
      phone: '555 1110'
    ,
      name: 'Andy'
      phone: '555 1111'
    ,
      name: 'Alice'
      phone: '555 1112'
  ]
  B: [
      name: 'Bam'
      phone: '555 1113'
  ]

lastNumberForLetter = (letter, directory) ->
  [..., lastForLetter] = directory[letter]
  {phone} = lastForLetter
  phone

lastNumberForLetter 'A', phoneDirectory
# 555 1112
```

Exercise 10.4.4

Suppose the `Tracking` class and `http` object are as follows:

```
class Tracking
  constructor: (prefs, http) ->
    @http = http
  start: ->
    @http.listen()

http =
  listen: ->
```

A potential `double` function follows:

```
double = (original) ->
  mock = {}
  for key, value of original
    if value.call?
      do ->
        stub = ->
          stub.called = true
        mock[key] = stub
  mock
```

This double function returns a mock version of the original object. It has all the same method names, but the methods themselves are just empty functions that remember if they've been called or not.

In other circumstances your test might call for a spy instead. When you spy on an object, any method calls still occur on the original object but are seen by the spy. A double function that returns a spy follows:

```
double = (original) ->
  spy = Object.create original
  for key, value of original
    if value.call?
      do ->
        originalMethod = value
        spyMethod = (args...) ->
          spyMethod.called = true
          originalMethod args...
        spy[key] = spyMethod
  spy
```

Depending on the test framework you're using, there may be both mocking and spying libraries provided for you. The pros and cons of using mocks, spies, and other testing techniques aren't covered here.

That's it for the exercises. Happy travels.

appendix C
Popular libraries

While learning to program in CoffeeScript, it's important to deal only in language concepts and to build up programs using only the raw building blocks of the language instead of leaning too heavily on specific libraries or frameworks. Having said that, once you *have* learned CoffeeScript, there are many occasions when it makes sense to reach for a well-known and supported library or framework that takes an approach similar to your own.

What follows is a list of useful libraries and relevant websites for learning about them. In some cases the libraries are not only useful in your CoffeeScript programs but are themselves written in CoffeeScript—those libraries are indicated here.

npm

Although you've had experience with npm (the package manager that comes with Node.js), there are many aspects of it (such as dependency management) that you haven't explored. Find out more about npm at http://npmjs.org/.

Testing

In chapter 10 you built up your own small testing framework. There are several excellent frameworks that can help to extend your testing prowess:

- *Jasmine*—Jasmine is the most popular testing framework for browser-based programs. Find out more at http://pivotal.github.io/jasmine/.
- *Mocha*—Mocha is one of the most popular testing frameworks for Node.js programs. Find out more at http://visionmedia.github.io/mocha/ or `npm install mocha`.
- *Chai*—Chai provides assertion matchers to help make your tests more readable. Find out more at http://chaijs.com/ or `npm install chai`.

- *Zombie*—Zombie provides a virtual browser (a mock browser) that you can use inside Node.js. Find out more at http://zombie.labnotes.org/ or `npm install zombie`. *Zombie is written in CoffeeScript.*

Modules

In chapter 12 you created your own support for Node.js module syntax in your browser-based program. There are a few alternatives to look at while you wait for JavaScript runtimes to support some native module system:

- *Stitch*—Stitch uses a setup similar to the one you built in chapter 12. Find out more at https://github.com/sstephenson/stitch or `npm install stitch`. *Stitch is written in CoffeeScript.*
- *Browserify*—Browserify provides a compiler to support Node.js modules. Find out more at http://browserify.org/ or `npm install gamma`.
- *Bower*—Bower provides a complete package system for your browser-based programs, similar to some of the features that npm provides on Node.js. Find out more at http://bower.io/.

Builds

In chapter 12 you used Cake to build your program. Although useful, Cake can be overly minimal for some needs:

- *Make*—Make is not specific to CoffeeScript, JavaScript, or Node.js, but it's one of the most widely used build automation tools. Although Make can be intimidating to novices, it's an important and effective tool that you should learn to use. Find out more at http://www.gnu.org/software/make/.
- *Grunt*—Grunt is a task runner that runs on Node.js. Find out more at http://gruntjs.com/.
- *Lineman*—Lineman builds on top of Grunt and is targeted at build automation for browser-based programs. Grunt is a task runner that runs on Node.js. Find out more at http://linemanjs.com/. *Lineman is written in CoffeeScript.*

Deployment

In chapter 12 you looked briefly at deploying your CoffeeScript program to a server with SCP. There are alternatives. DPLOY is a configuration-driven SCP deployment tool for your Node.js program. Find out more at http://leanmeanfightingmachine .github.io/dploy/.

Instead of deploying to a server where you configure the environment, you might find it easier to deploy your application to a host that manages the servers for you. The two most popular options for Node.js are Heroku (http://www.heroku.com) and Nodejitsu (http://nodejitsu.com/). To make the most of these, you'll need to be familiar with npm.

Frameworks

There are many competing web frameworks for Node.js, but the most popular is Express (http://expressjs.com/). The creator of Express has now also created a new framework based on generators called Koa (http://koajs.com/).

There are even more frameworks for browsers than there are for Node.js, but the ones you'll find most interesting are Backbone.js (http://backbonejs.org/) created by CoffeeScript creator Jeremy Ashkenas and batman.js (http://batmanjs.org/), which is written in CoffeeScript.

Asynchronous programming

In chapter 9 you learned techniques for dealing with asynchronous programs. The most interesting development in this area is generator support in ECMAScript 6. But another interesting library to look at is bacon.js (https://github.com/baconjs/bacon.js), which uses functional reactive programming to move your event-driven code away from imperative and toward functional. *Bacon.js is written in CoffeeScript.*

Physical computing

Cylon.js is a framework for physical computing with Node.js. It has hardware support for many popular platforms including Arduino and Raspberry Pi. Find out more at http://cylonjs.com/ or `npm install cylon`. *Cylon.js is written in CoffeeScript.*

On GitHub

The popular web-based hosting service for projects that use Git is a good place to explore interesting new CoffeeScript programs. See popular recent programs written in CoffeeScript at https://github.com/trending?l=coffeescript&since=monthly.

Finally, be sure to keep track of the official CoffeeScript website at http://coffee-script.org, the CoffeeScript wiki at https://github.com/jashkenas/coffee-script/wiki, and the source code for *CoffeeScript in Action* at https://github.com/boundvariable/coffeescript-in-action.

index

Secrets of the JavaScript Ninja

by John Resig, Bear Bibeault

ISBN: 978-1-933988-69-6
392 pages
$39.99
December 2012

Node.js in Action

by Mike Cantelon, Marc Harter,
   T.J. Holowaychuk, Nathan Rajlich

ISBN: 978-1-617290-57-2
416 pages
$44.99
October 2013

Rails 4 in Action
Revised Edition of *Rails 3 in Action*
by Ryan Bigg, Yehuda Katz, Steve Klabnik

ISBN: 978-1-617291-09-8
600 pages
$49.99
August 2014

For ordering information go to www.manning.com

MORE TITLES FROM MANNING

Third-Party JavaScript

by Ben Vinegar, Anton Kovalyov

ISBN: 978-1-617290-54-1
288 pages
$44.99
March 2013

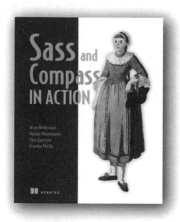

Sass and Compass in Action

by Wynn Netherland, Nathan Weizenbaum,
Chris Eppstein, Brandon Mathis

ISBN: 978-1-617290-14-5
240 pages
$44.99
July 2013

HTML5 in Action

by Rob Crowther, Joe Lennon,
Ash Blue, Greg Wanish

ISBN: 978-1-617290-49-7
466 pages
$39.99
February 2014

For ordering information go to www.manning.com